AGAINST THE LAW

CONSTITUTIONAL CONFLICTS

A Series by the Institute of

Bill of Rights Law at the

College of William and Mary

Edited by Rodney A. Smolla

and Neal Devins

AGAINST THE LAW

Paul F. Campos • Pierre Schlag • Steven D. Smith

DUKE UNIVERSITY PRESS   DURHAM AND LONDON 1996

© 1996 Duke University Press

All rights reserved

Printed in the United States of America

on acid-free paper ∞

Typeset in Minion by

Keystone Typesetting, Inc.

Library of Congress Cataloging-in-Publication

Data appear on the last printed page of this book.

CONTENTS

PREFACE

T WAS STEVE's idea. It was Pierre's organization. It was Paul's passion. And so this book—a product of a rather odd and improbable combination of authors—came together.

There were doubts throughout.

Steve was concerned that the relentlessly critical tone of the book would be damaging. He worried half seriously, half in jest, that a conservative thinker would become associated in a joint enterprise with one of the most irreverent and intellectually radical (if not nihilistic) thinkers on the contemporary American legal scene. Indeed, he had already received negative and cautionary reactions from older, wiser colleagues at another law school: "Stay away from those street toughs."

Pierre too was concerned. He had been told not to publish with the other two. Yet here he was publishing with one of the most conservative (if not reactionary) constitutional thinkers in American legal thought. He was told that this would be deeply confusing to readers. And he worried that the book would simply be exhibit A in the usual left or liberal charge that ultra-intellectualism is simply neoconservatism by any other name.

Paul, who refused to divulge his political orientation to anyone (including the other two authors), didn't worry at all.

And all three of us decided to go forward with the book.

One reason, of course, was a shared sense of the deadening quality of contemporary political orthodoxies and their disputes. In some sense, each of us has been unwilling to simply toe the line of *any* political orthodoxy—reactionary, conservative, liberal, or radical. None of us seems to be very good at being a foot soldier. And being in Colorado, we are much too far away from anywhere to feel the civilizing effects of the great institutions.

A second, perhaps more profound reason is that despite our widely different political visions, there are certain things we share in common—certain understandings of the shortcomings of American legalism. We all think that legalism is aesthetically, ethically, and intellectually lacking in rather profound ways.

And we all think that it is important to point this out in the most ecumenical manner possible.

Hence, this book.

Oddly, perhaps—and certainly against the odds—we have looked on our widely disparate political and intellectual inclinations as an advantage. We very much hope that we are not the only ones.

Paul F. Campos
Pierre Schlag
Steven D. Smith
Boulder, Colorado
November 1, 1995

ACKNOWLEDGMENTS

W E WISH TO THANK the many friends and colleagues who have contributed to this book. We give special thanks to Sandy Levinson for suggesting and conducting the interview, "Waiting for Langdell," and to Leonard Levy for graciously acquiescing in our use of the same title he used in his book, *Against the Law.*

Different versions of the essays in this book have appeared in various law reviews and are published here with their permission. Pierre Schlag, "Normativity and the Politics of Form," 133 *U. Pa. L. Rev.* 801 (1991); Paul Campos, "Against Constitutional Theory," 4 *Yale J. L. & Human.* 279 (1992); Steven Smith, "Idolatry in Constitutional Interpretation," 79 *U. Va. L. Rev.* 583 (1993); Pierre Schlag, "Clerks in the Maze," 91 *Mich. L. Rev.* 2053 (1993); Paul Campos, "A Heterodox Catechism," 11 *Const. Comm.* 65 (1994); Paul Campos, "Secular Fundamentalism," 94 *Colum. L. Rev.* 1814 (1994); Steven D. Smith, "Nonsense and Natural Rights," *S. Cal. Interdisciplinary L. Rev.* 000 (1995).

INTRODUCTION

T HE PAST THIRTY years have witnessed a curious development in the American legal academy. Thirty years ago almost all legal academics were engaged in something that could be called "doing law." They were writing articles identifying true and correct rules of law. They were working with the official legal materials put out by courts, legislatures, and agencies. They paid respectful attention to new judicial opinions, tried to make sense of them, and tried to integrate them into their own understanding of the law.

Generations of legal academics—and not a few lawyers—have looked to law not merely as a way to coordinate transactions and resolve disputes, but as a source of moral or ethical guidance. They have sought to conduct their lives in accordance not only with particular laws but with "the law"—with a lawlike aesthetic, a lawlike frame. They have taken cognizance of ethical and political issues in a lawlike way. They have used lawlike techniques to identify and define problems. And they have employed lawlike arguments to achieve lawlike solutions: norms, prescriptions, recommendations, and so on.

It was easy for the legally trained to fall into such habits. It was alluring as well, for the law promises to its practitioners all manner of good things. It promises a solid form of analysis (called "thinking like a lawyer"). And it promises that if its practitioners live by its spirit, they will act according to the fundamental authoritative principles of their culture, including, but not limited to, justice, fairness, order, due process, notice, neutrality, and impartiality.

But something has happened.

Indeed, a great many leading American legal thinkers have now mostly abandoned "doing law." Instead, they are pursuing enterprises that they might call "legal theory" or "interdisciplinary studies" or some such thing. These legal thinkers are no longer "doing law" in the sense that they are no longer devoting their professional lives to canvassing and systemizing the sundry acts of American officialdom. On the contrary, leading legal thinkers now try to distance themselves from the uninspiring world of bureaucratic decision making. They do so in various ways. For some the flight is into abstraction. The details of official bureaucracy are left behind in the course of an ethereal abstraction of law—one that renders it much more pristine and elegant. For others the flight is in the opposite direction. They find comfort in the familiar formal and aesthetic qualities of classic legal artifacts: they celebrate the craft of the judicial opinion. For all, the flight is accomplished through a profound idealization and romanticization of what they still think of as "the law." These are people who have to a certain extent recognized the legalist maze for what it is and have tried, as best they can, to get out.

We understand very well the motivations that would lead such legal thinkers to avoid that maze. Indeed, there is little that is appealing—intellectually, ethically, or aesthetically—in sifting through the bureaucratic morass produced by the various agencies of officialdom. Yet one thing puzzles us: These legal thinkers, who exhibit so little interest in doing law themselves, nonetheless continue to dedicate much of their scholarly enterprise to the justification, the celebration, and the idealization of an enterprise they have to a large degree abandoned.

This is a troubling inconsistency. It does not rise to the level of a logical contradiction (and in any case, such a contradiction could be easily explained away). Rather, we suspect a certain dissonance of character here. These leading legal thinkers seem to want to avoid doing law. But their strategy to avoid doing law lies, ironically, in producing normatively pleasing and aesthetically elegant representations of law that serve, whether intentionally or not, to celebrate doing what they themselves have abandoned. It thus seems that there is a certain tension between the constative and the performative dimensions of their enterprise. That is, if one looks at what these scholars are *doing* (and, more to the point, *not doing* anymore), it seems they have lost much of their faith and even their interest in law. Yet, if one listens to what these scholars are *saying*, they seem bent on trying to maintain a vigorous belief in that same law. To put it another way, they seem to think that while doing law is not good for them, it is nonetheless good for others.

Another very large group of legal academics has also, to a great extent, abandoned the task of doing law. This is the group of legal scholars who remain committed to the reverential and meticulous study of the sundry decisions of officialdom. This is the group that dutifully continues to read the advance sheets as if these documents will inform them of what "the law" is. This is the group that pays close attention to minor doctrinal changes, to technical statutory reforms, to the minutiae of rules and regulations.

This group of legal thinkers is still on line. They are still absorbing, in massive doses, some part of the almost limitless quantity of legalism that issues daily from the capitals of officialdom. They are still on line, but they are no longer on the phone. The great silent majority of the law professoriat no longer has any influential connection with the decision-making agencies of law. Felix Frank-furter (and the revolving door between Harvard and Washington, D.C.) is now a distant memory—and the image of what he and those like him represented grows increasingly irrelevant. The phone has gone dead.

And so, not surprisingly, many members of this silent majority have given up on doing law as well. That is why they are silent. They do not write. They do not speak. Once again, we think we understand why this group has become silent, why these people have abandoned doing law. Doing law, after all, is not a rewarding hobby; it is not the sort of thing people undertake because they find the activity itself intellectually stimulating or morally edifying. We do not know any lawyers who are so impressed with the aesthetic qualities or the ethical insights of contemporary American law that they write briefs in their spare time. There is no reason to do law unless one is forced to do so, or unless one hopes to achieve certain instrumental results. No one, we believe, could mistake the current practices of our hypertrophied legal system for an appealing form of life, or a desirable mode of human association.

We understand very well why the silent majority of doctrinal thinkers has become silent. But once again, we detect a certain inconsistency. For like their more theoretically inclined brethren, many of these thinkers have plainly given up on doing law themselves, and yet they nonetheless continue—in the class-room, in the faculty lounge, at the bar convention—to insist on what they still see as law's almost limitless virtues. Once again, we are inclined to wonder: If these legal thinkers do not believe that doing law is good for them, why do they continue to celebrate this law as good or ennobling for others? Here too there is a certain dissonance. No doubt, with the help of a few distinctions, it could be rationalized away.

In this book we too make no attempt to "do law." Rather, we present the reader with three interrelated accounts of how the American academic study of law is in certain respects becoming a disillusioned and demoralized discipline, and we point toward the intellectual possibilities that this same disenchantment is helping to create.

Consider that most typical product of what Pierre Schlag has identified as normative legal thought: the one-hundred-page, five-hundred-footnote law review article advocating the "extension," or the "reform," or even the "trans-formation" of some large sector of American legality. It is becoming more and more evident that this amicus brief to no one in particular—this judicial opinion-in-waiting—has almost no chance of effecting any of its carefully crafted recommendations. How could it? For, as Schlag points out,

> [while] the legal brief is almost invariably addressed to some agent who
> has the jurisdiction and the power to grant the relief requested, normative
> legal thought is almost invariably not. That too explains why the conclu-
> sion in normative legal thought is such an anxious moment. In the border-
> lands of consciousness, there is a sense in which normative legal thinkers
> know their prescriptions and recommendations are not going anywhere.
> In the borderlands of consciousness, legal thinkers know that within the
> tens of thousands of pages of volume 1 to 103 of the *Harvard Law Review*—
> for instance—there is an abundance of prescriptions and recommenda-
> tions that have gone nowhere and do nothing but serve as an occasion for
> repeating argument structures and forms we now look back on with an
> odd mixture of amusement, disdain, and humbling self-recognition.[1]

Still, tenure must be granted, panels at scholarly conferences must be filled,
student editors must be kept busy, and the normative legal thinker must have
something to do. The peculiar enterprise of telling complex social practices
how to reform themselves in jargon-ridden articles published in unread legal
journals rolls on like some great unstoppable machine, full of almost comically
grandiose statements of the type "the interpretive principles suggested here are
intended for the President, regulatory agencies, and Congress, as well as for the
courts."[2]

And yet the suspicion arises that, given the probability of success for such
suggestions, normative legal thinkers are now to a great extent just going
through the motions. All that rhetorical passion, all that display of reformist
zeal or revolutionary ardor, is being spent on the production of prescriptions
whose contents remain almost completely sealed off from the corridors of
power. What are the social and psychological consequences of devoting one's
professional life to such an instrumentally dubious and intellectually truncated
enterprise? What sort of discipline could we expect to find organized around
such a set of practices? These are among the questions that animate Schlag's
essays, "Normativity and the Politics of Form" and "Clerks in the Maze."

Or consider the academic cottage industry devoted to the production of
theories of legal interpretation. Paul Campos suggests that these theories routinely overlook the ontologically deficient character of the texts on which such
lavish interpretive efforts are expended. The textual products of legal bureaucratic practice are often empty or impoverished receptacles exhibiting little or
none of the semantic richness imputed to them by interpretive theorists. A very
few legal texts can become sites for a modern brand of theological hermeneutics, where the sacral impulses of an essentially secular culture can be projected
onto the detritus of the past. "The protean mutability of such texts blends with

the imperishable marks of the writing within which they are encoded to create a cultural icon whose meaning is always changing but whose essence is mystically felt to remain the same. . . . A text—any text—is subject to the caducity and corruption of all mortal endeavors: the Constitution is not. The constitutional text might be the work of malevolent demiurgi or mere men, but the Constitution itself—protean, unchanging, responsive to our endless needs—could only be the work of a god."[3] Such interpretive practices may work well enough when manifested within the rather special context created by our ritualistic invocations of an essentially mythologized cultural artifact, but what relevance do they have to the work of almost all lawyers—and for that matter, of the great bulk of legal academics? What kind of interpretive practice will flourish under conditions in which essentially mindless bureaucratic texts are treated as if they were repositories of rich semantic meaning? What effects, psychological and social, are to be expected from attempts to deploy the equivalent of a theological hermeneutics on contemporary Supreme Court opinions, or on administrative agency regulations, or the arcane provisions of the tax code, or the bureaucratized verbal mazes of the Congressional Record? Campos presents and explores these themes in "Against Constitutional Theory" and "A Heterodox Catechism."

The story is told of a Baptist farmer who, when asked if he believed in baptism by total immersion, replied, "Believe in it? Hell, I've seen it done." In Steve Smith's work, the sense of emptiness and futility that haunts both much of normative legal thought and its offspring, legal interpretive theory, is linked explicitly to nothing less than the metaphysical crisis that generates the dark humor of the farmer's comment. His essays "Nonsense and Natural Law" and "Idolatry in Constitutional Interpretation" endeavor to show that normative legal interpreters have for the most part lost their faith in the metaphysical presuppositions necessary for a belief in a sufficiently transcendent law, and even for a belief in such crucial jurisprudential artifacts as "principles." Smith argues that if certain legal texts are to be taken as worthy of the respect that conventional legal ideology demands we give them, then nothing less is demanded of the interpreter than a belief that those texts were authored by some superhuman agency—a demand to which, of course, the modern interpreter cannot consciously accede. Here, the idolatrous character of many of the practices described in Schlag's and Campos's essays is made explicit, and is explicitly problematized:

> The modern idolater still must do what idolaters have always had to do—
> endow a mundane object with supernatural attributes and then forget or
> deny the human source and imaginary quality of those attributes. But the

secular idolater must do more: he must deny not only the idol-making process but also its conclusion. In a legal world that aspires to be secular, no appeal to transcendent authority and no Kierkegaardian leap of faith are permissible. Consequently, the legal idolater must at the same time tacitly affirm and explicitly deny (even to himself) the qualities that he imaginatively ascribes to law in order to make it worthy of being "interpreted" and obeyed.[4]

What are the consequences for legal thought of engaging in a theological enterprise without an enabling deity—of practicing what Campos calls a kind of secular fundamentalism? What sort of "reasoned dialogue" will take place under such conditions?

These essays, then, present our diagnoses of the present situation in American legal thought. For the many normative legal thinkers who engage in a variety of essentially idolatrous interpretive practices, law has become a substitute for, or a continuation of, other kinds of faith. Understandably, perhaps, these thinkers would prefer not to ask certain questions—questions whose answers might lead to the death of yet another god. But that is not a state of mind that lends itself to critical inquiry. It is, as one of us has written, part of a perspective "that knows how to question its gods, its values, but dares not do so for fear of confronting a loss it knows, on some level, has already occurred."[5]

"In heaven," wrote Grant Gilmore, "there will be no law. . . . In Hell there will be nothing but law, and due process will be meticulously observed."[6] We have written this book partly out of the conviction that the present moment is crucial for American law and for American legal thought. We believe that "the law" has become so hypertrophied, so inauthentic, so lacking in any sense of its own limits, so totalizing in its claim to rule all human relations, so fraught with transaction costs, and so laden with possibilities for harassment, intimidation, leverage, coercion, and bad faith that it has become necessary to speak against that law. This is, of course, disturbing, but it also presents legal thinkers with a tremendous opportunity. Any attempt to study a complex ideological system for what it is, rather than simply accepting that system's prelapsarian understanding of itself, is best undertaken at moments of profound crisis, alienation, and doubt. American legal thinkers are being cast out of their garden, but the world is all before them; and out of what once seemed Eden we must make our solitary ways.

A HETERODOX CATECHISM

Paul F. Campos

Let me try to state in a nutshell how I view the work of judging—my approach, I believe, is neither liberal nor conservative. . . . As Justice Oliver Wendell Holmes counseled, one of the most sacred duties of a judge is not to read her convictions into the Constitution. I have tried and I will continue to try to follow the model Justice Holmes set in holding that duty sacred.
—Ruth Bader Ginsburg

WHAT DID JUDGE GINSBURG promise the assembled multitudes? That she would judge rather than legislate; that her views on all matters pertaining to the meaning of the Constitution would not affect her views concerning the Constitution's meaning; that this paradoxical task was not only possible but indeed a sacred trust best illustrated by the restrained judicial activism manifested in the constitutional jurisprudence of that Nietzschean Christian, that pacific warrior, Oliver Wendell Holmes; and that she was neither liberal nor conservative but would be both and neither, as her oath of service to the law required.

What reaction did these promises elicit?

Universal cries of hallelujah, unto us a judge is given.

Is it possible to enumerate the sources of this splendid unanimity?

Such sources included, but were not limited to, the judge's gender, which elicited from that mostly male consortium a chivalrous reserve reminiscent of bygone days of errantry; the still fresh recollection of similar proceedings involving then Judge, now Justice Clarence Thomas and then Professor, now Saint Anita Hill, and the concomitant unhappiness which resulted from that less than optimal display of what might charitably be characterized as the tangled passions of a human heart, as well as the feminine reticence or even revulsion with which that display was met; the even more distasteful memories of the unforgettable auto-da-fé featuring then Judge, now iconic victim of an unscrupulous smear campaign Robert Bork; the tedium which any examination of questions of constitutional practice and theory naturally generates in everyone associated with or subjected to such questions; the certain knowledge that the principled distinction between law and politics was fully appreciated by the guest of honor; and (not least) the power that wishful thinking always exercises over the affairs of men.

Did certain questions germane to the issues at hand then go unasked?

They did.

What examples come most readily to mind?

First, some inquiry into the ontological status of that object of veneration yclept The Constitution, to which everyone (senators, judges, presidents, popes, emperors, Antichrists) must swear a most solemn oath to uphold, come hell or high water (subject, it goes without saying, to those procedures for amendment exhaustively described in Article 5 of that self-same document), and to no other earthly or infernal power world without end amen.

What makes such an inquiry desirable?

The confusion resulting from an inability or unwillingness to identify the meaning of that document with some set of semantic intentions emanating from an identifiable agent.

Does not the text of the document provide an adequate source of emanating signification?

No.

Why not?

Because of the perverse semantic plurality of natural languages, which provide an infinite play of signifiers to which more than one meaning may always be attached.

Does the attribution of meaning through the act of identifying that meaning with the semantic intentions of a particular author or group of authors adequately specify the meaning of the text in question?

Yes. However, the functional inadequacy of intentionalist accounts of constitutional interpretation are too well known to suffer repetition.

What assertions will be made in the course of suffering that repetition?

That among the innumerable sins of originalism might be counted the epistemological breakdown almost certain to occur when future generations attempt to determine just what someone meant or did not mean when employing human speech across the unbridgeable chasm of the obscuring centuries; the interpretive crisis occasioned by the ineluctable modality of human experience—to wit, the unimpeachable fact that the authors of that cryptic document failed to consider such cultural and technological wonders as wiretaps, interstate telephone lines, facsimile machines, condoms, the inflammable nature of national symbols, and the secularization of Christian holidays via the implacable logic of consumerism, not to mention the unforeseen consequences flowing out of an ever-broadening stream of interstate commerce that would come to include (among other things) cows, wheat, lottery tickets, slaves, compact disc players, certificates of deposit, greeting cards, treasures from furthest Araby, financial quotations, photographs of naked women engaged in crimes against nature, electronic signals bearing discrete parcels of information amenable to interpretation via a binary code as first envisioned by that enigmatic genius of the cryptographic art Alan Turing, baseball gloves, Japanese ceramics, sheet music, the unwritten history of the future, and the tangled passions of a human heart (see infra); the conceptual impossibility of reconciling the various conflicting intentions of the Framers, the Ratifiers, and the People Themselves; the natural repugnance felt by all at being forever within the clammy grasp of the past's dead hand; the obvious reluctance of the contemporary American public to accept what would then be the inescapable truth that the state of Connecticut is not constitutionally prohibited from violating the sacred precincts of the marital bedroom; and the simple yet embarrassing fact that no one whose opinion in these matters counted had given sustained attention to what the problematic authors of the Constitution, however defined, had meant by the words of that document since *Marbury v. Madison* or time immemorial, whichever came first.

Do the previous decisions of the United States Supreme Court, ennobled by the ineffable dignity that the principle of stare decisis lends to these fragments we have shored against our ruin, provide, in and of themselves, an authoritative source of constitutional meaning?

No, because this Court always stands ready to correct its errors, even though of long standing, those errors being all but incorrigible to legislative remedy.

To what additional sources of signification did Judge Ginsburg allude, given the evident failure of constitutional text, authorial intention, and judicial precedent to provide adequate sources of contemporary constitutional meaning?

She alluded to a jurisprudential method.

How will this method affect her constitutional practice?

Evidence can be adduced from the judge's own opinions, produced via the Federal Circuit Court for the District of Columbia.

What evidence does a cursory examination of this jurisprudential product yield?

That the then judge, now justice will employ the procrustean methods of her generation's jurisprudential mentors, Henry Hart and Albert Sacks, progenitors of *The Legal Process* (tentative draft, 1958), in order to better achieve the aspirational goals of our constitutional order through a scrupulous interpretation of an infinite variety of ambiguous legislative acts, conflicting lower court rulings, and (especially) the complex directives of administrative agencies, so as to lend formal certainty to social interactions of every kind, do what substantial justice requires, and, in general, make the world safe for bureaucracy.

What judicial procedures do these methods involve?

They involve, first, a careful, not to say exhaustive, review of all the relevant legal materials whose meaning, properly interpreted, might throw light on the proper resolution of the sorts of cases and controversies that courts display a special institutional competence toward resolving; second, the formulation of various complex, interlocking directives by means of which the properly interpreted meaning of the materials may be made synonymous with those interpretations that flow from the proper deployment of those interpretive methods which give the meaning of those materials a public and formal character, thereby making that meaning accessible to everyone who has undergone a socialization process resembling that to which students at elite American law schools were subjected circa 1958; third, the acceptance of the pragmatic yet principled dictum that law is a purposive activity which continually strives to solve the basic problems of social living; fourth, the full recognition of the indispensable role played by that most lawyerly virtue, procedure, in assuring a kind of objectivity to what would otherwise degenerate into an unconstrained act of judicial fiat; fifth, the establishment of the principle or public norm that decisions which are the duly arrived at result of duly established procedures for making decisions of this kind ought to be accepted as binding on the whole society unless and until they are duly changed; and, sixth, the sobering realization that the only alternative to regularized and peaceable methods of decision is a disintegrating resort to violence.

Can an example be given of a methodological directive that these methods presume to compel?

Yes. That a statute ought always to be presumed to be the work of reasonable men pursuing reasonable purposes reasonably.

What does the substance of this particular conclusion indicate?

That the methods propounded by *The Legal Process* (tentative draft, 1958) depend on the tautological or even shamanistic invocation of the signifier "reasonable"; that reasonable men will seem reasonably reasonable only under conditions that generate sufficient ideological consensus as to what reason requires; that the elite American law school circa 1958 was indeed such a place; that the now mind of the then student Ruth Ginsburg appears to represent a paradigmatic product of that environment; and that this mind's subsequent legal career provides a performative demonstration of the almost fanatical worship of technocratic rationality which that environment apparently induced.

What is the central tenet of this form of worship?

That law is a rational and self-conscious activity.

What heretical suspicion must then be suppressed at all subsequent costs, intellectual, psychological, and economic?

That we have no idea what we are talking about.

How is this suppression achieved?

Through the painful evocation of those fine and careful distinctions that mark the work of the legal craftswoman as she pursues with an almost Sapphic passion a jealous mistress along those well-trodden paths formed by the thrilling tradition of Anglo-American law, as this law strives to fulfill that glorious destiny foreordained by its place in the structure of American institutions as a voice of reason, charged with the creative function of discerning afresh and of articulating and developing impersonal and durable principles of constitutional law.

What other phrase describes this activity?

Boring your audience into submission.

What jurisprudential virtues did Judge Ginsburg's testimony exemplify?

Powerful intelligence, as demonstrated by her manipulation of many a Solomonic puzzle prepared for her by the Judiciary Committee staff; great patience, as manifested by her willingness to endure stoically the torrent of verbal nonsense issuing forth from the committee's chair, the Honorable Joseph Biden of Delaware; surprising candor, in regard to her answers concerning the constitutional status of abortion rights, whether located, as we feel they are, in the general vicinity of the Fourth, Ninth, and Nineteenth Amendments, or alternatively, as suggested by the judge herself, in a dynamic reinterpretation of the equal protection clause; and political acumen, as illustrated by her deft deflection of various potentially problematic questions regarding the practice of judicial review.

What jurisprudential vices did that same testimony point toward?

A certain rigidity of intellect, displayed, for example, in Judge Ginsburg's willingness to assert that her personal views on capital punishment would not influence her judicial evaluation of that practice; a powerful ability to tolerate cognitive dissonance, as evidenced by such assertions; an evident failure to comprehend that the sacred text of her generation of academic lawyers, *The Legal Process* (tentative draft, 1958), signaled the arrival of the characteristic crisis of modernism into the cathedral of American legal thought; and a resultant uncritical manifestation of the cognitive style exemplified by the substance of that text.

In what way does Judge Ginsburg's jurisprudential Ur-text, *The Legal Process* (tentative draft, 1958), indicate the arrival of the characteristic crisis of modernism in the history of American legal thought?

In its eternal status as a tentative draft rather than a published text.

What does this tentative status signify?

That God is dead.

How does the failure to publish one's work in any way indicate the necrotic condition of the erstwhile Almighty Creator of heaven and earth?

By signaling a sudden realization on the part of various erstwhile subcreators, including, but not limited to, novelists (Kafka), philosophers (Wittgenstein), architects (Gaudi), and legal process scholars (Hart and Sacks) that this (their work) is as good as it is going to get, and that the sudden exaltation of human creative labor into the sphere of the quasi- or pseudodivine implicitly requires of that work nothing less than perfection, despite the overwhelming evidence that perfection is not, has not been, and never will be a human attribute, and that therefore their appointed task is impossible, absurd, and yet absolutely necessary.

What does this realization generate?

A kind of paralysis.

What is the source of this paralysis?

A neurotic compulsion to devote one's life to the attainment of an unattainable goal.

Such as?

Creating sacred texts in an irremediably secular world, solving the fundamental mysteries of human existence, designing places of worship that will adequately honor a being who does not exist, and discovering the meaning of the Constitution.

With the help of?

The best minds of my generation.

Including?

Ackerman's paradigms, Bollinger's tolerance, Chemerinsky's anger, Dellinger's doctrines, Ely's democracy, Freeman's delusions, Grey's pragmatism, Halberstam's sister, Idolatry's cousin, Jacob's ladder, Komesar's politics, Levinson's theory, MacKinnon's machismo, Nagel's unhappiness, Omnipotence's blessing, Peller's critiques, Q's weapons, Regan's philosophy, Sandalow's skepticism, Tushnet's diatribes, Unger's priesthood, Van Alstyne's disease, Weschler's principles, Xerxes' divisions, Yudof's lucre, and Zeno's last paradox.

What, then, does the practically unanimous ascension of Judge Ginsburg portend for the next decade of constitutional commentators?

That the more it changes the more it will stay the same.

What emotions attend this realization?

Anger, frustration, resignation.

Why anger?

Because an increasingly meaningless bureaucratized discourse will continue to become ever more obscure, complex, and indeterminate.

Why frustration?

Because a surfeit of cultural angst will impel lawyers and, especially, legal academics to proclaim with increasing fervor and decreasing conviction that everything is for the best in this, the best of all possible jurisprudential worlds.

Why resignation?

Because of the evident absence of that instrumental power of reason over the course of human events which an age of reason believes rationality by its very nature must manifest.

Why is this instrumental power absent?

Because the falcon cannot hear the falconer.

What, then, is the answer?

To begin to question the instrumental power of rationality.

How well has this particular attempt succeeded?

Less than hope allowed, more than fear permitted.

What parable sums up the essence of our present constitutional condition? This one:

> They were offered the choice between becoming kings or the couriers of kings. The way children would, they all wanted to be couriers. Therefore there are only couriers who hurry about the world, shouting to each other—since there are no kings—messages that have become meaningless. They would like to put an end to this miserable life of theirs but they dare not because of their oaths of service.—Franz Kafka

WAITING FOR LANGDELL I

Interview of the Authors by Sandy Levinson

LEVINSON. I should explain the background for this. I had the great pleasure of reading a slightly earlier version in manuscript for the Duke University Press, and I very enthusiastically recommended publication because I thought all the essays were extremely interesting. This is an unusual book in the sense of three people coming together and writing essays. I think readers will have some curiosity as to what extent you actually agree or disagree with each other. Also, in reading it I was brought back to some questions I had thought about earlier in regard to my own work and, in particular, a controversy that raged about ten years ago or so in regard to an article that Paul Carrington wrote in the *Journal for Legal Education.* Roughly, the question would go like this: To what extent can the issues you raise or the positions you take easily be conveyed to law students without undercutting the basic enterprise of legal education? This comes to the question of the title, *Against the Law,* because certainly one of the questions raised by Carrington in his article was that if one is against the law, why teach it? Or, what does it mean to teach it?

I should say that I tried to suggest an answer to this because, generally speaking, I would identify myself as sympathetic with the enterprise that Carrington was attacking—a certain skepticism toward the standard pictures of legal analysis and the legal system. Indeed, in a book that I published in 1988 called *Constitutional Faith* I tried to present the defense for my continuing to teach, in a law school, much the same thing I had previously taught in a department of politics. Now, it was an important feature of Carrington's argument that he didn't say that people like me, or people like us, ought not be welcome within the academy generally; rather, he raised very specific questions about being within the legal academy. And I would at least like to begin our conversation by exploring some of these questions.

Let me begin by asking about your relationship to this title, and why don't we follow the famous alphabetic principle and begin with Paul?

CAMPOS. I would like to say first off that the alphabetic principle is somewhat misleading in this regard: this is really Pierre's title; none of us wants to take responsibility for the title, but I think Pierre really has to. It's a great title, which is the one thing that everybody who has had an encounter with this manuscript has agreed upon. That's the short and somewhat trivial answer, although I would want to express my gratitude to Pierre for allowing us to ransack his title for these purposes. I think of the title of *Against the Law* as being an expression of discontent with the notion of "the law," not as a social organization mechanism or dispute resolution process, but rather with the idea of "the law"—the almost theological, basically metaphysical idea of the law that is, I think, part of the standard orthodoxy of what is taught to students in American law schools. To me the title *Against the Law* implies that it would be better if this thing were called "social coordination and dispute processing" rather than "the law."

LEVINSON. The alphabetic principle picks up Pierre next.

SCHLAG. For me the title *Against the Law* is meant to indicate a certain direction. This book is written by three legal academics in an environment in which practically all legal academics are busy celebrating the law and are essentially engaged in activities of legitimation. We have a different orientation.

With respect to Paul Carrington's question, I think that it is useful to law students—to people who are going to become lawyers, who are going to be working with law—to take a certain amount of distance from the enterprise in which they will be engaged, particularly given the character of positive law today.

LEVINSON. We'll certainly return to Carrington. Steve?

SMITH. It is probably true that in any community or any civilization, there are going to be mechanisms for resolving disputes and making collective decisions, and the people who are responsible will give their reasons for resolving the dispute the way they have done or for making the decision that they have made. These decisions and reasons will probably be collected, organized, and used in the future. If that's what we mean by "law," then it is hard to be "against the law."

But there is something else that "the law" connotes. I have sometimes tried to use the term in uppercase and lowercase (The Law and the law) to try and distinguish between these two things, although they are so intermingled that they can't really be separated. The Law would probably be what Holmes had in mind when he talked about the "brooding omnipresence in the sky." It's the notion that there is some ontologically real and objective thing that is The Law.

Of course, almost all lawyers (and certainly law professors) who confront that notion directly would say of course they don't believe in that—they are not naive. "We're all legal realists now," and so forth. But at the same time, they may go about doing things that make no sense except on the presupposition that there *is* something like The Law. So I guess I view this book as trying in various ways to criticize that presupposition, and to point out how, whatever we may say, the presupposition does run through a lot of our activities and our writing and thinking. That's what I understand the *Against the Law* title to mean.

LEVINSON. One could imagine a book entitled *Against Morality*. This might seem like a shocking title, and yet the authors might say, "We mean to be making an ontological argument that there is no morality there. But for God's sake, don't you go thinking we are against morality. We merely have a conventionalist view of morality." So, one way of hearing you is to say that you're ontological skeptics and you want to undercut any notion of the ontological reality of law. In that sense you are "against the law." But, hey, this doesn't mean you are opposed to the legal system, to the American constitutional order; it's just that you want to emphasize that these things are practice based and convention structured rather than hooked up with some transcendental reality. Would that be a fair way of interpreting what you just said, Steve?

SMITH. I'm not sure. I think actually we're a bit ambivalent on that point. One of Paul's essays and one of mine try to develop what somebody might take to be intended as a really fundamental criticism of constitutional interpretation. But then these essays end by saying that we're not opposed to constitutional interpretation; we're arguing that it is incoherent or idolatrous, but we're not trying to get rid of it. I suspect that readers might wonder whether our disclaimer is serious. And in fact we may feel ambivalent about the question. I would say at this point, I'm agnostic in not positively trying to confine the criticism, but not necessarily being definite in extending it either.

CAMPOS. I've always found the conventionalist argument about morality to which you alluded completely unsatisfactory. It seems to me to be a sort of pragmatist cop-out to say, "Well, yeah, you thought that 'morality' referred to some kind of ontological reality, but it actually just refers to a bunch of social conventions. But there is no reason that those social conventions shouldn't have the same amount of weight or workability just because we don't happen to believe what they used to be attached to." That answer for me just doesn't work at all, and so I would, I think, go a little further than Steve in saying that if you don't believe in this metaphysic of law, a bunch of practices within the legal academy certainly don't make sense, and I think they are just the practices to which Pierre was referring. Steve actually elaborates on this theme in one of the essays, of course.

SCHLAG. If I may add one thing, there are implications in all of this for practice. These aren't the sorts of implications that take a normative form in the sense of proposing solutions, but there are clear implications for practice, one of which is to recognize the absurdity of the situation in law. If I can elaborate on what Paul said, once you give up a certain metaphysics of law and you go to a sort of neopragmatic or conventionalist stance, there is no reason to believe anymore. I think all three of us are agreeing on that—that once the metaphysic is gone, we are indeed in deep intellectual difficulty. Once the metaphysic supporting law, once the metaphysic supporting morality, is no longer credible, one simply can't, as an intellectual matter, go on pretending that we can just use the same words to mean the same thing in pretty much the same old way. As an intellectual matter, that will not work. Now, it may well work—*work* being a technical term here—in a personal sense, in one's daily life, but as an intellectual matter, it simply won't work.

SMITH. This might be a good place, I think, to tie this discussion into your question about Carrington. Because I guess I think that you *can* say that a given community can function with the kind of discourse that presupposes certain things, even though those things are not real in the sense that the community presupposes, so long as they believe it. They may be able to carry on an enterprise, and even from an outside standpoint you might be able to say it's performing a valuable social function. I suppose anthropologists would be very used to thinking in this way about cultures that they don't participate in themselves.

In Brian Simpson's article on common law and legal theory, he argues that the common law basically was this kind of system. It works so long as you have a fairly small group of people who are socialized in the same way, who share common practices, beliefs. But as soon as you don't have that situation anymore, then it won't work.

So it seems to me that Carrington's position could be right in a given set of circumstances. I've often at least jokingly told Pierre that Carrington *was* right—Pierre *should* be drummed out of the legal academy—and I probably should be too.

LEVINSON. But you're less certain about that.

SMITH. Yes. And in reality the answer is that we don't have that kind of cohesive, uniformly socialized legal profession anyway now. So although Carrington's argument could be right in a certain context, it isn't right in our context. He's already too late.

LEVINSON. In *Constitutional Faith*, one of the things I suggested was that our era is seeing the death of constitutionalism as an informing vision in a way that, arguably, the nineteenth century, at least among intellectuals, saw the death of

God as a certain sort of informing vision. To what extent would you commit yourself, at least descriptively, to accepting the notion that we are caught in what Matthew Arnold called "the long withdrawing melancholy roar"—of either constitutionalism specifically or law more generally. Owen Fiss wrote an article about ten years ago, very critical of Critical Legal Studies, called "The Death of Law?" which for Fiss was a very bad thing indeed. So I am curious as to whether you would agree, at least descriptively, maybe even normatively, with the statement that the task of the intellectual is to tell the truth, and the truth is that these old informing visions no longer work. We have to find something else.

SMITH. It's hard to say. Sometimes my perception is that as a descriptive matter, the faith in the constitutional vision is dying out. It seems to me that there is a kind of demoralization, for example, about constitutional law. How do we teach this anymore? What are we supposed to do? But then this might just be another instance of the pervasive phenomenon where people you happen to talk with naturally tend to think some of the same things that you do, and so you get a skewed perception of reality. It may be that this faith just springs eternal. Constitutional scholarship goes on, and the Supreme Court keeps going on. And there are even signs of a bit of retrenchment. Critical Legal Studies has faded away. And originalism, which you might have thought would have faded away a couple of decades ago, has revived and you see signs of retrenchment.

But my perception, I guess, is that in the retrenchment there's a kind of desperation, a kind of awareness that this game is going to disappear unless we really make an effort to save it. And that already reflects a sense that it's a losing battle at this point.

CAMPOS. Yeah, I want to agree with what Steve said, although I think perhaps I would go a little bit further than he. I think what Steve says is indeed happening. And it's already happened to the Langdellian vision. If you look at the way those guys wrote seventy to eighty years ago, nobody believes in the kind of law they believed in. That's gone! I also think that the very efforts that have been buttressed up to replace it are suffering the same thing. The most common move is the claim that law is a sort of postrealist, instrumental power game, politics with a special vocabulary; as if political rhetoric and political metaphysics were in such great shape that we could just keep doing politics as usual in this special language. That won't work.

SCHLAG. Yes. I think that talking about the problem in terms of the Nietzschean situation is a good way of talking about it. I want to add two things to what Paul said. It seems to me that there are two things that make the situation for law and the legal academy particularly acute.

First, law is, by virtue of its observance of precedents and canonical authorities, extremely backward looking. The identity of law is based very much on authority. And the fundamental aesthetics of those authorities are set way back in the eighteenth century and the nineteenth century—the eighteenth century by virtue of the constitutional founding, the nineteenth century by virtue of the professionalization of the American law school, the establishment of Langdellianism. Legal academics have no control over this fundamental aesthetic. What's more, legal academics are not in control of the present production of authoritative materials. If anyone is in control of the production of these authoritative materials now, it is judges and legislators. And these people need not be, by vocation or avocation, intellectuals. They don't need to be interested in anything intellectual. They have certain legal tasks to perform, right? And the tasks they have to perform are not defined with a view to achieving intellectual perfection, truth, or any other cognitive virtue. Now, the problem is that legal academics have identified with these actors. Legal academics have patterned their professional identities after judges and legislators and the like. This means that law has never really achieved the status of an intellectual discipline. Legal academics have not been in control of the materials; we have not been in control of any method; and so it's not a surprise that after a while, one should turn around and find that there is not much there. This is what's happening now.

Now, the second thing. Critics of the enterprise of law, legalism, or legal thought have been rather systematically marginalized throughout the history of the American academy. One can speak here of the marginalization of the critics. One can tell the same story about the realists. The critics have in a sense been kept on the outside and the enterprise has continued to reproduce itself on the supposition that the true belief is true. But this true belief has been sustained essentially by political acts—by personnel actions (or nonaction)—and the result at this point is that we have arrived at a kind of belief in the legal academy which is not very vital and not very appealing

SMITH. Could I ask you a question, Pierre? From what you said, it seems to me someone might infer that there need not be any Nietzschean crisis in the *practice* of law. There is a crisis within the academy. But there is also a really deep split between the way legal academics talk about things and the way lawyers, judges, and politicians talk about them. The practitioners might go on perfectly well. They don't need, as you say, truth anyway, and so there's no reason why they need to suffer from any crisis of faith.

SCHLAG. That poses a very difficult question which we sometimes talk about. The question is to what extent does a social system depend on its being logical, coherent, and conceptually appealing. And that's something that we have not answered, I think. My assumption is that a social system can indeed survive and continue to reproduce itself amid large degrees of incoherence, contradiction, paradox, and the like.

SMITH. I was thinking that Sandy's analogy to religion might be helpful here as well. Because one might say that the "death of God" creates a crisis within certain intellectual classes, but as far as people generally are concerned, there's no reason why a religion can't go on and flourish as well as it ever did.

LEVINSON. Both in fairness to Paul Carrington and also to grasp some of the paradoxes of contemporary legal education, it was Carrington as dean who hired Stanley Fish at the Duke Law School. And one has to assume that he read Fish before welcoming him to Duke and giving him a joint appointment at the Law School and the English Department, even though quite obviously Fish did not hold a law degree and did not have the standard credentials. So part of the question of trying to understand what's happening in the academy involves the fact that even in ostensibly conservative schools with ostensibly conservative deans, there has been a certain welcoming of some kinds of criticism. But then I guess the point of these comments is to ask you perhaps to elaborate a bit your own stance relative to somebody like Fish, because certainly many of our colleagues across the land would see Fish as somebody who is against the law, who is part of the attack, the loss of faith, and so on. But there he is at the Duke Law School, hired by Paul Carrington. Now is this a deep paradox? Or are there indeed interesting differences between Fish's sort of critique of the law and your own that would make it explicable why Paul Carrington would hire Fish but maybe not one of you?

CAMPOS. I think that's quite true. I think that Fish would not see himself as being against the law, I mean, in the sense that you're referring to. But I think that I would see myself—and perhaps all of us—as being in some way in a similar position to his. We are saying something along the lines of, "Are we against unicorns?" No, we're not against unicorns, we're not against the study of unicorns, we're not against the worship of unicorns. What we do want to point out, though, is that if you want to use a unicorn to mow your lawn by eating the grass, some problems are going to arise. Now, we think that's a legitimate kind of thing to point out within a university. Still, Carrington brings up a troubling point. It may be that for the replication of the social system we call law to "work" you have to have people who really believe that unicorns are biological, as opposed to literary or mythological, phenomena. I think that's a very difficult question to answer, and I certainly don't think he has the answer to it. Carrington's willingness to hire Stanley Fish speaks very well to his breadth of intellectual interest, but it also speaks, I think, to the sense that a lot of people have that it's too late at this juncture to be saying, "You must believe." Look, once you are saying, "You must believe," the game is pretty much over. You just don't believe anymore. By contrast, if you believe, then you believe. But if you're saying, "Well, I'm not sure if I believe, but I *should* believe," that's not belief, that's simulated belief. And I think we have a lot of simulated belief in legal academia right now in which people believe on Tuesday but don't believe on Friday, believe in front of a classroom but don't believe in the lounge, believe with the left side of their brain but don't believe with the right side. I think Stanley Fish wouldn't find this surprising at all. He'd say, "Well, what did you expect?" Right? And I think that's something worth saying, and that maybe in a very different way we're saying a similar sort of thing.

SCHLAG. I think it's important to point out another paradox, which I think has been already hinted at. And it's this. In one sense, Carrington might be right; it may be that in order to sustain the enterprise of law you need people to have faith and to have belief, and therefore you should drum out those people who don't have faith or belief. It may also be the case that for the success of the enterprise of law you need people who are rather radical in their assessment of the enterprise and who have very strong criticisms to make. That's also just as plausible. I don't think anybody has ironclad answers to these kinds of questions. Most of us in the university are committed to reason in the sense of discussing these things. And it seems to me that both positions are plausible and that the appropriate approach is to engage in arguments back and forth. To invite one side or the other to depart from the academy doesn't seem to me to be an appropriate move.

LEVINSON. This, for me, brings up a question relating to how Judge Harry Edwards, in a much discussed article in the *University of Michigan Law Review,* seemed to make some arguments along Carringtonian lines, and I should emphasize again in fairness to Paul Carrington that he has disowned some readings of his own article about, for example, whether he would drum people out of the academy. He says he would not—that this was an unfair reading. But some people did read it that way, and so my reference in part is to the text rather than necessarily to what Paul Carrington's views happen to be. But there was a tone in Edwards's piece that the legal academy has fallen into the hands of too many people who just don't take the traditional legal enterprise seriously, and this is a terrible thing. He then either said or can be read as saying not that he is opposed to the presence of *some* people who have these understandings, rather that there are just too many such people. There is some sort of ideal balance in the team called a law school faculty, and he fears that there are now too many left tackles and not enough fullbacks, or whatever.

SMITH. One Pierre Schlag on a faculty is enough?

LEVINSON. Well, this is an important question. Richard Posner, who delivers a withering attack on Edwards, also at times uses a team metaphor, and there is, I think, something very appealing about that notion, that you don't want everybody to have the same views, and so on. But it does boil down to the question: Would you say that it's very important that there continue to be people who accept the traditional apparatus, who pray before the icon of law every day, who don't have the kinds of doubts that you express? Or would you want a law school faculty composed entirely of people broadly speaking with your take on our present situation?

SCHLAG. You know, I don't think there's much risk that there will be many people like us in the academy.

LEVINSON. But that's a bit of an evasion.

SCHLAG. Yeah, it's an outright evasion, but I happen to think it's quite true. The question, really, for most of the history of the academy was whether there was going to be *any* critical perspective. I think a review of the legal academy starting with Langdell in 1871 would bear that out.

Putting that aside, one of the things I think we need to talk about is whether or not the sort of extraordinarily refined doctrinal approach that someone like Judge Harry Edwards champions is producing anything of value. Is it producing anything of value in the academy and is it producing anything of value in the law? That is, what do we have to show for all this doctrinal complexity apart from a massive piling on of transaction costs? Is there anything to show for it?

Now, what has happened in the past is that these kinds of questions weren't raised very radically and people would answer the questions in doctrinal terms. They would say, "Of course the doctrine is good. Of course it makes sense." Why? "Because, look at this other doctrine. The doctrine is necessary because it's hooked up with this other doctrine; and if we don't have that doctrine, then. . . ." Anyway, it was basically rather naive circles of doctrine justifying more doctrine.

For my part, I have very serious doubts about the value of the kind of legal process doctrinalism that Judge Harry Edwards seems to champion—both in the academy and in practice. Now, by virtue of the fact that judges like Harry Edwards seem to be wedded to doctrinal analysis of this extraordinarily over-wrought variety, it is something that we have to teach to our students. But I doubt, to put it in Paul's earlier terms, whether it is a good system of dispute processing, whether we are getting anything of value, anything that is normatively appealing, anything that is economically efficient, anything that is illuminating. I think, rather, that all this doctrinalism, all this legalism, has deleterious effects.

LEVINSON. Okay, but as I hear you, I hear you saying that, really and truly, if you could design a law school adequate to our present situation, you would not really want any doctrinalists around. I think one way of reading Richard Posner's *Overcoming Law*—and particularly the first chapter, which contains a savage, wonderfully vibrant, con brio attack on Herbert Wechsler and the notion of neutral principles and balancing and the like—is that Posner would have real doubts about hiring Wechsler or many Wechslerians, except maybe as museum pieces; and Posner is actually a very generous person. There is, in fact, a list in which he indicates lots of people he thinks are valuable, but I don't have the feeling that he really thinks Wechsler is one of them. Duncan Kennedy is part of the list; Mary Ann Glendon is part of the list. And I really don't hear you finding any place in the academy for those who are "traditional doctrinalists."

SCHLAG. No, I wish to correct that misimpression. The reason to have doctrinalists in the academy has to do with the fact that this is a kind of law that is practiced by our courts. If it were not a kind of law practiced by our courts, then I doubt doctrinalism would have much appeal. But since it is practiced by the courts, it's necessary to have doctrinalists, and it's necessary to have doctrinalists who are good at doctrinalism. And that presumably means people who, at least in part, believe in it.

CAMPOS. But not too good.

SMITH. Mediocre doctrinalists?

CAMPOS. Yeah. Mediocre doctrine is okay. But the terrible thing is the level of sophistication that the doctrinal enterprise has achieved. I think it's fine to have doctrinalists around for the reasons that Pierre says, and also I would want to emphasize again that this whole conversation is taking place at the level of the hypothetical and is rather absurd. I mean, we have ten thousand doctrinalists and three guys writing a book called *Against the Law* . . .

SMITH. Soon to be drummed out of the academy. . . .

CAMPOS. The point is that "advocating" mediocre doctrine would be the zenith of normative utopianism—the kind of zany notion that the world would be made perfect if only we got rid of the Third Amendment and moved the Sixth over on the other side of the Eighth, and then we'll have a perfect Constitution, to use Henry Monaghan's wonderfully sarcastic phrase. So, I would say that, leaving aside the completely unreal question of whether or not there should be doctrinalists in the legal academy, I would nevertheless like to see doctrinalists who have a certain attitude that is not reflected by the kind of thing that is produced by the law clerks to the judges on the D.C. Circuit or the Supreme Court, where you have this basically neurotic practice of elaborating massive picayune mazes—to use Pierre's words—in a vain attempt to try to figure out "the law." Doctrinalism is like hot fudge—it's fine in its own place, and it has its uses, but we've got way too much of it and it's way too complicated, and I think that many lawyers are beginning to get a feeling that this stuff isn't working because there's too much of it, it's too complex, nobody can understand it, it's too expensive to deploy, and it's really kind of distasteful on all sorts of levels. So I would say, yes, we should have doctrinalists, but not *fanatical* doctrinalists.

SMITH. On the general theme of the conversation, I think that a criticism like Harry Edwards's gets a lot of force from a general societal dissatisfaction with the legal profession. Everybody seems to believe now that there is lot of dissatisfaction with the legal profession; the O. J. Simpson trial is sort of a focal point for this right now. It's only natural that this, in turn, causes a lot of soul searching and criticism of the legal academy. And a criticism like Edwards's can sound like it's resonating with this general dissatisfaction. But the irony here is that the popular dissatisfaction with the law has to do with precisely the kind of highly developed or aggravated state of affairs that a fanatical doctrinal approach produces. The public, I think, is dissatisfied with the proceedings in the O. J. Simpson trial not so much because they think these lawyers are too theoretical these days, or lacking in faith in the law. The public is concerned that the lawyers are *too lawyerly*—too good at making distinctions and running the procedures out indefinitely. And if this is the source of the natural concern within the legal academy, it seems to me a real mistake to think that a move in the direction that Edwards suggests—or, for that matter, the MacCrate Report— will be responsive to those problems. If anything, a more reflective, theoretical approach would seem to be a better response to those kinds of concerns.

CAMPOS. Yes, and I'd like to add that, in classic doctrinal terms, what we need are worse lawyers. We need people who don't find the eighty-fourth argument, who don't dig through the administrative regulations, who don't pile on the transaction costs, as Pierre puts it. In the essay "A Heterodox Catechism" I argue that it's no coincidence that Hart and Sacks weren't able to publish *The Legal Process*. They literally *couldn't* get to the end. They literally couldn't stop. I try to tie it in with a kind of modernist illness that since you have to be God and you have to get it right, you can never actually do it. So you have all these modernist thinkers, artists, and so forth, who leave these abandoned works around that they can never actually complete, and *The Legal Process* is an example of this.

What saves the legal system so often is simply scarcity. It's simply the fact that time is limited, money is limited, judgment has to be rendered, something has to be done, and so the thing gets processed more quickly than it otherwise would. What to me is most interesting about the O. J. Simpson case is that this is how the legal system, on some level, is *supposed* to work. If you have all this money available, and you have all these resources poured into the thing, it will just go on forever. And you'll get this thing that makes you wonder, well, is this good? The reason, after all, we have to plead things out or settle the case is because we have a system that, if it were routinely activated, it would simply collapse. So we activate it only on rare occasions, and then this kind of sacred monster grows up before our eyes.

SCHLAG. What procedures should we use to decide what procedures we should use to instruct the jury on the procedures they should use to decide the case?

LEVINSON. I want to take up for a moment a related topic. If one reads Harry Edwards, or Mary Ann Glendon's quite influential book *A Nation under Lawyers,* the claim is made that in essence the academy is being taken over by— Glendon talks about advocacy scholars, Edwards about interdisciplinarians who just aren't interested in helping judges out, or whatever. Now, your perception is that people with what I would describe as "our point of view"—because I am certainly broadly and maybe even narrowly sympathetic to the work you're doing—are being ever more marginalized and the doctrinalists are still in control. Yet if you look at some analysis citation counts or publications in prestigious law journals, you find that, at least in recent years, the most heavily cited articles have tended to be nondoctrinal articles. Every article in this book was published in a highly prestigious venue, and I think it is generally thought that if you write a classic doctrinalist article trying to get something straight, you will be condemned to a second- or third-tier review and are, in fact, not likely to be very much cited except by those relatively few other people who are doing doctrinal articles. How does one put together, if at all, these wildly conflicting images of the present state of the legal academy?

CAMPOS. I don't necessarily see any contradiction. Everyone is besieged. Everyone is, to some extent, correct in perceiving that they are besieged.

SCHLAG. I agree with Paul. I don't think there is a contradiction. I think in the last five to ten years we have seen the exhaustion of what were once some extraordinarily vital schools of thought. Legal theory is nowhere at present. It has suffered by virtue of the fact that the courts, regardless of their political orientation, paid no attention to legal theory. Critical Legal Studies is no longer really on the scene. Law and economics has perfected itself to such a state of sophistication that it is no longer accessible to the general run of legal academics. The people who do law and economics now have Ph.D.s, and they mostly write to each other. They are, in a phrase used by George Priest, in their "own bubble." So you have the exhaustion of a terrific number of previously vital schools of thought. So that's fairly demoralizing.

Then, as a general matter, there is a tremendous gap between what legal academics are doing and what the courts are doing; the courts are not paying attention to what legal academics have to say. This is extraordinarily demoralizing for many people—particularly the doctrinalists. I mean, if the courts are not listening, why on earth would one write doctrinal articles? Why on earth would one write such things? Writing doctrine is certainly not rewarding in and of itself. It is not as if doctrine has an appealing aesthetic. Lawyers don't write briefs in their spare time. Why should legal academics? The demoralization of the doctrinal enterprise is very significant because in the American legal academy, doctrinalism is demographically dominant. And yet, as an intellectual genre it is exhausted. That's not a good combination.

So I think in the last five or ten years, legal academics have realized that basically they don't have a great deal of power. And so there is a tremendous amount of demoralization on all sides.

SMITH. Well, it depends, I guess, on how you classify people and how you classify articles, and which are doctrinal. I would think that the articles that get published the most, and that get cited the most, *are* doctrinal in a broad sense. They may not be a certain kind of old-fashioned doctrinalism—there is a little theory, a little policy thrown in—but they are focused on doctrines or formulas. They prescribe solutions for rights or solutions for particular problems, and so forth. My own experience, certainly, is like that. Maybe I'm just complaining about not getting cited very often. But the things that I have done that I think were fairly doctrinal—they criticized a particular establishment clause doctrine or prescribed something else—tend to get cited more than ones that I think of as more historical or conceptual or theoretical. So it seems to me that there is quite a big market for doctrinal work. I think in some ways that is unfortunate.

LEVINSON. I think that is a valuable point, to pick up on Pierre's article and the theme he has been stressing for quite a while. What you are describing are normative articles. And there are a variety of ways to be normative. Some say the best understanding of the cases just leads you to this conclusion. Others say the cases are really rotten, they should be overruled. For example, one of the most highly cited articles published in the last ten years is Mari Matsuda's article on hate speech. And that is a law reform article. It tells you what to do. I think you are probably right that relatively few articles that don't have a normative payoff are highly cited, or for that matter even highly likely to be published in the prestigious venues. Some will, but probably there is still this desire that you tell the reader how to make the world better. And certainly Pierre has emphasized very, very strongly that that's nothing the legal scholar should view as part of the job description. Do both of you agree with Pierre on that point?

CAMPOS. Yes.

LEVINSON. Well, one of you agrees. Steve?

SMITH. I agree that it should not be part of the job description. I would not go so far as to say—and I'm not sure Pierre would either, but maybe he would—that it is inappropriate for legal scholars to write normatively. I do think it is very unfortunate that a normative element is basically an expectation. If you write an article that doesn't do that in the end, people tend to say, "Yeah, okay, fine, but in the end what should we do?" As I've said in the preface of my book, it is like playing the first seven notes of the scale and stopping. People think you can't do that. You have to finish. I think that is very unfortunate.

SCHLAG. I just cut down some parasites on my ponderosa pines. And if somebody were to ask me, "What are you going to put in its place?" I'd say, "Nothing. Haven't I done enough?"

NORMATIVITY AND THE POLITICS OF FORM

Pierre Schlag

If the sociology of the system of education and the intellectual world seems to me to be fundamental, this is because it also contributes to our knowledge of the subject of cognition by introducing us . . . to the unthought categories of thought which limit the thinkable and predetermine what is actually thought: I need merely refer to the universe of prejudice, repression and omission that every successful education makes you accept, and makes you remain unaware of, tracing out that magic circle of powerless complacency in which the elite schools imprison their elect.—Pierre Bourdieu[1]

WHAT SHOULD BE done? How should we live? What should the law be? These are the momentous questions. These are the hard questions. These are the questions that animate virtually all of contemporary legal thought—from the most modest doctrinal reform proposals to the most ambitious utopian speculation. In our classes and in our writings we speak ceaselessly of ways to improve law. We seek to bring law into greater consonance with moral value, or the public interest, or justice, or some other worthy conception that celebrates its own take on the social good.

Because we are constantly engaged in this great prescriptive effort to better law, our thought often appears extraordinarily ennobling. Indeed, our contributions to legal thought routinely affirm that we are working on the side of the good, the right, the just—at least as we understand those concepts. We are part of a laudable enterprise, and in our teaching and writing we seek to enlist others, our students and colleagues, in this notion that law can be perfected, can be improved through reasoned argument about the good, the right, the just, and the like.

It must thus come as quite a shock to discover (as one invariably does) that this passionate normative life of the law has no readily apparent relation to the actual structure or content of legal practice. For our students, the transition is extremely abrupt. For three years, the talk is of bringing law into accord with purposive reason, of refining the efficiency calculus, of being very pragmatic and oh, so contextual. Rudely, however, these three years are brought to a close by the vulgar reality principle of the bar exam. This is quickly followed by one (quite possibly) last, exceedingly hedonistic vacation.

This vacation typically ends badly, with the law graduate finding himself confined in a small, cool cubicle with a window, a couple of diplomas, one potted plant, and a very bad view. From that cubicle law begins to seem far less genteel, far less intellectualized, and, most of all, far less respectful of its own inner normative text than it did in law school. In that cubicle (and in tens of thousands like it), the student-become-lawyer will learn, and learn quickly, that law is a power game. In that cubicle, doctrine, arguments, causes of action, defenses, and the like will undergo an almost magical metamorphosis. They will be recast as the rhetorical moves that allow lawyers, clients, and courts to get more of what it is they want. In legal practice, the noble values immanent in positive law will lose much of their moral sheen. They will be recognized for what they effectively are: part of the arsenal of rhetorical levers by which institutional authorities can be instrumentally summoned to visit coercion on selectively named parties.[2] The normative values embedded in law will become part of the prime cultural set pieces by which lawyers manipulate the self-image of jurors, clients, judges, and other lawyers to get more of what it is the lawyers ostensibly want. For many students-become-lawyers, this will seem a very glamorous and exciting game—one that smacks of real consequences, real power, and real life. And it will continue to seem glamorous and exciting so long as the student-become-lawyer continues to believe that he is in control of the power game. It will not be until much later (if at all) that the student-become-lawyer will recognize that it is more likely the other way around.

If this seems like an unusually dark vision of the practice of law, it is likely to be so only for those whose understanding of law is informed principally by the dreamy normative narratives that issue routinely from the legal academy. Practicing lawyers are likely to find this vision unexceptionable: practicing lawyers experience law as a complex network of bureaucratic power arrangements that they have learned to manipulate.[3] That is what legal practice is about. Words get used, arguments get made, institutional pressure builds, situations become increasingly intolerable, somebody gives, and a settlement is reached or a contract is signed or a jury comes back with a verdict. It's law. It's power.

Against this backdrop of bureaucratic power games, it becomes interesting to try to determine just what all of our passionate and very moral normative conversation does or does not contribute. Against the backdrop of this power game of law, our normative conversation can seem exceedingly polite, given to a rather unbelievable romanticization of the enterprise we call "law."

Many legal thinkers understand this dramatic conflict in terms of an opposition between the "realities" of practice and the "ideals" of the legal academy. For these legal thinkers it will seem especially urgent to ask once again: What should be done? How should we live? What should the law be? These are the hard questions. These are the momentous questions.

And these are the wrong ones.

They are wrong because it is these very normative questions that reprieve legal thinkers from recognizing the extent to which the cherished ideals of legal academic thought are implicated in the reproduction and maintenance of precisely those ugly realities of legal practice the academy so routinely condemns. It is these normative questions that allow legal thinkers to shield themselves from the recognition that their work product consists largely of the reproduction of rhetorical structures by which human beings can be coerced into achieving ends of dubious social origin and implication. It is these very normative questions that allow legal academics to continue to address (rather lamely) bureaucratic power structures as if they were rational, morally competent, individual humanist subjects. It is these very normative questions that allow legal thinkers to assume blithely that—in a world ruled by HMOs, personnel policies, standard operating procedures, performance requirements, standard work incentives, and productivity monitoring—they somehow have escaped the bureaucratic power games. It is these normative questions that enable them to represent themselves as whole and intact, as self-directing individual liberal humanist subjects at once rational, morally competent, and in control of their own situations—captains of their own ships, each the Hercules of his own empire, the author of her own text.

It isn't so.[4] And if it isn't so, it would seem advisable to make some adjustments in the agenda and practice of legal thought. That is what I will be trying to do here. Much of what follows will seem threatening or nihilistic to many readers. In part that is because this article puts in question the very coherence, meaningfulness, and integrity of the kinds of normative disputes and discussions that dominate legal thought.

One question will no doubt recur to the reader throughout this essay: But what *should* we do? That question is not going to receive a straightforward answer here, and I would like to explain why at the outset. Suppose that you are walking on a road and you come to a fork. This calls for a decision, for a choice. So you ask your companions, "Which fork should we take? Where should we go?" You all begin to talk about it, to consider the possibilities, to weigh the considerations. Given these circumstances, given this sort of problem, the questions Where should we go? and What should we do? are perfectly sensible.[5]

But now suppose that it gets dark and the terrain becomes less familiar. You are no longer sure which road you are on or even if you are on a road at all.[6] So you ask, "Where are we?" One of your companions says, "I don't know—I think we should just keep going forward." Another one says, "I think we should go back." Yet another says, "No, I think we should go left." Now, given the right context, each of these suggestions can be perfectly sensible. But not in *this* context. Not anymore. On the contrary, you know very well that going forward, backward, left, or in any other direction makes no sense unless you know where you are. So, of course, you try to figure out where you are. You look around for telltale signs. You scan the horizon. You try to reconstruct mentally how you got here in the first place. You explore. You even start thinking about how to figure out where you are.

If your companions keep asking in the meantime, "But what should we do? Which road should we take?" you are likely to think that these kinds of questions are not particularly helpful. The questions that seemed to make so much sense a short time back have now become a hindrance. And if your companions keep up this sort of questioning (Which road should we take? Which way should we go?), you're going to start wondering how to get them to focus on the new situation, how to get them to drop this "fork in the road" stuff and start using a different metaphor.[7]

One metaphor that recurs throughout this essay is that of the theater. Now, you might reasonably think that it's a bit difficult to get from the "fork in the road" metaphor for normative legal thought to the metaphor of law as theater. But it's not really that difficult—especially if you understand at the outset that those individuals who keep saying, "Where should we go? What should we do?" are themselves *already doing* a kind of theater. They are engaged in a particular kind of dramatic action appropriate for a particular kind of scene, agon, and actors. They are doing the kind of theater that is particularly appropriate for forks in the road.

One problem with normative legal thought is that it is constantly representing our situation as a fork in the road—calling, of course, for a choice, a commitment to this way or that way. You might think: well, this is not so bad. At least we get to choose. We are free and we can choose which way to go. But, of course, we are not free. The rhetorical script of normative legal thought is already written, the social scene is already set, and play after play, article after article, year after year, normative legal thought requires you to choose: What should we do? Where should we go? We are free, but we must choose—which is to say that we are not free at all. On the contrary, we (you and I) have been constituted as the kind of beings, the kind of thinkers, who compulsively treat every intellectual, social, or legal event as calling for a choice. We must choose.

What should we do? Where should we go? Such questions are no longer helpful. It's time to do a different kind of theater. And the first thing to do is figure out where we are and what we're doing. What we're doing, of course, is normative legal thought.

The orientation of American academic legal thought is pervasively and over-whelmingly normative. For the legal thinker, the central question is, what should the law be? Or, what should the courts do? Or, how should courts decide cases? Or, what values should the ubiquitous (and largely nonreferential) "we" (i.e., us) believe? Or, how should . . .

These questions and their doctrinal derivatives constitute, organize, and circumscribe the tacit agenda of contemporary legal thought. The key verb dominating contemporary legal thought is some version of *should*. Sometimes this *should* does not quite rise to the moral *ought* and remains merely an instrumental, technical, or prudential *should*. Sometimes it is a covert *should*—hidden beneath layers of legal positivism. But the fact remains that *shoulds* and *oughts* dominate legal discourse. And the question of whether any given *should* is a true moral *ought* or another instrumental *should* turns out to be just another internecine squabble among competing normative perspectives.[8]

The normative orientation is so dominant in legal thought that it is usually not even noticed. No doubt the very pervasiveness and dominance of this thought have enabled it to escape conscious thematization. Indeed, while the concept "normative legal thought" is hardly unknown or unintelligible to American legal thinkers, its precise significance, its precise movements in social or intellectual space, remain largely unrecognized and undetermined. The understanding—or rather, understandings—of normative legal thought within the legal academy are not nearly as refined or contested as the understandings, for instance, of legal formalism, legal realism, legal process, law and economics, Critical Legal Studies (CLS), or the like.

Nonetheless, normative legal thought did not arrive on this scene without a history. On the contrary, normative legal thought arrived an already loaded term—one that had already been engaged in jurisprudential skirmishes with conceptualism, positivism, and nihilism. Indeed, our image of normative legal thought is already a product of some cognitively and professionally sedimented distinctions,[9] between normative legal thought and (a) descriptive thought (as in, for instance, the opposition between descriptive and normative law and economics); (b) conceptualism (as in, for instance, the claim that normative legal thought is value conscious, open-ended, and nonauthoritarian in contrast to conceptualism); or (c) nihilism (as in, for instance, the claim that either law is a normatively meaningful enterprise or we face the abyss of a bleak and chaotic nihilism).[10]

These distinctions and the patterns of argument structures associated with these distinctions have played significant roles in fashioning our preconscious, prereflective understanding of the character and location of normative legal thought. As I have argued elsewhere, however, these distinctions and their attendant arguments collapse whenever intellectual attention is turned their way. The result is that descriptive thought, conceptualism, and nihilism remain pervasively normative in character. As I have argued previously, even legal thought that strives to be "purely" descriptive is nonetheless value-laden.[11]

Normative legal thought thus turns out to be much broader and more sweeping than legal thinkers might have imagined. All this raises an interesting question: Are we in a position to attempt an understanding of normative legal thought?

My sense is that we are, but not by way of the conventional strategies typically deployed in contemporary legal thought. The usual strategies identify the object of inquiry by providing "definitions," "models," "ideal types," and the like. It is our practice as legal thinkers to discuss aspects of legal thought by first reducing them to an objectified, stabilized, usually essentialized object-form—located invariably somewhere "out there." Indeed, even today, among many legal theorists, this sort of objectification, stabilization, externalization, and essentialization of thought continues to be considered good form—an integral aspect of what it means to be intellectually "serious."

But, arguably, this conventional approach is no longer intellectually serious. I would like to avoid objectifying normative legal thought *in this way.* I want to urge that normative legal thought cannot be considered *simply* as a kind of thought that is "out there," already reducible to a set of ideas, propositions, theories, and definitions of its content or character. To reduce normative legal thought to an object-form, to a definition, to a genre, to a specification of boundaries, or to a definite location in social and intellectual space is to misunderstand and miscast not only the thought to be inquired into but the thinking that is to pursue the inquiry itself.[12] Such a reduction of thought to object-forms is a bad business.[13]

If we were to reduce normative legal thought to a set of ideas, theories, or models, or any other conventionally reified space for thought, we would be led into making certain kinds of mistakes—mistakes that are, ironically, characteristic of normative legal thought itself. I will mention two kinds of mistakes engendered by the usual objectifying practices of contemporary legal thought.

The first kind of mistake is that this objectification immediately situates the subject (here, you and I) as already *outside* the reach of the object under inquiry. In this one move of situating oneself outside the form of thought, two transformations are accomplished instantaneously. First, the inquiry has just been tremendously simplified. Second, the value of the inquiry and the interest in whatever it might produce have just been radically reduced (to close to zero). And the reason is this: to situate oneself *outside* the thought to be inquired into is in effect to stabilize a naive subject-object relation whereby the subject (here, you and I) eclipses from consideration and critical inquiry what we, as authors and readers, have already contributed in the construction, in the formulation of the object of inquiry. In the case of "normative legal thought," for instance, our attempts to "define carefully" a "precise" object of inquiry might amount to little more than a mindless and self-indulgent rehearsal of our own stereotyped discourse on an empty signifier known as "normative legal thought."

There is a second kind of mistake engendered by premature objectification. If we indulged in a reductive objectification of normative legal thought, we would be led away from recognizing that normative legal thought is not just theory, ideas, substance, and outcomes, but is simultaneously practice, activity, form, and process. When a normative legal thinker writes, she is not just recommending some course of action. She is rehearsing a style of argument—one that reinforces certain social relations between author and reader, one that reinforces a certain aesthetic representation of social life—of who the key actors are; of how they are related; of the status of discourse, communication, and reason; of the relations of theory and practice, form and substance, outcome and process.

Thus, if we are to understand normative legal thought, we must try to resist as much as possible the conventional reifying practices of contemporary legal thought. But now, ironically, this caution turns out to have an unexpected implication. If we take seriously the observation that the practice of objectification is conventional and prereflective—an aspect of the very form of our legal thought—we cannot dispense with objectification simply by defining our terms carefully or engaging in other such conventional conceptualistic exercises.[14] On the contrary, to understand that legal thought is a practice, that it is conventional in character, and that it is a process is to recognize that objectification is sedimented not only in normative legal thought, but in us as well.

Objectification is in some senses unavoidable. Not only is it unavoidable, it is in some senses obviously helpful in allowing us to communicate. The question, then, is not whether one objectifies, but how.[15] Now, in some sense, normative legal thought is already self-objectifying: it reenacts consistent and recursive strategies that solidify in visible and stereotyped patterns. Consider, for instance, the following quotes rudely excerpted from the conclusions of articles in volume 103 of the *Harvard Law Review*:

> *Let us not fall victim to* the paralysis of neutral analysis. Instead, we must meet and talk together. . . . *We must talk* specifically about the kinds of community we would fashion.[16]

> *The real problem with* contemporary doctrine is not that it fails to attain some overarching reconciliation among these competing considerations . . . but rather that it fails to articulate with sufficient clarity what is actually at stake in the definition of public discourse. *We need to establish* a domain of public discourse. . . . *Doctrinal formulation should assist* courts in the evaluation of these considerations, rather than masking them under wooden phrases and tests.[17]

> The traditional understandings of statutory construction are inadequate. . . . *The interpretive principles suggested here are intended for the President, regulatory agencies, and Congress, as well as for the courts.*[18]

> *Scholarship should reveal and debate* the Court's value choices. . . . Ultimately, *the decisions must be defended or criticized* for the value choices the Court made. *There is nothing else.*[19]

> *The system will function better when doctrine reflects reality.* . . . *What is needed* is a single event that will crystalize the developments that have already occurred and focus judicial attention on a new line of development. A sweeping Supreme *Court opinion might work,* but a more *promising solution is a statute.*[20]

> *If one unequivocal conclusion follows* from this review of the law of the mentally retarded parent, it is that *the formal classification should be abolished* as a basis for state interference with the parent-child relationship. . . . *What follow are some specific recommendations.*[21]

There is a recursive quality to the patterns of legal thinking evidenced in these excerpts, a prescriptive, normative quality to the form of this legal thought. And indeed, these recursive patterns are not new; they have been in place a long time.

It is interesting to compare these concluding statements from volume 103 of the *Harvard Law Review* with concluding statements taken from volume 1 of the same journal, published in 1888 during Langdell's tenure as dean of the Harvard Law School. What is striking in making such a comparison is how little the grammar of academic legal thought and the role of the academic legal thinker have changed since the days of Langdell:

In conclusion . . . *this proposition, it is hoped, will find favor* with the reader in point of legal principle. *It can hardly fail to commend* itself on the score of justice and mercantile convenience.[22]

In the present opinion of the author *such would be the best way out of the difficulty. . . . He would, therefore, close with the suggestion* of three statutes, whose rigid enforcement might, with due adjustment to meet evasions, be expected to meet the case.[23]

The theory that State laws "unreasonably" affecting foreign or interstate commerce may be held unconstitutional . . . *is objectionable. . . . In the opinion of the writer* . . . the purpose or intention of the State Legislature . . . is the only criterion . . . *and the difficulties of the law would be greatly lessened if* the Courts would clearly and in express terms adopt this criterion.[24]

Some cynic, who has had the patience to read so far, will, no doubt, remark that the legal profession is not a charitable institution, and that men practise law to get money . . . and not from philanthropic motives. To this I answer that no profession can be great unless the money-making aims of the individual are leavened by a sense of the importance of his vocation and of the dignity of the body that pursues it. . . . *This is the quality which we need to foster.*[25]

These are the questions upon which the justice of the proposed legislation depends. Till they shall have been understood, considered, and argued by those competent to the task, *it will never truly be said that George has been refuted.*[26]

It is preposterous to attribute any such sweeping effect to the [Fourteenth] amendment. . . . [I]t has not yet been decided or provided that the independence as to local matters, which forms the strongest bulwark against that disintegration so often predicted . . . is to be subjected to the surveillance of the national courts. *And it is to be deplored that the Supreme Court of the United States,* upon which chiefly rests the responsibility for preserving the proper relation of dependence and independence between things national and things local, should have adopted a course which may tend to countenance such an idea.[27]

[I]t is only just that the bill-holders, whose debt has not yet been extinguished, should be allowed to prove against it in competition with the other creditors. *Of the four views presented the last would seem to be the only one consistent with justice and the intention of the parties.*[28]

The relentlessly prescriptive character of American legal thought has not gone wholly undetected. Legal thinkers have themselves reflected on the dominant patterns:

> With monotonous regularity, law review articles attempt to speak to courts deciding today's legal issues, in the hope that some legal actor, such as a lawyer, will refer to the article in a legal argument and persuade some judge (or, more likely, law clerk) to adopt the conclusions and analysis the article advocates.[29]

> When viewed as an academic discourse, the most distinctive feature of standard legal scholarship is its prescriptive voice, its consciously declared desire to improve the performance of legal decisionmakers.[30]

> The reason for this irreducible normativity is that the subject of legal scholarship is law, and law is a mechanism through which our society operationalizes its normative choices. In a society like ours, moreover, these choices are a matter of conscious and continual debate.[31]

> Legal academics often style themselves as judges—above, beyond, neutral with respect to the interested party or practitioner, and after or innocent of the messiness of legislative or sovereign choice. . . . [W]e may even style ourselves as judges of the judiciary, making assessments in teaching and writing about cases which were "correctly" or "incorrectly" decided.[32]

> Most of our writings are not political theory but advocacy scholarship— amicus briefs ultimately designed to persuade the Court to adopt our various notions of the public good. In one or another form this has been the staple of legal scholarship and at least has the claims of tradition.[33]

Clearly, some legal thinkers understand the patterned character of their own normative legal thought. Below I try to describe the character of this normative legal thought in terms of a set of family traits. I have deliberately left the problem of objectification unstable and unresolved. Hence, the list of traits can be read as describing the paradigm case of a piece of normative legal thought. It is also possible, however, to understand them as an attempt to trace the network of forces and relations that constitute normative legal thought as a process. Based on the discussion thus far, and on our own already immersed understanding of normative legal thought, the latter might be described as an aggregate and an aggregation-in-process of the following family traits:

Normative legal thought is *prescriptive*. It recommends some identified doctrine, theory, attitude, institutional framework, hermeneutic methodology, or the like to the reader.

Normative legal thought is *monistic;* it has a single-norm orientation. Insofar as normative legal thought is prescriptive, it seeks to prescribe a single authoritative norm to rule within the defined jurisdiction of the enterprise. Even when it advocates pluralism (e.g., contextualism) or dualism (e.g., dialectical thought), normative legal thought will nonetheless envelop such potentially nonmonistic stances within a monistic form.

Hence, normative legal thought strives for a textual formalization that will produce a single norm. The aim is thus to articulate or develop a norm that is *complete, self-sufficient, discrete, separable, trans-situational, noncontradictory,* and *nonparadoxical* within its intellectual or legal jurisdiction.

In turn, the self-sufficient, discrete, and trans-situational character of the norm selected is associated with the *positive* character of normative legal thought. Even critical (negative) moments are usually presented as being in the service of the construction of some positive norm. So even when normative legal thought is concerned with changing insights, attitudes, temperaments, epistemic frameworks, and so on, it does so by advocating a *positive* norm-form.

The single-norm orientation also implies a *conclusion oriented* enterprise. What matters to both the reader and the author of normative legal thought is the conclusion; the process of argumentation is not valued intrinsically, but only insofar as it potentially validates or invalidates the conclusion.

The single-norm orientation also implies that much of the work of normative legal thought lies in *norm selection,* that is, the selection by some reader or ultimate addressee of the favored norm from a number of possible, extant or hypothetical, options.

Normative legal thought is thus *choice oriented;* it acknowledges that the reader is entitled to choose norms, attempts to enlist the reader in choosing the norm, and then attempts to channel (as much as rhetorical effectiveness will permit) the reader's choice to the norm favored by the author.

And because the reader is constructed as one called on to engage in ethical, moral choice, much of the work of normative legal thought consists in *norm justification*—in justifying the author's favored norm to this choosing reader.

Normative legal thought also has *practical, worldly ambitions.* It seeks to have the favored norm not just adopted by the reader, but put into effect—even institutionalized or realized in social practice.

Choice oriented norm justification means that the practical realization, the actualization of the norm, is deferred. It is up to the reader to take the further steps necessary to put the norm into effect. Normative legal thought is thus *action deferring,* contemplating that the action necessary to give effect to the norm will be done by the reader or someone connected with the reader after the reading is completed, outside the text, yet nonetheless subject to the norm and the arguments proposed by the text.

The stance of much of normative legal thought is produced within a self-defined adversarial context, thus requiring *adversarial advocacy* in favor of the selected norm. Indeed, the argument structures are often reminiscent of those employed by lawyers in appellate argument, with litigation techniques of fact recharacterization and issue framing often deployed even in the context of otherwise sophisticated intellectual argument.

Because of the adversarial advocacy and the conclusion oriented stance of normative legal thought, it tends to be *reader centered.* In other words, normative legal thought strives to respect and reflect (as much as possible) the presumed belief structures, assumptions, ideals, and self-image of the imagined reader.

In sum, then:

Normative legal thought is an enterprise of
    norm selection
    norm justification

This enterprise deploys a rhetoric that is
    prescriptive
    value oriented
    reader centered
    adversarial advocacy
    choice oriented
    action deferring
    single-norm oriented
    conclusion oriented

The rhetoric of normative legal thought aims to produce, recommend, and institutionalize norms that are:

    practical, worldly
    complete
    self-sufficient
    discrete
    separable
    trans-situational
    noncontradictory
    nonparadoxical
    positive

These characteristics are the family traits that describe and constitute normative legal thought. At times, some traits become more dominant or more visible than others. Normative legal thought thus does not have a static and fixed identity. It has no pregiven boundaries. And that is because normative legal thought is not simply an object-form or a genre, it is also a process—a kind of rhetorical economy of relations and forces that channels and organizes American legal thought. It is a decentralized economy that, despite the lack of any fixed or stable center, nonetheless exerts gravitational force on the production of legal thought, enabling and leading it to become typically the kind of thought described by the conjunction of traits above.

That much of contemporary legal thought should exhibit a conjunction of these traits is not surprising. Many of the traits are mutually entailed—metaphorically and rhetorically.[34] The repeated coalescence of this same set of traits is precisely what gives normative legal thought the appearance of a genre. It is this repeated coalescence of the same set of traits that makes law review articles almost always look the same: law review articles are extremely easy to identify precisely because they—as products of the rhetorical economy of normative legal thought—already arrive on the scene in a highly stereotyped form.[35] "We must do this." "They should do that." And so on.

The process of normative legal thought typically (though not necessarily) yields its paradigmatic object-form, but the power, the relations, and the forces of this process exceed the paradigmatic case of the object-form. Normative legal thought shapes, enables, and distorts all legal thought, including the sort of thought that (like my effort here) seems far removed, from the paradigmatic case.

HOW TO BE NORMATIVE, WIN FRIENDS, AND
INFLUENCE CONNECTIONS

One of the consequences of the unquestioned dominance of normative legal thought in the academy is that there has been little or no articulate consideration of just how this thought produces or expects to produce its effects. Yet normative legal thought clearly represents itself as having practical, worldly ambitions. Much normative legal thought reveals an expectation and a desire for its own realization in judicial or statutory law (for formalists) or by effective action in the social sphere (for realists). While this much is clear, what is not clear, and indeed has not even been seriously questioned, is how normative legal thought expects to realize these ambitions.

That this question should arise only now is unsurprising. For most of the history of American legal academic thought, it would have been unthinkable to ask such a question. It is only now, when the effectiveness of normative legal thought is in doubt, when the receptivity of judicial (and other) audiences is questionable,[36] when the very identity of any fixed paradigm for legal thought is uncertain, that the question can arise. And because the question is arising seriously for the first time, we are without any strong, self-conscious, widely shared theoretical frameworks to help our inquiry. Still, we are not entirely without markers or resources. If we pay close attention to the normative legal thought that emerges from the academy, we may yet understand how normative legal thought thinks it produces its effects. The more popular normative legal theories, for instance, indirectly reveal a great deal about what normative legal thinkers believe they are doing with their normative legal thought. Instead of reading normative legal theory in terms of what it means for adjudication or "law," we can usefully read these theories for what they reveal about the enterprise of normative legal thought. Indeed, many of our contemporary jurisprudential theories can easily be seen as instances of projection in which authors and readers displace onto the judiciary their own idealized self-images as legal thinkers.

Not surprisingly, the theories that are most popular within the legal academy are those that project the most attractive self-image. Consider, as an example, Ronald Dworkin's theory of law as integrity and his depiction of the ideal judge as Hercules.[37] Regardless of whether Hercules is an accurate or a desirable model for the appellate judge, he certainly resonates profoundly in the self-image of the contemporary legal academic. Indeed, it is easy to understand Hercules as the projection of the legal academic's idealized self-image onto the character of the appellate judge. Similarly, Dworkin's theory of law as integrity can easily be understood as a projection of the kind of elegant theory construction that characterizes the most esteemed legal scholarship onto the appellate judicial opinion-writing process.

And, of course, as self-images go, the one provided by Dworkin is extremely flattering: "Judges who accept the interpretive ideal of integrity decide hard cases by trying to find, in some coherent set of principles about people's rights and duties, the best constructive interpretation of the political structure and legal doctrine of their community. They try to make that complex structure and record the best they can."[38] As a conceptual field for projection by legal academic readers, one of the great advantages of Dworkin's theory is that it can slide easily from concrete and determinate interpretations to extraordinarily moving and generous abstractions about what "making the law the best it can be" might mean.[39] Dworkin's theory is thus constructed as a tour de force that permits both author and reader to oscillate between sophisticated (though thin) and meaningful (though controversial) readings.[40]

Although these points about the ambiguity or ambivalence of the Dworkin-ian theory could easily be turned into objections, that is not my point here. Rather, my claim is that Dworkin's theory articulates indirectly something very important about what many legal academics believe courts do. His theory gives an extremely eloquent, sophisticated, and respectable voice to the otherwise simple legal academic belief that judges who experience precedent, law, and doctrine as constraint, nevertheless often do, and likely should, strive very hard to "read" this law, to "stretch" this doctrine in order to do the right thing. At the same time, Dworkin's theory also gives voice to the typical legal academic concern with judicial imperialism by insisting that the reading and the stretch-ing be done in a principled and coherent manner. Dworkin's theory delivers what legal academics want: neither mechanical jurisprudence nor freewheeling utopia—but rather the middle way.

Hence, Dworkin's text gives sophisticated and respectable expression to pre-cisely this sense of what adjudication is and should be. In turn, this sense is a projection of what legal academics themselves do in their scholarship. Indeed, the vast bulk of contemporary legal scholarship attempts to read and organize authoritative legal materials in such a way as to make a normatively pleasing arrangement. Legal academics stretch the cases—sometimes very far, some-times hardly at all. But they virtually always try to arrange them in a coherent and principled manner.[41]

The main points of difference among legal thinkers turn on what they think constitute "the authoritative legal materials," how they rank or organize con-flicting values, what import and spin they place on aesthetic criteria like co-herence and consistency, and the extent to which they understand these vari-ables to be interpenetrated and interactive. All of this is to say that whatever its relevance for judges and adjudication, *Law's Empire* is an extraordinarily so-phisticated account of what the vast majority of contemporary legal academics think they are doing with their legal thought. Indeed, the paradigm of contem-porary legal thought—whether in treatises, articles, or the classroom—is the rendition of an interpretation of precedent, doctrine, theory, and law that will make them better, more just, more fair, and more efficient in a principled and coherent way. What Hercules does is what legal academics do: they apply their intellectual faculties to the rewriting of the law so as to make it more principled, coherent, and morally appealing.

Indeed, the Dworkinian jurisprudence is such a good idealized account of the self-image of legal academic thought that it even serves as a sort of cere-monial exorcism of some pervasive ambivalences of legal thinkers. Its oscilla-tion between sophisticated (though thin) abstraction and concrete (but contro-versial) meaningfulness at once simulates and defuses the ambivalence that

most legal thinkers experience in reconciling established legal tradition and
moral principle, truth and politics, law and utopia, order and morality. Part of
Dworkin's success is attributable precisely to the fact that he places the concerns
of legal academic thinkers in the foreground and manages to allay these concerns in a "relentlessly interpretive" approach that represents itself not only as
coherent but as the very rule of principle on earth.[42] But what do the normative
legal thinkers think they are doing when they are being Hercules? What do they
think is being accomplished by this discursive enterprise of norm selection and
norm justification? Here, I want to give an empathic, sympathetic account of
the experience of doing normative legal thought. Again, Dworkin is an excellent guide.

What does Hercules want to do in his empire? Like the legal academic, he is
relentlessly interpretive, we know. But at what does all this interpretation aim?
If it is not exactly clear what Hercules seeks to accomplish (render a decision?
write doctrine? issue an appellate opinion?), there is the same sort of ambiguity
among legal thinkers. What we do know is that normative legal thinkers want to
persuade an important institutional actor (usually a judge) to adopt a particular norm. Their self-conscious motive is thus norm adoption.

While the normative legal thinker typically does not imagine himself as
serving a particular named client (in either the lawyerly or the social theoretical
sense), neither does he envision himself as choosing proposed norms in a
normative or political vacuum. On the contrary, the normative legal thinker
has a rich picture of the legal field—the argumentative framework and the
beliefs and perceptions of the relevant audience: its fears, hopes, aspirations,
and much more. The normative legal thinker also has a set of political or moral
values.

Both the representation of the field and the moral and political values are to
some extent plastic, but not infinitely so. The plasticity of the field depends in
part on the differing capacities of legal thinkers for reformulating both their
representation of the field and their own political or moral values. Typically, the
normative legal thinker understands himself to be choosing a norm based on
his representation of the legal field and his normative values. Typically, the
normative legal thinker looks for channels of argument within the legal field
that can support norms consonant with the legal thinker's own moral or political values.

All sorts of trade-offs are possible here. For example, a legal thinker may
decide to pursue a particularly promising channel of argument within the legal
field even though it appears to be only partially consistent (if at all) with his
own values.[43] Another legal thinker, on the other hand, may be so committed to

a particular political or moral stance that she will develop that stance in adverse conditions, even though the argument possibilities in other areas or for other norms appear to be much more favorable.[44]

Thus, choosing which norm to support is, for the normative legal thinker, already a question of norm justification; the choice of which norm to support is already being decided by thinking about how and whether the norm can be justified according to the (legitimate) reasoning criteria of the internalized external audience. Again, what counts as "justification" and what counts as "(legitimate) reasoning criteria" differ among legal thinkers and are subject to reformulation. While the normative legal thinker typically experiences norm justification as governed in part by the beliefs of his readers (the external audience), he also shares many of those beliefs himself (the internal audience). Thus, though it is true that the normative legal thinker may sometimes advance arguments that he does not believe or considers makeweight or trivial, that certainly does not describe the whole or even the main part of the norm justification experience. On the contrary, for the normative legal thinker, the process of norm justification is never simply, never just, a matter of public relations or rhetorical manipulation.

The appeal of normative legal thought is grounded precisely in the fact that it is rational, deliberative, authentic, and noncoercive. Normative legal thought appeals to shared values and shared understandings of what law is and what it ought to be. As Frank Michelman puts it, "The *persuasive* character of the process depends on the normative efficacy of some context that is everyone's."[45] It presupposes "that such a fund of normatively effective material— publicly cognizable, persuasively recollectible and contestable—is always already available."[46]

In this account of normative legal thought, two crucial assumptions are being made: (1) there is some normatively charged context that is both retrievable and universally shared, and (2) the fund of normatively charged beliefs and ideals is normatively efficacious. The first assumption is crucial if normative legal thought is to avoid collapsing into authoritarianism or coercion. It is precisely this assumption that allows normative legal thought to claim that it is respecting the dignity of the individual. The second critical assumption allows normative legal thought to claim that its normative content is not epiphenomenal but does, in fact, regulate and guide the practices of legal thinkers, judges, and their institutions.

While normative legal thinkers typically hold to these assumptions, they are nevertheless aware that their arguments and thought operate in a rhetorical field. This poses a problem for my empathic account of normative legal thought. On the one hand, to suggest that normative legal thinkers believe that their thought cuts through the field of rhetorical manipulation would be to treat them as naive, out of touch. What's more, on some level it would be wrong: normative legal thinkers show some recognition of how the rhetorical power of legal thought lies and how this power is deployed to achieve in- strumental ends. But now here's the problem: if normative legal thinkers are aware of the rhetorical, of the power dimensions of normative legal thought, they can no longer claim that their thought is *outside* the field of coercion and manipulation.

Normative legal thought seems to be in a quandary here, and it's not at all clear how normative legal thinkers resolve this tension. It may be that I have been misled in my empathic attempts to describe what it is that normative legal thinkers think they are doing, and that the self-understanding of normative legal thinkers is much more along the lines of Plato's "noble lie."[47] Perhaps. For the most part, normative legal thinkers typically try to avoid the problem with moves like this: "Participants in argument cannot avoid *presupposing* that the structure of their communication both excludes all force other than that of the better argument and neutralizes all motives other than the cooperative search for truth. These presuppositions may be counterfactual; still, *the cost of giving them up* is what Habermas, following Apel, calls a performative contradic- tion."[48] The intimation is that we must give up the recognition that we are involved in a rhetorical enterprise, lest we get caught up in "performative contradictions." The obvious bootstrap character of this move seems to have largely escaped notice.

But this is no surprise: Generally, normative legal thought has not paid much attention to its own rhetorical situation, and thus it has not given much serious thought to this problem—or even recognized it as one. In part, this oversight helps account for the upbeat and cheery character of normative legal thought. Typically, normative legal thought exhibits a confident Enlightenment vision, largely oblivious to the challenges that modernist and postmodernist thought poses to its status as "serious" discourse. And, as we have begun to see, norma- tive legal thought is not terribly self-conscious or self-critical. Indeed, only the rudest, the most sudden shocks to the system seem capable of jarring normative legal thought out of its complacency.

L.A. LAW'S EMPIRE

On Thursday, March 29, 1990, at approximately 10:00 P.M., Stuart Markowitz was arrested for DWI. Stuart Markowitz is a fifty-year-old mid-level partner in a small Los Angeles law firm—a bit of a buffoon, something of a schlemiel, soft around the edges, but not entirely spineless.* He is one of the less ego-centered, more principled characters on *L.A. Law*.† He is even (at times) surprisingly politically correct on gender issues.

As you might expect, it was an incredible shock to witness Stuart, this soft, kind, harmless man, being rudely arrested. You can picture the scene. The cop is a predictable six-foot-something, a Nordic blond Visigoth sporting the ubiquitous standard cop-issue aviator glasses. Clear protofascist material. The shock of Stuart's arrest is compounded by our having learned just moments before that Stuart and his wife, Ann, planned to go off to a motel to do (as Stuart announced in his best muffled baritone voice) "some unbelievably sinful things."

In a few short TV frames, the promise of innocent sex is violently and definitively crushed by the powerful long arm of the law. If you are a member of the legal community, this scene has particular resonance for you: it evokes the iconic intrusion into the marital bedroom condemned in *Griswold v. Connecticut*;[49] Orwell comes to mind. Note the image of law here: it is on the wrong side, unaccountably random and awesomely powerful.

Stuart's breathalyzer tests reads 0.09.‡ This comes to us as somewhat of a surprise. True, Stuart had been sipping wine with Ann moments before the arrest, but he certainly did not look drunk, and besides, it's not in Stuart's character to drink and drive. Fortunately, we discover, Stuart will be represented by Michael Kuzak, Stuart's brash, young, sexy, terribly competent, and ruthless partner. In fine form, before taking Stuart's testimony, Michael sits down with Ann and Stuart to explain the law:§

---

*See *L.A. Law* (NBC television broadcast, March 29, 1990). *L.A. Law* is a television show depicting the lives, foibles, and failures of lawyers in a contemporary small Los Angeles law firm. The show's romanticization of the legal profession in terms of sex, power, and money was informally believed among legal academics in the late 1980s to have played some part in producing the otherwise inexplicable upsurge in law school applications.

†Not that this is a highly principled or selfless crew, you understand.

‡California's DWI statute reads in pertinent part: " (b) It is unlawful for any person who has 0.08 percent or more, by weight, of alcohol in his or her blood to drive a vehicle. . . . In any prosecution under this subdivision, it is a rebuttable presumption that the person had 0.08 percent or more, by weight, of alcohol in his or her blood at the time of driving the vehicle if the person had 0.08 percent or more, by weight, of alcohol in his or her blood at the time of the performance of a chemical test within three hours after the driving" (Calif. Vehic. Code § 23152[b] [West Supp. 1991]).

§Consider the ethical implications of such advice: "A lawyer who advises a witness about the law or about desired testimony before seeking the witness' own version of events comes dangerously near subornation of perjury; whether a violation is in fact committed is a question of the lawyer's intention and of his or her knowledge about the client's foreseeable reaction to the lawyer's information" (C. Wolfram, *Modern Legal Ethics* [1986], 648 [discussing lawyer interviews of witnesses in preparation for testimony]).

MICHAEL. Peter Himeson is the best toxicologist in the state. If he testifies for us, our stock goes way up. O.K., to the facts. . . . Now, you had a glass of wine minutes before leaving the restaurant, right?

STUART. Well, I had wine with lunch, so I guess, it was . . .

MICHAEL. Yes, but timing is very important. Let me explain something. It takes thirty minutes for a drink to get into your bloodstream. That means that if you had a glass of wine just before you got into your car, our expert witness could testify that it wasn't in your system when you were arrested. . . . This is very important testimony. . . . So . . . when do you think you had that last glass of wine?[50]

Stuart and Ann understand implicitly:

ANN. He drank it right before we left.

MICHAEL. Are you willing to testify to this?

ANN. Yes.

MICHAEL. Good . . . Very good.[51]

Note that Michael has just elicited precisely the testimony he would like the witness to give without once inviting any reference to the truth of the matter. Michael understands, of course, that his role is circumscribed. He cannot overtly suborn perjury—or, more precisely, he cannot knowingly allow Ann or Stuart to lie about the chronology of Stuart's drinking. On the other hand, there is no rule of law, no provision of the ethical code, nothing at all that compels Michael affirmatively to find out the truth about when the drinking occurred.

We thus come to understand that whether or not Stuart will be convicted for DWI has virtually nothing to do with whether or not he was legally drunk at the time of the arrest, and everything to do with the quality of the performances by the various actors (most notably, Michael, Stuart, Ann, the cop, the D.A., and the experts) within the stylized, sometimes highly circumscribed roles that the law has scripted and structured for them.[52] The image of law presented here is the performance of rhetorical moves within scripted, stylized roles that can be used by the various actors to invoke or suppress institutional power. There are ratios of power among the various actors, and depending on how all the actors deploy their power possibilities, *this* outcome rather than *that* one will be produced. So far, Michael Kuzak is performing his role well—so well, in fact, that he would like to make the case go away before trial. To this end, he has prepared the entire case before going to see the D.A. The provable facts are as follows:

1. Stuart had a 0.09 blood alcohol level, which is barely over the 0.08 DWI limit in California.

2. Two witnesses (Stuart and Ann) will testify that Stuart drank the wine just moments before he got into his car.

3. The state's top toxicologist—a highly respected person in the field—will testify that based on this time line, it would have been impossible for Stuart to be drunk at the time of the arrest.

Armed with these rhetorical obstacles to conviction, Michael Kuzak goes to see the D.A., a woman he knows by name. He tells her the provable facts. He adds that the case has been scheduled before Judge Matthews—a judge whom both Michael and the D.A. know to be a friend of the senior partner in Michael's firm. She looks skeptical. Michael pleads with her. He asks for a favor: "I need this one." Michael's tone implies: "Come on, please, just this one time . . ."[53]

Michael and the D.A. apparently have a "professional friendship," an informal relation that arises from the repeated contacts of their routines. Very likely they have had cases against each other before. It is this kind of professional friendship that sustains the vast informal network through which the long arm of the law does much of its work: plea bargains, settlements, consent decrees, and so on. This is the network of the law within the law—the "shadow law."[54]

The shadow law works smoothly and efficiently in the shadow of the unwieldy bilateral monopolies created by the state's statutory criminal law. The shadow law reduces transaction costs through an institution known as the "favor bank,"[55] a huge, constantly rearranging assembly of ties, loyalties, debts, and obligations. To outsiders, it is the secret economy of the law operating in the interstitial spaces left by the rational structure of explicit doctrinal law. The favor bank is in significant part a feudal institution—hierarchical in structure and operated on principles of loyalty and honor, and on ties of professional friendships like the one between Michael and the D.A.

In the end, the favor bank, the shadow law, and Michael's performance do their work: the charges are reduced to "reckless driving—dry."* And that's what matters to us: Stuart is just too nice a guy to be convicted. How does Michael come out? From the perspective of law in the books or law in the law school, Michael has engaged in some very questionable practices. Yet from a purely instrumental perspective, he has done a good job of it. Besides, this is what real law is like—playing the power ratios and manipulating the performances to get

---

*L.A. Law (March 29, 1990). And this is utterly predictable: "One statistic dominates any realistic discussion of criminal justice in America today: roughly ninety percent of the criminal defendants convicted in state and federal courts plead guilty rather than exercise their right to stand trial before a court or jury" (A. Alschuler, "Plea Bargaining and Its History," 79 Colum. L. Rev. 1, 1 [1979]).

the right result. And in our role as TV viewers, we know the right result: it is to get soft, kind, harmless Stuart out of the sex-hating, life-denying, fun-killing, Orwellian grasp of the law.

At the end of this episode, Stuart and Ann are back at their law offices and Stuart drops the inevitable bombshell. "I was guilty: three glasses of wine," he says.[56] This is a brilliant piece of script writing. It is brilliant because it confirms the central point that law is a game of power and manipulation. The lawyers manipulate and control. The law manipulates and controls as it tells its story through the mouths of the various legal actors—the lawyer, the D.A., the suspect, and the witness—all acting in their legal roles. And it is only when the long arm of the law is retracted and the choreographed legal roles have been dropped that Stuart can tell us that he was, in fact, drunk.

Did we see this coming? Probably. Could we have missed it? Sure: if we had insisted on believing that the statements made by Michael Kuzak, the lawyer, Stuart Markowitz, the suspect, and Ann Kelsey, the witness, were part of a field of undistorted rational discourse whose ultimate criterion is truth. We could have been taken in. But only if we indulged in one hell of a category mistake. We would have had to misconstrue a field of performances, of performative utterances, of power moves—that is, the field of law—for a field of undistorted rational discourse.

In our role as TV viewers of *L.A. Law,* we usually don't make that mistake. We understand that the law represented to us is not simply or even primarily a system of undistorted rational discourse. We understand implicitly that it is an institutionalized arrangement of performative roles and possibilities that both enable as well as delimit the possibilities for truth telling and deception. We understand that there is a great deal more going on than could possibly be captured by a medium that reduces law to stabilized "propositions," to rational arrangements of "ideas," to overarching "theories."

This is a world in which deceit plays an important part. Ann, Stuart, and Michael succeed in deceiving some of the other characters on the show (including each other). By the end of the show, Stuart is even deceiving himself: reflecting on the fact that by being able to pay $3,000 for a top toxicologist he was able to beat the rap, Stuart says to himself, "I'm just lucky, I guess." This is an extraordinary moment of self-deception. Indeed, it hardly classifies as luck for an upper-middle-class, well-connected, white male lawyer to be able to beat an isolated DWI rap. On the contrary, it's part and parcel of what it means to be part of that class. But Stuart abstracts himself away from this unwelcome bit of social self-knowledge, denies to himself that he is part of this web of social power, and avoids any reckoning with the social sources of his power: it's just plain, dumb, ineffable luck. Here we get a wonderful insight into how the average lawyer manages to deal with the web of social power in which he is enmeshed. Like Stuart, the typical lawyer denies that he is of the web. He claims that he is outside or above the web.

One of the striking aspects of *L.A. Law* is that, for all its obvious and not so negligible shortfalls, it is often a better approximation of the world of law practice than the routine academic productions of normative legal thought.[57] This perception is likely to be shared by anyone who has had any actual practice experience, anyone who understands that professional power is the juice that makes the wheels of the law bureaucracies run. Lawyers tend to see their professional power as resting "not on rules, but on local knowledge, insider access, connections, and reputation."[58] For instance, "lawyer regulars" within the criminal justice system maintain intimate relations with all levels of personnel in the court setting as a means of obtaining, maintaining, and building their practice: "These informal relations are the *sine qua non* not only of retaining a practice, but also in the negotiation of pleas and sentences."[59]

The favor bank and the shadow law, more than the reason of the better argument, are the stuff of law. The favor bank cannot be seen in *Law's Empire*, but only on *L.A. Law*. *Law's Empire* is predicated on the separation of law from the social and on the confinement of law to the space of the rational, the conscious, and the originary. Normative legal thought implicitly assumes that "we are a government of laws, not men."[60] *L.A. Law* reminds us that the obverse is also true. Practicing lawyers know very well that "it makes all the difference which judge is deciding a case."[61]

When a lawyer presents a case to a jury, the opening argument, the direct examinations, the cross, the objections, and the summation all typically aim toward the paramount objective of making the jury believe the lawyer's story line and disbelieve the other side.[62] To this end, the lawyer will establish her authority, credibility, and rapport with the jury. Moreover, she will not presume on them too much, but will construct a relatively clear and simple story line. This will be a prototypical story that resonates within the culture and evokes stereotypical responses such as pity, admiration, contempt, fear, and so forth. Each of the trial lawyer's actions in the courtroom will be designed to bolster, repeat, and reinforce that story line.[63]

For the trial lawyer, the substantive doctrine and the law of evidence and of civil procedure will serve two main functions. In one sense, they will be filters, the screens through which the stock story line must pass.[64] In this screening capacity, the positive law is obstructive. But the positive law is enabling as well: it organizes, echoes, and dignifies the lawyer's story line. In this second sense, the law signals to the jury that this is not just any story being told but one that fits a prototypical pattern (i.e., defendant intentionally harmed plaintiff), and that therefore the story warrants a prototypical response (i.e., jurors should make defendant compensate plaintiff).[65]

In crafting this story, the lawyer will consider the self-image of the jurors, their values, and their beliefs about themselves. The lawyer will frame the story with a simple rhetorical structure in mind: believe my story because it will confirm your sense of yourself as decent, courageous, sensible, and so on; disbelieve my opponent's story because in order to believe it, you will have to give up part of your favorable self-image.

Thus, for the effective trial lawyer, truth, rationality, and moral values play a role but only in an instrumental sense—only insofar as they aid the lawyer in effectively manipulating the jury to reach the predetermined desired outcome. Control and manipulation are the objective. What matters is not the rationality of a story but whether the story will rhetorically and cognitively produce the desired result; what matters is not moral value but the moralistic self-image of the jurors.

For the trial lawyer, the field is already in part constituted. As the litigation proceeds, countless factors increasingly limit the trial lawyer's possible strategies. The positive law sets the bounds of possible litigation. Discovery sets the bounds of the possible factual positions in the case. The identity of the judge sets the bounds of permissible evidence. Still, many of the power relations are the creation of the trial lawyer herself. She will establish a relation with the jurors and judge, and in doing so will influence the jurors' relation with the judge, with their task, and with opposing counsel.

Neither the truth, nor the rational content, nor the moral effect of this relation matters. What matters is the relation itself: who commands, who silences, who is believed, and so on. The trial lawyer knows all this. And the last thing she wants to do is re-present to herself all these relations in terms of a conventional separation and stabilization of truth, rationality, or moral value. On the contrary, to be effective, all this must be implicitly understood—indeed internalized—as a system of differentiated relations among power, truth, rationality, rhetoric, and deceit. As Edward Dauer and Arthur Leff put it: "A lawyer is a person who on behalf of some people treats other people the way bureaucracies treat all people—as nonpeople. Most lawyers are free-lance bureaucrats, not tied to any major established bureaucracy, who can be hired to use, typically in a bureaucratic setting, bureaucratic skills—delay, threat, wheedling, needling, aggression, manipulation, paper passing, complexity, negotiation, selective surrender, almost-genuine passion—on behalf of someone unable or unwilling to do all that for himself."[66]

All this, of course, *appears* to be very far from the reigning image of law on the contemporary normative legal thought channel. Listen to Dworkin and experience the dissonance: "What is law? . . . Law's empire is defined by attitude, not territory or power or process. . . . It is an interpretive, self-reflective attitude addressed to politics in the broadest sense. . . . Law's attitude is constructive: it aims, in the interpretive spirit, to lay principle over practice to show the best route to a better future, keeping the right faith with the past."[67]

Listen to Owen Fiss: "I continue to believe that law is a distinct form of human activity, one which, as Ronald Dworkin and others have insisted for some years now, differs from politics, even a highly idealized politics, in important ways. Political actors can and often do make claims of justice, but they need not. . . . Judges on the other hand, have no authority other than to decide what is just, and they obtain the right to do so from the procedural norms that surround their office and limit the exercise of their power."[68]

These visions of law offered by Fiss and Dworkin are a far cry from *L.A. Law*. Against that backdrop, the Dworkin-Fiss visions advertise an extraordinarily idealized, romanticized account of law—impossibly clean and orderly. They certainly seem quite distant from the vision of lawyering offered by Dauer and Leff.

And yet, is there really any contradiction between the two visions? Does the validation of the Dauer-Leff view of the lawyer-as-bureaucrat somehow falsify the Dworkin-Fiss visions? Or, correspondingly, do the Dworkin-Fiss visions somehow falsify the Dauer-Leff account? The answer, surprisingly, is no. What Fiss and Dworkin describe as the practice of law is what Dauer and Leff describe as the practice of law. We have to understand that when Dworkin and Fiss give their idealized or romanticized accounts of law, they are not talking about a separate reality: the Dworkin and Fiss visions are real—and they are realized every day in precisely the ways described by Dauer and Leff. "Laying principle over practice" and "making the law the best it can be" *is* the harassment, *is* the aggression, *is* the manipulation. All this stuff about "deciding what is just" and showing "the best route to a better future, keeping the right faith with the past," is exactly what Dauer and Leff's bureaucrat-lawyers say and do as they delay, threaten, wheedle, needle, manipulate, and otherwise kick people around.

Normative legal thought never quite manages to understand this point. Indeed, the continued viability, the continued respectability of normative legal thought as an enterprise in the academy *depend on* its failing to understand this point. Normative legal thought routinely fails to understand this point by relentlessly repeating two errors.

First, normative legal thought believes that in the abstraction of the normative terms from their bureaucratic setting on *L.A. Law*, their significance has nonetheless been preserved.[69] Normative legal thought tends to disavow its own performative dimension; it tends to hide from itself the kinds of social and rhetorical uses to which it is put. Rather uncritically and solipsistically, norma-

tive legal thought tends to concern itself only with its own "substantive" propositional normative content and its own normatively sanctioned uses. In this
sense, we can say that normative legal thought is not a "serious" enterprise, but
rather one that presumes uncritically that its main, or critical, significance is
self-determined.

This fixation of normative legal thought on its own substantive propositional
normative content is sustained by a second kind of prototypical mistake. Having abstracted its own discourse from the bureaucratic setting of *L.A. Law,*
normative legal thought tends to assume that its own substantive propositional
normative content somehow controls the way normative legal thought is
used—that somehow its propositional normative content regulates the ways
people get kicked around. Normative legal thought is thus prone to a naive
form of identity thinking in which the normative significance of a legal term in
the legal academy is blithely assumed to correspond roughly to the same normative significance in law practice. But it's not so.

And rhetorically, it is relatively easy to see that it is not so. We need only ask
what kind of role normative legal thought or Dworkin could play on *L.A. Law.*
The point here is not the usual one of trying to assess whether Dworkin's vision
of Law is right or not. Rather, the question is, what *role* can Dworkin *perform*—
what role can normative legal thought credibly *perform*—on *L.A. Law*? What is
the performative significance of normative legal thought?

It is not easy to see what role Dworkin could play. For one thing, it is
extremely difficult to imagine a normative thinker like Dworkin on *L.A. Law.*
To the extent that we understand Dworkin as the author of *Law's Empire* and
Taking Rights Seriously (as opposed to Ronald Dworkin, the man), it is implausible that he should become a regular character on *L.A. Law:* there is no role on
the show for a regular character whose primary (if not sole) mode of communicative interaction is "authentic" normative legal thought.

Perhaps, then, we should think along more modest lines. Perhaps we could
introduce Ronald Dworkin in a flashback. Michael Kuzak, faced with a very
difficult appeal on constitutional grounds, could remember his old professor
from law school. At a critical point in the case preparation, Michael would
remember his old professor's words and these would, of course, provide the
crucial missing link to win the case. "Yes—I've got it!" exclaims Michael. The
judge "constructs his overall theory of the present law so that it reflects, so far as
possible, coherent principles of fairness, substantive justice, and procedural due
process, and reflects these combined in the right relation."[70]

No. Dramatically, this does not work. It is not credible. Normative legal
thought cannot contribute to the practice of law *in this way.* Its prescriptions

and its subtle intellectual moves are simply not important to the practice of law in this way.

Perhaps, then, Ronald Dworkin could be allowed to make a speech at some bar convention about the rule of law and law's empire? Now, this dramatic option does work; this is credible theater. It can be scripted. Ronald Dworkin could even play the part himself. But there is something disturbing about this. The only role we have found for Ronald Dworkin or normative legal thought on *L.A. Law*'s empire is the ritualistic ceremonial one of providing the lawyering profession with a pleasing and admirable self-image. In other words, the one role dramatically possible for the normative legal thought of the legal academy is that of self-image maintenance for legal academics and lawyers.[71] This, of course, raises a disquieting question about the social significance of normative legal thought, suggesting that its primary significance is the performative one of providing and disseminating an appealing rhetoric and self-image for the lawyering profession.

In part, these observations bring us back to the early days of the CLS legitimation thesis, when legitimation was a description applied to legal thought, as distinguished from judge-made law. In the early days of CLS, Duncan Kennedy suggested that various kinds of legal thought were a kind of legitimation of existing legal institutions and practices.[72] As applied to academic legal thought, there is not much doubt that this legitimation thesis was and is right: virtually regardless of what is going on in the courts or the legislatures, most legal thinkers spend their intellectual energies rationalizing (i.e., making rational, coherent, appealing, etc.) whatever it is the courts are doing. Very often this legitimation effort takes the form of criticizing certain opinions or tendencies— but it is always in the effort to redeem, to celebrate, to validate the vast bulk of positive law, the legal institutions, and the thinking and practices of the contemporary American legal community.

While there can be little doubt that normative legal thought is always launched in the enterprise of legitimation, its role may go well beyond apologetics to the actual creation, production, and maintenance of the discourse and rhetoric that enable bureaucratic institutions and practices to organize themselves.[73] The normative legal thought of the academy may thus serve to keep the techniques and strategies of bureaucratic harassment, needling, wheedling, aggression, and so on in working order. There is a great deal to be said for this view. For one thing, it helps to explain how the Fiss-Dworkin visions are completely consistent with the Kafkaesque Dauer-Leff vision of bureaucratic lawyering: when lawyers harass, coerce, and intimidate, they do it with the nice words, the nice arguments, the nice jurisprudence crafted by normative legal thinkers.

In accordance with this last view, the primary role played by normative legal thought is to constitute students (and to a lesser extent, lawyers and judges) as polite, well-mannered vehicles for the polite transaction of bureaucratic business. *Law's Empire* spells out the proper etiquette for the actors on *L.A. Law's* empire.[74] This is not as surprising as it might first seem: remember that *Law's Empire* begins with and draws its inspiration from a discussion of courtesy.[75] Courtesy, of course, is nothing if not the studied observance of the idealized self-image of an existing social regime.

So it is certainly plausible to think that normative legal thought's crucial role goes beyond apologetics to the maintenance and refurbishing of the rhetoric deployed on *L.A. Law's* empire. But such a conclusion is hardly inexorable. After all, there is something quite unorthodox in trying to put Dworkin or any other normative legal thinker on the set of *L.A. Law*—they clearly do not belong there. And if I persist in trying to put them on the stage of *L.A. Law,* they will try vigorously to get off. This is quite predictable; we can expect normative legal thinkers to try to marginalize and deny *L.A. Law's* empire.

From the perspective of normative legal thinkers, *L.A. Law's* empire is "tosh";[76] it is a fallen and degraded world not worth thinking about or even recognizing. If the world of law practice has become *L.A. Law's* empire, then so much the worse for law practice—or so normative legal thinkers might argue. But this dismissive posture is not really available to them. Normative legal thought, after all, does not present itself as a mere intellectual exercise bereft of social or political ambitions. On the contrary, normative legal thought wears its worldly ambitions on its literary sleeve, as the names of its major productions— *Law's Empire* and *The Rule of Law*—indicate.

Owen Fiss reminds us eloquently of these worldly ambitions:

> The judge might be seen as forever straddling two worlds, the world of the ideal and the world of the practical, the world of the public value and the world of subjective preference, the world of the Constitution and the world of politics. He derives his legitimacy from only one, but necessarily finds himself in the other. He among all the agencies of government is in the best position to discover the true meaning of our constitutional values, but, at the same time, he is deeply constrained, indeed sometimes even compromised, by his desire—his wholly admirable desire—to give that meaning a reality.[77]

Owen Fiss is entirely right: normative legal thought demands and desires not merely to be performed, but to be enacted in some realm beyond itself—to be realized in the social realm. This sociality of law is true even of the most austere, ascetic formalist approaches that claim that law has an immanent moral rationality.[78] Even for such self-announced formalist accounts there is a demand that law be not simply thought, but enacted, realized.

To recognize the significance of these worldly ambitions is to recognize that normative legal thought cannot be indifferent to *L.A. Law*'s empire. On the contrary, normative legal thought's ambitions are precisely to rule over the domain currently occupied by *L.A. Law*, to submit the conduct of the various legal actors to some normatively appealing overarching rational pattern. Normative legal thought cannot so quickly dismiss *L.A. Law*'s empire—for that empire is the realm where law is enacted. *L.A. Law*'s empire may be a degraded, fallen world, but it is most assuredly not tosh.

There is another reason why normative legal thought cannot simply dismiss or deny *L.A. Law*'s empire: it is in some senses a more resonant and richer source of intellectual inquiry about law than many of the genteel productions of normative legal thought. Obviously, there are things that *L.A. Law* gets wrong;[79] it is, after all, prime-time TV. But despite its romanticization of law practice, the program, in comparison with normative legal thought, is much more consonant with what we are told by psychology, sociology, rhetoric, and even personal experience about the actual practice of law itself. In fact, one would have a very difficult time finding intellectually respectable sources of authority to credit the sort of psychology, sociology, and rhetoric that is (and must be) implicitly or explicitly assumed into methodological—and often ontological—existence by normative legal thought.[80]

Indeed, where is the intellectually respectable documentation to validate the main social and psychological categories of normative legal thought? Where is the psychological or sociological documentation to authorize normative legal thought's routine invocations of

>   the integrity of the sovereign individualist self?
>   the phenomena of choice, consent, free will?
>   the concept of unitary intent?
>   the notion of individual agency?

There isn't much. By and large, normative legal thought has assumed its own psychology, sociology, and rhetoric into existence. This sociology, psychology, and rhetoric assumed by normative legal thought are largely the unconscious concretization of its own *posited* aesthetic of social life—an aesthetic inherited from worlds now long since gone. There is little to support the social aesthetic of normative legal thought other than fiat and academic inertia. Unfortunately for normative legal thought, its *posited* understandings of the psychological, the

social, and the rhetorical are now stunningly anachronistic and strikingly discordant with much of what leading work in the humanities and social sciences
has to tell us about human beings and what they do.[81]

To the extent, then, that normative legal thought remains concerned about
the adequacy of its representations of the social sphere, it cannot afford to
dismiss *L.A. Law*'s empire. To the extent that normative legal thought is or
wants to consider itself an "authentic" enterprise, it must recognize the advanced bureaucratization of the practice of law and strive to understand how its
own psychological, sociological, and rhetorical maps are so discordant with
those on *L.A. Law*'s empire.

WHY HERCULES CAN'T DO *L.A. LAW*'S EMPIRE

Even if the dramatic requirements of *L.A. Law* do not leave much in the way of
roles for a Dworkin, normative legal thinkers continue to strive to communicate with the actors on *L.A. Law*'s empire. Normative legal thinkers write
articles, they write books, they seek to "intervene." And indeed, given their
worldly ambitions, the normative legal thinkers must strive to intervene. For
them, *L.A. Law* is a moral outrage—a fallen world, a bureaucratic shadow image
of "real" law.

How do normative legal thinkers intervene in and communicate with the
world of *L.A. Law*?[82] Well, they say some very normative things. They appeal to
conscience, to doing the right thing, to justification, to intellectual consistency,
to normative coherence. In one sense this is utterly unremarkable and routine.
Yet against the backdrop of *L.A. Law,* these sorts of interventions seem naive,
unworldly, and inappropriate. To try to engage in authentic normative legal
thought on *L.A. Law* is to recognize just how out of place it is. The dramatic
relations of *L.A. Law* are substantially more complex and richer than the stylized formalizations reproduced by even sophisticated normative legal thinkers.
What we get by trying to put Dworkin or any other normative legal thinker on
L.A. Law is a graphic depiction of the fragility of the assumptions that underlie
normative legal thought.

But now we must ask: What is it about normative legal thought that makes it
stand out as so obviously inappropriate for *L.A. Law*? The inadequacy of normative legal thought on *L.A. Law* stems from its routine and largely unconscious dependence on rhetorical assumptions that simply do not hold there.
First, normative legal thought assumes that its addressees are actually or potentially normatively competent. Second, it assumes that its own categories and
grammar resonate deeply and authentically within the culture in such a way

that normative legal thought can be effective in transforming and regulating the culture. These assumptions greatly simplify normative legal thought's academic mission. In making these assumptions, it has assumed into methodological and ontological existence a world mapped in its own image, a world charted in its own categories.

Most of this kind of thought is addressed (at least nominally) to judges, either directly or via the selective mediation of lawyers or clerks. While it is commonly assumed that legal thinkers "speak to judges and other formulators of law, helping them to understand and perform their job,"[83] this seems to be a case of wishful thinking. Perhaps at one time legal thinkers did speak to judges and did routinely help convey some useful prescriptions or helpful recommendations.[84] But it is difficult to believe that this is generally (or even often) the case now. Judges simply do not have the time, the inclination, or the patience to read this stuff.[85] Besides, normative legal thought tends to be just about as boring,[86] lifeless, and unedifying as the judicial opinions it reflects and refracts.[87] Not surprisingly, the vast majority of the prescriptions, recommendations, and solutions produced by this thought will never reach a judge, or any other legal actor.

Some of these prescriptions, however, may, and in fact often do, find their way into the classroom. They may even seem appealing or persuasive to the students.[88] But even then, it is exceedingly unlikely that they will survive the institutional frameworks within which the students become employed. To the extent that these normative arguments do survive, it will be precisely when they are least necessary—that is, when they already fit the preformed agenda of interests and worldviews of the client, the court, or the legislature. Normative legal thought (even if it seems to be all the rage among left-liberals) is thus an extremely conservative enterprise—conservative in the sense that it tends to reproduce whatever regime is already in place.[89]

And indeed, because normative legal thought is so miscast for this scene, it would be surprising if it did have much success pressing its recommendations and prescriptions on *L.A. Law*'s empire. Normative legal thought presupposes that its relation to its addressees is already regulated by shared commitments to values (like truth, good, right, and neutrality) and rational discourse criteria (coherence, consistency, authenticity, etc.). Accordingly, normative legal thought yields arguments that depend on the presence of shared values and criteria of discourse in the speaker and the listener. But if the aim is to regulate the actions and the actors on *L.A. Law*'s empire, these presuppositions are inappropriate in at least two major ways.

First, the values and discursive criteria presupposed by normative legal thought are not shared at a sufficiently concrete level to enable conclusions to follow in a relatively unproblematic manner. The values and concerns are far too abstract to enable an unproblematic resolution of serious disputes among the contestants. This point carries particular force when the community becomes thin and fragmented, as it is now. In those circumstances, normative legal thought will itself be incapable of recognizing, let alone reconciling, the concrete psychological, social, and rhetorical motivating forces that lead actors to disagree.[90] On the contrary, normative legal thought becomes increasingly epiphenomenal: the serious argumentative work is done at a preliminary stage, in the differing aesthetic accounts of social events and social action offered by the contesting parties.

There is a second way that the presuppositions of normative legal thought are inappropriate for *L.A. Law*'s empire. Normative legal thought routinely represents the scene in which it is operating in its own image, as if its values and its discursive criteria already occupied a distinct and regulative role. Hence, normative legal thought represents the forces and relations identified by terms like *rhetoric, psychology,* and *sociology* as domains somehow distinct from and subordinate to the normative vocabulary and grammar. For normative legal thought, the identity of the normative is always known and already stabilized: a normative position is either contaminated by power or it is not; it is either genuine or it is not. In this either/or way, normative legal thought not only represents itself as distinct and separable from the contaminations of power and deceit, but also as regulative of discourse and action.

What makes *L.A. Law*'s empire more interesting than the routine productions of normative legal thought is that on *L.A. Law*'s empire, normative argument is not assured of such a pre-scripted, regulative leading role. On the contrary, on *L.A. Law*'s empire, the very identity of the normative is in question. There is no implicit assumption that the legal discourse provides access to a normativity insulated from power, deceit, or rhetoric, and normative statements are just as likely to be received by the actors as rational persuasion as they are to be experienced as power moves.[91] The most troubling prospect for normative legal thought, then, is that its principal contribution to the world of *L.A. Law*'s empire might be to furnish an increasingly elegant, polite, and appealing rhetoric—a rhetoric that is itself already the production of unexamined exercises of power.

The divergence between normative legal thought's ambitions and the possibility of their realization is all the more apparent when one notes that normative legal thought is at once extremely ambitious and yet seriously out of touch with the world it seeks to rule and govern.

Normative legal thought often understands itself to be playing for very large stakes. *Law's Empire,* the leading popular work in jurisprudence, modestly confines itself to the study of "formal argument from the judge's viewpoint," yet nonetheless manages to bill itself as "Law's Empire" and to exalt the reader to become a legal Hercules. This is not the jurisprudence of modesty.

Such intellectual confidence might be justifiable if normative legal thought had a firm understanding of the social situation, or if there were some reason to think that the discourse of normative legal thought had tapped into the cultural sources that would allow us "to lay principle over practice to show the best route to a better future, keeping the right faith with the past."[92] But the gestures of normative legal thought do not map very well onto the scene of social and legal action.[93] The aesthetics of normative thought effect a rationalist simplification, stabilization, and subordination of the political, the social, the psychological, and the rhetorical. In normative legal thought, they have always already been subordinated to an overarching normative rationality that is already in command. In contrast, on *L.A. Law,* as in law practice, the political, the social, the psychological, the rhetorical, and the rational are all differentially related in complex ways.

Indeed, the various domains are difficult to distinguish from each other, and their relations are far from being stabilized in some preexisting hierarchy. On *L.A. Law,* as in law practice, it is often a real—that is to say, a dramatic—question whether acts of conscience are acts of morality or acts of rationalization, whether acts of persuasion are acts of rationality or acts of power, and whether the relations among the actors are overdetermined, undetermined, or determined at all. In contrast to *L.A. Law,* normative legal thought seems thin and two dimensional.

In one sense, then, the flatness of normative legal thought proves to be a peculiar advantage—one that enables normative legal thought to operate in a world it systematically represents as "first best."[94] Normative legal thought routinely assumes that it is operating in an epistemic regime in which the thinker already possesses a series of reasoning moves that are themselves secure, self-identical, and stable. It assumes a world of reasoning in which the medium and channels of communication are already established between author and reader, academic and judge;[95] in which the matrices carved by language and reasoning are already adequate to say anything worth being said. In this world, the autonomous self of author and reader is in control of its own thinking processes; it already stands whole, outside the duplicities of ideological and institutional distortion.

Now, as you might guess, to assume such a world of already secure, linear, nonparadoxical, and fully compliant communicative links simplifies the intellectual situation tremendously. The intelligibility and coherence of all the reasoning moves have been secured a priori; questions and inquiries can stand still; the impact, scope, and consequences of reasoning moves are predictable. In such a world, the only significant intellectual task is to police the formal relations between the premises and the conclusions and to ensure that they are correctly observed.

This sort of thought police work is extremely easy: the set of formalized symbols (legal categories) already bear a certain set of formalized relations to each other (consistency, coherence, etc.); they have already been codified. The basic legal object-forms (legal categories) have already been largely sedimented. The transformational grammar is fairly easy to learn. Duplicity, paradox, ideology, and instability have already been ruled out from the start as serious forces constituting or disabling the thought of the author and the reader. The thought and the thinker are already whole, competent, and unquestionably in charge of the production of the normative legal text.[96] What is more, the normative grammar ensures that nothing can really disrupt this formal rhetorical economy.[97]

But while in this sense normative legal thought is extremely easy, in another related sense, normative legal thought is very difficult. Its terminus is very demanding: normative legal thought must end on a concluding note that is nonparadoxical, noncontradictory, positive, and presumably capable of being adopted in *L.A. Law*'s empire. The conclusion is normative legal thought's moment of high anxiety: it is where the normative text hopes to forge a connection to social action. Consider, for instance, Robin West's normative recommendation that "progressive constitutionalists, as well as progressive legislators . . . try to create a viable progressive interpretation of the Constitution, congressionally and popularly supported, with the explicit aim of creating a modern 'constitutional moment.' "[98] This call for a constitutional moment, for the relocation of constitutional practice from the courts to the legislature, for "a Constitution that is at once more progressive, more political, more challenging, more just, and more aspirational than we have yet imagined,"[99] is deeply moving. And yet, it moves nothing. Missing from West's recommendations is what is typically missing from normative legal thought: any sense of how the prescription (we should all try for a constitutional moment) might realize itself in the social sphere. The connection between works of normative legal thought and the social situation is often not a connection at all but a rupture masquerading as a connection. Very often, the graft does not take—we are left with an aporia—and the normative recommendations, left unconnected to any social reality, simply drop off into the abyss.

As in virtually all the work of normative legal thought, the social, rhetorical, institutional, and professional mechanisms of realization are assumed to be present, functioning, and responsive to the ideational recommendations of normative prescription. It is as if the machinery of the social and political world were already constructed with a series of workers waiting at the levers for instructions from normative legal thinkers.

Now it is precisely this sort of widespread, sedimented understanding of the situation that enables normative legal thought to believe that its issuance of prescriptions constitutes serious intellectual or political work. Yet to proceed with such first-best world assumptions about the situation, character, and role of legal thought and thinkers is to begin thinking *after* the crucial issues have already been begged. The problem here is not that the structure of normative legal thought is an abstraction of the social or legal field. Rather, the problem is that it is the wrong sort of abstraction, one that, by way of selective essentialization, has succeeded in leaving behind most of the difficult and interesting problems.

In this sense, even though normative legal thought finds life very easy within its own simplified homeostatic matrices, life becomes very difficult when the problem is how to translate normative prescriptions into the order of things. There is a ratio operating here. The more the matrices of normative legal thought are stabilized, simplified, and reductively organized, the easier life will be within the normative system and the harder it will be to translate normative productions into the order of things. Formalism, including normative formalism, has advantages, but these ultimately have a cost: the cleaner, the more austere your normative conceptual universe, the less chance that you can achieve anything meaningful with it on *L.A. Law*'s empire. Applying this ratio to normative legal thought, we see that its prototypical matrices are so stylized and so insulated from any "outside" that its prospects for the realization of any normative prescription are questionable except perhaps when the prescription is so modest in its utopian leanings and hopes for change that it is already virtually an abstracted reflection of extant positive law.

If normative legal thought fails to understand its own rhetorical construction as a kind of formalism, it also fails to understand the character of *L.A. Law*'s empire. Indeed, the scene on which normative legal thought hopes to play is increasingly defined by an aesthetics of bureaucracy incommensurable with the aesthetic of an "authentic" normative discourse. Consider, for instance, the primary categories around which the grammar of normative legal thought currently organizes itself:

self-determination/self-governance/self-realization
free will/choice/consent/intent
culpability/guilt/blame
liberty/freedom
autonomy/dignity/respect/personhood
opportunity/privilege
rights/entitlements
duty/responsibility/obligation
community
necessity/coercion/duress
private
public

Compare these prototypical terms, which assume rational and normatively competent agents, with the scene of law—the law firm, the courtroom, the jail, the social realm—a world increasingly defined by bureaucratic practices such as

formalized rule regimes
routinized procedures
rationalized production/technical mastery
conceptual and organizational hierarchy
instrumental forms of consciousness/operationalized value systems
dependency on expertise
high specialization of functions
jurisdictional compartmentalization
fragmentation and sectorization of knowledges
strategic uses of linguistic and cultural resources

The incommensurability of the aesthetic of normative discourse with the aesthetic of bureaucratic practice suggests that opportunities for the exercise of any "authentic," normatively competent behavior are extremely restricted within bureaucratic forms of life. For one thing, the organizational structure of bureaucracy—its zero-sum quality, its diffusion of causal lines of responsibility, its incentive/disincentive structures, and its routinization of rationalization (*raison de bureaucracy*)—is often cast in a way that precludes and obstructs normatively competent behavior. For another thing, the incommensurability makes it unclear how one would recognize or name authentic normative bureaucratic behavior in the first place.

Once we notice our bureaucratic circumstances, the character, identity, and possibility of the ethical become highly problematic. As a simple example, consider whether traditional moral virtues like honesty, sincerity, loyalty, and honor of craft are "authentically" applicable or even intelligible in the context of bureaucratic institutions. To facilitate matters, consider the two lists of bureaucratic responses below and ask yourself two questions. First, which list most plausibly conforms to traditional moral virtues? Second, when you have personally experienced these responses, which set seemed closest to doing the right thing?[100]

> *Bureaucratic Morality I*
> It's not my job.
> Some other department.
> I don't make the rules, I just follow them.
> I'm sorry, this is not the proper form.
> I wish I could, but I simply can't . . .
>> do that.
>> answer that question.
> Come back tomorrow.
> Oh, I would never have said that.
> I'm sorry, your file is not in here.

> *Bureaucratic Morality II*
> I really shouldn't be telling you this, but if . . .
> No one will check on this.
> You can't do it that way, but if you call it this instead . . .
> Technically, it doesn't comply, but . . .
> Well, it's really supposed to be done that way, but what really matters is . . .
> I'm sorry your file is not in here.

My point is that absent further specification of the context (and often even with it), it is difficult to determine which set of responses more nearly corresponds to the traditional virtues.

The sort of uneasiness prompted by the presentation of these responses is a reflection, an instantiation of the incommensurability of our normative grammars and categories with the configurations of our present bureaucratic practices and institutions.[101] And while these normative grammars and categories continue to occupy our attention, the most thoughtful and sophisticated attempts to reconstruct the ethical in light of our modern or postmodern condition have the performative effect of revealing just how narrow and insecure the jurisdiction of the ethical has become.[102] This is why, in sophisticated accounts, the ethical voice often reduces to very fragile and highly abstract, almost mystical, pleas to heed, as Drucilla Cornell puts it, "the call to witness to the

Other,"[103] or the commitment "to the not yet of what has never been present, cannot be fully re-called, and therefore cannot be adequately projected." The very fragility, abstraction, and mysticism of our most thoughtful and sophisticated ethical thought are testimony to the retreat of the ethical from our world.

If we recognize the advent of bureaucracy and take it seriously—admittedly a difficult task—we are returned to the question of just who or what normative legal thought thinks it is addressing. What messages are being received and what roles do the normative messages serve? What sustains normative legal thought? How does it manage to seem so plausible and meaningful to so many legal thinkers? If the effects of normative legal thought are not what it imagines them to be, then what are they?

Strangely, these seemingly different questions all beget the same answers— answers that entail reorienting our attention. Normative legal thought's hegemony has directed us for so long to try to control, reform, and improve the legal order through normative good works that we have come to believe that the lines of force run predominantly one way (that way). What I want to show in the next section is that rather than thinking of normative legal thought as providing a starting point for critique, reform, or social change, normative legal thought instead reproduces its own aesthetic in ways that are intellectually as well as politically unhelpful. Normative legal thought sustains a kind of jurisprudential theater that in effect leaves legal thought arrested—the uncritical automatic production of academic bureaucracy and its inertia.

THE THEATER OF THE RATIONAL

Among the many reasons to put Ronald Dworkin's jurisprudence on *L.A. Law* is to draw attention to the theatrical aspect of legal thought.[104] It is very easy for legal thinkers to forget that they are performers in an enterprise whose characters, roles, and action are always already largely scripted.[105] In part that is because most legal thinkers do not see themselves as engaged in theater in the first place. And they do not think they are engaged in theater precisely because of the kind of theater they are already doing: they are doing the *theater of the rational.* The theater of the rational is precisely the kind of theater that is grounded in the forgetting of its own theatricality. To play a part in this theater is to rule out the recognition that one is doing theater.

Indeed, consider the dramatic scandal were Ronald Dworkin or Owen Fiss or even Bruce Ackerman to stop in the middle of his own work to contemplate *seriously* the historical, psychoanalytic, or cognitive scene of his own normative jurisprudence. Something would seem out of kilter, rhetorically askew. Reflexivity may be fine for Andre Gide or John Fowles, but it is not acceptable for a

Dworkin or a Fiss or an Ackerman: we simply do not expect this sort of critical reflexive act to originate from these particular agents, or any like them.[106]

While it is predictable that many schooled in the older jurisprudences will fail to engage in such critical reflexivity—that they will in their usual subject-object separations think that "theory" is "objective" and "independent" of the agents that produce "it"—what is striking is that this failure is by no means limited to orthodox thinkers. On the contrary, the failure to inquire into the constitution of the subject that produces legal thought is (virtually) universal in contemporary legal thought.[107] Ironically, this failure occurs even where the jurisprudential approach would seem to lead almost unavoidably to a serious examination of the scene of academic production. I will give three examples of this striking, though utterly routine, lack of critical reflexivity: one from the so-called right, one from the so-called center, and one from the so-called left. In each case, I argue that the jurisprudential approaches lead readily to, and would indeed benefit from, an articulate consideration of the scene in which their own thought is produced and disseminated. Yet no such consideration is forthcoming in any of the cases.

I draw my example of the so-called right from law and economics. One of the interesting contributions of law and economics work is its consideration of the comparative advantages and disadvantages of various social coordination systems. Ronald Coase, for instance, discussed ways of conceptualizing the comparative advantages of different types of social coordination mechanisms—most notably, the market, government regulation, and market bypass mechanisms such as the firm.[108] Coase argued that each kind of social coordination mechanism could be expected to be more desirable than the others in certain situations.[109] Coase's analysis found an echo and a normative elaboration in the work of Guido Calabresi, who developed the "cheapest cost avoider" approach to tort law. According to Calabresi, the function of tort law is to provide institutionally effective conceptualizations of the relevant actors and of the various cost-benefit judgments to be made so that the actor who is in the best position to make a certain kind of cost-benefit judgment is in fact led to make it.[110]

The approach pioneered by Coase and Calabresi has now blossomed into a number of sophisticated and complex variants. Much of this law and economics analysis strives to identify which institutional actor or social coordination mechanism can most efficiently acquire or manufacture the relevant choice information, make "correct" decisions, and act on those decisions.[111] Law and economics thinkers are thus extremely attentive to the sorts of informational advantages and disadvantages that the various competing social coordination mechanisms create.

Tellingly, however, even though law and economics thinkers are quite capable of recognizing that every social coordination mechanism has informational blinders that must be considered in assessing its desirability, there is one institutional framework that is always implicated in the choice and yet (virtually) never examined by the law and economics thinkers: their own. Like almost all other legal thinkers, law and economics thinkers routinely situate themselves, their discourse, and their institutional framework somewhere "outside" the problem posed, as if they had no informational blinders, cognitive deficits, or conceptual disabilities whatsoever that might affect or skew the choice among the available social coordination mechanisms.[112] What is strange about this, of course, is that once this simplifying supposition is brought to light, it appears to be not just wrong, but completely contrary to the very theory that law and economics thinkers deploy to assess the relative comparative advantage among the various social coordination mechanisms. Perhaps even more striking is the fact that the reliability of such assessments could only be enhanced by the consideration of the institutional advantages and disadvantages that law and economics thinkers experience in making such assessments.[113]

Law and economics thinkers are hardly alone in this kind of oversight. Many other jurisprudential approaches would seem to require, as a matter of their own intellectual seriousness, a critical examination of the scene in which their legal thought is produced; yet again, no such examination is forthcoming. Consider an example drawn from the so-called center—legal neopragmatism. Neopragmatists believe many things, and a brief essentialist description would hardly do justice to the many pragmatist themes that have emerged. Still, one belief legal neopragmatists seem to share is that truth is situated, practical, social, and contextual.[114]

Now, with all this emphasis on the situated, social, practical, and contextual character of legal thought, it would seem appropriate for legal neopragmatists to examine their own context: the social, cognitive, and rhetorical scene of their own thought, the scholarly situation within which their talks and articles and classes are being produced. But legal neopragmatism has yet to consider the scene of its writing in any serious manner.[115] Instead, it shuns what would have seemed to be among the most pragmatic of questions: What are the functions, character, and possibilities of legal academic thought?[116]

Two neopragmatists who come close to discussing these questions are Martha Minow and Elizabeth Spelman. They begin their recent article on pragmatism with exactly the right (that is, the pragmatic) question. "As we turn to address the meaning of 'context' in these contexts, we are pointedly aware of a plausible question likely to occur to a sensitive reader: What is the context for our inquiry?"[117] But then, rather than answering the question and exploring the context of academic legal thought or law review writing or conference papers, or any other aspect of their scene, they define the context of their inquiry in terms of three scholarly and rather conceptualistic definitions of context.

This failure to examine the scene of the writing is exactly the same pattern we observed in law and economics. In both cases, the jurisprudential commitments require examinations of the scene of writing, yet in both cases, having been brought to the brink (or beyond), the scene is left untouched and undisturbed, as if it had no impact on and no significance for the thought being produced.

This pattern is not restricted to the right or center. On the left, consider the radical project of deconstruction. While the politics of deconstruction continue to be generally in question, in the legal academy deconstruction is generally associated with the CLS left. In France, deconstruction has often been characterized (and criticized) as a kind of radical and extreme intellectual movement.[118] Deconstruction, as a postmodern phenomenon, thus arrived on the shores of America in opposition to liberal humanism and its centerpiece, the sovereign individual subject. Derrida's own description of deconstruction proclaims as much: "Deconstruction does not consist in passing from one concept to another, but in overturning and displacing a conceptual order, *as well as the nonconceptual order* with which the conceptual order is articulated."[119] Given this radical project of displacing and overturning not just the conceptual order but also the nonconceptual order within which the conceptual order is articulated, it would seem particularly appropriate for deconstruction as it is imported into American legal thought to examine the scene in which it is operating—or rather, to displace and overturn the conceptual and nonconceptual matrices and forces within which it is received.

We might expect deconstruction, for instance, to attempt to displace the legal advocacy mentality so prevalent in academic legal thought, as well as to displace and overturn the authority structures of legal thought. We might expect a displacement of the sovereign legal author, the matrices of his thought, or the like. Little of this has occurred. On the contrary, rather than turning deconstruction loose on the scene of legal academic thought—which would correspond to Derrida's own deployment of deconstruction on the scenes of structuralism, Plato's philosophy, and academic thought generally—virtually all the legal deconstructionists, like the law and economics thinkers and the neopragmatists, have shied away from such a critical turn on the scene of their own writing. Instead, they have compressed deconstruction into an utterly traditional legal role: in their hands, deconstruction has become just another legal resource, just another set of reasoning moves, just another "analytic tool" for the legal academic to deploy at will against opponents.[120] As with the other two approaches, this failure of deconstruction to disturb its own relation to the scene of legal thought has produced a domestication of what might be a helpful and intellectually interesting contribution to legal thought.[121]

What is striking here is the repetition of the same pattern in three ostensibly very different jurisprudential approaches. In each case there is a manifest failure to question the scene of legal thought, even though each approach would seem to warrant a thoroughgoing examination or even disturbance of this scene. But there is something about the way the theater of contemporary normative legal thought is defined or established that leads legal thinkers away from taking cognizance of the scene in which they are acting or the kind of action in which they are engaged. Within the unspoken norms of legal thought, it is not considered legitimate, relevant, or serious to draw attention to this scene.

As you might imagine, this is an interesting recognition to achieve at this point because the very enterprise pursued here is precisely the sort that normative legal thought considers beyond inquiry—illegitimate, irrelevant, and unserious. What I am writing about in this essay is thus the same thing as the resistance to what I am writing; I am trying to reveal the network of social, cognitive, and rhetorical forces that shape our thought and yet remain unconscious. I am trying to reveal the character of the legal unconscious. And we have now encountered a serious blockage—an unwillingness, an inability of legal thinkers to consider the scene of their own thought even when such a move would seem at once intellectually obvious and obviously beneficial.

This blockage is easily understandable in practical terms. For any of these approaches to question the cognitive, rhetorical, or social scene of their own writing would immediately place in question their present formal configuration. It would—at least from their perspective—immediately trouble their intellectual authority and legitimacy (as these terms are currently understood). For an economist to draw attention to the comparative advantages and disadvantages of her discourse, or a neopragmatist to focus on the academic conventions that have produced and validated her discourse, or a deconstructionist to destabilize the very conceptual and nonconceptual frameworks that allow him to import deconstruction into the academy, would be to challenge the very discursive scene that enables each of these kinds of thinkers to claim intellectual authority and legitimacy in the first place. It would be, in short, to challenge the very conceptual-institutional-rhetorical system that allows the claims to be articulated and heard.[122] But while these are obvious risks, the critical reflexive turn also offers obvious intellectual rewards. Nonetheless, the reflexive turn is virtually never taken. Why not?

The very way the question has been framed here presupposes what is routinely presupposed in legal academic thought: that legal thinkers (you and I) are sovereign individual subjects who choose their own discursive positions and thought processes and announce these positions within a self-sufficient and weightless medium of communication; that you and I as sovereign individual subjects make rational decisions about such questions as whether or not to take a reflexive turn.

It is precisely these pervasively sedimented assumptions that prevent us from understanding why the critical reflexive turn is not taken. We have thus reached the critical point in this essay where the same rhetorical constructions that disable legal thinkers from taking the critical reflexive turn are also disabling us (you and I) from understanding why the critical reflexive turn is not taken. Our thought, our theater, and our selves are rhetorically constructed so that the critical reflexive turns become (virtually) unthinkable. The very form and practice of our thought already establishes us as such competent conversants in an already rational and rationally legitimated discourse—as such relatively autonomous, coherent, integrated, rational, and originary individual subjects—that, for the most part, we are simply not capable of even entertaining the requisite doubts to investigate how we are socially and rhetorically constructed. Indeed, even as you read this, and as I write it, it is difficult for each of us to remember that it is the way you and I think that is being put in question and that, therefore, at this very moment, there is no safe external place for you or me to go to adjudicate the truth or falsity of what is being said by recourse to some set of preestablished, noncontroversial criteria.

We are no longer having the usual sort of stereotypical scholarly conversation in which we can somehow separate ourselves from the conversation that is taking place. On the contrary, we are in a conversation aimed at demonstrating the ways in which our rhetoric shapes us and the way we think about legal thought. And the very difficulty of the last paragraph is in part attributable to the fact that the intense critical reflexive turn—the one you are experiencing now—is quite foreign to our rhetoric. It can even be experienced as annoying and coercive.

Indeed, as you read, you may experience this conversation as an attack on the self—your self. But that is the point: it is perfectly understandable that you should feel assaulted. The rhetorical turn here is leading you, the reader, to deal seriously with the question of your own autonomy as reader. And, of course, this is not easy or pleasant because you, as a legal thinker, have already been rhetorically constructed to think of yourself as an autonomous, self-directing, rational, choosing entity, and this text, in its very form and rhetoric, is disturbing that self-image. It is rather rudely, without asking your permission, leading you to question the status of your self-image as an autonomous entity.

Believe me, at this moment we are most definitely not having a rational conversation among rational, autonomous, choosing entities. Rather, you are being manipulated, and in a way you may not find particularly pleasant. For even as you recognize that you are being manipulated, you are also being reminded—even as you read the next word of this sentence—that you are not the autonomous, rational, self-directing, choosing entity you assume yourself to be. Part of what makes this text so trying is its refusal to honor, even in the most superficial ways, the conceit that the reader is a rational, self-directing, choosing subject. And we (you and I) are so invested in and invested with that self-image that I almost feel I should apologize to you for breaching some unspoken rule of author-reader courtesy. There has been a breach of good form here. And that is because the challenge posed here is not just a substantive, remote, theoretical challenge; it is a challenge to the very form and practice of the thinking of the rational, self-directing, choosing self—your self.

This rhetorical assault on the self as rational, self-directing, and choosing occurs right on the surface of the text, right up front, in plain view, openly. Part of the reason it is so open is to demonstrate that this tacit practice of good form is also the way the rational, self-directing, choosing self was constructed in the first place. Indeed, your expectation as a reader is that you will be treated with a bit more deference, respect, and courtesy than you have received here. No exhumation of some deeply buried generative structure is required to recover the rhetorical construction of the autonomous, rational, coherent self. Rather, the social and rhetorical construction of the sovereign individual subject occurs under our very noses—in the open movements of the form, the practice of our own thought.

We don't notice this process of social and rhetorical construction of the self—not because it is deep and far removed from the everyday, but because our rhetoric is itself structured to suppress such inquiry, because it is our process, form, and practice not to pursue inquiries into the process, form, and practice of our own thought. We (you and I) as legal thinkers are constructed and reconstructed as sovereign individual subjects even at the moments when the sovereign individual would seem to be most at risk—when we are reckoning with conventionalism, social constructivism, deconstruction, and the like.

Indeed, even when legal thinkers come close to recognizing that the individual subject may well be a vastly overstated rhetorical, cognitive, or linguistic construction, the very form of their thought nonetheless succeeds in situating their selves and the selves of their readers outside this recognition.[123] In fact, it is just that tension—between the recognition that the self is socially and rhetorically constituted and the conflicting one that the self remains autonomous—that leads to the construction I have called the relatively autonomous self.[124] In the end, while this self concedes both its own autonomy and its social construction, it is autonomy, rationality, and the like that come out on top.

Inasmuch as we are constructed as sovereign individual subjects, the very idea of troubling the process, form, and practice of our own thought simply does not, and often cannot, occur to us. And insofar as it doesn't occur to us, it becomes our process, form, and practice not to inquire into the process, form, and practice of our thought. If we take a look at the field of legal thought, it is apparent that it is already constructed in our own image. The very process, form, and practice of legal thought systematically situate both author and reader in a rhetorical field that represents itself as an already extant, self-sufficient, virtually complete mode of rational discourse—just waiting to be put to good use by sovereign individual subjects (conversant in the field). The rhetoric constructs both reader and author as the beneficiaries of an already constituted, nonproblematic, nonparadoxical, already rationalized mode of argumentative strategies, reasoning moves, and the like—not just as a potential, but as an already realized, already in place, first-best world of reasoning and communication.

This, in a sense, is the crowning success of Enlightenment epistemology. But there is an ironic twist: Enlightenment rationality has become so successfully ingrained in our processes, forms, and practices that, ironically, we have (almost) completely lost the quintessentially Enlightenment capacity to question, to criticize our processes, forms, and practices themselves. To put it plainly, if somewhat misleadingly: We have come to believe in our own rationality in a fundamentalist manner; we have come to believe it implicitly, in a manner that goes without saying, in every saying. The rationality of the Enlightenment has become so successful, so hegemonic, that it has become immobilized through its own institutionalization.[125] The Enlightenment commitments to reason, to criticism, and to rebellion against unreasoned convention have themselves become firmly embedded as a barely visible, largely unquestioned, almost unquestionable convention.

Indeed, the process of rational thought is not just pervasive but self-reinforcing. The taken-for-granted sense that legal discourse is already sufficiently rational for its tasks in turn authorizes the deprivileging of form. There is no particular reason to examine the form of legal thought in a serious way because the form of legal thought is already assumed to be adequate for its purposes and to be within the control of relatively autonomous subjects. The form within which legal thought is produced is considered to be weightless and inconsequential, such that the vocabulary and grammar of legal discourse are assumed to be adequate and sufficient to allow any important or legitimate substantive message to get through. In consequence, what is considered central, crucial, and important in legal thought is almost invariably conceptualized as substance. Hence, even on the rare occasions when form is made the *primary* focus of inquiry, it is only after form has been reconceptualized in terms of the categories of substance. Inquiry into form—in the sense of inquiry into the formative framework within which legal thought is produced—remains, at this point, largely beyond the possibilities of contemporary legal thought.

Inasmuch as it is substance, and not form, that matters, legal thought also privileges outcomes at the expense of process. Legal thought is supposed to materialize into outcomes, and process is supposed to be subservient to the attainment of that goal. This privileging of outcome at the expense of process is a mimesis of the representation of legal discourse as an already in place, self-sufficient, shared, rationalized mode of discourse ready for deployment by a relatively autonomous subject: insofar as the process of rationalist discourse is already established as satisfactory, the only action in legal thought lies in the deployment of this system to produce outcomes—hence the usual fixation of legal thought on the production of ideas, theories, positions, models, and other such conventionally reified terminal thought analogues.

Inasmuch as the goal of legal thought is to produce (substantive) outcomes, in what is admittedly an ongoing process, theory must already be in a position to regulate practice. This is implicit in the assumption that legal discourse is already a self-sufficient and rationalized field of discourse enabling relatively autonomous subjects to control their own thinking. Hence, in legal thought, theory is routinely depicted as being in control of or as informing practice. Indeed, theory is very often depicted as the source of constraint or restraint on legal interpretation, the source of normative outcomes, and the generative origin of substantive intellectual visions.

The privileging of substance over form, outcome over process, and theory over practice is recursive. The rationality of legal thought and the sovereignty of the relatively autonomous subject are preserved because that which could potentially destabilize them is always already relegated to the excluded or marginalized region of the subordinate term (i.e., form, process, practice), and thus immediately put beyond view or subjected to control. Yet, this establishment of the field in terms of a privileging of theory over practice, substance over form, and outcome over process is itself excluded from view because the work of field definition (exclusion) is itself performed in the excluded regions. It is our practice to deprivilege our practice. It is our form not to inquire into our form. It is our process not to question the process of our thought. It is not just that we (you and I) *think* this way. We *are* this way.

Sometimes this hierarchy of privileging and deprivileging acquires a form that is (virtually) absolute. But it is important to understand that the privileging/deprivileging usually takes many forms at once, some of which are far from absolute.[126] And it also important to understand that any piece of legal thought often partakes of a plurality of relations among the privileged and deprivileged terms at once.

This description of rationalist rhetoric is consonant with the earlier description of normative legal thought, and with the previous understanding of how normative legal thought hopes to accomplish its ends. Such a rationalist rhetoric is precisely the sort of generative discursive environment in which we would expect normative legal thought to thrive, and it is precisely the sort of rhetorical framework that we would expect normative legal thought to establish, entrench, and maintain. This reciprocal constitution of normative legal thought and rationalist rhetoric, this consonance and mutual entailment, is evident in various ways.

It is apparent that virtually all aspects of normative legal thought are suited to the rhetorical reproduction and maintenance of the sovereign individual subject. As Charles Fried puts it, "Before there is morality there must be the person. We must attain and maintain in our morality a concept of personality such that it makes sense to posit choosing, valuing entities—free, moral beings."[127] This insistence of normative legal thought on the importance of a morally competent, normative subject is quite consonant with the rhetorical construction of the legal thinker as a sovereign individual subject. Indeed, this rationalist rhetorical construction is at once a prefiguration and an entailment of what Fried calls "choosing, valuing entities—free moral beings."

The normative enterprise of *norm selection* and *norm justification*—with their emphases on *choice orientation, value orientation,* and *prescription*—is keenly suited to keeping the sovereign individual subject in the driver's seat. Likewise, the *single-norm, conclusion-oriented* character of legal thought, with its fixation on end products and its requirements that these end products be *practical, nonparadoxical, noncontradictory, complete, self-sufficient, discrete, separable, positive,* and *transsituational,* is conducive to deflecting any serious interrogation of either the rhetorical practices, forms, or processes that constitute the sovereign individual subject or his rhetorical enterprise. Hence, we are drawn toward the meticulous dissection and examination of what the legal subject has produced and whether these end products have been produced in the right (noncontradictory, nonparadoxical, linear, authority-driven) way. And in turn, this orientation draws attention away from the legal subject who is producing all this stuff in the first place.[128]

The *action-deferring* and *reader-centered* character of normative legal thought likewise ensures that no serious challenge is posed to the identity or character of the sovereign individual subject. The texts of normative legal thought are supposed to have their effect by appealing to the intellectual faculties of the reader. The texts are supposed to honor the reader's already preformed views, ideas, prejudices, and aesthetic representations of social and political life. There is to be no overt disabling or subversion of *her* identity or role. For instance, within the rationalist rhetoric of contemporary legal thought, it is permissible to write articles *about* Derridean deconstruction of legal thought—but to actually *practice* Derridean deconstruction will evoke resistance, misunderstanding, and incomprehension. The expectation is that any author will, of course, explain and justify any significant departure from the default positions and will refrain from any rhetorical exercise that might actually require active change on the part of the reader.

Finally, the *adversarial advocacy* orientation of normative legal thought—which is attributable, at least in part, to the conflation of the role of lawyer and legal academic—does much to insulate the sovereign individual subject and its rhetorical supports from scrutiny. Because so many legal academics understand their legal thought to be positional in character—on behalf of some (intangible, often very worthy, but poorly identified) client-surrogate—much of legal thought is produced within the explicit context of adversarial advocacy among academics and is devoted to advancing or defeating this or that position. Many normative legal thinkers understand themselves to be engaged in "passionate advocacy" on behalf of some cause. Now, of course, there is no tribunal listening; no one is empowered to put all this normative passion into effect. But that does not mean that this passionate advocacy is therefore without effect: on the contrary, it often succeeds in bracketing any serious questioning of the rhetorical system that enables such aimless passionate advocacy to be produced in the first place. Indeed, when one is engaged in passionate arguments to an imagined tribunal, one is hardly likely to question the argumentative structures that allow the arguments to be framed and presented in the first place.

Not only does normative legal thought conduce to the maintenance of the sovereign individual subject and his rationalist rhetoric, but one can see the reverse process at work as well. Indeed, if normative thought occupies so much attention in the legal academy; if normative legal thought seems like the obvious, the "natural," thing to do; if the What should we do?/What should the law be? question seems so important; and if normative legal thought seems veritably like law itself, it is because the rhetorical situation—the default settings—has already enabled us, constituted our discourse, and configured our roles so that we will produce normative legal thought.

Think about it this way: suppose that, contrary to my intimations, you really are a sovereign individual subject. Suppose further that you already are in communication through an undistorted medium (known as law) with other very powerful sovereign individual subjects (otherwise known as judges and legal academics). Suppose as well that all sovereign individual subjects (including judges and legal academics) are not only receptive to but are obliged to follow rational argument—to put theory in charge of practice. Finally, suppose that these judges and academics face a series of problems that hurt a lot of people, waste human resources, or otherwise injure the community. Given these assumptions, why not engage in normative legal thought? Why do anything else?

It is important not to underestimate the importance or the resilience of this embedded rationalist rhetoric: it is this rhetoric that successfully deforms not only modernist but also postmodernist thought within the legal academy.[129] The resistance of the rationalist rhetoric is both conscious and embedded in the very form and rhetoric of normative legal thought. Indeed, when confronted with challenges from modernism or postmodernism, the recursive move of normative legal thought has been to ignore the implications of modernism and postmodernism by encasing these implications within its same old rationalist conceptual and rhetorical structures. Normative legal thought treats modernism and postmodernism as new "substance" ready for assimilation within the same old unreconstructed rationalist rhetoric.[130]

Even in sophisticated legal thought one sees the effects of this rationalist rhetorical structure on the reception of postmodern thought. For instance, consider Robin West's attempts to enlist Foucault in the service of what she calls "progressive constitutionalism." She uses Foucault to underwrite the notion that "modern progressive political theory begins with a central, even definitive, insight: conservative *deference* to communal authority—whatever form it takes—directly implies a parallel deference to the clusters of social power that invariably underlie it."[131] West then cites various works by Foucault.[132] But West's point is not Foucault's point at all. Foucault's argument is Nietzschean, not normative, and his point is not that various social groups like "conservatives" give *deference* to social power, but that social groups, their configurations, and their identities are themselves effects of truth/power. Robin West's use of the term *deference* implies that conservatives are somewhere outside social power—somewhere sufficiently distinct and separate from social power that they can apparently choose to *defer* to social power. This logic of deference and choice is not the Foucauldian understanding, but is instead the conventional rationalist separation of power from the categories of truth and normativity.

West continues: "They may have power, in turn, because they are right (and thus have survived centuries of critical inquiry) or, as Foucault's social 'archaeologies' have aimed to reveal, they have power *for some other reason,* such as that *they serve* the interests of dominant social groups."[133] Again, this is not so much Foucault as a distortion of Foucault's thought through the conventional rationalist rhetoric of the legal academy.[134] Foucault does not talk of social groups as having power for "some other reason," or for any reason, for that matter. On the contrary, following the Nietzschean inversion, Foucault's enterprise is precisely to demonstrate that reason and reasons are themselves the productions of power.[135] So when West says, "In any case, normative authority *rests* on some form of social power,"[136] she is not following Foucault at all. On the contrary, it is precisely the conceptualization of normative authority *as distinct from* and as *resting on* social power that Foucault repeatedly questions.[137] But it is not just normative authority that West separates from social power; she separates the subject as well. Hence, for West, "when the conservative embraces, preserves, respects, and defers to the teachings of communal authority, he or she necessarily, whether or not intentionally, embraces the social power that underlies it."[138] This is not the Foucauldian understanding, but the envelopment, the encasement, of Foucault's thought within the channels of rationalist normative rhetoric.

Ironically, this is precisely the sort of intellectual-institutional effect of truth/power that would have interested Foucault himself. It is interesting precisely because it is emblematic of the reception extended by normative legal thought to most modernist or postmodernist work. Within normative legal thought, the postmodern decentering of the self is immediately transformed from what might be described as an activity, an engagement, or a process into a "thesis," a "position," an "idea"—a "theory," in short, into the very sort of intellectual entity already so stabilized and so encased in the rationalist object-form that "it" is guaranteed to leave the self of the normative legal thinker and the very form of his thought unchallenged and undisturbed.

In this way, normative legal thought continues to play well in the academy: we have all already been constructed as actors in the theater of the rational. The setting is in place, the parts are written, and it's all so convincing that far from questioning the scene, we have forgotten that it is theater. And, of course, now, having lost our bearings (almost) entirely, it is theater that is doing us: "What should we do?" "Where should we go?"

THE POLITICS OF FORM

What are the politics of normative legal thought? Political stasis and intellectual syndicalism. One consequence of the dominance of the normative, its positive prescriptive aspect, and its value orientation is that legal thinking becomes subordinated to political value commitments. I am not saying that legal thought has now become politicized in contrast to some imagined prior period when legal thought was supposedly free from politicization. Rather, the claim is that legal thought has now become politicized along rather static, fairly blunt, and normatively oriented lines.

For instance, consider this familiar division of the field: law and economics, mainstream doctrinalism, liberal legal theory, feminist jurisprudence, CLS. Virtually each of these groups of legal thinkers depicts its situation and its intellectual approach as embattled—as engaged in a struggle for the direction of law. This configuration of the jurisprudential field is quite familiar to all of us. I could call it "premature politicization" or "the politics of nostalgia." I am going to call it both.

Premature Politicization

The field configuration seems to be a kind of premature politicization in the sense that it leaps from a now relatively widely shared notion that law is politics to a shallow, yet apparently utterly definitive conceptualization of politics. The notion that law is politics has de facto taken on the sense that law is informed by normative value choice and normative value commitments. The jurisprudential field then becomes organized around this largely archaic understanding of politics as the value choice of individuals about how the legal or political order ought to be constituted. The left, the liberals, and the conservatives of the academy then come to be defined in terms of their value choices, their value orientations, or their stances on the importance of making value choices. This is not confined to the intellectual plane; it has become the hegemonic regime within which the production of legal thought occurs. This politicization is premature in the sense that its operant understanding of politics has yet to encounter the current forms and practices of power. The pathways, the directions, and the effects of power are rarely, if ever, subordinate to "value choices."[139]

The Politics of Nostalgia

I am tempted to call this configuration the politics of nostalgia as well because every political group in the legal academy wants to present itself in terms of some worthy political tradition with strong resonant symbols. For example, CLS thinkers have identified themselves as intellectual guerrillas, or even compare themselves to insurrectionary figures like Che.[140] Indeed, much of CLS thought was inspired by a drive to repeat, revive, and reenact the new left politics of the sixties.

If this political self-identification seems a bit out of touch, conservatives and liberals fare no better. Liberals still draw their inspiration consciously (at this point, more likely subconsciously) from a political text that must read a lot like *A Theory of Justice*.[141] By and large, they are still writing articles for the Warren Court (or wishing they could). They still think of the great political problems of the age in terms of the individual versus the community.[142] What the liberals fail to notice is that while they are talking about the individual versus the community, the reproduction and extension of bureaucratic practices routinely traverses back and forth across the public/private distinction without giving that venerable liberal distinction a moment's thought—thereby extinguishing *ab initio* the liberal version of both individualism and community. It turns out that being a liberal means that you worry a great deal about getting just the right combination of individual freedom and community while getting neither.

As for conservatives, they have this absolutely uncanny capacity to arrive on the scene way too late. Conservatives always appear bearing the gifts of tradition and the past, asking us to conserve these gifts and thereby preserve our communities,[143] and perhaps even our very identities.[144] It is no doubt pleasant to stand up in support of worthy traditions and the great constructions of the past, but conservatives almost always forget that access to the past is always and already mediated by the present. And in our present there is not a great deal left to conserve, and not many social practices that will help conserve whatever is worth conserving. We live, as Baudrillard suggests, in an epoch of simulation: simulated culture, simulated intellectual life, and, perhaps most vexingly for conservatives, simulated conservatism.[145] And the simulations have almost already lost their ability to refer back to the "real thing."

What I am claiming here is that within the legal academy (and perhaps outside it as well), not only the political programs but also the political identities of the left, liberals, and conservatives are now very much in question. The left-CLS glorification of the Sartrean individual subject helps produce a self that in its high Sartrean moments recognizes its own absolute freedom,[146] but for the rest of the day is shaped and driven by precisely the same market-bureaucratic practices that conservatives and liberals are also helping to establish, expand, and entrench.[147] Liberal humanism, with its insistence on legalizing all aspects of social intercourse through its "rights" rhetoric, is in effect imposing a politically correct, totalitarian sameness on everyone. They can be called "rights," but that does not immunize them from becoming a kind of bureaucratic social control device. The conservative call seeks to preserve "our" traditional values, but because the call is too late, it helps entrench precisely the sort of market-bureaucratic state that has already rationalized, regimented, and effaced those same values.

In this way, the "value orientation" hegemony of legal thought does promote a kind of political stasis. Indeed, in the maintenance of this hegemony there is a great deal of unconscious complicity among the various groups. Conferences, colloquia, and symposia are typically arranged along the usual normative break lines among the camps such that all camps have to be represented. The militancy of each group serves to police and regiment not only its own forces but, ironically, the forces of the other camps as well. There is a tremendous degree of intellectual and political reductivism among all the groups. What we get is a kind of intellectual syndicalism, in which the jurisprudential order is maintained and the intellectual or research agenda is stabilized by an ironic yet tacit agreement among openly antagonistic parties.

No one chooses this state of affairs. The old intellectual elites are burdened with the call of an onerous political responsibility to their followers. They regret the loss of intellectual freedom. The young intellectual elites are burdened with honoring (or honoring in the breach) conceptual systems, intellectual styles, and political stances that they do not believe and no longer find useful. In the name of scholarship, dialogue, thought, academic freedom, political responsibility, moral responsibility, and seriousness, we have an academic regime that induces massive amounts of repression and compelled production. Most of contemporary legal thought is currently the outgrowth (one way or another) of bureaucratic domination.

Slippage and Resonance

Precisely how is this system of normative legal thought maintained? The question has a certain bite here because the conventional, benign answers on which normative legal thought sustains itself are no longer available. On the contrary, my claim is that the prescriptions of normative legal thought *rarely* produce any significant effects—except to provide an occasion for the reproduction and reinscription of the rationalist aesthetic, its rhetorical organization of law and social life, and indeed our very selves.

Thus, the claim is not that normative legal thought is without effect, but that the politics of normative legal thought are not what normative legal thought imagines them to be: its politics are in its process, the practice of its construction, and the form of its dissemination. Thus, it is only a little ironic that I close this discussion by examining beginnings—how normative legal thought constructs itself and the theater of the rational.

As I have tried to show, the very ways that normative legal thought repeatedly reinscribes itself are also the ways it insulates itself from challenges. This is a *politics of form* that establishes itself through the related processes of *slippage* and *resonance*. These processes are difficult to describe because they are themselves the processes that produce the stabilized matrix of legal thought that enables us to think as we do. Hence, to attempt to locate or define such processes (slippage and resonance) within the usual established categorical matrices would be to confuse these processes with their effects.

It turns out, however, that we already have some familiarity with slippage and resonance. Slippage has been going on throughout this essay. We witnessed slippage earlier when I claimed that the dualism of descriptive/normative thought slides into legal formalism/realism, which, in turn slides into the dualism of technical doctrinalism/moralist jurisprudence. Slippage is the slide of the same force (and the reproduction of the same effects) across our sedimented and reified conceptual structures; it is a kind of transposition that occurs unconsciously. Slippage is *intellectual.* Slippage is what occurs when *L.A. Law,* the television program, becomes a metaphor for law practice (*L.A. Law*'s empire), then the rhetorical vehicle for a demonstration of how legal argument does its work, and finally a stage setting for an aesthetic evaluation of normative jurisprudence. Slippage is *rhetorical.* Slippage is also what occurs throughout this essay when the text shifts from philosophy to sociology, from fiction to truth, from low culture to high culture, and so on. Slippage is *cultural.* Moreover, slippage is what happens throughout this essay when it is read as one continuous movement from a politics that claims to be a politics of substance, of values, of theory, and of results, to what in this section turns out to be the politics of form. Slippage is *political.* Slippage is the diagonal, transverse movement of the same force (and the same effects) across the conventional reified sectors that mark our world—sectors like the intellectual, the rhetorical, the cultural, and the political. Slippage does its work in all directions—moving from fiction to truth (and vice versa), from the material to the ideal (and vice versa), from reality to appearance, and so on. You may have noted that slippage has been occurring even as you read and I write this paragraph.

Resonance is the echo made by what slippage has inscribed. If slippage has been pervasive, then there will be a great deal of resonance. For instance, if the distinction between formalism and realism or between rules and standards seems important or true, it is because these distinctions resonate virtually everywhere. If the dichotomies usually associated with Plato (fiction/truth, ideal/material, reality/appearance) resonate, it is because they have been inscribed pervasively in our philosophy, in our rhetoric, in the indexing systems of libraries,[148] in the definition of the jurisdiction of the intellectual disciplines and subdisciplines that have organized themselves around these dichotomies and so on. Resonance describes that part of the rhetorical organization of this essay where each part echoes the others in different ways.

Slippage and resonance cannot do their work when they meet with resistance. For instance, as we saw earlier, neopragmatism, deconstruction, and comparative institutional analysis are all arrested by the resistance of the rationalist rhetoric and the disciplinary defenses of the sovereign individual subject. Each of these jurisprudential approaches could beneficially undertake inquiries into its own situation, but the rationalist rhetoric is stronger, and slippage is arrested. Resistance has been present as a strategy here as well. The attempt to put Dworkin and normative legal thought on *L.A. Law* is a clear example of resistance, because it is clear that Dworkin and normative legal thought won't take on *L.A. Law*.

Slippage, resonance, and resistance by themselves have no conventional moral or political value. They organize the world and our selves and allow us to operate in ways that are sometimes helpful and sometimes not. Now that the conceptual structure of these processes is explicit, I want to show how they help construct, stabilize, and order our legal and social world. I understand this construction, stabilization, and ordering to be the politics of form. This is a politics, of course, that does not leave much room for the legal academy's current normative thought as a politically meaningful enterprise. So it goes.

Nesting

One of the classic ways the normative rhetoric extends and insulates itself from displacement is through "nesting," a process by which views, forces, and phenomena that could potentially destabilize the system of normative rhetoric are reconfigured within the rationalist form so that their disruptive potential is neutralized. We have already seen this process at work with neopragmatism, comparative institutional economics, and deconstruction: neopragmatism becomes formalized as a set of ideas, theories, or approaches to be applied; comparative institutional economics is deployed from a purportedly supra-institutional vantage point; and deconstruction becomes transformed into a set of operationalized techniques. In each case the various approaches are in effect reconfigured within the rationalist normative rhetoric and are thereby stripped of their destabilizing potential. In effect, whatever is admitted within normative legal thought becomes encapsulated within the rationalist rhetoric in a way that ensures compatibility.

This rationalist nesting process neutralizes challenges to the orthodoxy by representing them in much less salient or threatening forms—a kind of juris-prudential inoculation.[149] Hence, for instance, the social construction of the subject is often represented as an idea the sovereign individual subject can accept or reject without having to confront it as the truth of her being. Like-wise, deconstruction is represented as supporting a form of radical individual subjectivism that turns out to be at once untenable and politically harmless, or as a set of argumentative techniques that can be wielded at any time for any reason by any individual. The price of acceptance for any destabiliz-ing intellectual movement in the legal academy is a kind of self-deformation in which the movement conforms to the existing matrices of the dominant rationalism.

Not surprisingly, the effects of the rationalist nesting process are not con-fined to the intellectual plane. The very process of continuous and repetitive rationalist nesting of so many disparate intellectual currents reconfirms the universality of rationalism, and thus entrenches rationalism cognitively and rhetorically. Rationalism becomes the universal mode of discourse, confirming its validity each time it admits (and covertly neutralizes) the disruptive poten-tial of any new approach.

Its success and its embeddedness ensure that only those modes of thought most amenable to the rationalist form will be integrated into legal discourse. It is no accident that the most successful interdisciplinary approaches to legal thought have been those most rigorously formalized in the rationalist image: microeconomics and American Anglo-Saxon moral philosophy. Even within the ostensibly destabilizing influences that comprise CLS thought—neo-Marxism, phenomenology, structuralism, deconstruction, existentialism—the most successful strains of contestatory thought have been those most config-ured in the image of rationalism: structuralism and Sartrean existentialism.[150]

The rationalist nesting process works on basic descriptions or understand-ings of social reality as well as on intellectual approaches—it is, for instance, one way by which legal thinkers and their legal thinking are abstracted from the complexities of *L.A. Law*'s empire. We have already seen this abstraction at work. *L.A. Law*'s empire's complicated mass of differentiated relations among power, truth, rationality, deceit, and rhetoric is reconfigured by abstracting the various relations through and into a rationalist form. Regularities are identified, relations are established, and the field of regularities and relations becomes stabilized as if it were the controlling schema governing the occurrences on *L.A. Law*'s empire.

Once this rationalist schema of relations becomes emancipated from its social context, it becomes cognitively and rhetorically embedded. The complicated mass of differentiated relations of power, truth, rationality, deceit, and rhetoric are represented as organized in accordance with the network of rationalist relations. As a result, while they are recognized as important components, power, deceit, and rhetoric are nonetheless represented and encapsulated as isolated instances (very often deviations) subordinate to the overarching and controlling framework of rationality.

This sort of abstraction and stabilization of the social field is believable (and believed) because rationality does have some connection to the social field; there is some resonance. Moreover, because the rationalist framework becomes cognitively and rhetorically embedded as a discursive formation, those in whom it has become embedded lose the ability to understand the social field in any other way. For legal thinkers, the rationalist aesthetic soon becomes all there is. This is why critiques of rationalism like the one offered here (or, indeed, the modernist and postmodernist assaults on rationalism) are so often apprehended and experienced as threatening, as signaling a total loss of order and meaning, as nihilistic.

Once the rationalist aesthetic becomes cognitively and rhetorically embedded, slippage continues from the cognitive and the rhetorical to the social and the professional. Indeed, to think within the rationalist aesthetic is to acquire all the distance as a human being from others that is implicit in the distance that normative legal thought takes from *L.A. Law*'s empire. To think as a rationalist is not just to *think* in a particular abstracted way, it is to *be* one who deals with others in a particular abstracted way. The more rationalist one's form of thought, the more one's dealings with others are mediated by prefigured, invariant, and sharply drawn conceptual categories. This is why Duncan Kennedy and Mark Kelman are correct in their observation that individuals who are more rulelike (read here "more rationalist") tend to favor substantively individualist regimes.

Between the rationalist rhetoric of the law school classroom and the ether of the eightieth floor of the Wall Street office building, there is the process of slippage, of mimetic repetition. And in the end, it is the rationalist character of normative legal argument and its self-satisfied distancing from the complexities of *L.A. Law* that enable the lawyer on the eightieth floor—sharply dressed and well manicured, his memoranda clean, crisp, and error-free—to save or ruin barely known lives with magisterial detachment. These stereotypical (but, indeed, requisite) accoutrements—the manicure; the crisp, freshly laundered, cuffed shirts; the fixation on typo-free papers—are all vehicles and echoes of distancing between the self and the action. In the psychoanalytic idiom, they are the vehicles of denial that make the dirty work possible.

If the eightieth floor of the Wall Street law firm does not seem in some sense an outrage, a grotesque episode, it is because the eightieth floor is itself a resonance, an architectural and social inscription of the same rationalist form of thought, cognition, and rhetoric practiced in the law school classroom. The relation of the eightieth floor on Wall Street to the dirty harbor indistinguishable below, the relation of the clean, white, typo-free brief to the lives of the parties, the relation of the theater of the rational to *L.A. Law*'s empire, the relation of the law school classroom to life itself—these are all the same relation. And the same relation is regularly slipping from one sector to the other—from the intellectual to the rhetorical to the professional to the social, and back again.

Rationalist forms of thought produce just the sort of rhetoric, just the sort of "self," that enables the formation of a professional corps of lawyers cognitively and psychologically capable of running the sort of abstracted social coordination mechanisms known as "Wall Street law." Similarly, Wall Street law creates the sort of stabilized, routinized, and recursive socioeconomic institutions and practices that make the stabilized and abstracted character of rationalist normative rhetoric possible. What we have in both cases is a process of slippage. The rationalist form in one sector slides (without conscious effort) into another sector, and then another, and so on.

This process of slippage from one sector to another in turn entails the cognitive phenomenon of resonance. If the eightieth-floor Wall Street firm seems normal to the incoming associate rather than an outrage, it is because the relation of the eightieth floor to the people below is a mimetic replay, an echo of the relation of the rationalist normativity of the classroom to life itself. The eightieth floor seems right because it resonates with the rationalist normative rhetoric. Similarly, the rationalist normative rhetoric seems like a helpful way to think because it resonates with the eightieth floor. Resonance allows the rationalist normative rhetoric to maintain itself. There are correspondences between rationalist normative rhetoric and the constitution of the social field. The rationalist normative rhetoric is thus not so much completely wrong in its conceptualization of social life as it is systematically incomplete, overstated, and overextended.

This mimetic repetition and successive embedding of the same rationalist normative rhetoric in different sectors of social life (the intellectual, the professional, and the social) occurs as our attention is focused on other matters—on prescriptions, recommendations, substance, conclusions, theories. On the intellectual plane, nesting colonizes, defuses, and distorts destabilizing forces (such as deconstruction or postmodernism) by admitting and reconfiguring intellectual challenges in the rationalist format. Thus, for instance, before neo-pragmatism will be considered by orthodox legal thought, its contributions must be reformulated as distinct propositions, ideas, and theories. It must be recast in object-form artifacts that the normative rhetoric (and normative thinkers) can recognize. The rationalist rhetoric, however, does not replicate itself just by nesting. Some challenges and some dislocations must simply be kept *outside* the rationalist rhetorical system altogether.

Border Patrol Jurisprudence: The Uses of the
Inside/Outside Distinction

Through its privileging of theory over practice and substance over form, contemporary legal thought represents itself as "theory" and "substance." Theory and substance in turn are typically represented as

> rationality
> reasoned elaboration
> dialogue
> discourse
> interpretation
> judgment

(all of which are also often represented as law).

Excluded from the self-representation of legal thought are

> power
> social force
> blind convention
> social necessity
> social contingency
> historical accident

(all of which are often represented as concededly important to the development of law, but not law itself).

When presented in this graphic manner, this either/or form of thinking looks quite crude and unbelievable. That is because it *is* crude—in the sense of basic, unrefined, and not yet mediated by critical reflection. But while crude in these senses, this either/or form of thinking is hardly unbelievable. On the contrary, it is believed over and over again, even in the highest reaches of jurisprudential thought. Indeed, this sort of either/or thinking has a long and distinguished (albeit not always enlightened) history in jurisprudence, where it is routinely featured in the famous dichotomy between "the internal perspective" and "the external perspective."[151]

This distinction is critical to the formation of *Law's Empire* and to its insulation from *L.A. Law*'s empire. One of the striking things about *Law's Empire* is that while it claims to be just that (i.e., Law's Empire), the technical definition of its jurisdiction turns out to be exceedingly narrow, almost trivial. Dworkin's exclusionary technique is utterly classic. As he is engaged in the *constative* enterprise of defining the object of his inquiry, he is also engaged in the *performative* enterprise of excluding unwanted complications. From the very beginning of his book, Dworkin excludes troublesome or potentially destabilizing considerations through a series of either/or vacuum boundary oppositions.[152] Dworkin starts by announcing that he does not "discuss the practical politics of adjudication." He is "concerned with the issue of law, not with the reasons judges may have for tempering their statements of what it is."[153]

This is the first of several major either/or oppositions. With this one, Dworkin announces that he is concerned with *law,* as opposed to *nonlaw*—the quite possibly frivolous reasons judges may have for tempering their statements of what the law is. Hence, Dworkin is concerned with the "real" law, not the distortions that judges and lawyers may make of it on *L.A. Law.* Dworkin continues:

> My project is narrow in a different way as well. It centers on formal adjudication, on judges in black robes. . . .
>
> Some critics will be anxious to say . . . these arguments obscure—perhaps they aim to obscure—the important social function of law as ideological force and witness. A proper understanding of law as a social phenomenon demands, these critics say, a more scientific or sociological or historical approach. . . .
>
> This objection fails by its own standards. . . . Of course, law is a social phenomenon. But its complexity, function, and consequence all depend on one special feature of its structure. Legal practice, unlike many other social phenomena is argumentative. Every actor in the practice understands that what it permits or requires depends on the truth of certain propositions that are given sense only by and within the *practice.*[154]

Dworkin has set up a second either/or here. There is something that is called legal practice, and it is bounded: indeed, "every actor in the practice"—that is, any *insider*—knows very well that legal propositions are given their legal sense only "*within* the practice." So, one can think of law *within* the practice of law or *outside* it. But either way, law has an *inside* and an *outside;* it is bounded. Dworkin does not argue this; it is simply an aesthetic consequence of the conventional deployment of the inside/outside distinction, or what George Lakoff and Mark Johnson call "the container metaphor." It is so conventional, so familiar, to think that law is bounded, that it has an inside and an outside, that one might not even notice that something rather contestable has just been asserted.

This is the second major either/or in less than a page. By this point, the book begins to have some rhythm. Nothing complex, you understand. Nonetheless, the reader is prepared to anticipate and accept Dworkin's thought in either/or terms. And Dworkin exploits this anticipation, for he is about to formulate the killer either/or—the one that will be ritually invoked throughout his production to eliminate any threats to the theater of the rational or to *Law's Empire* itself:

> People who have law make and debate claims about what law permits or forbids. . . . This crucial argumentative aspect of legal practice can be studied in *two ways* or *from two points of view.* One is the *external* point of view of the sociologist or historian. . . . The other is the *internal* point of view of those who make the claims. . . . This book takes up the internal, participants' point of view; it tries to grasp the argumentative character of our legal practice by joining that practice and struggling with the *issues of soundness and truth* participants face. We will study formal legal argument *from the judge's viewpoint* . . . because judicial argument about claims of law is a useful paradigm for exploring the *central, propositional* aspect of legal practice.[155]

Now, as an aside, consider that on the stage of *L.A. Law's* empire this monologue would be wildly implausible, verging on the incoherent. In *L.A. Law's* empire, judges are hardly "central" to legal practice. And if there were a single central aspect to legal practice, it would hardly be "propositional" in character. And as for the issues with which the participants or the actors struggle, these can hardly be accurately represented as "issues of soundness and truth."

But in the theater of the rational, Dworkin's statement is eminently plausible. Indeed, his statement is almost coterminous with the structure of the theater of the rational itself. His either/or establishes that one can try to make sense of legal practice from the *inside* (the internal point of view) or from the *outside* (the external point of view).[156] This move authorizes the author (Dworkin, here) to locate the boundary between the internal and the external points of view in social and intellectual space. That is, it authorizes Dworkin not merely to make an abstract distinction, but to allocate the baggage of the world on one side or the other. And that, of course, is precisely what happens. Dworkin situates virtually everything that could possibly destabilize or threaten his empire on the outside. Sociology, history, legal practice itself, the perspective of lawyers, and so on are all already on the skids, already located on the *outside*, where they can have no significant disruptive effect on what is on the *inside*, most notably "formal legal argument from the judge's viewpoint . . . the central, propositional aspect of legal practice."[157] In effect, the inside/outside distinction has severed these devalued aspects of law (sociology, history, etc.) from *Law's Empire*.

This severance is made possible by another conventional effect of the inside/outside distinction: it essentializes what is on the inside and separates "it" from what is relegated to the outside.[158] In our case, we would expect Dworkin's rhetoric to essentialize the internal point of view, to map out its scope and fill in its content. But actually this has already been accomplished in the quote above. Indeed, it is amazing how quickly Dworkin's assertion that there actually exists an "internal point of view" to the practice of law is reductively essentialized to the "study [of] formal legal argument from the judge's viewpoint."[159] The point so far is not that Dworkin has committed some argumentative faux pas. On the contrary, the point is to recognize that the rhetorical conventionality of the inside/outside distinction and its derivative, the internal/external perspective, have enabled controversial matters to be assumed into and out of existence without ever being questioned.

While the internal point of view is essentialized, the inside/outside distinction is performing other important rhetorical work—important exclusionary work. Excluded from Dworkin's rendition of the "internal perspective" are exactly those social features such as power, force, blind convention, history, psychology, and sociology that would threaten his enterprise if considered.

Take sociology, for instance. Because Dworkin's deployment of the internal/external boundary always already excludes sociology, he can always already dismiss it as an external perspective. Thus Dworkin does not have to consider the sociology of legal thought, the ways in which sociological forces constrict legal thinkers such as judges and himself. And indeed, this sort of argument is repeated routinely throughout Dworkin's book, serving to deflect challenges to his account of what he calls law. Yet this marginalization of the social and the historical seems—now that we think about it—clearly wrong. It seems clear that a competent judge (or legal academic) would want to think about the social and historical location of her own thought processes.[160] Why, then, do we almost automatically believe Dworkin when he tells us that sociology and history are part of the external perspective?

In part, we believe because Dworkin is hardly the first to use the internal/external perspective in these ways. He is following a long, well-sedimented convention of legal thought. H. L. A. Hart, for instance, found it useful to distinguish the external point of view of the "observer who does not himself accept" the legal rules from the internal point of view of the "member of the group which accepts and uses them as guides to conduct."[161] For Hart, the external point of view could be useful to predict the behavior of members of the group, but it could not reproduce "the way in which the rules function in the lives of certain members of the group."[162]

It is precisely the embeddedness of this distinction that routinely leads us to represent law as if it has a boundary (1) that can be located in social/intellectual space, (2) that separates law from destabilizing inquiries and knowledges, and (3) that stabilizes the realm of law by encasing it in objectivist form. Not surprisingly, this sedimented rationalist distinction reproduces itself automatically, without anyone questioning whether it is a useful or accurate way of representing law. The thought of those who think about law arises from within the sedimented intellectual practices of those who have left their marks before. Kent Greenawalt, for instance, writes:

> In trying to develop a satisfactory account of law that appropriately treats both normative and conventional elements, one can usefully distinguish an outsider's, or sociologist's, view from that of a participant who must actually decide what the law is. It is no coincidence that Hart, while emphasizing the "internal point of view" taken by officials, has been mainly interested in the former and Dworkin the latter. Because convention looms larger in a sociologist's view of law than a participant's, and normative elements are more central for a participant, Hart's focus has led him to stress convention, and Dworkin's focus has led him to concentrate on normative evaluation.[163]

There is nothing wrong with Hart focusing on convention and Dworkin stressing normative evaluation—nothing wrong so long as the distinction between the internal and the external perspective is as helpful as it is cracked up to be. But it is not clear that it is. One of the consequences of allocating the world's intellectual baggage to one side of the dichotomy or the other is that this procedure eclipses some interesting questions about the connections between sociology (Hart's focus), on the one hand, and normative evaluation (Dworkin's interest), on the other.

If one is constantly operating in a world in which these are seen to be two different and relatively unrelated enterprises, then the lack of connection is established and sanctified from the very beginning. This leaves us with a sociology of law that is largely immunized from normative argument, and a normative evaluation that has no ready correspondence to what sociology tells us about who we are. It leaves us, that is, precisely where we were when we noted that the aesthetics of normative legal thought are discordant with the aesthetics of bureaucracy that define the social sphere. It leaves us with the awesome dissonance we earlier experienced between *Law's Empire* and *L.A. Law*'s empire. And it is precisely the conventionally entrenched and normatively defended distinction between the internal and the external perspective that systematically enables and legitimates legal thinkers not to think about, or even recognize, this otherwise stunning dissonance.

Moreover, this aesthetic distinction slides over into the social field. We begin by thinking of law as bounded on aesthetic grounds; we end up thinking of the social phenomenon of law itself as a kind of bounded object. The problem, of course, is that the issue of whether or not the social phenomenon of law is bounded is quite controversial. Yet, the "aesthetic" supposition of internal and external perspectives succeeds in presupposing this problem away; it succeeds in establishing into existence social facts that are little more than the predictable result of conventional metaphorical usage.

The insulation and segregation of knowledge happen at the intellectual, cognitive, and professional levels. As Kent Greenawalt anticipated, the intellectual/cognitive effects of the distinction between the internal and external perspectives are translated into professional formations/deformations.[164] Unfortunately, the professional intellectual divisions created and maintained by the internal/external perspectives may not be particularly helpful to serious intellectual endeavor. For example, the split between law and social science is associated with a rather unbelievable (albeit all too real) professional polarization. As Lawrence Friedman puts it:

> Probably no serious scholar clings absolutely to either one of the two polar positions; nobody thinks that the legal system is totally and absolutely autonomous; and nobody (perhaps) seriously puts forward the opposite idea, that every last jot and tittle, every crumb of law, even in the short, short run, can be and must be explained "externally." But most lawyers, and a good many legal scholars and theorists, tend to cluster somewhere toward the autonomous end of the scale. Social scientists interested in law,

and legal scholars with a taste for social science, tend to cluster somewhere toward the other end.[165]

If Dworkin's invocation of the internal/external perspective works so well, if it seems so plausible, it is in part because the distinction resonates so well with the present configuration of the university—the divisions of departments, disciplines, and subdisciplines. The sorts of distinctions Dworkin makes are not only professionally but also physically inscribed. The entire university is carved up into departments that are housed in separate buildings.

This division of the university into disciplines can seem perfectly sensible. Within each discipline and subdiscipline we find complex formalizations that appear to be helpful, productive, and "serious." But as one gains distance from any particular discipline or subdiscipline and tries to make sense of the entire assembly, a new picture emerges. It suddenly looks as if each discipline or subdisciplinary group has carved up its own jurisdiction, its own intellectual territory, so that all the truly difficult and interesting questions—all the major intellectual obstacles—are located outside, beyond the boundaries of each discipline and subdiscipline. From a distance, it looks as if there is (virtually) no intellectual action to be found on the inside—just the mindless rehearsal of disciplinary discourse moves. It looks as if the jurisdictions have been defined so as to avoid and externalize all intellectual challenges or dilemmas, as if the department structures and the various disciplines and subdisciplines have all been mapped out so as to maximize the possibilities for formalization and minimize encounters with aporias, contradictions, paradoxes, and the like. It looks as if the disciplines are organized to frame intellectual problems in a way that minimizes the necessity for significant thinking.

In other words, the disciplines and subdisciplines quite literally organize themselves *around* aporias and paradoxes. They achieve a respectable formalization not because they "know" anything, but because they are organized so that they don't have to know about the contradictions, aporias, and paradoxes that surround them and that effectively define and limit their intellectual jurisdiction.

As an example, consider the role of the performative contradiction. Until very recently, the worst thing one could do in academic thought was to get caught in a performative contradiction. Not surprisingly, after decades of striving to avoid performative contradictions, we have a sedimented academic structure and sedimented "knowledges," all nicely arranged in discursive formations constituted to avoid performative contradictions. But after decades of avoiding performative contradictions, there is now a new concern: Where don't you go and what do you miss if you keep trying to avoid performative contradictions? And, of course, there is a political angle to all this. After all, fear of performative contradiction discourages and marginalizes reflexive inquiry into the status of our own statements and our own knowledges. Fear of performative contradiction thus has a conservative effect. And what is conserved, of course, is the jurisdictional and structural integrity of our knowledges. But because this integrity depends on such a truncated definition and establishment of the knowledges and the disciplines, it is almost a joke: integrity as joke.

Consider, for instance, that the jurisdiction of legal thought is delimited largely by reference to the doctrinal pronouncements of appellate judges. This reductive equation of the "internal perspective" on law with the pronouncements of the appellate judge is at once routine and bizarre. Why should the appellate judge—typically a passive, infrequent, thoroughly manipulated, and generally inaccessible participant in the production of law—serve not just as the main, but as the only referent point for "the internal perspective"? Why not the lawyer, the legislator, the bureaucrat, or the average citizen? And why, for that matter, should we routinely attach so much importance to what judges think about law? Can anyone imagine trying to make sense of the automobile market by adopting "the internal perspective"—and then equating the internal perspective with the dealer's point of view?

And there are political as well as intellectual, cognitive, and professional effects and implications that result from the deployment of the internal/external perspective. In Dworkin's case, the internal perspective presents an unbelievably appealing vision of contemporary law while relegating its less admirable aspects to the professional oblivion of the external perspective. Thus Dworkin both begins and leaves us with a highly romanticized vision of law as an appealing form of rational thought. This is not hard to do so long as one is rhetorically astute in ways that we, as participants in the theater of the rational, are already prepared to accept.

The theater of the rational comes with its own grammar for the suppression of disbelief; Dworkin needs only to hint at this theater to get the audience to participate. Dworkin is very good at this theater: he describes a minuscule fraction of the realm of law and makes it out to be *Law's Empire*. Rather than alerting us that the law about which he writes is far removed from the law as it is practiced by lawyers in late twentieth-century United States, Dworkin repeatedly invites the audience to confuse and conflate *Law's Empire* with what we know to be *L.A. Law*'s empire. The (not quite) final irony of this recursive rehearsal of the internal/external perspective is that external perspective is forgotten as the internal perspective comes to represent everything that "really" matters.

Meanwhile, the internal/external perspective slides well beyond the *intellectual* borders of the theater of the rational.

The Birth of the Clinic

The reverberations of the internal/external perspective do not stop in the genteel ether of intellectual thought. On the contrary, the internal/external perspective is marked and echoed in the very topography of the law school. The external, the *L.A. Law* stuff, is almost always located in and sharply confined to a rigidly demarcated space, a space known as "the legal clinic." The clinic is almost always to be found in a basement or an annex or in some other peripheral, typically devalued site located outside the place where the main event—the traditional class—is held.

And there should be nothing surprising about this correspondence between the fancy jurisprudential dichotomy of internal/external perspective, on the one hand, and the graphic, physical separation of the traditional classroom and the clinic, on the other. The latter is simply a material inscription of the already extant and ruling dichotomy between the internal and the external perspectives, a dichotomy that has already been inscribed at the cognitive, professional, and political levels. Before the legal clinic became a place, before "legal clinic" became a metonym, it was an idea. In order to end up in a separate, peripheral, largely devalued place, the legal clinic had to be seen as a separate, peripheral idea—an idea separable from the idea of the traditional classroom.[166] And given the standard cognitive, professional, and political inscription of the internal/external perspective, it was, of course, easy for law faculties to see legal clinics as not belonging in the classroom.

Indeed, to recognize the work of the legal clinic as something that does belong in the classroom would be to surrender professional and political benefits already secured by the sedimentation of the internal/external dichotomy. That is, such a recognition would entail, for the traditional legal faculty, extensive revision of the classroom script (a lot of hard work) and increased intellectual risk as legal "knowledge" became subject to the vagaries, complications, and uncertainties of actual practice (a lot of ego risk). On the political level, to allow the clinic into the classroom would mean that the traditional faculty would immediately have to surrender the pleasant political fantasy that they are helping prepare lawyers for an always already noble and admirable enterprise (something akin to *Law's Empire* or the *Rule of Law*).

This separation between the theater of the rational and *L.A. Law* thus finds one of its most material, and hence most durable and indelible, inscriptions in the division between the legal clinic and the traditional classroom.[167] The physical separation authorizes student role differentiation. The social significance of this separation is that it constructs students who behave as if the two worlds— the legal clinic and the traditional classroom—have little to do with each other. Students quickly learn that anything assimilated in the legal clinic is irrelevant to the traditional classroom, where the law is explored from "the internal perspective." The student learns that she can be one kind of law person in the clinic and a completely different kind of law person in the classroom. She learns one of the key lessons the legal academy imparts to its students: internalize and defuse contradiction by compartmentalizing the self.[168]

This ability to compartmentalize the self in terms of performative roles becomes very important to the student once she becomes a lawyer—it is the technique by which the student-become-lawyer resolves the contradictions that practice presents. It is the technique by which ugly actions are insulated inside a compartment of the self and rationalized away. As the saying goes, "it's just my job." It is in this way that the lawyer is constructed to become a key site for the management of social contradictions.

Given the way the internal/external perspective becomes inscribed in the structure of the self, it really is no surprise that this jurisprudential distinction should resonate. It is relentlessly recursive and reenacted at various levels, all of which, by virtue of their synchronicity, tend to confirm each other. So, not surprisingly, after being relentlessly projected and subsequently inscribed at the levels of the cognitive, professional, political, material, and self, the distinction between the internal and external perspectives just simply seems true. In a psychoanalytic, rhetorical, and theatrical sense, the internal/external perspective is relentlessly acted out.

Now, there are a few points I want to emphasize about how the internal/external perspective works. First, to the extent that this inscription of this distinction slips from the cognitive, through the professional and political, to the material levels, the dichotomy and its organization of the world become more difficult to undo. More difficult in the crude sense that the distinction acquires greater social weight. Once the clinic is located downstairs or in the annex, it becomes more costly to try to integrate it into the classroom. More important, however, once the clinic is downstairs or in the annex, it becomes difficult even to imagine putting it in the classroom. Thus, slippage works in the reverse direction as well. Once inscribed at the level of the material or professional, the embedded inscriptions of internal/external—such as classroom/ clinic and regular faculty/clinical faculty—in effect confirm the "intellectual" validity and plausibility of the dichotomy. In this sense, the internal/external perspective resonates in the material and professional organization of the law school. Once inscribed in that organization, it is a powerful material confirmation of the idea that clinic and classroom carry on distinct activities. The process of resonance confirms the sense that the internal/external perspective is indeed anchored in "reality." The internal perspective of *Law's Empire* is in the classroom, and the external perspective of *L.A. Law* is in the clinic. In short, the internal/external dichotomy and its asserted content gain intellectual validity precisely because they have been inscribed at the cognitive, professional, political, and material levels.

What we learn, then, by taking the internal/external perspectives dichotomy seriously is that the kind of theater it supports, the theater of the rational, is itself constituted by a series of cognitive, professional, material, and intellectual practices of questionable rationality. If normative legal thought is now in trouble, it is because it has been the main production of a kind of theater that is fast losing its credibility.

CONCLUSION

Normative legal thought is conclusion oriented. Among other things, this means that normative legal thought works very hard to reach this point (the "Conclusion"). This is the point where the payoff is to be found—the what to do, the prescription, the recommendation. This is so clearly the site of the payoff that many legal thinkers routinely turn to the conclusion first in order to decide whether or not it is worth reading a piece. Why, after all, endure an arduous journey through scores of pages if the payoff is not warranted?[169]

Conclusions are the point at which normative legal thought is supposed to graft its thought onto a social or juridical reality outside the text. For normative legal thought, the conclusion is the anxious moment when thought ceases and the prescription, the recommendation, is urged on the reader. This is where the reader is supposed to choose whether to accept or reject the conclusion. If the argument has been good and the prescriptions fit the argument, then the expectation of both author and reader is that the latter will adopt the conclusion as her own.

All of this, of course, is déjà vu. It resonates not just with the practices of reading and writing normative legal thought in the academy,[170] but with a more primal experience: the structure of the appellate brief. There is in the form of normative legal thought a mimetic replication of the structure of the lawyer's brief. The lawyer's brief begins with a statement of jurisdiction, which is followed by a statement of the issues, the discussion of the facts, the argument of law, and then the request for judicial relief. Normative legal thought closely tracks this structure, and when it is complete, there is a conclusion. The conclusion in normative legal thought is thus the mimetic counterpart of the lawyer's prayer to the court for remedy, for decision.

The big difference, of course, is that the legal brief is almost invariably addressed to some agent who has the jurisdiction and power to grant the relief requested, whereas normative legal thought is almost invariably not. That too explains why the conclusion in normative legal thought is such an anxious moment. In the borderlands of consciousness there is a sense in which normative legal thinkers know that their prescriptions and recommendations are not going anywhere. In the borderlands of consciousness, legal thinkers know that within the tens of thousands of pages of volumes 1 to 100-something of the *Harvard Law Review,* there is an abundance of prescriptions and recommendations that have gone nowhere and done nothing but serve as the occasion for repeating argument structures and forms we now look back on with an odd mixture of amusement, disdain, and humbling self-recognition.

But not perfect self-recognition. Not perfect, because if you look back at those pages of the *Harvard Law Review,* it is apparent that the old-school academics, those who wrote in the earlier part of the twentieth century, identified themselves much more successfully with the courts and the judges than we do today. The old-school academics took themselves to be speaking to judges, to be helping judges along. They identified with the mode of judicial thinking. It is easy to conclude that, for much of the earlier part of the twentieth century, legal academics were far more successful (at the very least) in fooling themselves that their work had some effect on the judiciary.

Currently, of course, this sort of supposition is hardly believable. For some legal thinkers, this recognition is the occasion for nostalgia. For others, it is nothing of the sort. Who wants to prescribe or recommend things to judges anyway? That sounds like a recipe for formalism.[171] What's more, if one enters the bureaucratic maze of doctrinal restatements restated, one ends up with restatement consciousness. And why do that? Because it's law? Doubtful.

Sometime in the future the ALI will publish the Third Restatement on Everything. It will be a comprehensive compilation of four-part balancing tests all based on key terms that will themselves be defined in terms of four-part balancing tests, and so on in such a way that the Third Restatement on Everything will have achieved the first totally comprehensive, totally closed system of totally self-referential four-part balancing tests. It will be great. Then it will turn to mud.

Law has apparently transformed itself into a bizarre bureaucratic life-form that reproduces itself, not just without consulting us or our wishes but by shaping us and our wishes. What is the role of normative legal thought relative to bureaucratic practice? But that is already the wrong question. Normative legal thought isn't somewhere else, where it could then be relative to this practice. Normative legal thought is that inseparable aspect of bureaucratic practice that persists in mistakenly thinking that it is separate and distinct and then compounds this error by thinking that it rules over bureaucratic practice. Normative legal thought is at once an abstraction of and indistinguishable from the operations and practices of bureaucracy.

There is no stable referent behind the bureaucratic practices' own self-representation and self-effectuation in normative thought. Normative legal thought has thus had the effect of retarding our understanding of our social situation within the academy.

Normative legal thought, of course, is also a mode of social control—both within and without the legal academy. As I've argued throughout this essay, the rhetoric of normative legal thought establishes the identity and polices the bounds of legitimate legal thought. And as this essay itself demonstrates—constatively and performatively—normative legal thought is breaking down, is losing its appeal. This is what enables me to think and write this essay, and what enables you to read and understand it.

There are enough dislocations and disruptions within normative legal thought and within our social order that we can actually begin to re-cognize (that is, to cognize again and differently) that normative legal thought is not as it represents itself to be; that its main significance lies in the rehearsal and the inscription of a false social aesthetic; that its politics are seriously out of date; that its contributions to the construction of social and legal reality are ambivalent at best, noxious at worst.

But what should we do? This question arrives on this scene predictably enough, but really much too late at this point. It's already being done. We've been doing it since the beginning of this essay, and even before. We've been trying to show a whole series of routine normative agendas, questions, and frameworks the way off the jurisprudential stage. They are not helpful anymore. More accurately, more mildly: their *dominance* is not helpful anymore.

Needless to say, this essay is not a glowing report of American legal thought. Yet it is not meant as criticism. It is more in the nature of an attempt to help destabilize normative legal thought. Here and elsewhere, a whole way of thinking about the law is being dismantled and displaced. For those who want to continue to live in the old ways, this process is not pleasant. Indeed, it's rarely pleasant to inhabit a social practice that is being changed without your consultation. *But don't let that distract you.* It happens all the time. It's happening now. With and without this essay. It's the law.

NONSENSE AND NATURAL LAW

Steven D. Smith

We hold these truths to be self-evident, that all men . . . are endowed by their Creator with certain unalienable Rights.—The Declaration of Independence

Natural rights is simple nonsense . . .—nonsense upon stilts.—Jeremy Bentham[1]

W E CANNOT FULLY make sense of the Constitution, or of the ways we talk about the Constitution, unless we understand the Constitution from within a natural law–natural rights framework. So argues Roger Pilon,* among others,[2] and although the argument is obviously controversial, I want for now to accept it. But I also want to suggest that this claim points to a dilemma that lies at the heart of contemporary constitutional discourse. The first prong of the dilemma, once again, is that we cannot make sense of a good deal of constitutional discourse *outside* a natural law–natural rights framework. The second prong of the dilemma is that *we* cannot talk sensibly about the Constitution from *within* a natural law–natural rights framework, because this sort of framework gains its sense from a worldview that is no longer permitted us. The unhappy conclusion, it seems, is that we cannot talk sensibly about the Constitution.

I will elaborate this dilemma in three stages. First, I will explain what I mean by "nonsense." Second, I will say a little about the worldview within which the Constitution was initiated. And, third, I will explain how the loss of this worldview makes the eighteenth-century concepts of natural law and natural rights nonsensical, and thereby precludes us from making sense in much of what we say about the Constitution.

THE POSSIBILITY OF NONSENSE

The crucial first step in my argument asserts that it is possible to talk nonsense. This possibility is one that lawyers and legal scholars have often acknowl-

*This essay was originally given as a comment on a talk by Dr. Pilon presented at a conference on Natural Law and the Constitution, held in November 1994 at the University of Southern California Law School.

edged—and, some would say, demonstrated. In his well-known article "Transcendental Nonsense and the Functional Approach,"[3] Felix Cohen suggested, ambiguously perhaps, that a host of legal terms—*tort, crime, corporation, property, rights in rem*—may be meaningless or nonsensical. To put it differently, Cohen could be understood as saying that these terms are "just words"—that they refer to or name nothing real. In a similar vein, Karl Llewellyn in his early work criticized lawyers' use of "words that masquerade as things."[4] Much legal discourse, he feared, "is in terms of words; it centers on words; it has the utmost difficulty in getting beyond words."[5]

Much earlier, an astute judge and philosopher, Francis Bacon, had made a similar point: "The idols imposed by words on the understanding are . . . names of things which do not exist (for as there are things left unnamed through lack of observation, so likewise are there names which result from fantastic suppositions and to which nothing in reality corresponds)."[6]

This critical judgment—that something is "just words"—is one that most of us make at times; we might also express it by saying that a statement or conversation (or maybe even someone's life's work) is "nonsense." The grammar and syntax may be impeccable. And as with a catechism (or a Gilbert's) recited by habit or rote, there may be recognizable patterns of assertion and response. But the words just don't seem to mean anything. We might even be able to replicate or enter into the conversational pattern ("If *she* says X, *I'm* supposed to say Y— or perhaps, in an ironic tone, Z") and yet confess, "But I really don't know what we're talking about."

What Is Nonsense?

Although this sort of judgment or statement ("it's all nonsense"; "it's just words") is familiar, it is not easy to make the notion of "nonsense" more precise. Cohen, for example, was influenced by the logical positivists, who sometimes suggested that all meaningful statements fall into two categories— empirical statements and analytical or tautological propositions—and that any statement not falling into one of these categories is therefore nonsensical.[7] But this scheme seems too simple. And philosophers like Hilary Putnam have argued that the logical positivists' verification test for detecting nonsense is itself nonsensical by its own standard.[8]

Conceding the difficulty of the task, I offer the following tentative suggestion: All of us have, at least implicitly, a worldview or ontology that functions as a sort of catalogue of the kinds of things we believe to be "real," or to exist, and of the various properties and relations of which these things are capable. The words and sentences that we use in conversation are meaningful to the extent that we can locate them within, or give an intelligible account of them by reference to, our ontological catalogues. Conversely, if we cannot give an account of our words or statements in terms of what we regard as real, then we are speaking nonsense—just words.

But I must quickly note two complicating factors. First, since our worldviews or ontological catalogues differ, judgments of "nonsense" are relative; a statement that is nonsense for one person or culture may not be nonsense for another person or culture. (This is not to concede, of course, that all beliefs are equally valuable or true, or that "truth" is merely relative.) So we should be cautious about issuing the judgment of "absolute nonsense."

Second, our ontological catalogues are typically complex; they contain sections for different kinds of things: "material objects," "ideas" or "concepts," "social practices and conventions," and so forth. This complexity might suggest that we cannot unwittingly speak nonsense after all; all our terms will necessarily refer to "real" things, even if these things can be located only in the category of "concepts" or "beliefs." Indeed, to say that something is just words is already to locate it in a particular section of our ontological catalogue—the section for "words," or perhaps "language games."

The quick answer to this objection, I think, is that questions such as "Is the abominable snowman real?" or "Does God exist?" are typically intended and understood as asking whether the entity in question exists in some particular or understood sense. By the same token, judgments of "nonsense" assert that a term does not denote anything that exists *in the sense the speaker supposes* or *in the way the thing would need to exist in order to justify some action or practice.* For example, suppose I invite you on a safari to hunt unicorns, and you answer, "That's nonsense. Unicorns don't exist." If I respond that you are metaphysically naive and that unicorns *do* exist—you can find them in the category of "legendary beasts"—I will have missed the point.

In the same way, I suspect that disappointed children who are comforted with explanations of how Santa Claus really does exist in a metaphorical or ethereal sense (perhaps as a cultural personification of the spirit of generosity) know perfectly well that they are being subjected to a bald equivocation. Subtleties will not salvage the reality of *their* Santa Claus. At least, after hearing our second-grade teacher's thoughtful, delicate explanation along these lines, I don't remember that anyone in my class responded: "Gee, now I understand. Santa is so much richer, so much more truly *present,* than I had supposed. How simpleminded I was to have felt upset."

So the complications just noted do not preclude the possibility of talking nonsense. For some purposes, to be sure, there may be better ways to describe the kind of problem being addressed here. For example, the problem might be described as a sort of ontological gap between a person's or culture's *explicit* or *owned* ontological assumptions and the *implicit* or *presupposed* ontological assumptions—the assumptions about which things would need to be real in particular ways in order for the person's or culture's discourse and behavior to be sensible or rational. For present purposes, however, the notion of "nonsense" seems a satisfactory and more accessible way of approaching the problem.

But the discussion thus far also suggests that although nonsense is possible, there can be no simple, all-purpose test for diagnosing it. Instead, the detection of nonsense involves an examination to determine whether our words and sentences can be supported with an adequate account relating them to our beliefs about reality.

The Socratic Inquiry

Fortunately, we have an outstanding example of just this sort of examination—the most Socratic, so-called aporetic dialogues of Plato. Typically, these dialogues revolve around a question such as "What is courage?" or "What is justice?"[9] When Socrates professes not to know the answer to this question, his interlocutors (usually sophists or citizens of Athens) are astonished; they are sure that they can easily supply an answer. And indeed, they *are* familiar with the conventional usage of the term and are able to give instances of what is conventionally regarded as courage or justice. An accomplished sophist, such as Protagoras, can give eloquent speeches about the virtue in question—speeches that leave his listeners "spellbound."[10] But under Socrates' examination, these answers are found to be deficient. So the dialogues end in perplexity, or aporia, with even Socrates reasserting that he does not know the answer to the question.

The aporetic dialogues have generated a huge array of interpretations. For our purposes, however, two points are significant. First, it is plausible to understand Socrates as engaged not in a *semantic* project, but rather in an *ontological* inquiry.[11] Socrates is not quibbling over words, as his detractors contend;[12] he is not asking merely for a synonym or a definition or even a correct proposition. Instead, Socrates wants his interlocutors to "give an account" of the quality or entity in question.[13]

But why is Socrates so intent on having "an account"? Terry Penner has helpfully suggested that when Socrates asks about justice or temperance or virtue, he wants to know *the thing itself*.[14] Thus, for Socrates, "we must know the reference of 'virtue,' not just the meaning."[15] Such knowledge would be expressed through an account that would not merely tell how a term is defined or used, but would explain the real nature of whatever it is in reality that the term refers to. Socrates wants to know, in other words, whether and in what sense courage or temperance or justice is *real*.[16]

The second significant observation is that in pursuing his ontological inquiry, the Socrates of the early dialogues does not offer his own ontology, as Plato later would with his theory of Forms. Instead, as Gregory Vlastos has argued, Socrates tries to determine whether an account of ethical terms can be given within the conventional ontology of his own culture.[17] This investigation typically ends in failure and perplexity. Greek ethical discourse fails, in short, on its own terms.[18]

In sum, although the sophists and the Athenians confidently deploy terms such as *justice, courage,* and *virtue,* they cannot intelligibly connect these qualities to anything that they themselves regard as real. They are, as Socrates tells Callicles, "playing with words but revealing nothing."[19] By this interpretation, therefore, the conclusion of the Socratic examination is that within the Greeks' own worldview, Greek ethical discourse is nonsense. It may be elegant and erudite nonsense, but it is nonsense nonetheless.

THE JEFFERSONIAN ONTOLOGY

If it is possible to talk nonsense, then a question arises: Is talk of "natural law" or "natural rights" meaningful, or is this kind of talk merely nonsense? Jeremy Bentham famously asserted that natural law is "nonsense on stilts."[20] Was Bentham right? The preceding discussion suggests that this question cannot be answered absolutely or in the abstract, but only by reference to the worldview or ontological catalogue prevailing in a given period or for a particular group of people. In this section I will speak to this point by briefly describing an essential aspect of the Jeffersonian worldview within which rights discourse flourished during this country's founding period.

The Jeffersonian worldview did not begin with Thomas Jefferson. In his classic *The Great Chain of Being,* Arthur Lovejoy described a philosophy that in different versions has appeared again and again throughout the history of Western thought. Lovejoy traced this philosophy back to Plato, and in particular to the *Timaeus.* The essential recurring ideas can be stated briefly. First, the world was created by an originating mind—the demiurge, or, more commonly, God—who by virtue of being perfectly good and self-sufficient could not know envy, and hence chose to confer existence on everything that it could conceive of.[21] Second, because the originating mind could not but choose to give existence to everything that it could conceive of, the universe is rich with the greatest possible variety of entities—Lovejoy called this idea the "principle of plenitude"—which together form a continuum from the lowest and most inanimate to the highest and most intelligent. This hierarchy is the Great Chain of Being.[22] Third, because everything that exists is the product of mind, not of chance, there is a reason why each thing exists in the particular way that it does.[23] Following Leibniz, Lovejoy called this idea the "principle of sufficient reason."[24]

Lovejoy also showed how much of Western thought has consisted of the working out and the reworking of these themes. Of course, the variations on these general themes have been virtually infinite. The central unifying element, however, is the notion expressed by Plato: in the constitution of the cosmos, *mind*—or soul, or God—is primary. Nature is derivative and created, and it operates in accordance with the design of the originating mind, or God.

This general way of conceiving of the world reached its culmination, Lovejoy argued, in the eighteenth century.[25] So it would not be surprising to find this conception in the thought not only of American Christians during the founding period, but also in the thinking of more "secular" citizens such as Jefferson. And studies by historians such as Daniel Boorstin and Henry May confirm this surmise.

In a study (aptly entitled *The Lost World of Thomas Jefferson*) of the "mindscape of ideas" that informed the Jeffersonian worldview, Daniel Boorstin shows that Jeffersonian thought was firmly anchored in a version of the Great Chain of Being philosophy.[26] This worldview was pervasively manifest, both explicitly and implicitly, throughout Jefferson's thinking on subjects from religion to science to history and politics.

Boorstin notes that "Jefferson on more than one occasion declared 'the eternal pre-existence of God, and his creation of the world,' to be the foundation of his philosophy."[27] Henry May confirms this view: "Jefferson's universe was as purposeful as that of [Yale president and aggressive Protestant] Timothy Dwight and presupposed as completely the existence of a ruler and creator. The world was intelligently planned, benevolently intended, and understandable."[28]

As May's observation suggests, the Jeffersonian deity was not the wholly transcendent, inscrutable God of the Calvinists. Rather, God was benevolent and, most important, eminently intelligible.[29] Because the general Jeffersonian orientation was above all pragmatic, the Jeffersonian God was of necessity a very usable deity; and the Jeffersonians made constant use of him in all branches of their thinking.[30]

For example, the Jeffersonians assumed that if the world was the product of a supremely wise and benevolent Providence, then there could be no significant distinction between *is* and *ought*.[31] Hence, the "Jeffersonian cosmology" worked by "blending the world as it is with the world as it ought to be."[32] In this cosmology, "all facts were endowed with an ambiguous quality: they became normative as well as descriptive."[33]

From a modern perspective, perhaps the quirkiest and hence most revealing manifestation of this fusion of *is* and *ought* occurs in Jeffersonian thinking about what we would regard as scientific questions.[34] In the Jeffersonian view, the facts of nature conformed to, and hence must be explained by reference to, the providential plan. The world had been created in a single, brief creative period; the Creator did not need thousands or millions of years to accomplish his ends.[35] Moreover, since the world as created already conformed to the divine design, it could not change in fundamental respects. Thus, in response to the contention that the earth evolved slowly and in response to natural agents such as steam, Jefferson objected:

> I give one answer to all these theorists. . . . They all suppose the earth a created existence. They must suppose a creator then; and that he possessed power and wisdom to a great degree. As he intended the earth for the habitation of animals and vegetables, is it reasonable to suppose, he made two jobs of his creation, that he first made a chaotic lump and set it into rotary motion, and then waited the millions of ages necessary to form itself? That when it had done this, he stepped in a second time to create the animals and plants which were to inhabit it? As the hand of a creator is to be called in, it may as well be called in at one stage of the process as another. We may as well suppose he created the earth at once, nearly in the state in which we see it, fit for the preservation of the beings he placed on it.[36]

This view of the natural world was not merely an abstract thesis; it could be applied to specific scientific questions. For example, in his "Notes on Virginia" Jefferson addressed the question whether mammoths still exist. Although fossils of mammoths had been found, some people hypothesized that these animals might have become extinct. But Jefferson rejected this possibility a priori: "Such is the economy of nature, that no instance can be produced, of her having permitted any one race of her animals to become extinct; of her having formed any link in her great work so weak as to be broken."[37] Given this necessary inference from the order of nature, Jefferson considered possible empirical evidence of the mammoth's persistence to be inconsequential.[38] In making this deduction, moreover, Jefferson was not being original or innovative; other thinkers (such as Spinoza) working within the Great Chain of Being framework had likewise found this sort of argument compelling.[39]

For present purposes, however, the more important consequence of the Jeffersonian worldview is that it informed, and indeed was the necessary foundation for, thinking about ethics, government, law, and rights. The Jeffersonians believed, Boorstin explains, that "uniform and objective moral principles" were inherent in human biology itself.[40] Moreover, God has impressed these principles on the human heart; they are equally known to the plowman and the professor by means of a moral sense that God gives to every human being.[41]

With respect to the government of society, likewise, the Jeffersonians believed that God ordains principles for society and that the purpose of political theory is to discover "the plan implicit in nature."[42] The proper ends of society are not for human beings to determine; they are given in the divine plan, and the duty of government is simply to ascertain and conform to that plan. Thus, the Jeffersonian theory of government amounts to little more than deference to the Creator's plan.[43] As Henry May notes: "A benign God, a purposeful universe, and a universal moral sense are necessary at all points to Jefferson's political system."[44]

The notion of individual rights, so central to the Declaration of Independence and to Jefferson's political legacy, was for Jefferson likewise grounded in the divine scheme. As the Declaration says, "rights" are conferred on humans by "their Creator." For Jefferson, "no claim [of rights] could be validated except by the Creator's plan."[45] For similar reasons, modern worries about conflicts between rights, or about balancing competing rights against each other, or about the excessive or socially corrosive character of rights did not afflict Jefferson. "Faith in the Creator's design," Boorstin explains, "was what saved the persistent iteration of 'rights' from seeming an anarchic individualism."[46]

RIGHTS AND THE MODERN MIND

The preceding discussion suggests that for the Jeffersonians, natural rights were closely connected with a Creator who conferred such rights on human beings. But were these theistic trappings actually necessary to Jeffersonian rights discourse? Perhaps the same basic ideas and the same basic discourse could flourish as well or even better if the providential wrappings were discarded.

The question is urgent because the Jeffersonian, providence-centered worldview is no longer authoritative in legal and academic contexts. Appeals to God or to the providential design are generally not admissible. James Boyd White has observed "a peculiar division between academic and religious thought in our culture. In the academic world we tend to speak as though all participants in our conversations were purely rational actors engaged in rational debate; perhaps some people out there in the world are sufficiently benighted that they turn to religious beliefs or other superstitions, but that is not true of us, or if it is true, we hide it, and it ought not be true of them. Ours is a secular academy and, we think, a secular state."[47]

As White's statement intimates, the situation is complex. The providential worldview has not been relegated to the historical scrap heap, like, say, the Ptolemaic view of the cosmos has. Surveys indicate that nearly all Americans believe in God, and this number no doubt includes many academics. *Academic culture*, however, typically does not allow for appeals to supernatural explanations; and the exclusion of religion as a ground of argument or explanation seems particularly operative in the context of legal argument, where, according to one view, the exclusion has a constitutional basis.[48] Hence, *if* rights discourse makes sense only within the providence-centered worldview, then it would follow that if we continue to engage in this discourse we are talking nonsense— at least, relative to us.

I want to argue that rights discourse *does* depend for its meaning on the providence-centered worldview. I will state the central argument crudely, and then try to elaborate and qualify it. My central contention is that rights depend on law, and law depends on a legislator or lawgiver. If we have human legislators, we can talk sensibly about human or positive law, and hence legal rights. But we cannot make sense of "natural" rights, rights that are independent of or transcend positive law, without an extra-human lawgiver.

Rights and Law

One way to approach the claim that rights depend on law is to ask what is the difference between, on the one hand, *wanting* or even *needing* something (such as freedom of speech, a minimum income, or equal concern and respect), and, on the other hand, *having a right* to that thing. Within an established legal order, this question seems answerable. Among the many interests, desires, and needs human beings may have, there are some interests that are legally recognized and protected. We can distinguish these protected interests from other, unprotected interests by calling them "rights."

So, if I am asked to give an account of what I mean when I say I have a property right in my car, for example, I can say that I have an interest in possessing and using my car and that the legal order now in place prohibits other people from interfering with that interest (except, of course, under certain conditions, such as my failure to make the payments). I have interests in other things—life, freedom of speech, and so forth—that are similarly protected, to one degree or another, by the law. But I may have many other interests—in clean air, in having an enjoyable and lucrative job, in *your* car—that are not protected. I can use the term *rights* to distinguish my legally protected interests from other interests and to indicate that someone who interferes with the first kind of interests transgresses a legal prohibition. In saying this, I give an account of the term *rights;* I explain what it means to say that something is a right.

Conversely, if we cannot refer to a legal order in place, then it becomes difficult to give a satisfactory account explaining what it means to have a right, or how a right differs from other interests, desires, or needs that are not "rights." Of course, we might still talk about morality, or about how people ought to treat each other, but this sort of talk does not easily lend itself to assertions about rights.

Let me try to clarify this assertion. It is true that as our worldview changes (or as over time we exchange an old ontological catalogue for a newer one, so to speak), we can still use older terms to refer to new entries in our current catalogue. There is nothing nonsensical about this practice in itself. But insofar as the new entries are not equivalent to the old ones, they will not have the same properties and implications. And if we overlook these differences and continue to use our terms as if they *could* do the same work, we risk falling into nonsense. For example, I can still talk about Zeus as an existing thing—existing not as a muscular philanderer operating out of Mount Olympus, but as a literary or mythical character. But given my worldview (and, I trust, yours), if you ask me why I am sacrificing a bullock and I answer, "To calm the wrath of Zeus," you will have good grounds to suspect that I am committing nonsense. Zeus still exists, but not in the sense that my statement and conduct presuppose.

In the same way, we *can* use the word *rights* without reference to a legal order. For example, we might use it as a label for the conclusions of certain of our moral or prudential inquiries.[49] So we might argue as follows: The state should not restrict my speech; it would not be right for the state to restrict my speech; therefore, I have a "right" to freedom of speech. But this sort of talk does not quite capture all we typically want to say when we make assertions about rights. In much traditional rights talk, at least, claims about rights function as *reasons* or *premises*—not as *conclusions* or as labels for a conclusion. *Not* "Government should not restrict what I say—therefore, I have a right to freedom of speech"; *but rather* "I have a right to freedom of speech—therefore, government should not restrict what I say."[50] Indeed, if we really understood the term *rights* as nothing more than a label for the conclusions of other sorts of moral or practical inquiries, it would be hard to understand why so much attention is paid to the concept.

In short, we *can* use the term *rights* without reference to a legal order, but then the term comes to lose much of its meaning. Analytically, rights come to seem like mere conclusions or labels for conclusions, not reasons. Rhetorically, the invocation of rights seems merely a way of giving emphasis to a demand. ("I want this *and I mean it.*")

The Lawgiver and the Law

If we cannot speak sensibly about rights without assuming *law,* we cannot speak sensibly about law without assuming a *lawgiver.* The conception of "law" as a set of commands or rules issued by an authoritative sovereign or legislator is conspicuous in our images of law, modern and ancient: We imagine Congress passing laws for the citizens of this country, Solon giving laws to the Athenians, God giving the law to Moses, and Moses in turn giving it to the people of Israel. Conversely, when we try to imagine "law" without reference to any lawgiver or legislator, the notion becomes hazy or mystical—Holmes's "brooding omnipresence in the sky."[51]

Not surprisingly, therefore, most theories of law include a legislator as an essential element. This element is perhaps most central in positivist theories such as that of John Austin: Law consists of the general commands of the sovereign.[52] But even in theories different from or critical of Austin's, the lawgiver typically plays a necessary role. Thus, Thomas Aquinas defined law as "an ordinance of reason for the common good, *made by him who has care of the community,* and promulgated."[53] The legislator is only one element in this definition, but he is nonetheless an essential one.

More recently, Holmes criticized Austin's scholarship, but he did not discard the idea of the sovereign lawgiver; even his theory that law is merely a prediction of what judges will do arguably just confers the position of lawgiver on judges.[54] Lon Fuller was a persistent critic of Austin, of legal positivism, and of the concept of sovereignty. But his views did not so much deny the *necessity* as the *sufficiency* of a legislator for making law. In order to count as "law," Fuller insisted, a rule needs to be more than a command; it needs to conform to the "internal morality" of law.[55] But in Fuller's clearest and best known exposition of this internal morality, the image of the lawgiver—King Rex making rules for his subjects—remains central.[56]

This recurring theme is not fortuitous. We can give an intelligible account of law by reference to a lawgiver. Conversely, in the absence of a lawgiver it is difficult to explain what law is, how it arises, or what gives it (whatever "it" is) the status of "law" as distinguished from moral or prudential discourse in general.

Rights without Providence?

This analysis suggests that Jefferson's insistence on linking rights to Providence was more than a rhetorical trope. Jefferson's providential worldview recognized a supreme legislator—the Creator, or God—who constructed the world and governs it according to a divine design. This view can support an account of natural law—which can be understood by reference to the providential design— and, perhaps, of natural rights. Natural rights might refer to those human interests and concerns that rank highest in the providential scheme and with which others are forbidden by Providence to interfere. For example, if in the providential scheme life is sacred and the taking of human life is accordingly prohibited, then we might say that human beings have a "natural right" to life.

Remove the extrahuman legislator and the providential scheme, however, and it becomes difficult to explain what it means to say that something is a "natural right." We still have human legislators, of course, so we can still talk of *positive law* and of *legal rights*. And we can still make policy arguments—and perhaps, though this seems more controversial, moral arguments—to the effect that human governments ought to protect particular interests by creating legal rights.[57] But it is difficult to give an account of just what we mean when we say that something should be recognized as a legal right *because it is a natural right*.[58] Rights rhetoric seems to be nothing more than a sort of exclamation mark added to ordinary moral or prudential arguments.

This conclusion runs counter, of course, to a vast quantity of modern rights discourse, most of which defends, or more often assumes, the reality of "human rights" (as opposed to merely legal rights in a positivist sense) without supposing any need for providential assumptions. In this brief essay no survey is possible. But it will be helpful to focus on the arguments made by Roger Pilon because these offer forceful, crisp versions of the two major strands of modern rights thinking. One argument, reminiscent of Locke, traces rights back to a state of nature that culminated in a social agreement creating, and conferring limited powers on, the state. The other argument, reminiscent of Kant, tries to derive rights from an application of formal logic to human behavior.

The Lockean argument. Consider first the state-of-nature argument. In the natural state, or "the pre-government world," Pilon argues, every individual enjoyed the right to rule himself. This right was not a gift of government; rather, government arose only later and hence can claim only those rights that individuals have conferred on it.[59] A familiar objection to state-of-nature– social-contract arguments is that the state of nature is a fiction—it never existed—and you cannot derive actual rights from a fictitious condition that culminated in a fictitious contract or transfer. But my immediate objection is in a sense just the opposite of this: Dr. Pilon does not take the fiction of the state of nature seriously enough. Pilon's state of nature, it turns out, wasn't all that natural or primitive; it was already filled with rights—most important, the right of self-rule. But in a state of nature worthy of the name, it is hard to understand how the idea of "rights" would even arise or what the idea would mean.

In a genuine state of nature, it would seem, people want what they want and do what they do. People might rule themselves, but what sense would it make in that context to say that they have a "right" to rule themselves? We might as well say that the sun has a right to shine, or that cats have a right to chase mice. Rights talk seems natural to us because we have a legal order in place, and this legal order is the framework that gives rights their meaning. But when we project rights into a state of nature we are like baseball fans who show up in the middle of a tennis match and ask what inning it is or whether there have been any home runs.

The crucial move in this argument is from the premise that in a state of nature no one has a right to rule over others to the conclusion that everyone has a right to rule over himself or herself. Once this right has been brought into existence, the rest is relatively easy: The right, created *ex nihilo,* can now be reworked, assigned, transferred to the state in whole or in part. But the argument is flawed. Its premise—that in a state of nature no one has a right to rule over others—seems plausible because in a state of nature it is not clear what it would even mean for anyone to have rights at all. But the conclusion—that because no one has a right to rule over others everyone has a right to rule himself—is implausible, and for exactly the same reason.

Or perhaps you could insist that there *are* rights and law in the state of nature—since the condition is hypothetical it is wonderfully receptive to alternative descriptions—but then you have not solved the problem of rights; you have merely stipulated the problem out of existence.[60] Most important, you still have not given an account explaining just what it means to say that something is a right or in what sense rights actually exist.

The Kantian argument. Pilon's more Kantian argument tries to account for rights by applying formal logic to human actions. We can say that someone has a right if the denial of that right would involve the doubter in self-contradiction.[61] Pilon gives the following example:

> Quite simply, what we can say to the murderer, the rapist, and the robber is that in involving us involuntarily in a transaction with him, he himself is acting voluntarily and for purposes which seem to him good, which he is *claiming implicitly as rights for himself* in that his purposes justify his acts

to him. In acting conatively, that is, he is *implicitly claiming to have a right* to act voluntarily and purposively, which are the generic features that characterize action as such and hence that *necessarily* characterize it. Because he necessarily accepts these right-claims which are rooted in action for himself, he must accept the implication that every other actor and hence everyone else has these same rights, or else he will contradict the claims he necessarily makes for himself. Thus he must accept that others have the same rights he necessarily claims, to act voluntarily and purposively and hence not to be coerced by others by being involuntarily involved in transactions with them.[62]

Once again, although this argument purports to demonstrate the existence of rights, it actually works by assuming them a priori. Unless you assumed in advance that there are such things as rights and that human actions are grounded in claims of right, what sense would it make to assert that every human action necessarily makes an implicit claim of right?

The crucial move in *this* argument, I think, is from the assumption that every person who acts voluntarily acts for a reason or purpose "that seems to him good," to the conclusion that every person implicitly but necessarily claims a *right* to act as he does. This seems a non sequitur, and it is just at this point that the question is begged. A person's reason or purpose for acting might, and usually does, take some form other than a claim of right. For example, the robber might explain his action by simply saying, "I'm robbing you because I need money." This sort of *instrumental* reason does not involve any logical self-contradiction.

So far as I can make out, Pilon suggests two possible responses to this objection. He might say that an instrumental reason—"I need money"—would not "justify" the robbery, and that only a rights claim will do that. But this response would equivocate, I think, on the notion of "justification." The robber's instrumental reason "justifies his acts to him" in the sense that it gives him a sufficient reason or motive for undertaking the robbery. Of course, the instrumental reason might *not* justify the robbery in some other sense. It would not "justify" the robbery in a court of law, of course, nor would it satisfy the standard of ethical justification that Pilon or his mentor in this matter, Alan Gewirth, would impose on the situation. But that observation provides no basis for accusing the robber of *self-contradiction,* because it does not follow from the fact of purposeful, voluntary action that the robber is either consciously or "necessarily" committed to offering *that* kind of justification. The most that might necessarily follow from his purposeful action is that he has a reason, or "justification," that satisfies *him.*

A different response would suggest that even the instrumental reason—"I need money"—is self-contradictory, perhaps because it entails a general maxim for action such as "Rob when you need money," and this maxim self-destructs because it means that the robber himself risks being robbed and deprived of his money. But this response is vulnerable to a criticism that has been made of Kant's categorical imperative:[63] The "maxim" for a given action (assuming there needs to be a maxim) can be formulated in several ways, at least some of which are not self-contradictory. For example, the robber's maxim might be something like "People in my situation [carefully specified] should rob." Or, secure in his strength and cunning, he might act on the maxim: "Rob if you can get away with it." That rationale may be less than admirable. And, of course, the robber might be mistaken about his own invulnerability. But the rationale does not entail any logical self-contradiction, and most important, it does not take the form of a rights claim.

Perhaps more fundamentally, it is hard to understand what sort of thing this "implicit" claim of right that Pilon discusses could even be. What sort of reality does this claim enjoy, or in what sense can the claim be said to exist at all? Although Pilon attributes the claim to human actors, he does not suppose that they are typically *conscious* of making any such claim. So the rights claim evidently does not exist in the form of a "mental state." Instead, the claim is located in some other realm of existence—the realm of formal, logical "necessity." But the ontological status of this realm seems quite mysterious, particularly since this is a necessity that actors such as robbers are apparently able routinely to disregard.

The clearest account of the status of the "implicit claim of right," I would suggest, is that the claim exists within and by reference to a conceptual scheme of justification that Pilon and like-minded thinkers such as Gewirth impose on human actions. That scheme dictates that all purposeful human actions must be justified, and that justification must take the form of a rights claim. So if we begin by assuming the validity of this conceptual scheme, then *of course* every purposeful action necessarily entails an implicit claim of right; the scheme does not demonstrate the existence of this claim but merely stipulates it. And the problem, once again, is that you cannot prove and explain the existence of rights by simply stipulating them.

In short, the denial of rights entails a logical self-contradiction only if you assume in advance that rights exist, that all actors are somehow committed to justifying their actions, and that the only adequate form of justification consists of a rights claim. But that is simply to assume the point in question.

More generally, it seems that Pilon offers both his Lockean and Kantian arguments on the assumption that the primary problem for natural rights talk is *epistemological*. Our challenge, in other words, is to determine *what rights we have;* and the Lockean and Kantian arguments are devices for making that determination. But although natural law and natural rights talk might well pose an epistemological problem in some contexts, in our context such talk encounters a prior, *ontological* challenge. The question *for us* is whether and in what sense it is meaningful to say that natural law or natural rights exist at all. By focusing on the epistemological problem we may overlook the more basic ontological problem, and in doing so we risk falling into nonsense.

CONCLUSION

My discussion does not suggest that talk of natural law and natural rights is absolute nonsense, but only that such talk is nonsense *to us.* The sort of worldview within which such talk makes sense is one that we no longer accept—or at least that the assumptions and restrictions of our academic culture no longer permit us to invoke. So when we speak positively or prescriptively about "natural rights" or "human rights," we speak a language, so to speak, that *we* have no right to speak. To put the point differently: Rights, like Santa Claus, sound like nice things; consequently, we may devoutly wish to take rights seriously. But without the metaphysical resources to give substance to natural rights, our rights talk inevitably collapses into sophistry—"playing with words but revealing nothing."

If my claim of nonsense is correct, and if Pilon is also correct (as I suspect he is) that our constitutional discourse depends on notions of natural law and natural rights, then those of us involved in constitutional law will just have to reconcile ourselves to speaking, or at least to hearing, a good deal of (often quite intricate and learned) nonsense. This situation may be unsettling, but it is not unprecedented. For example, I suspect that Socrates would feel right at home.

AGAINST CONSTITUTIONAL THEORY

Paul F. Campos

NOBODY CAN AGREE on what the Constitution means. Some argue
that it prohibits states from banning abortions; others claim that it
says nothing about abortion, or that it prohibits abortion. The Constitution is said to abolish the death penalty and to specifically authorize the
death penalty; to ban segregated schools and to be indifferent to segregation; to
require that we exempt religious believers from laws that burden the practice of
their religion and to prohibit governments from granting such exemptions; to
eliminate the possibility of a thirty-one-year-old president and to welcome this
possibility.

Two beliefs about this perplexing document, however, do not appear controversial. All commentators seem to agree, first, that the Constitution is a text,
and, second, that understanding it is primarily a matter of deploying the proper
theory of textual interpretation. The purpose of this essay is to demonstrate
that those beliefs are largely mistaken. I am aware that readers of this text will
consider such a claim highly counterintuitive, and may dismiss it out of hand. I
can only prospectively ask for your patience. Reading, Barthes has noted, is an
intimacy between strangers; and perhaps, like all intimacy, it requires an initial
gesture of faith from both author and reader.

I

*No one can articulate a syllable which is not filled with tenderness and fear, which is not, in
some language, the powerful name of a god.*—Jorge Luis Borges[1]

In his story "Pierre Menard, Author of the Quixote" Jorge Luis Borges creates a
character whose life goal is to write *Don Quixote*. Menard's goal is not "to
compose another *Don Quixote*—which would be easy—but *the Don Quixote*."[2]
He first considers a straightforward approach: "Know Spanish well, recover the
Catholic faith, fight against the Moors or the Turk, forget the history of Europe
between the years 1602 and 1918, *be* Miguel de Cervantes."[3]

Menard rejects this method as too easy. For Cervantes at the beginning of the seventeenth century, the writing of *Don Quixote* "was a reasonable . . . perhaps even unavoidable" undertaking;[4] for Pierre Menard to write the same book in the twentieth century is a considerably more arduous, and therefore, for Menard, more interesting task.

Menard partially succeeds in his absurd enterprise: he finishes two chapters and parts of a third of the famous novel. Borges's narrator notes that despite appearances the two works are not the same. While "Cervantes' text and Menard's are verbally identical [Menard's] is almost infinitely richer." The narrator quotes Cervantes: "truth, whose mother is history, rival of time, depository of deeds, witness of the past, exemplar and advisor to the present, and the future's counselor." Written in the seventeenth century, this is, according to the narrator, "a mere rhetorical praise of history." He then quotes Menard: "truth, whose mother is history, rival of time, depository of deeds, witness of the past, exemplar and advisor to the present, and the future's counselor," and is swept away by the contrast:

> History, the *mother* of truth: the idea is astounding. Menard, a contemporary of William James, does not define history as an inquiry into reality but as its origin. Historical truth, for him, is not what has happened, it is what we judge to have happened. . . .
>
> The contrast in style is also vivid. The archaic style of Menard—quite foreign, after all—suffers from a certain affectation. Not so that of his forerunner, who handles with ease the current Spanish of his time.[5]

The narrator concludes that Menard has created a new technique to enrich "the halting and rudimentary art of reading": "This new technique is that of the deliberate anachronism and the erroneous attribution. . . . This technique fills the most placid works with adventure. To attribute the *Imitatio Christi* to Louis Ferdinand Celine or to James Joyce, is this not a sufficient renovation of its tenuous spiritual indications?"[6]

Borges demonstrates that it is possible for the same combination of words to constitute two radically different texts. What is it that allows this phenomenon to take place? The short answer is captured by the word *context:* the context within which we read Menard's *Quixote* is utterly dissimilar from the context we bring to Cervantes's verbally identical text. But, as Steven Knapp and Walter Benn Michaels have pointed out, what is context but another way of saying *authorship?* Following the antitheoretical work of Knapp and Michaels, I will argue that to read a text is to try to determine what its author intends to say, and that any other description of textual interpretation is incoherent.[7] I will claim further that this conclusion suggests that theories of interpretation (that is,

general accounts of how one goes about getting good interpretations) are
pointless and can have no heuristic value. I will then suggest that these conclusions lead to no obvious normative implications for the project of legal, and
specifically constitutional, interpretation.

One way of seeing why reading a text must mean trying to determine what its
author intends to say is by attempting to imagine how one would go about
reading a text without reference to authorial intention. Suppose you are walking along a trail on a dusty plateau near the border of Arizona and Mexico. You
notice, etched in dust by the edge of the trail, what appear to be four letters that
seem to form the word *real*. A resident of the area who is with you explains that
marks which appear to be words often show up near this part of the trail. Some
people, she explains, believe that the swirling desert winds create such marks;
others believe that someone surreptitiously makes the marks in the sand.[8]

It is clear that your attitude toward this "text" will be a product of the
assumptions you make about its authorship. If you believe that the marks are a
product of the desert wind, you will conclude that what looks like a word is not
a word at all: the marks merely resemble a word. On the other hand, if you
believe some person has traced the marks in the sand, you will ask what the
word they form means. Under the circumstances you might wonder whether
you were reading the English word *real* or the Spanish word *real* (royal). But
this question is in fact meaningless unless it refers to what the author of the
word meant, at the elementary level of determining what language the author
meant to employ.

Several objections to this account of textual meaning come immediately to
mind: doesn't a mark that only appears to be a text become a text when we treat
it as such, and can't we still read a text even if we make mistaken assumptions
about authorial intention? Furthermore, even if we think we know what the
author meant, can't we consciously choose to substitute our own "reading" of
the text?

Suppose that you become convinced that the marks in the sand were produced by random fluctuations of the desert wind. You can still insist that the
wind has created a "real" word, but only if you adhere to one of two positions.
Either you believe in some combination of linguistic formalism and metaphysical realism that simultaneously denies the conventional nature of semantic
meaning and affirms our access to a transcendental semantic order,[9] or you can
claim that even if the marks were initially meaningless, they now have a meaning *for you*. Few would be willing to admit to the former position, and the latter
claim merely confuses the issue. For if the marks were initially meaningless but
have become meaningful through your ascription of meaning to them, then it is

precisely through that ascription that they have become a text: a text of which you are the author.

In the alternative, suppose that you assumed that the marks were made by an English speaker who intended by the word *real* the opposite of *imaginary*. You later discover that in fact the marks were made by a Spanish speaker who meant by *real* roughly what an English speaker would usually mean by *royal*. Wasn't your initial assumption a reading? Yes it was, but it was a particular type of reading: a misreading, by which you misunderstood what the author actually said. Misreading is always possible, but it alters neither the text's meaning nor our interpretive relation to it.

Or imagine that you subsequently discover that the marks were made by a monolingual English speaker, but because of an aesthetic preference (you think the Spanish word is prettier) or a political longing (you would prefer the text to be the work of a cryptic monarchist), you choose to treat the marks as if they formed a Spanish word. Of course, this is a perfectly possible procedure. I will call this sort of conscious disregard of the author's text *reauthoring*. This is exactly the procedure that Pierre Menard revealed through his reauthoring of *Don Quixote,* the technique of "deliberate anachronism and erroneous attribution [that] fills the most placid works with adventure."

If this account of textual interpretation is correct, then a text always means what its author intends, and any reading of a text must perforce be an attempt to discover that intention. We have seen that it is possible to do things with words other than read them: we can misread them (by incorrectly understanding the author's meaning), we can write with them (ascribing the meaning we choose to words without reference to another author), or we can reauthor them (consciously ignoring what we know about the author's—and hence the text's—meaning in favor of our preferred understanding of the words he or she employed).

Although there is little or no linguistic difference between writing and re-authoring, a critical theoretical distinction does exist, as a matter of social practice, between the two: in our culture only reauthoring can successfully claim to be a form of textual interpretation.

It is important to emphasize that this is not a methodological, let alone a normative, prescription for how one should read texts. To imagine that one *should* read a text so as to discover what its author intended by it is to mistakenly assume that it is possible to do anything else. But since any reading of a text that really is a *reading* of that text simply consists of a search for authorial intention, statements such as "The supreme court . . . *should* have accorded interpretive primacy to original intent in ascertaining the 'meaning' of the constitution,"[10] if they are statements about the Constitution *as a text,* are both tautological and methodologically empty.

The fact that similar claims are routinely made by theorists of all persuasions, either fervently demanding or cautiously recommending or openly deploring the use of authorial intention as a tool for ascertaining the meaning of the constitutional text,[11] helps locate the main source of the confusion that envelops contemporary debates on constitutional interpretation. The confusion arises because we imagine that intention is something one either does or does not add to a reading of a text in order to extract a meaning from it. Once one sees, however, that meaning and intention are not separable, and are in fact identical,* appeals to authorial intention, whether celebratory or condemnatory, lose most of their force and interest.

The question then becomes: Should we read the Constitution or should we do something else with it?

II

I know of an uncouth region whose librarians repudiate the vain and superstitious custom of finding a meaning in books and equate it with that of finding a meaning in dreams or in the chaotic lines of one's palm. . . . This dictum, we shall see, is not entirely fallacious.
—Jorge Luis Borges[12]

Utopia Park is the pride of Erewhon. Its many winding paths are frequented by joggers, bicyclists, and townspeople who simply want to take a leisurely stroll. Recently, many pedestrians have complained that certain bicyclists ride down the paths at dangerous speeds, reducing the tranquility of the park. Matters came to a head last week when a collision with a fast-moving bike put an eight-year-old girl in the hospital with a broken wrist. Two nights later, the girl's parents appeared at a town council meeting and angrily demanded that the council ban bicycles from the park. They pointed to an ordinance passed by the council nearly thirty years before, which states "No vehicles shall be permitted in the park," and claimed that this ordinance prohibits bicycles from entering the park. Several other opponents of bicycles in the park voiced their agreement and insisted that the council enforce the law. The council's three members, Henry, Michael, and Ronald, promised to answer these demands at the next

*That is, semantic intention and semantic meaning are identical. As Knapp and Michaels point out, "Not all intentions are intentions to mean (not all acts are speech acts)" (S. Knapp and W. B. Michaels, "Against Theory," 8 *Critical Inquiry* 723 [1982]).

council meeting, after they had given the matter further study. On the night before the meeting they reviewed the history of the ordinance's adoption and enforcement.

The ordinance was passed on November 11, 1963, by a vote of 2 to 1. Council members James and Lawrence had voted in favor of passage; Conrad had voted against. The minutes of that meeting reveal that the ordinance was passed primarily to keep motorcycles out of the park.

The original council had also debated how broadly the term *vehicle* should be defined. James stated that it should mean anything that could move fast enough to harm a pedestrian. Someone in the audience had asked whether that included bicycles. James and Lawrence thought it should; Conrad subsequently refused to vote for the ordinance because he didn't believe that bicycles should be banned from the park.

For the first few years after the ordinance was passed, no bicycles were allowed in Utopia Park. But by 1970 the composition of the council had changed, and bicycles began to appear again on the park's paths. Indeed, although the ordinance was never formally revised, no one had been cited for riding a bike in Utopia Park since 1973. Very few people even remembered that the ordinance had once been understood to prohibit this activity.

The three members of the present council agreed that, as a practical matter, bicycles had to be allowed in the park. They could not, however, agree how to go about interpreting the ordinance so as to produce this result. By the next morning, each had developed a distinctive interpretive strategy that would allow the council to announce the outcome that all its members wanted to reach.

Henry's argument was comparatively straightforward. For Henry, it was simply nonsensical to claim that the ordinance could be interpreted as allowing bicyclists in the park. The authors of the ordinance had considered and rejected that possibility. However, he reasoned, if a text cannot be interpreted in a manner that generates the result desired by the interpreter, an interpretive (or one might say an *anti-interpretive*) option remains: the reader can choose to ignore the text.

Henry argued that although it was absurd to imagine that the ordinance permitted bicycles in the park, it would be even more ridiculous to enforce the ordinance at this time. The customs, practices, and recent history of Erewhon all argued against such a result. Everyone now assumed that one could bring bicycles into Utopia Park. Enforcing the ordinance would not only damage the economic future of Erewhon, it would upset a well-settled group of expectations that the community had developed and now relied on. For Henry, the answer to the interpretive problem was simple: if an aspect of the meaning of the ordinance has become fundamentally unacceptable to the community, then the community should refuse to enforce that aspect.

Michael found Henry's solution elegant but unacceptable. He believed that to refuse to enforce the ordinance was a form of public dereliction which could eventually undermine the rule of law. In Michael's view, it was necessary to enforce the true meaning of the ordinance in such a way as to continue to allow bicycles into the park.

Michael reasoned that although the authors of the ordinance had specifically intended to ban bicycles from the park, this specific intention was not the product of an arbitrary impulse. It had been generated by a more general intention: to ban those vehicles from the park that unreasonably endangered pedestrians and other persons enjoying the park's facilities. Michael argued that in order to enforce the original meaning of the ordinance properly, the council had to honor this more general intention of the law's authors. He claimed that if James and Lawrence were to be confronted with Erewhon's present economic and social condition, they would agree (given the benefits that bicycles might bring to Erewhon, as well as the citizenry's customary use of bicycles in Utopia Park) that bicycles do not pose an *unreasonable* hazard to other persons in the park.

But Michael's interpretive strategy contained a much more audacious claim: he held that even if James and Lawrence were to disagree with the present council members on the reasonableness of bicycles in Utopia Park, it was up to the present council to determine the most accurate understanding of James's and Lawrence's general intention. James and Lawrence had intended to ban unreasonably dangerous vehicles from the park, and the council was bound by the rule of law to follow that intention. It remained, however, the duty of the present council—and *only* the present council—to determine what the best present understanding of that general intention entailed.

By deploying the proper interpretive method, Michael claimed, the council could simultaneously enforce the original meaning of the ordinance and address the problems generated by the ever-changing context of the present interpretive moment.

Ronald rejected the approaches of both his colleagues. While Henry seemed willing to abandon all hope of rehabilitating the ordinance, and Michael appeared obsessed with producing an interpretation that could be characterized as faithful to the ordinance's original meaning, Ronald's concerns were somewhat different. He was just as convinced as his fellow council members of the desirability of permitting bicycles in Utopia Park, but in contrast to Henry's pragmatic approach and Michael's concern with historical integrity, Ronald wanted to generate a justification that would be, for lack of a better phrase, aesthetically pleasing.

To that effect, he argued that the ordinance should be treated not as evidence of a singular political event (i.e., the council vote of November 11, 1963) but as a textual object whose meaning changed over time. The goal of the object's interpreters should be guided by a political aesthetic to make the ordinance the best ordinance it could be within the genre of political events to which it belonged. Ronald stressed that the council members were far from wholly unconstrained in this task: they were limited by the language of the ordinance itself and by the political history of its interpretation. For instance, if the ordinance had happened to say "No bicycles are permitted in the park," or if it had been consistently understood by everyone as forbidding bicycles, it would be difficult to generate the necessary interpretive "fit" for an argument claiming that the ordinance actually allows bicycles in the park.

The language of the ordinance, however, was providentially ambiguous, and nothing in its interpretive history precluded the reading that they all longed to justify. Everyone on the council agreed that the most desirable understanding of the ordinance would permit bicycles in the park; Ronald argued that his strategy of interpretation would allow the ordinance to fulfill its potential as a legal object. The text could be interpreted in a plausible and aesthetically pleasing manner and still achieve the social goals that were the object of the genre of textual objects to which it belonged.

III

A blasphemous sect suggested that the searches should cease and that all men should juggle letters and symbols until they constructed, by an improbable gift of chance, these canonical books.—Jorge Luis Borges[13]

The foregoing arguments will no doubt seem familiar to those acquainted with recent disputes concerning constitutional interpretation. It is a field in which a classic interpretive conundrum is repeated over and over again: the text of the document generates a result which, in terms of contemporary law and politics, seems wholly unacceptable.

I will now discuss in a less oblique manner three grand strategies designed to deal with the constitutional text in such situations. These strategies, or some variation on them, make up a broad, though not exhaustive, typology of modern constitutional argument. As will become clear, two unifying characteristics link the three methods: all demand that we obey the Constitution, and none recommends that we read the constitutional text.

Henry Monaghan is the perfect originalist. His acerbic observations on the utopian arrogance of legal scholars have hit too close to home and are naturally dismissed out of hand; nevertheless, his suggestion that the Constitution itself might be the product of human beings remains a troubling thesis.

Monaghan effectively criticizes theories of constitutional interpretation which obscure or deviate from the idea that the meaning of the constitutional text is inseparable from the intentions of those who wrote it.[14] He is then faced with a sharp dilemma and the challenge that arises as a consequence of it. Monaghan admits that the meaning of the constitutional text cannot be reconciled with much of modern constitutional law. He acknowledges the validity of Paul Brest's claim that, at a minimum, all decisions that apply aspects of the Bill of Rights to the states, as well as the whole line of "right to privacy" cases and virtually all recent First Amendment decisions, are inconsistent with an accurate reading of the constitutional text.

This situation leaves Professor Monaghan with a major interpretive problem. He rejects out of hand Brest's elegant solution: "Why, [Brest] asks, should the constitutional text be authoritative at all for successor generations? It is, I recognize, logically possible to maintain some ground other than the written constitution as the first principle in constitutional theorizing; but I simply find this argument to be a barren one. . . . For the purposes of *legal* reasoning, the binding quality of the constitutional text is incapable of and not in need of further demonstration."[15] Monaghan treats as axiomatic the assertion that "the body politic can *at a specific point in time* [i.e., by encoding its will in a text] definitely order relationships, and that such an ordering is binding on all organs of government until changed by amendment."[16] This is, for him, the essence of a written constitution. Monaghan's dilemma, then, is a sharp one. He recognizes that reading a text means trying to determine what its author(s) intended to say, and that it is a fundamental claim of our legal rhetoric that the text of the Constitution is binding law on all branches of government. Enforcing an accurate reading of the constitutional text, however, would inevitably result in a massive destabilization of constitutional law because such a reading would necessarily overrule a substantial portion of modern constitutional doctrine. Yet if constitutional law cannot tolerate engagement with the constitutional text because of the state of constitutional doctrine, exactly what role is the word *constitutional* playing in this sentence? Monaghan's answer would no doubt be: certainly not one that is semantically coherent or politically edifying.

His own suggestions on how best to solve the dilemma remain tentative. Although he explicitly rejects Brest's proposal that we ignore the constitutional text when it seems prudent to do so, Monaghan's interpretive strategy is in the end difficult to distinguish from the program of his colleague: "The expectations so long generated by this body of constitutional law render unacceptable a full return to original intent theory in any pure, unalloyed form. While original intent may constitute the starting point for constitutional interpretation, it cannot now be recognized as the only legitimate mode of constitutional reasoning. To my mind, some theory of *stare decisis* is necessary to confine its reach. Of course, this is to accord an authoritative status to tradition in 'supplementing or derogating from' the constitutional text."[17] Monaghan concedes the great difficulties inherent in formulating such a theory but stops short of admitting that there would be little practical difference between it and Brest's "general, nontextual mode of constitutional analysis."[18] Indeed, the only real difference between the two theorists' approaches seems to be how much bike riding would have to take place in the park before each would declare the relevant ordinance irrelevant.

When it deals with the classic conundrum of the unacceptable constitutional text, original intent theory—even in Monaghan's strongly stated form—reverts to a kind of pragmatic anti-interpretation that has much in common with just those versions of constitutional theory that it finds most unacceptable. When reading the constitutional text will not do, ignore it: this radical idea is elegant and descriptively satisfying, but it fails to address precisely those concerns about judicial legitimacy that Monaghan identifies as the most compelling reasons for reading the Constitution rather than doing something else with it.

Michael Perry claims to have solved Henry Monaghan's dilemma.

Perry advocates "sophisticated originalism."[19] His interpretive strategy makes the following assertions: (1) a judge should enforce a constitutional provision according to its original meaning; (2) the meaning of a provision may have relatively specific aspects and a relatively general aspect; and (3) enforcing a provision means enforcing both the specific and the general aspects of that meaning.[20]

Perry uses the equal protection clause of the Fourteenth Amendment for illustrative purposes. He asks us to assume that a specific aspect of the meaning of the clause is that no state may discriminate on the basis of race, and that

> the most general aspect of the original meaning—the broadest articulation
> of the most general aspect warranted by the relevant materials—is that no

state may discriminate on the basis of "irrational prejudice." Assume also, however, that it is *not* a specific aspect of the original meaning of the equal protection clause that no state may discriminate on the basis of sex. . . . Given those assumptions, originalism authorizes a judge to enforce, in the name of the equal protection clause, not only the (relatively) specific principle that no state may discriminate on the basis of race, but also the (relatively) general principle that no state may discriminate on the basis of irrational prejudice.[21]

It makes no difference, according to Perry, whether or not the authors of the Fourteenth Amendment thought gender discrimination was a form of discrimination based on irrational prejudice. Perry admits that in all likelihood they did not. What matters is the underlying principle: "[That the ratifiers] did not believe that they were prohibiting a practice does not mean that the correct application of a principle they established does not prohibit the practice."[22]

The specific/general, narrow/broad, concept/conception move is an extremely common one in constitutional interpretation. Monaghan's dilemma is solved by specifying authorial intent at whatever level of generality is necessary to overcome the embarrassing implications of the text. This method allows the interpreter to discover that even if the authors of the Constitution specifically intended to allow a practice, the general principle from which they derived their specific intention might in fact prohibit that practice. For instance, in the context of the Eighth Amendment, Perry argues for the possibility that the death penalty "is *truly* a cruel or unusual punishment—notwithstanding that the ratifiers of the clause did not so believe."[23] I do not intend to offer a full-scale critique of Perry's interpretive account. Instead, I will argue that he cannot accurately be characterized as an advocate of *reading* the constitutional text when faced with the classic interpretive conundrum.

Perry claims that his brand of originalism is "elaborated *entirely without reference to authorial intentions*" (his emphasis).[24] This claim, of course, could not in a logical sense be strictly true: even if Perry's method actually advocated ignoring authorial intent (which it does not), such a method would still *refer* to the author(s), if only in an oppositional or dismissive manner. But Perry does not advocate ignoring authorial intent; he advocates discovering a dichotomy between the author's general intent and his or her specific intent, and then systematically privileging the former over the latter.

The distinction between specific and general intent is not completely empty. Take the question of cruel punishments. If I enact a statute barring cruel punishments, I might or might not consider capital punishment cruel. Suppose

I do not think it is cruel. It is clear that when I said "cruel punishments," then, I did not mean capital punishment. My general category of cruel punishments did not include the specific example of capital punishment. Now, suppose I later change my mind and come to believe that the death penalty *is* cruel. Has the meaning of the statute that I enacted changed? As a matter of interpreting my previous intentions, and hence the text I produced, clearly it has not: at the time, I used the general term *cruel* to capture a set of specific practices, which didn't include capital punishment; if I were to use the term now, it would include capital punishment. What has changed is what I *now* mean by "cruel," not what I *then* meant.[25]

But even if I were to concede that by changing my mind about cruelty I have somehow changed the meaning of the statute I previously enacted, this would not affect Perry's argument. For Perry, what counts is not what the text means by "cruel," or even what the author now thinks is cruel, but rather, what the interpreter thinks would be the best elucidation of the general principle that the author was invoking.[26]

To see why this is so, we can examine Perry's description of four varieties of originalism in the context of capital punishment and the Eighth Amendment. Perry presents three possible situations. In situation 1, the authors of the Eighth Amendment intended (or would have intended if they had considered the issue) the Eighth Amendment to prohibit the death penalty. In situation 2, the authors did not intend the Eighth Amendment to prohibit the death penalty because they never considered the possibility, and if they had considered the possibility they would have been uncertain as to whether or not it did (i.e., as far as its authors were concerned, the Eighth Amendment had nothing to say about the death penalty). In situation 3, the authors intended, or would have intended had they considered the issue, for the Eighth Amendment *not* to prohibit the death penalty.[27]

Perry then identifies what he considers the "four basic versions of original-ism." (1) In the strictest version of the theory, a court should invalidate capital punishment only in situation 1. (2) A less strict version would allow a court to invalidate capital punishment in either situation 1 or situation 2 if the court believes capital punishment violates the general principles that underlay the specific intentions of the Eighth Amendment's authors. (3) An even looser version of originalism would allow a court to invalidate capital punishment in all three situations if the court concludes that the death penalty violates the general principles behind the authors' intentions. (4) The least strict version of originalism is identical with the third version, except that in this manifestation a court would *not* invalidate capital punishment even in situation 1 if the court

concludes that capital punishment *does not* violate the general principle underlying the authors' specific intentions.[28] According to this version, it would be
perfectly legitimate for a judge to hold that the Eighth Amendment permits
drawing and quartering—even though the authors of the amendment specifically intended to prohibit that practice—if the judge believes that drawing and
quartering is not inconsistent with the relevant general principle.*

Perry asserts that it "is difficult to identify originalists today who defend
the first version of originalism, or even the second version," and claims that
even Robert Bork's latest elaboration of originalist theory rejects the first two
versions and "seems underdeterminate with respect to the choice between
the third and fourth versions." As for Perry himself, he is mildly inclined
toward the third version, but he suspects that in terms of actual political consequences "the difference between the third and fourth versions probably is not
great."[29]

I suspect that Perry is correct. An account of originalism that allows us to
"read" an amendment so as to prohibit capital punishment, even though the
authors of that amendment intended to allow the death penalty, will not differ
significantly in its actual consequences from an interpretive account that allows
us to "read" the amendment in a *less* prohibitory fashion than the authors
intended. Both methods are flexible enough to solve interpretive conundrums
that, after all, only arise because of the constraints of authorial (i.e., textual)
meaning.

We can easily understand the attractiveness of "sophisticated," or "moderate," originalism. It is a strategy that allows the interpreter to claim that he or
she is interpreting the author's text and no other, and yet at the same time to
generate readings that are in direct opposition to the author's meaning. It
allows us to combine, in a way that Monaghan's approach does not, ancestor

---

*At another point in his paper Perry states that "if the ratifiers believe that a particular practice
violated a constitutional provision . . . a court may not rule that the practice does not violate the
provision even if, in the court's view, the practice does not violate the general aspect of the original
meaning of the provision" (M. Perry, "The Legitimacy of Particular Conceptions of Constitutional
Interpretation," 77 *Va. L. Rev.* 669, 698 [1991]). Perry, then, apparently advocates version 3 of
originalism over version 4. (He in fact says that version 3 "may make the most sense.") Version 3,
Perry says, allows "the development (but not contradiction) of the original meaning of a constitutional provision (ibid.). Perry fails to explain why prohibiting a practice that the ratifiers specifically wished to allow (version 3) counts as the *development* of a constitutional provision, while
allowing a practice that the ratifiers specifically wished to prohibit (version 4) counts as a *contrac-
tion* of the original meaning. For instance, to a Kantian retributivist, allowing drawing and quartering (if the moral law demanded this punishment for certain crimes) would obviously count as a
development of the Eighth Amendment's meaning.

worship with pragmatic politics, and to practice "interpretation" as a form of textual rehabilitation.

But if a text means only what its author intends it to mean—no more and no less—then how does one characterize a program which demands that we stick to the author's text but not to the author's meaning? Such an interpretive strategy requires that we *systematically misread* the text. Only a program of systematic misreading allows us simultaneously to retain the author's text and our meaning within the same interpretive matrix. By specifying authorial intent at a level of generality that is nearly meaningless,[30] the systematic misreader can generate interpretations that are diametrically opposed to the author's meaning, yet claim fidelity to the general principles that must underlie any specific belief.

When reading the constitutional text leads to unacceptable consequences, Professor Monaghan suggests that we ignore the document, while Professor Perry provides us with a system of almost Ptolemaic complexity by which we may systematically misread it. In what could perhaps be characterized as the final stage in an evolutionary series of hermeneutic gestures, Ronald Dworkin refuses either selectively to ignore or tentatively to rehabilitate the offending text; instead, he boldly jettisons the object of interpretation altogether.[31] What Monaghan and Perry only hint at in a partial or indirect fashion, Dworkin asserts in brazenly pragmatic style: the interpretive dilemma is best solved by severing the Constitution from its authors.

Dworkin considers the possibility of treating the Constitution (or any other statute) as an act of communication, and then rejects this idea, which he calls the "speaker's meaning" theory of interpretation: "The speaker's meaning theory begins in the idea . . . that legislation is an act of communication to be understood on the simple model of speaker and audience, so that the commanding question in legislative interpretation is what a particular speaker or group 'meant' in some canonical act of utterance."[32]

What counts for Dworkin is not what a statute meant, but rather what it can plausibly be made to mean:

> [An ideal judge] interprets not just the statute's text but its life, the process that begins before it becomes law and extends far beyond that moment. He aims to make the best he can of this continuing story, and his interpretation therefore changes as the story develops. He does not identify particular people as the exclusive "framers" of a statute and then attend only to their hopes or expectations or concrete convictions. . . . Each of the

political considerations he brings to bear on his overall question, how to make the statute's story the best it can be, identifies a variety of people and groups and institutions whose statements or convictions might be relevant in different ways.[33]

For Dworkin, then, the text of a statute is of relatively little importance. The task of the judge is to attach those meanings to the words of a legislative enactment that will make the legislation "the best it can be."[34] The wise judge "interprets history in motion, because the story he must make as good as it can be is the whole story through his decision and beyond. He does not amend out-of-date statutes to suit new times, as the metaphysics of speaker's meaning would suggest. He recognizes what the old statutes have since become."[35]

The question that Dworkin never directly faces (because of either pragmatic reticence or formalist confusion) is how old statutes acquire new meanings. If the speaker's meaning does not account for the statute's meaning, then what does? Dworkin's answer appears to be: the interpretive process. For Dworkin, once the statute has been severed from its author(s), it is free to "enter into new relations" with its interpreters.[36] Their task is then to make the autonomous textual object the best it can be while taking into account the constraints of history, language, and politics that all interpreters must operate within.[37]

The good interpreter, then, reauthors the statute, jettisoning the offending text and replacing it with a text that makes for a better story. Dworkin's own work provides many enchanting examples of this very process. For instance, the authors of the Fourteenth Amendment wrote: "Nor shall any state deprive any person of life, liberty, or property, without due process of law; nor deny to any person within its jurisdiction the equal protection of the laws."[38]

Written by a group of upper-class white males in the middle of the nineteenth century, this is mere rhetorical praise of formal equality. It does not prohibit segregated schools,[39] or address the rights of women,[40] or have anything to say about matters of sexual preference.[41]

On the other hand, Dworkin's Fourteenth Amendment reads: "Nor shall any state deprive any person of life, liberty, or property, without due process of law; nor deny to any person within its jurisdiction the equal protection of the laws."[42]

The contrast is astounding. Dworkin, a contemporary of John Rawls, does not define equality as a series of formal gestures, but as a state in which the sovereign treats each individual with equal concern and respect.[43] Such an approach clearly prohibits segregated schools.[44] Nor are women ignored: while the original text speaks of "persons" and sees only men as political actors,

Dworkin's text comprehends gender discrimination as a basic affront to the concept of equal protection.[45] An even more startling contrast is to be found in the attitudes of the two texts to questions of sexual orientation: the nineteenth-century document completely ignores the issue, while Dworkin's amendment easily encompasses such questions at its core.[46]

Through the process of *reauthoring* Dworkin offers us an aesthetically pleasing, if complex,[47] way out of the labyrinth of the classic interpretive conundrum. By detaching the Constitution from its authors, the object of interpretation becomes available for many pleasant procedures that help make it the best Constitution it can be. The good interpreter "recognizes what the old statute [has] since become";[48] that is, he or she pours the old textual meaning out of the Constitution's linguistic skin and pours in the new wine of enlightened political theory—in the form of a reauthored text.

IV

There is no intellectual exercise which is not ultimately useless.—Jorge Luis Borges[49]

Why must a text mean what its author intended it to mean? After all, Professor Dworkin has observed, "we can understand the equal protection clause as forbidding racial segregation without supposing that any particular historical statesman or draftsman intended that it should do this. We can read *Hamlet* in a psychodynamic way without supposing that Shakespeare either did or could have intended that we do so."[50] Now it must be admitted that Dworkin's objection seems intuitively plausible. If we *can* seem to do these things, what becomes of the claim that a text means only what its author intended? I submit that Dworkin's claim appears to be coherent (let alone plausible) only because we commonly confuse two distinct entities: on the one hand, the *text,* and on the other, the *writing* within which the text is encoded.

Consider Dworkin's own example. The text of *Hamlet* is a speech act. It is a communicative gesture or series of gestures by which a certain author expressed a number of thoughts, beliefs, aesthetic impulses, and so forth. Can we read the text of *Hamlet* as a dramatic commentary on Freud's ideas concerning the Oedipal complex? To do so, we would have to assume that Shakespeare was familiar with Freud's work; otherwise, it would be impossible for the text of the play to make such an implicit allusion. Dworkin believes that an alternative reading is possible: we can ignore what Shakespeare meant by the marks that constitute the text of *Hamlet,* and devise an "interpretation" of those marks which assumes they are making Freudian allusions. While one can readily admit that such a *reauthoring* of the marks is possible, the question remains, Does such a procedure count as an interpretation of the *text* of *Hamlet*? Apparently, Dworkin believes that it does, because he fails to make a distinction between a text (the singular speech act of a particular author) and a writing (the particular set of marks that make up a text).

For instance, I could begin an essay on suicide with the words "To be or not to be: that is the question." Obviously, I am not the author of the first sentence of Hamlet's famous soliloquy. My sentence and Shakespeare's are verbally identical, yet they are two separate texts. Although it is logically possible to read Shakespeare's text as if it contained an allusion to my essay, it would be empirically absurd to do so.

The realization that the same set of marks, the same *writing*, can contain two or more texts solves the puzzle of Dworkin's objection. Once we realize that language is always a set of constantly shifting conventions—that nothing exists between the meaning of speech acts and the meaninglessness of marks—and that therefore a particular set of marks can mean anything, we will not make Dworkin's mistake of confusing the text with the marks that compose it.

Another way of characterizing Dworkin's error is to describe it as the imagining of a *preinterpretive state* in which texts exist in temporary autonomy from both author and reader: "Justices who are called liberal and those who are called conservative agree about which words make up the Constitution as a matter of preinterpretive text."[51] But there can be no preinterpretive text, because even identifying certain words as constituting a particular text—and not some other text that uses the same words—is itself an interpretive act. The mere act of *identifying* a text as a text requires that we simultaneously identify, on some level, its author(s).

I repeat these points because I am well aware that the idea that a text means only what its author intended it to mean strikes many people as deeply counterintuitive. In our culture we habitually force our ideas about language into an essentially formalist paradigm.[52] This paradigm produces the fiction of the autonomous text, free from both author and reader, whose very autonomy makes it available for interpretation, or, more precisely, for the proper "interpretive method." When even as subtle a thinker as Ronald Dworkin routinely conflates the putative object of interpretation (the text of the Constitution, the text of a statute, the text of *Hamlet*) with the physical marks that encode the interpretive object, it is not surprising that the claim that a text means only what its author intended it to mean seems bizarre, or even dangerous.[53]

At this point, it would be natural for those, like Dworkin, who assert that a text can mean things the author never intended it to mean to claim that my account of textual meaning merely splits semantic hairs. I use the term *text* (so this objection would say) in a limited sense: I mean by it roughly what Dworkin means by "speaker's meaning." Those who prefer a hermeneutical approach use the term *text* to signify both what I have called the text and what I have termed the writing within which the text is encoded.

Such an objection fails to take into account two related points. First, the statement that a particular account of textual meaning "merely" splits semantic hairs implies that clarification of the terms of debate is not an important function (some modern philosophers would say *the* most important function) of intellectual discourse. Identifying just what we are talking about when we talk about texts is a necessary precondition to coherent debate about textual interpretation. The second point is an illustration of the first: if the distinction between a text and a writing is properly maintained, it becomes clear that while one may prefer to deal with a writing rather than with an author's text, it is nevertheless impossible to *interpret* a writing in the sense that one interprets texts.

If a text means what its author intended it to mean, then *interpreting* a text means, by definition, trying to determine what its author meant. It follows logically that the words that form any text could, in principle, mean anything at all (since the meaning of a text is identical with its author's intention, which itself is not amenable to theoretical regulation), and that no writing could mean anything whatsoever (because the marks themselves, separated from their author's intention, are meaningless).

If this account of textual meaning is correct, two general implications for the interpretive theory of texts follow. The first is that there can be no such theory: that is, there can be no general methodological prescription for how one goes about getting good textual interpretations. Hence, the project of producing a *theory* (that is, a general method) for determining the best way to read a text becomes empty when we realize that reading a text means trying to figure out what its author intended to say, and nothing more. And this task can have no theoretical content: it is essentially empirical.*

Second, we cannot interpret *a writing* because a writing in itself has no

---

*Since there is no limit to what someone can intend something to mean—or, to put this another way, since anyone can use anything to mean anything—there is no point in trying to devise a *general* interpretive procedure, an interpretive *method,* that will help resolve interpretive controversies. The object of every interpretive controversy, when it really is an interpretive controversy, is always and only a particular historical fact, and there is no general way to determine what any particular historical fact might be. No general belief, or if one prefers, no *theory* about the nature of interpretation offers any help in deciding the meaning of any particular text" (S. Knapp, "Practice, Purpose, and Interpretive Controversy," in *Pragmatism in Law and Society,* ed. Michael Brint and William Weaver [1991], at 323).

meaning. "Interpreting" the Constitution as a set of marks rather than as a text is identical with "interpreting" the Grand Canyon or marks made by the desert wind. The Grand Canyon can be made to mean anything at all with equal validity by everyone who views it because, like the physical marks that constitute a writing, it has no a priori meaning.[54] Considered as a writing, the Constitution—like any other writing—means nothing (or, if one prefers, anything) at all. Considered as a text, it can mean only one thing: what its authors intended it to mean.

In other words, although we may well disagree about what the author of a text *meant*, we cannot in any meaningful sense disagree about the best *way* to interpret a text. Such a disagreement would have significance only if a valid distinction could be maintained between the meaning of a text and the author's meaning.

Imagine, reader whom I imagine, that you are a practitioner of "constitutional interpretation." If my argument seems plausible, then the situation appears bleak. On the one hand, the constitutional text has been unmasked as a speech act or acts; that is, as the limited mental product of limited minds—minds limited by the knowledge, the prejudices, the historical circumstances, and the inevitably disappointing capacities of a certain group of human beings; in other words, by the qualities of its authors. On the other hand, the writing which contains the constitutional text offers no help at all to those who believe that law—even constitutional law—should authorize or constrain or at least guide the legal decision maker.

Even the most passionate proponents of originalism admit that the text of the Constitution is an inadequate source for much of contemporary constitutional law. Even the most fervent supporters of "presentminded interpretation" admit that some form of textual constraint must exist in order to give constitutional law legitimacy.[55] Yet if nothing exists between the inevitable semantic limitations of the constitutional text and the semantic emptiness of the writing within which that text is encoded, the whole enterprise of contemporary constitutional interpretation would seem to be founded on a mistake. No one, it turns out, actually recommends *reading* the Constitution: instead we are asked to ignore or misread or reauthor that troublesome text.

But where, we might well ask, does this leave the question of legal and political legitimacy? It seems like a strange ritual indeed: our most sacred secular text is continually honored by our cultural rhetoric as all the while we devise ever more complex strategies for avoiding contact with its meaning.

Now I wish to introduce the following idea. For the purposes of constitutional adjudication, the Constitution is not a text; it is a sacred or canonical writing. That is, it no longer functions primarily as a speech act, but as a cultural artifact which mimics a text and provides occasions for misreading and reauthoring. Sacred and canonical writings are, by their nature, required to perform work within a culture that is beyond the capacities of a mere text, and although they begin their lives as texts—as speech acts—they inevitably become detextualized as they gain sacred or canonical status.

Prime examples of this phenomenon are provided by the Bible and the works of Shakespeare.[56] Of course, the Bible is, within the context of Western culture, the paradigmatic instance of a sacred writing. It is a text that has been all things to all the peoples of our culture, and it continues to metamorphose to meet the needs of the present day. Shakespeare, at least to English-speaking peoples, represents the best example of a canonical writer: a man whose writings have achieved such status within his culture that they are analogous to a kind of literary sacred text. When we consider Shakespeare's unmatched position within the hierarchy of secular culture, it is perhaps not surprising to discover that his texts, too, have been transformed by a multiplicity of "interpretations" into whatever we need them to be. The following examples represent the tiniest fraction of this phenomenon: whole libraries could be, and have been, filled with the products of a cultural imperative that demands of these writings more than any text could possibly give.[57]

According to Hans Walter Wolff, the multiplicity of the Old Testament texts "resists any principle of exposition which seeks to determine the contents of the texts according to a predetermined schema."[58] John J. Davies believes that the Bible is a unitary text and can be properly understood only if it is read with its overall unifying schema already in mind.[59]

Edgar McKnight has discovered that the Bible is best interpreted through the lens of modern literary theory;[60] James Smart asserts with equal vigor that literary theory is useless if one seeks an accurate reading of that text.[61]

Walter Bradley and Roger Olsen, physical scientists and Christian believers, examined the evidence and concluded that the Creation story told in Genesis is not intended to be taken literally: for them, the text speaks of metaphoric "days" that represent geological epochs.[62] Henry Morris retorts that the text demands to be taken literally, and that the Genesis story is incoherent unless the word *day* is intended to mean, in this context, the period between the rising and setting of the sun.[63]

Proponents of liberation theology have discovered that the Bible is a product of its sociohistoric setting and can only be understood as such.[64] The Jewish theologian Martin Buber knew that the Bible is "an infinite Book" that contains "eternal reality" in its text and argued that temporally limited readings obscure or pervert the text's true meaning.[65]

Virginia Mollenkott has affirmed that the Bible reveals God to be an essentially maternal presence in a feminine, nurturing universe. She holds that the Bible is replete with images of a feminine Godhead that protects and comforts Her people.[66] Phyliss Trible argues that the biblical text unveils a world of patriarchal terror where misogyny, rape, and the total subordination of the Feminine are the norms.[67]

These examples, I repeat, represent the merest glimpse of a tiny fraction of some of the conflicting contemporary interpretations brought to bear on the biblical text. And this amazing heterogeneity of understanding is not a situation peculiar to contemporary readings of the Bible. According to medieval theologians, every passage of Holy Scripture needed to be interpreted in four distinct fashions: literally, morally, allegorically, and anagogically.[68] This method led, naturally, to an endless series of disputes over the true meaning of key passages in the biblical text.

A glance at Shakespearean scholarship reveals a similar interpretive situation. For instance, Bernard Grebanier claims that *The Merchant of Venice* is a sensitive treatment of a moneylender who happens to be a Jew,[69] while J. L. Cardozo sees the play as an anti-Semitic tract.[70] The distinguished critic Frank Kermode argues that Shylock is the consistent villain of the drama;[71] his equally distinguished colleague Harold Goddard claims that the play's text reveals Shylock to be the essentially innocent victim of his hard-hearted Christian neighbors.[72]

Similar conflicts of understanding are replete in the criticism of every Shakespeare play. For example, Marianne Novy sees in *The Taming of the Shrew* a celebration of patriarchy;[73] Coppella Kahn reads that play as a subtle critique of patriarchal practices within marriage.[74] And when King Lear expires with dead Cordelia in his arms, O. J. Campbell argues that the old king dies of joy, believing Cordelia to be alive. Campbell finds in the text of the play a reassertion of divine justice: "Lear has found in [Cordelia's] unselfish love the one companion who is willing to go up with him . . . to the throne of the Everlasting Judge."[75]

James Stampfer draws a different conclusion from the drama's climax: "Even those who have fully repented, done penance, and risen to the tender regard of sainthood can be hunted down, driven insane, and killed by the most agonizing extremes of passion."[76] Stampfer examines Lear's death and concludes that the text is telling us that "we inhabit an imbecile universe."[77]

These examples, again, merely scratch the surface. It is safe to say that every well-known passage in all of Shakespeare's plays has generated a multitude of contradictory interpretations.

What special quality or qualities do these texts have that results in this extraordinary interpretive situation? How can different interpreters conclude that the very same words claim that the world is six thousand and four billion years old; that the universe is patriarchal and matriarchal; that there is a supreme moral world order and that we live in a nihilistic void? I submit that it is no particular quality of the texts themselves, but rather a quality of the interpretive situation into which the texts are subsumed that leads to this endless multiplication of contradictory meanings.

In the case of a sacred writing, the interpretive situation dictates that the holy text remain inerrant, or at least essentially true, in the midst of fundamental cultural shifts concerning questions of religion, morality, science, and politics. Hence the same words of God have been found to support capitalism and communism, patriarchy and feminism, creationism and evolution, and many more mutually exclusive dialectics within the synthetic conflict that passes for human truth.[78]

A canonical writing fulfills a similar function within the realm of secular culture. Shakespeare is "our" greatest writer: it is only natural that we would find the crucial beliefs and taboos of the contemporary interpretive situation faithfully mirrored in his obliging text. The issues of the moment become, as it were, canon fodder for our interpretations of writings that have been granted a kind of sacred place within the current cultural hierarchy.

As a writing becomes sacred or canonical it necessarily absorbs many texts besides that of the author. Today, we can with some effort recover pieces of Freud's Shakespeare, Coleridge's Shakespeare, Johnson's Shakespeare, and even Shakespeare's Shakespeare.[79] It is a commonplace to acknowledge that the Bible of the Israelites is not the Bible of the modern Jews, which in turn is not the Bible of Martin Luther, which is still less the Bible of Saint Thomas Aquinas.[80] In all these cases, the ineluctable demands of belief required that the author's text give way before the misreadings and reauthorings of different cultures and different times. The protean mutability of such texts blends with the imperishable marks of the writing within which they are encoded to create a cultural icon whose meaning is always changing but whose essence is mystically felt to remain the same. It is this paradoxical quality of the sacred or canonical writing that allows it to produce the cultural cohesion and sense of unity that is beyond the power of any text. And it is this same quality that enables the Constitution to fulfill its function as a unifying cultural artifact—not as a text, but as a canonical writing.

I close this text by answering two imaginary objections posed by my imaginary reader. The first is of a descriptive nature: perhaps, the argument goes, these baroque speculations have some validity in relation to the cabalistic jurisprudence of the First or Eighth or Fourteenth Amendments, or of the commerce clause, but surely we still read the constitutional text when it proclaims that the Senate "shall be composed of two Senators from each State," or that a President "shall hold his office during the term of four years," or that the Twenty-first Amendment repeals the Eighteenth.

I freely admit that we do still read the constitutional text when it proclaims such things; and it is precisely because we still read these clauses (as opposed to ignoring or misreading or reauthoring them) that they do not provide occasions for constitutional adjudication and "interpretation." More than one observer has in effect argued that if it should suddenly become highly desirable, for example, that someone less than thirty-five years old run for president, the relevant portion of the constitutional text might well be jettisoned in favor of whatever ingenious misreading would do the necessary "interpretive" work to allow this result.[81] That is to say, portions of the Constitution are still texts to the extent that they remain irrelevant to the resolution of contemporary cases and controversies.

The second objection is, inevitably, normative. Fancy ideas about intention and meaning are all very well, objects my well-meaning, well-intentioned, but predictably misguided interlocutor. Yet we chosen ones, we happy few, we legal academics, have a special responsibility of awesome dimensions. Our interpretations, especially our constitutional interpretations, march on "a field of pain and death,"[82] and we must therefore always keep in mind that a "false" interpretation is not necessarily a "bad" interpretation.[83] Perhaps if we were to examine the question very closely we would discover that we don't actually advocate reading the Constitution, but might it not be better, after all, to keep this knowledge even from ourselves?

Such an objection makes at least two unwarranted assumptions. It posits, quite unreasonably, that the insights of intellectuals have a regular or predictable impact on the power relations which exist in a culture that routinely ignores them. And it assumes that the normative implications of this particular insight are self-evident. I believe a text can mean only what its author intended it to mean, but the normative consequences (if any) that this belief has for the practice of constitutional interpretation remain unclear. Perhaps if this account of textual meaning were to become widely accepted we would discover that "reading" a canonical writing should involve looking for the best synthesis of the texts it has encompassed. Perhaps some would conclude that a legal document that plays the cultural role assigned to our Constitution must inevitably be read, then misread, then reauthored, and finally rewritten in an interpretive cycle that ends where it began: with an author's newborn text. For my part, I am inclined to accept the tolerant wisdom of an imperial poet:

There are nine and sixty ways
Of constructing tribal lays
And every single one of them is right.[84]

Those who long for justice require certitude. The intolerable inadequacies of language are captured in G. K. Chesterton's eloquent words: "Man knows that there are in the soul tints more bewildering, more numberless, and more nameless than the colours of an autumn forest. . . . Yet he seriously believes that these things can every one of them, in all their tones and semi-tones, in all their blends and unions, be accurately represented by an arbitrary system of grunts and squeals. He believes that an ordinary civilized stockbroker can really produce out of his own inside noises which denote all the mysteries of memory and all the agonies of desire."[85]

It is absurd to imagine that a single instance of human speech, limited by the contingencies of history and pure chance, could demarcate the ultimate boundaries of a people's fundamental law. A text—any text—is subject to the caducity and corruption of all mortal endeavors: the Constitution is not. The constitutional text might be the work of malevolent demiurgi or mere men, but the Constitution itself—protean, unchanging, responsive to our endless needs—could only be the work of a god.

The cold eye of rationalism mocks such assertions and demands that we face the reality of political choice with no illusions about our ancestors, our texts, or ourselves. Such skepticism fails to reckon with the human need for some semblance of communion with the divine. It laughs at the lines of reverent pilgrims who file past the fading symbols on a piece of parchment that, for them, in some way embodies who they are.

Before we tear away the veil of sacredness that obscures a merely human text from our view, we might remember Elijah and Moses, who covered their faces before God; Isaiah, who was terrified when he saw the One whose glory fills the Earth; the rabbi Simeon ben-Azai, who saw Paradise and died; the Midrashim, who will not speak the Shem Hamephorash, the Secret Name of God.

We may choose to utter impious words until the Constitution is nothing but its transitory text; we may reject the seeming absurdities and superstitions of our cultural practices; and we may find that we do not need sacred or canonical writings, and that the constitutional text itself is adequate to our state. But I suspect that if the Constitution ceases to exist, it will, once again, become necessary to invent it.

LEVINSON. I'd like to hone in more now on what it is you do when you teach, because one of the questions that has plagued me is how to figure out what I'm doing in the classroom, given that I have a certain skepticism about the legal enterprise as traditionally defined, et cetera. I am curious, whether you teach constitutional law or property or whatever, about the following: given the views you express in the book and have now repeated in our conversation, what is your self–job description in terms of your role as a teacher of students who want to be lawyers?

CAMPOS. Well, I've been thinking about this, partially because I knew you were going to ask a question like that. So I think I have actually managed to formulate a little bit more of a self-description than I would have before. And it has two parts. First, I see my job as giving the students whatever equipment I can give them to begin to make them protolawyers. I teach them a rhetoric, and I teach them how to manipulate that rhetoric, which is a starting point for a lawyer, but obviously just a starting point. But I don't believe I can teach them much more than that within the context of the law school classroom. Second, I try to get them to see the legal categories and vocabularies and concepts that they are learning to manipulate in an unhabitual way. Almost immediately in their legal education, they are habituated to a certain way of thinking about law, and the role I see myself as having here besides habituating them to think about law in that way is to unhabituate them to thinking about law in those sorts of ways. It's hard to describe, but the student who can read a plain meaning argument without a sense, on some level, that this is a strange kind of game, that it seems strange when you step away from it, is a student that I haven't reached, at least in my legislation class. I think that this second thing, this unhabituation, is actually quite practically useful to them, and might actually be more practically useful than the rhetorical habituation which I initially give them, in my first-year property class.

LEVINSON. This generates one paradox which I find myself going through almost every year. I teach a constitutional law course that is deeply influenced by my colleague Philip Bobbitt and his notion that there is a set of what he calls "modalities" that constitute what Jack Balkin calls "the grammar of law talk"; that to be a lawyer means to learn this grammar and say well-formed sentences in law talk. This is very different from most of my colleagues' courses. Almost invariably, in the third or fourth week of the course, one hears what in the Book of Exodus is called murmurings of the students; why am I doing this to them while other sections are marching through cases learning doctrines, and so on? And one of my responses is a version of yours. "Look, believe it or not but trust me, it is true. I'm making you better lawyers, because one of the things you are going to discover when you go out in the world is that all that it means to be a lawyer is to be able to use the modalities. And sometimes doctrinalism is going to be a great modality, and I'll teach you how that kind of argument works, but sometimes you are going to need to make originalist arguments and prudential arguments and plain meaning arguments. You've got to know how all of these work, and I'm really your friend and your ally. I'm trying to make you the best lawyer you can be."

Now, I always feel guilty after making this talk, because, among other things, it presupposes that being a lawyer is a terrific thing to be. What this boils down to is an implicit claim that we really have figured out the best way to train good lawyers, and we are just happily going into our classrooms saying, "I am delighted to be preparing another generation of students to march into Covington and Burling or Legal Services offices, or whatever it is they choose to do." But the whole point of these remarks is that I do feel a certain angst and tension because I have all sorts of problems with what it is that lawyers do and whether really and truly I want to be spending my life training people to be "effective lawyers." Do you feel any of these tensions?

CAMPOS. Yes, I do feel these tensions. I would like to think, and sometimes I do think, that in training people to be good lawyers I am also training them to have a certain distance from the rhetoric that they are deploying. Because in my mind the lawyers who do the most damage are not crooked lawyers, are not incompetent lawyers, but are the true believers—are the ones who are charging out there, waving the First Amendment or whatever it might be—shouting, "There is a fundamental right to this, and if we have to blow up this social edifice in order to validate this right we are going to do it because the law requires it to be so."

Here I think the relevant analogy is that of the religious fanatic. Somebody who has no doubts about what God is requiring that he do is a dangerous person. And somebody who has that same attitude about the law is also a dangerous person. So I like to think if they acquire a certain degree of distance from the enterprise to which they are being habituated and which they are learning to manipulate, they will not be the kind of lawyers who do the sort of damage that is done by the zealot.

SCHLAG. My approach, I think, is very similar to Paul's. In a real sense, I try to teach the students how the law is put together. I try to afford students the possibilities of not believing in the law, of disbelieving the law, of thinking this is not a very good way to solve problems, not a very good way of running a social system. And I give them the opportunity to think about these things. I explore these issues because I think it is much better to explore those issues in law school than to explore them twenty years after being a lawyer, or a judge, or anything else. I think students are owed a certain degree of candor about what the practice of law is and how it differs radically from the self-congratulatory representations of law they encounter in case law and legal scholarship.

Here it might help to analogize to a different domain. What is taught at West Point? What is taught about how to conduct a war? I mean, do teachers basically talk only about honor and the virtues of war? I hope not. In the same sense, I don't think that, in law school, one should constantly be celebrating the aspects of law and constantly crafting pleasing normative fantasies about what law can do—any more than one ought to be creating pleasant fantasies about what can be done with an army.

LEVINSON. At this point I simply have to insert that there are many things I like about this collection, but one of them is the particular section of "Normativity and the Politics of Form" on *L.A. Law*'s empire, which I read and immediately assigned in a legal profession course, because it raises so many rich questions about this assumption. That being said, I am still left with the question of whether I wanted students to end up saying, "Well, you know, I really think I'm going to find something else to do with my life," or whether they should simply assimilate it and say, "Oh, yeah, I can handle this," and go off unchanged in terms of their conception of being a lawyer.

SCHLAG. I also think, and this might be a cop-out, but some degree of responsibility has to rest with the student for choosing law. Now, there is at least one sense in which this is a real cop-out, and that is this: the image that college students have about what it is to be a lawyer are completely unrealistic. The culture sells an image of what it is to be a lawyer that is radically unrealistic. But nonetheless, I think some degree of responsibility has to be placed upon the student for deciding to go to law school.

SMITH. I am just wondering whether this might mean that maybe the answer to your question, Sandy, is just the opposite of the one that you said you sometimes adopt. The question is why is it appropriate for you to add a lot of theoretical content to your course that students might not be getting in other constitutional law courses? And your answer is that it will make them better lawyers, and it's a good thing to be a better lawyer. But the answer might be that you will make them worse lawyers in a certain sense, and it will be better to be a worse lawyer; a much more self-doubting kind of lawyer might be a better kind of person and have a better life to lead than someone who is really a better lawyer.

LEVINSON. I think one could well argue that the kinds of decisions now made by people called lawyers who are defined by having received a certain kind of legal education would be better made by people who'd gotten a different sort of education. I'm very sympathetic to that notion; but that, in some ways, is different from focusing on what it is that lawyers do when acting as advocates for clients and things like that.

SCHLAG. I want to go back to the point at which you started talking about the angst that is implicit in telling students that you are training them to be better lawyers. I think I have that sort of angst too. I sometimes give the kind of response you have described. I think there's a much more generalized problem, though, with law school teaching. And we, the three of us—the four of us—are not exempt from it. But neither is it limited to people like us. I think there was once a time in which legal academics and lawyers believed that they could represent private interests—the interests of clients—and at the same time serve the public good: maintain the rule of law. So you had this happy coincidence between the pursuit of private interests and public good. And within the legal profession there was a time when this was just taken as being self-evident. Now, by contrast, I think it is self-evident that this is not the case at all. Now, having a good lawyer, in the sense of having someone who will effectively represent you, is understood to have nothing whatsoever to do with the public good, except to the extent that your lawyer will represent your private interests as being the public good. This is a question which I am interested in writing on. I haven't seen much of anybody pay *serious* attention to this question: What is the relation between the representation of the interest of a client—a private client— and the achievement of the public good? I haven't seen much serious discussion of that. I think there can't be any serious discussion by those who are committed to the rule of law. And that's because the answer is obvious: There is a wide gulf between the two.

In terms of training lawyers, I don't think that too many people in the legal academy are really very serious about teaching students to become effective lawyers in the sense of teaching effective representation of the private interests of clients. I think there's a reason for that; in fact, several. One reason is that if you are committed to the effective representation of the private interests of clients, you have to engage in actions that most academics would find reprehensible—what Leff and Dauer call "wheedling, needling, intimidation, harassment and the like." This is what lawyers do today, and, very often, this is what they must do. I think legal academics don't want to teach such skills. They shy away from this, even though that's what the practice of law is today. Besides, they probably don't know how to teach such things.

LEVINSON. Well, but to come, in a sense, closer to home in the courses we do teach, lawyers, on occasion, do write briefs or do make arguments to judges or administrative officials, in addition to the wheedling and needling, and one of the ways I define what I'm doing is teaching them law talk and increasing the probability that they will be able to write an effective brief for whoever hires them, whether it's the slave owner or the member of the underground railroad protecting the fugitive slave, because I, in fact, spent a lot of time on slavery. You talk about choice, and at one level I profess myself indifferent to the choices they make. It's like teaching them how to speak French, that I'm going to teach them the grammatical structure and then whether they say—and I don't speak French, so—"*Je t'aime*" or "All Jews should be gassed" is irrelevant so long as they get the grammar right. And I can say, "Well, yes, you've got the subject-verb agreement, you've got the cases right," or whatever; or, "No. Your sentiment, 'peace should come to the world tomorrow'—noble sentiment, you got the grammar wrong," as opposed to the perfectly well-formed abhorrent sentiment.

I think part of our own idealism that took us into law was that there was some linkage between a well-formed sentence in law talk and goodness in the world. And what we have all reacted to is a loss of belief in that connection. At best, it is an entirely contingent connection. I think it would truly be the source of despair if we thought the necessary connection ran the other way, and I'd be interested if any of you think the connection runs the other way; that is, to engage in law talk is necessarily to make the world a worse place. My own view is simply that there's no reason to think it necessarily makes the world a better place, and very often will make the world a worse place, because these are rhetorical techniques that can be used for good or for ill, the way French grammar can be used for good or for ill.

Ought one feel comfortable with this kind of formal indifference to how our teachings will be used? Quite obviously, it's not going to help if we say, "Now, students, I certainly hope you never use these for bad purposes." That's just claptrap that our students will legitimately dismiss. We know that what we're teaching can be used for ill as well as for good. Is this simply part of being an adult that we have to realize that and go on with our normal lives, our normal lives being the training of people to fill the social role of lawyers being hired by private clients who are themselves indifferent to the public interest?

CAMPOS. I'd like to respond to that. In my legislation class, I have to deal, of course, with this question of private interest versus public interest. I have to confess I think the structuring of political discourse in that way is pretty incoherent under present circumstances. I don't know what the public interest is, and I don't know how one would go about talking about the public interest as being something which has a kind of identity which can be separated out from that plural and political world out there. Now that's sort of a side point to my main reaction to your statement. I've come from a somewhat different cultural background than most people who go into legal academia in that all of my family, with the exception of my immediate family, were born and have always lived in Mexico. And in Mexico it is simply understood that the function of law is to maintain the present power structure so that the rich can remain rich and the poor can remain poor, and anybody who would think otherwise would be considered somewhat naive. So I guess I have a certain degree of cultural inoculation, perhaps, to the more highly idealized and romanticized view of law that I believe many people in the legal academy came in with. But to pursue something that Pierre said earlier, it's not merely that legal academics—certain types of legal academics—tend to equate the rule of law with producing good things: it's that they see the instantiation of law in society, the activation of legal mechanisms, to be almost a good in and of itself. It's as if you had military strategists who believed that machine-gunning enemy villages is *in itself* a desirable thing. It's as if you had oncologists who believed that people should have chemotherapy for breakfast as a matter of course, whether or not they happened to be sick. Now, that doesn't mean that machine guns and chemotherapy are necessarily immoral. Far from it. I would assume that most people think that military force is something that needs to be exercised, and needs to be exercised well from time to time, and that chemotherapy is something that needs to be available and needs to be used properly, but that nevertheless the deployment of these things is always to be done with a certain degree of regret.

SMITH. There's another side to this, though. You've invoked Grant Gilmore, and maybe even Gilmore would say, "Well, yeah, if there are going to be disputes in society, then we're going to have to have some way to resolve them. But it would be nicer if we didn't even have them. So in that sense it would be better if we didn't even have law at all." But social coordination is more than just dispute resolution. So in opposition to Gilmore, someone could invoke, say, John Finnis, who would say, "No, law *is* a good thing. We need it not just because people fight and hurt each other, but because it allows for coordination of joint efforts, and without it you couldn't have that."

You could compare this to teaching somebody French. You don't know whether they're going to use it for good or bad, but there is still something good about giving people skills that will allow them to communicate with other people. By and large, communication seems to be prima facie a good thing, even though it might be abused. And, to a point, I think, that might be true of law also if you tie it into social coordination.

Then, of course, there comes a point on the continuum—nobody knows just where it is—where law starts to become a bad thing, as Paul and Pierre have described. So there's still plenty of room for angst. But I think it's not the same kind of angst that comes from believing that this is a neutral thing, and you just have no idea whether it could be completely good or completely bad. It's sort of more of both, you know, inherently more of both.

SCHLAG. Angst may be the natural condition of law—one that is necessarily denied. What is required of lawyers is to engage as authentically as possible in an inauthentic discourse. You are to act as if you believe. The things that you must say as a lawyer must be said as if you believe them. You must even try to get yourself to believe them. Perhaps you even *do* believe them. But then you stop being a lawyer, and somebody asks you, "Do you believe this?" And you say, "I was making an argument! Look, I was filing a complaint!" "Do you believe in complaints?" "I believe if I file a complaint, that's the way to start a lawsuit." "Yes, but do you believe in complaints?" That's not a real question to a lawyer. The same thing is true, to some extent, with respect to a legal argument made by an appellate advocate. "Do you believe in this argument?" "Of course I believe in this argument!—this is a press conference." Outside: "Do you believe in this argument?" "Are you asking me whether I believe in it as the lawyer of my client, or are you trying to have some sort of confidential, off-the-record conversation with me about whether I really, *really* believe the argument? Who are you talking to here?"

It's a very bizarre sort of practice. Part of the problem—this gets back to the Nietzschean point—part of the problem is that we are asking students to believe and practice a metaphysic which we as law teachers largely do not believe, except when we are in role. We are asking them to believe in a metaphysic which people in other departments—sociology, psychology, anthropology—do not believe and would, indeed, find laughable. Nonetheless, we ask, we train the students to believe this metaphysic. One of the tragedies for law students is that they often take this metaphysic (which we do not believe) to be not only what one has to say as a lawyer, but to be a valid description of social reality.

SMITH. Is that the tragedy? Or is it more tragic to deprive students of that belief? Maybe if no skepticism were ever imparted to them, they could go out and joyously do this thing without feeling this kind of doubt.

SCHLAG. I disagree with that. I think that by the time they get to practice, the experience of young lawyers is very different from the representation of law that they were given in law school. It is at that point that they become very cynical, very demoralized, and very upset with their law school for teaching what they will then call "theory," even though it was really doctrine.

SMITH. But on the other hand, maybe the opposite is true. It could be that students, while in law school, absorb a fair amount of skepticism. But when they get thrown into practice, these kinds of questions are not really raised, and they just have to go out and do the job, and the advocacy mentality takes over, and then they just believe it. It's just not a question anymore.

SCHLAG. In most law school courses the implicit representation is that a brief and a memorandum of points of authorities are filed to persuade the judge to rule in your favor, in accordance with your prayer for relief. In practice, you use briefs for all sorts of reasons: to harass the other side, to make them say something, to keep them from saying something, because you need to hold a press conference, because you want to divulge information, to put the other side between a rock and a hard place—for any number of reasons. Practice is, in some sense, much richer and much more interesting than the law as it's represented in law school. When students get out in practice and they remember their first year class in . . . and they line up the cases on their side, and the judge says, "I don't really want to hear about these cases. I'm just going to rule"; well, then they get very demoralized.

SMITH. That's not law.

SCHLAG. Of course it's law! It's law at the superior court!

SMITH. But that's probably what they end up saying. In other words, the practice is disillusioning to the extent they may have gotten some kind of ethical idealism in law school. Practice will probably shatter *that* illusion. But whether it shatters an illusion about law being somehow real, I'm not sure. I think what happens many times is, as they're writing the brief they really *do* think they're telling the law to the judge. Then if the judge says, "I don't want to hear it, I disregard this argument and rule on some other basis," one common response to that, I think, is, "He misunderstood the law!" So it doesn't necessarily result in a kind of skepticism about there being law.

CAMPOS. Yeah, but this is what Pierre would call dissonance, right? Both things are there, and I think one thing we've been emphasizing here is this disjunction between legal practice and what gets done in the law school. But I think we also need to point to the very important synergistic relationship between what gets done in practice and what gets done in the law school. Because what gets done in the law school is to produce a certain ideology of law which, at this point, I think we would to some extent all agree, is out of control. So I don't think we should leave the impression that we believe that there is no relation between the idealized, romanticized ideology of the law school and the actual structure of legal practice. To the contrary, there is a relationship. It just happens to be a completely different relationship from the relationship envisioned by many legal academics.

SCHLAG. Basically, the harassment, the needling, the wheedling, the intimidation is all done with very nice words. I mean, it's all . . .

CAMPOS. Legal words . . .

SCHLAG. Legal words that are very clean, very noble, very proper. And, to some extent, what is done in the legal academy is to bring this very pleasing vocabulary, this very pleasing language, up to date, up to speed. Some academics seem to think that this language is then regulative of practice, but that relation, I think, generally doesn't hold. Instead, all sorts of uses are made of those very pleasing words—uses that are often not so noble.

LEVINSON. Two comments. One is simply a reference. Tony Kronman wrote an article a number of years ago pointing out that a principal difference between law school and graduate school is that graduate students, by and large, in the best of all worlds, would want in due time to replace their professors; and professors, in turn, were trying to prepare students to replace them. That was my own experience in graduate school. Whereas, what Kronman argued is that, by and large—maybe the Yale law school is quite literally the one exception to this, but—by and large, students don't want to be law professors, and law professors have, as one of you suggested a few minutes ago, quite consciously chosen not to be lawyers. And that sets up inevitable tensions that are quite different from whatever tensions are present in graduate education. I am assuming that it is an existential need to be able to look at yourself in the mirror and feel more or less proud of the life you have chosen. It does seem to me that ultimately what is driving my questions, and what I think makes this such a powerful book, is the question of how, if at all, people with, broadly speaking, our set of views can have a high degree of self-respect for the particular job of the law professor—to teach and prepare lawyers.

One final observation. My impression is that thirty years ago law professors were really delighted to prepare people for the practice of law. That there was a notion of the majesty of the law. That this was all a big system in which law professors played the quite happy role of preparing people to be lawyers. So it kind of all worked out. But I think the sixties did this in. I think that you find far fewer people who have this theory. And at least for me, and possibly because I am the oldest among us, this existential question takes on more bite, as to where, if at all, the source of pride and self-respect of being a law professor in the American law school training people to be lawyers, where that comes from.

SCHLAG. I think that one of the sources of self-respect comes from basically facing up to the paradoxes and the contradictions which we have discussed, and doing a good job of doing that.

SMITH. Is that more as a scholar, though?

SCHLAG. No, as a teacher. That is, doing a good job of presenting to the students what law is, how it is put together.

SMITH. Let me just ask you about that, though. Suppose you were engaged in teaching people and preparing them for something that you regarded as a really vicious profession—one that would make them unhappy or would be bad for society. Suppose you had somehow or other stumbled into this, and now this was the job you had. You hadn't realized the character of it before, perhaps, but now you have. How much self-respect would you be able to get from saying, "But, unlike everyone else, I *tell* them this is a vicious . . ."?

SCHLAG. You know, that is exactly right. And this reminds me of something I wanted to say earlier about your earlier comment. What we are dealing with here can be conceptualized as problems of frame. That is, is it a good thing to be a law professor as opposed to being whatever else one might be?

LEVINSON. A professor of legal studies in a sociology department or a history department or a political science department?

SCHLAG. Right, or a carpenter or . . .

LEVINSON. Here, I am assuming the life of the scholar dedicated to training people other than law students.

SCHLAG. Is it a good thing to be a law professor? And, of course, there is the narrower question: Having decided to be a law professor, what is a good way of going about it? And that is close to the question that you asked. Now, the more you think it is just absolutely awful to be a law professor, in an aesthetic or in a moral sense, the less you will be able to justify or vindicate your existence by then saying, "Well, I'm doing a really good job at it. And I'm trying to be as ethical as possible." So, yes, there is this problem.

I have to say, however, that academics tend to think of their roles too much in departmental terms. Part of what is going on is that we are all intellectuals in the university. We happen to be associated with different departments. The division of the university into departments may reflect organizational necessities, but it doesn't necessarily reflect present intellectual needs or opportunities.

CAMPOS. The point Sandy is making reveals a deep tension in what we do. I don't have any kind of a satisfactory answer to it. We are part of the university, but we have a very, very difficult structural problem in just the way you describe. We don't have graduate students. We don't teach undergraduate students as part of their broader edification. Instead, we have a particular social role to play—the production of these kinds of persons. And that is problematic on the grand level of the moral and the aesthetic, to the extent that producing these kinds of persons is adding to the elaboration of the system, which is highly problematic in itself; but it is also problematic, I think, in the more manageable and perhaps more interesting way that Sandy spoke of, which is that there is a real tension in the relationship between a professor and his or her students. I find that to be a real problem in teaching, and I think that to the extent that our critique of the present state of the legal academy is at all correct, it's going to become more and more of a problem, because in order to make the scholarly and the academic and the intellectual side of law viable, it will have to become more and more like the rest of the university. But that won't help—in fact, it will exacerbate—the situation between the professors and their students.

SMITH. To answer Sandy's question directly, though, I guess I would say that we're not entitled to feel a lot of self-respect. If at one time law professors thought, "We are doing a wonderful thing by preparing people to go into a very rewarding and noble career . . ."

LEVINSON. We were teaching "the wise restraints that make men free."

SMITH. I think we're not entitled to feel that. The best we can do, I think, is to find small ways in which we can say, "This enterprise is going on anyway. I didn't create it and I didn't make the choice for any of these students to come to law school. Based on, maybe, a series of accidents, I find myself situated in this right now. I'm going to do it as honestly as I can, and I'm going to try to prepare students not only to be able to do it well, but to be alert to some of the pitfalls. And to some extent I may be doing a good thing, a very limited good thing, by being a drag on what might otherwise be some really bad tendencies." Actually, I sometimes take that view about legal scholarship as well. And I don't think that view entitles you to much, well, certainly to much pride. But for me, I think that's a problem to struggle with, and that's about the best I can do with it.

SCHLAG. This is a really good question—and maybe we should spend more time on it. I think there has been a general demotion of the status of the law professor. At one point it was an extraordinarily noble calling. It's no longer that, obviously. It may be a desirable position, but it's no longer a noble calling.

CAMPOS. This is what Posner emphasizes in his discussion of Wechsler at the beginning of *Overcoming Law*. Posner manages to evoke the aura of a certain grand eloquence that seemed completely natural to Wechsler's generation. Now, today, when you look at the Harvard Law School, which has become a sort of intellectual Beirut, you just can't imagine that these people—well, not these people, of course, but their predecessors—once had a vision of themselves doing something that was as ennobling as the more extreme legal process rhetoric would have you believe.

SCHLAG. Certainly the legal process teacher cannot feel particularly gratified having to practice legal process on today's materials. I mean, what can't you make out of these materials? What can't you say with these materials?

CAMPOS. As Steve mentioned earlier, this is related to something that Brian Simpson emphasizes in his historical work. We start to lose all cultural context and forget that what is called "the common law" was at any one time something like thirty or forty guys from the same, very small slice of English society getting together to resolve some disputes, and naturally enough thinking in very similar sorts of ways. It was an operation whose total scale was comparable to a medium-size American law firm. That was the common law. And then you take that model and push it into a multicultural country of 260 million people, and you see the same kinds of disjunctions that result from thinking that Periclean Athens has an enormous amount to tell you about the United States in 1995 in terms of something called "democracy," because the word *democracy* is used in both contexts. They used the word *law* in the Inns of Court in 1717, and we use the word *law* in the Municipal Court in Chicago, Illinois, in 1995, and we think we're talking about the same thing, but we're not.

LEVINSON. It seems to me that one of Posner's most insistent themes is a basically sociological analysis that there's just a phenomenal amount of diversity within the legal profession, and the more diversity, the less consensus, and there seems to be no solution to that problem, assuming a solution would be desirable. To bring this phase of our conversation full circle, during the Carrington controversy, Bill Van Alstyne and his colleagues at Duke wrote a letter—and this comes back to your title, *Against the Law*—saying that it would be very odd if somebody interviewing for a position in the sociology department walked in and said, "You know, I really think that sociology is worthless as a way of analyzing the world or studying the world." Not simply, "I think that structural functionalism really doesn't make much sense, but Marxism really does"; or, "Marxism doesn't make much sense, but some sort of interpretive hermeneutic sociology, that's the way to go." That's a fairly pained critique, but if someone said, "Look. I looked at them all. None of them make any sense, and

I'd like a job in your department to train students to be sociologists," Van Alstyne suggested this would really be rather wacky. Why is it any less wacky if somebody says, "I really think the whole legal enterprise is just bankrupt"?

SCHLAG. If I were a sociologist in the sociology department, I'd vote to hire this person. I don't think it's wacky at all.

LEVINSON. And why would you vote to hire this person?

SCHLAG. Because if I were a sociologist, and sociology is bankrupt, I'd like to know about it. I'd have a real interest in knowing why it's bankrupt. If it's bankrupt, I'd like to know it. Now, if somebody is just going to come in and hurl insults at me, then I can understand Van Alstyne's point. But if the person is going to come in and demonstrate why, indeed, this is a discipline that ought to go the way of phrenology (my current interest), then . . .

LEVINSON. But then, of course, the solution is to dissolve the department, so that after next year nobody will be hired in sociology, because nobody will be admitted to study it.

SCHLAG. But this is a very liberal idea. This is the exercise of dialogue, of reason at work. If we are wrong in our critiques, in our assessments, or in our descriptions, then there are certainly more than enough legal academics bound to disagree with us who can make very reasonable arguments as to why we are wrong. But that's what should happen.

LEVINSON. But this is the devil's advocate.

SCHLAG. Well, no. No, it's not, because we believe what we're saying.

SMITH. But to make Pierre's point—here's another way of trying to make it. Maybe what you've described sounds wacky in sociology, although Pierre disagrees with that. But in a philosophy department, it shouldn't seem strange if somebody said, "Philosophy means a lot of different things, and it has meant certain things in this century, and I think all of those things make no sense. And I would like a position on your philosophy faculty." I don't think it would seem at all strange to say, "Yeah, let's hire him. He may be very good." Lots of important philosophers have essentially done just that.

CAMPOS. I think that's precisely correct. In fact, to concretize this, I remember reading Habermas's claim that the main function of German sociologists was to state continually, in what he called "a typically German manner," that there was no such thing as sociology. So there isn't anything necessarily unusual about having somebody say—in fact, it's really a fairly conventional move—"There is no such thing as sociology," which is supposedly an even more radical claim than to say it's bankrupt, right? But here I think we're again dealing with a certain kind of semantic confusion. Just because Professor Van Alstyne has a certain view of a series of an extremely complex set of social practices which he calls "law," that doesn't make it law, does it? And when someone says, "You've got the wrong view of what this stuff is all about," that's not a claim that there's no such thing as law or that law is necessarily bankrupt or anything like that. It's just a claim that you've got a bad model for thinking about a really complicated form of social interaction.

LEVINSON. This suggests that the title of your book, though it might be somewhat more awkward, is *Against the Current Conception of Law and in Favor of a Better One.*

SCHLAG. We considered that one.

CAMPOS. Yeah, but I think that's quite accurate, I think that's quite right. Obviously, we're not anarchists, except for Pierre.

SCHLAG. No, I am not an anarchist.

CAMPOS. Obviously we are not anarchists . . .

SCHLAG. We're going to have to edit this very seriously.

CAMPOS. . . . and I think it should be clear from context that when we say *Against the Law* we're saying something like that, right? The title is catchy and seems a little inflammatory, but I think one thing all of us feel deeply is a certain degree of resentment about this game of semantic capture of the flag, in which you've got people saying, "Well, you know, I'm for law, and you're against law, because I have this idea of law, and you have a different idea of law, and therefore I'm for law, and you're against law." That's a complete non sequitur.

SCHLAG. Yeah, like some of the responses to the normativity critique. You know, much of the normativity critique can be reduced to the view that normativity is not what it claims to be. And the response seems to be, "What do you mean, there's something wrong with normative argument—that's evil." I understand that kind of response as a non sequitur.

LEVINSON. I think it may be slightly facile for you to say, "Well, look. None of this is anarchy, none of us is an anarchist." At least in some of the things you say both in the book and in the conversation, there's a really significant critique of certain standard views, a real desire that they be replaced by others, and, at least on occasion, clear overtones that it might not be a bad idea to minimize the amount of law. Maybe there's no getting rid of it, but by and large, whenever there's a choice between law and something else, the *burden of proof* should be on the person who wants law. Concomitantly, there should always be a *presumption* in favor of no law. Is that unfair as an interpretation—not necessarily *the* interpretation—but *an* interpretation of this book?

SMITH. Let me add one further distinction, then maybe we can answer your question. We've talked already about how *law,* the term, is understood in quite different ways, and that may be the aspect of the title that you're focusing on.

But you could focus on the other word, too, *against*—in what sense is somebody against this? Paul, for example—I'll speak for him—might say, "I am against certain notions of interpretation, of what interpretation means, on a certain level, a kind of intellectual level. I think they're incoherent." It doesn't follow that Paul is against the sorts of practices that people are trying to describe. They may or may not be good things. So that's at least a further complication in asking about this title and about in what sense we're "against the law."

LEVINSON. The one thing I hear in what you just said is overtones of Stanley Fish—that there are no consequences; that this is entirely a metadiscussion, but philosophy leaves everything as it is, there's a world of practice, so don't worry that there are practical consequences in accepting or rejecting these metaviews, and I'm not sure . . .

SMITH. But I was saying that more in response to your suggestion that there might be some kind of across-the-board presumption. I was not trying to say that there are no consequences, but that to the extent there is any across-the-board presumption, or some fairly sweeping presumption of againstness, I think that would be more applicable to certain very widely held presuppositions behind talk about law on an intellectual level. There's no disclaimer of practical consequences. But I think we are much more agnostic, and there's probably much less consistency among the three of us, as far as what the practical consequences are.

SCHLAG. Many of the arguments I make are against the law in the sense of coming from a direction that is against the law. The thing that gives me difficulties with your formulation is precisely the references to presumption and burden, which are legalistic terms. One of the things that I have not done—for understandable reasons, I think, given the normativity critique—is talk about just how far these arguments against the law go, or what implications they have for decision making in this or that particular case. I think if I were going to do that, I would be engaged, again, in *doing* law, in phantom judging, something which I'm against.

CAMPOS. Try to imagine somebody in the legal academy writing a book called *For the Law.* That would seem like an absurd title. Perhaps ours seems like an absurd title, too, but that would be a particularly absurd title. Now, why would it be absurd? Would it be absurd for people to title a book *For Liberalism*? It would be problematic, because people would say, "Well, what liberalism are you talking about? Are you talking about this version, that version?" There are lots of liberalisms. People would recognize that right away. But it wouldn't strike them as at all problematic for someone to write a book saying *For Liberalism as Opposed to These Other Things.* But to write a book called *For the*

Law would—certainly within the traditional American law school—that would be considered absolutely bizarre. It would be like writing a book called *For Happiness*. And all we are trying to point out is that there isn't anything necessarily bizarre about writing a book called *For the Law*, or writing a book called *Against the Law*, for that matter.

SCHLAG. Though there is an ironic sense in which many legal academics have written nothing else: *For the Law*. They just haven't called it that.

IDOLATRY IN CONSTITUTIONAL INTERPRETATION

Steven D. Smith

Man cannot exist without bowing before something. . . . Let him reject God, and he will bow before an idol.—Fyodor Dostoevsky[1]

There are more idols than realities in the world.—Friedrich Nietzsche[2]

FOR MORE THAN a generation, constitutional scholars have exhibited a virtual obsession with the problem of interpretation. One conspicuous source of this obsession is *Brown v. Board of Education*, a decision that was at once monumental and yet difficult to justify in conventional terms. The challenge has been to articulate a theory that would explain what few have doubted—that *Brown* was a correct decision. Herbert Wechsler accepted the challenge and, by his own admission, failed.[3] Alexander Bickel gave it a try.[4] More recently, Bruce Ackerman, Robert Bork, Ronald Dworkin, and Laurence Tribe have all attempted to explain why the *Brown* Court correctly interpreted the Constitution.[5]

Initially, most post-*Brown* thinking about constitutional interpretation fell into one of two competing camps, often called "interpretivism" and "noninterpretivism." The camp of interpretivists included both scholars like Robert Bork and Raoul Berger, who understood constitutional interpretation as a search for historical meaning, and scholars like Ronald Dworkin, who favored a more creative and present-oriented approach to interpretation. In the noninterpretivist camp, theorists such as Thomas Grey and Michael Perry posited that although much of modern constitutional law cannot be justified as interpretation of the Constitution, noninterpretive judicial review that does not purport to be merely interpreting the text of the Constitution is legitimate and desirable. Although the former noninterpretivists now claim that their methodologies are interpretive after all,[6] the essential competing positions remain. Grey and Perry, along with other scholars, simply began to use the term "interpretation" in more expansive and exotic ways.

"Interpretation," it now seems, describes a category of intellectual operations at once more capacious and less commonsensical than even sophisticated scholars like Grey and Perry at first supposed. The pursuit of the newly discovered potential of interpretation has led legal scholars to explore other fields such as literary criticism and philosophical hermeneutics. As the scope of what could count as interpretation expanded, theories of interpretation proliferated. This escalation of theorizing does not appear to have generated any consensus about how constitutional interpretation does or should operate, however, and thus contributions to the debate continue to multiply.

In their wide-ranging study of interpretation, legal scholars have inevitably noted analogies between legal interpretation and religious interpretation. For example, Sanford Levinson and Thomas Grey helpfully discuss the parallels between Protestant and Catholic approaches to Scripture and competing theories of constitutional interpretation.[7] Michael Perry similarly stresses the analogy between modern judicial review and the biblical prophetic tradition.[8] And in reflections that have provoked and guided this essay (reflections not confined to constitutional interpretation), Joseph Vining emphasizes the affinities between law and theology.[9]

Scholars have approached these parallels gingerly, however, and have typically taken care to maintain a respectable distance from the religious ideas or traditions on which they draw. Perry defends his conception of judicial review by articulating a vision of community that he describes as "religious," but he hastens to add: "I do not use the word in any sectarian, theistic, or otherwise metaphysical sense."[10] The connection between law and theology that Joseph Vining describes consists largely of parallel problems and "methodological affinities"; both disciplines, he emphasizes, are centrally concerned with interpreting texts created by hierarchical authorities.[11] Vining does not argue that legal interpretation actually is a religious activity, except in a very loose sense;[12] indeed, he emphasizes that the "profitable juxtaposition" is between law and theology, not between law and religion.[13] Vining thus compares the methodologies of studying law and religion, but he does not go so far as to admit that legal theory shares the faith in transcendent authority found in religious belief.* Levinson and Grey use religion as an "analogy" or "metaphor" in thinking about law;[14] they do not directly challenge the prevailing view that law is, and should be understood as, a rational, secular enterprise.[15] Indeed, Grey's political secularism "insists that power be justified in terms that are rational at least in the weak sense that no ultimate mysteries be invoked to legitimate its exercise—no transcendent authority, no Kierkegaardian leap of faith."[16]

In this essay I will suggest that scholarly discussions comparing constitutional interpretation to theology or religion are illuminating beyond their own

---

*In light of writing by Vining since this essay was written, I am less confident about this statement. See Joseph Vining, *From Newton's Sleep* (1994).

intentions. There is a connection, as these discussions indicate, between constitutional interpretation and religion, but the connection is not merely an analogical or metaphorical one. Rather, many versions of modern constitutional
interpretation can best be understood by recognizing their implicit dependence
on what Grey and others disavow—a belief in "transcendent authority" and a
"Kierkegaardian leap of faith."

In short, modern constitutional interpretation—that is, interpretation as
practiced by the Warren and Burger Courts and as still practiced and endorsed
by leading constitutional scholars—is a religious enterprise in the sense that it
depends on the (usually tacit) assumption of transcendent authority. More
precisely, inasmuch as the transcendent authority on which these theories implicitly rely is illusory, legal interpretation can most accurately be understood as
a species of idolatry. Moreover, the leading temple devoted to this idolatrous
practice is not the so-called civil religion of Constitution worship attributed to
popular culture, but rather the legal academy itself.

Although mistaken, scholarly protestations that the relation of constitutional
interpretation to religion is merely analogical are also revealing. Those assertions reflect a conspicuous quality of the current academic and legal environment—its aspiration to secular rationality—that in turn suggests a reason for
our seeming inability to understand and settle on any account of what interpretation is or how it works. If modern constitutional interpretation has an
essential religious element that legal scholars cannot openly acknowledge, then
it is hardly surprising that the scholarly community would be ever theorizing
but never coming to a satisfying understanding of what constitutional interpretation entails.

THE PUZZLE OF LEGAL INTERPRETATION

The character of constitutional interpretation can best be appreciated after
reflecting on the nature of legal interpretation generally. Despite our habit of
thinking of legal interpretation as a rational and secular practice, there is something about the practice that mocks mundane rationality.

A First Look: The Strangeness of Our Interpretive Practices

The activity of law is devoted to the interpretation of authoritative texts: judicial
opinions, statutes, regulations, and constitutions. This devotion may seem entirely natural simply by virtue of its familiarity, but from a more detached
perspective the practice of legal interpretation has a puzzling aspect. There are,
after all, more straightforward and more obviously sensible ways of solving

problems or resolving conflicts—hardheaded, forward-looking pragmatism, for example. So why do we entrust the governance of our lives to a practice of reading meaning out of or into texts? Noting that textual interpretation is the law's principal resource, Joseph Vining remarks on the "oddness of it":

> Asked by others what to do, what the law would want a person to do, American lawyers will go off and find what a few old men scattered about the country thirty, fifty, a hundred years ago, sitting on intermediate appellate courts in Pennsylvania or in a town in the mountains of Kentucky, said they thought the law was at the time they spoke. They come back, put it all together, and say, "That is the law. That you ought to obey." They expect to be paid for producing such an answer and do not expect their inquirer to exclaim "Ridiculous!" and turn on his heel and stalk away.[17]

After offering other, similar illustrations, Vining concludes: "Looking up what some old men said, jumping when some new men speak—these things need to be explained."[18]

This sense that our practice of legal interpretation is something that from a detached perspective appears distinctly strange, and hence needs to be explained, may be sharpened if we imagine how the practice might look to the proverbial visitor from Mars. Suppose this visitor has been given a panoramic view of various terrestrial methods, past and present, of conflict resolution and problem solving. The Martian then reports back: "The people of this planet solve problems in various and sometimes remarkable ways. In some cultures, they have tried to obtain guidance by examining the entrails of birds. In other cultures, they look for counsel in the configurations of the stars, evidently assuming that the movements of gaseous bodies situated billions of miles away somehow speak to their earthly concerns. In still other cultures—American culture, for example—they read meanings into ancient texts (and especially into one ancient text that they call 'The Constitution') and then treat these meanings as dictating their present and future actions. The more astute among them do not suppose that these meanings represent the actual or conscious decisions of the authors of those ancient texts. Nonetheless, they allow these meanings to govern their individual and collective lives."

From our perspective, this description may seem to have missed something critical, and hence to have wrongly assimilated what we view as a rational practice—legal interpretation—to nonrational practices of augury and astrology. But can we plausibly defend the rationality of our practice and explain how it is essentially different from those with which the Martian visitor has equated it?[19]

The Requirement of an Author

One obvious and essential difference, it may seem, between astrology, say, and textual interpretation is that a text is the expression of a mindful author. The positions of the stars, in contrast, seem to be the result of chance in either of two senses. There may be no author, or no mind, determining the positions of the stars. Alternatively, there may be a celestial author or mind; but even if there is, we have no reason to suppose that in positioning the stars this cosmic mind is contemplating or attempting to address the questions the astrologer is asking. So even if some cosmic mind does direct the stars, their positions are still merely fortuitous with respect to the astrologer and his terrestrial concerns.

This contrast reveals an essential presupposition of textual interpretation. The practice of interpretation can seem to be a sensible one, and one essentially different from what we regard as nonrational or superstitious practices such as astrology, only on the premise that the text is the expression of a mindful author. The presupposition of a mindful author is implicit in our practices of studying texts, trying to determine what they mean, and seeking guidance or insight—or, in the case of legal texts, binding direction—from them. To be sure, we also study other objects without assuming that they are the products of a mindful author—rocks, for example, or stars. But we ask different kinds of questions about such objects, questions about how they work, what caused them to be the way they are, what their effects are. We would not ask of a rock formation, "What does this mean?" in anything like the sense in which we ask that question of, say, a newspaper column or the due process clause. And we surely would not suppose that the rock formation might be a source of answers to questions about how we should live our lives.

The essential presupposition of an author is emphasized by the interpretive theory (or, as they would have it, the objections to any interpretive theory) advanced by Steven Knapp and Walter Benn Michaels and, following them, Paul Campos. These scholars argue that "the meaning of a text is simply identical to the author's intended meaning."[20] In support of this controversial position, they reflect on how we would treat marks of unknown origins that resemble words.[21] Campos offers the following example: Suppose that while walking in the desert near the Arizona-Mexico border you see, in the sand, marks that appear to spell out the word *real*. In order to "interpret" these marks, you would need to make assumptions about a possible author. If you assume the marks were made by a Spanish-speaking author, you will interpret the marks in one way. If you believe they were produced by an English-speaking author, you will ascribe an entirely different meaning to them. But if you think no one made the marks, and that they are simply the bizarre effect of a fortuitous interaction of sand and desert wind, then you will not regard the marks as a "text," and you will not suppose that they have any "meaning." Or if you do ascribe meaning to them, then it would be more accurate to say that the marks had no meaning and did not constitute a word or a text until you came on the scene; and at that point you became the author of their meaning.[22]

In a somewhat different way, Joseph Vining also insists on the essential presupposition in textual interpretation of a mindful author. Vining argues persuasively that there would be no point in treating texts as we do unless we assumed that they are a product of a communicative mind. Writings, he observes, "command our respect and serious attention only to the extent that we hear a person speaking through them. Their authority rests upon the sense of mind behind them."[23]

The foregoing discussion suggests that the presupposition of a mindful author is implicit in all textual interpretation. In legal interpretation, however, even more is required. That is because we treat legal texts, unlike most other texts, as provisionally binding us in our present and future actions. A major purpose of legal theory is to explain how legal texts can claim this authoritative status. We must ask, as Philip Soper maintains, not simply "What is law?" but rather "What is law that I should obey it?"[24] What qualities must the author of a legal text possess, in other words, that would induce us to make decisions in conformity to that author's decree rather than simply making our own best judgment?

To this question, of course, theorists and citizens give different answers. To some, it may be enough that the author speaks for a majority of citizens whose will is registered in accordance with some conventionally accepted set of procedures. Henry David Thoreau, however, was hardly the only human being for whom it was not self-evident that a group acquires moral authority to command merely by virtue of numerical superiority.[25] More seems to be needed. Recognizing that "there is no reason to obey what just anyone says," Vining suggests that we must be convinced "that the voice means what it says, . . . that *it* believes in what it is asking another to believe in."[26] In a similar vein, Soper argues that the law will lack authority unless its authors are acting in good faith in the interests of the entire community.[27]

These requirements of authenticity and good faith seem sound but still insufficient. No one, it seems, would yield control over his life to, say, someone who is feeble-minded just because that person always speaks sincerely and charitably. Ideally, one might wish for an author possessed of special wisdom and foresight. Indeed, pressing the argument, one might arrive at a conclusion that has been widely held in some periods: No mere human being can plausibly claim to have the authority to direct the lives of other human beings. Only someone who has greater-than-human wisdom and virtue could claim such authority; human institutions, if they have legitimate authority, would have to derive it from that higher source.[28]

Fortunately, it is not necessary to resolve this difficult and perennial issue here. The critical point at present is that for textual interpretation to be understood as a sensible practice, the practice must presuppose that a text is the expression of a mindful author. Further, for legal interpretation to make sense, not just any author will do. Rather, the author presupposed in legal interpretation must also be able to claim whatever qualities might be needed to endow him and his textual productions with authority. So a question arises: Where can we find the author who is needed if our practices of legal interpretation are to make sense?

Authorial Candidates—Historical and Artificial

The bare requirement of a mindful author may seem easily satisfied. After all, virtually everyone acknowledges that legal texts do have authors. Sometimes, as with ancient common law doctrines, we may not know who the author was. In other contexts, we may argue about whom to regard as the official author. For example, is the author of a statute the draftsperson, who may have been a lobbyist or an unelected staff attorney, or is it the sponsor of the bill, or perhaps the entire legislature? Despite these questions, no one supposes that any legal text somehow generated itself spontaneously without the help of a flesh-and-blood author. Hypothetical scenarios about monkeys randomly striking typewriter keys or poems washing up on beaches are just that—hypothetical.

For some kinds of legal interpretation, the historical author arguably provides sufficient justification for our interpretive practices. In statutory construction, for example, courts often purport to search for, and then implement, the "intent of the legislature," and they routinely consult legislative history in an apparent effort to discover the actual intent of the legislators. To the extent that courts can actually discern what legislators meant, the "historical author" account might explain the sense and purpose of statutory construction.[29]

For modern constitutional interpretation, in contrast, a "historical author" account is untenable. That is because, although constitutional provisions do have historical authors, our interpretive practices pervasively show that it is not primarily the historical author's voice we are trying to discern. Michael Klarman suggests that this move away from the historical author—the effective severing of constitutional interpretation from original intent—may have been *Brown*'s larger jurisprudential consequence. "To strike down public school segregation," Klarman observes, "required the Justices consciously to burst asunder the shackles of original intent."[30] And once broken, the primacy of original intent could not be reestablished:

> By the 1960s only one Justice, John Marshall Harlan, continued to evince serious concern with the Fourteenth Amendment's original understanding. . . . On those sporadic occasions where a Warren Court majority opinion undertook historical exegesis, the elicited conclusions were sufficiently implausible to suggest virtual contempt for the integrity of the historical record. By the 1970s, moreover, a markedly more conservative set of Justices scarcely batted a collective eyelash at extending meaningful equal protection review to groups—women, aliens, and nonmarital children—plainly not among the contemplated beneficiaries of the Fourteenth Amendment.[31]

In a similar vein, Henry Monaghan has observed that "few of the present generation of constitutional theorists are concerned with what the relevant history 'really' shows with respect to original intent. . . . They simply do not care."[32] In short, for a generation or more it has been evident that a wide range of decisions under the religion clauses, the free speech clause, and the due process and equal protection clauses have almost no connection to any decision, intention, or expectation of the natural authors of those clauses—unless, that is, the authors' intentions are described in such broad and abstract terms that the distinction between following the authors' intent and simply doing what seems best disappears.[33]

It is fair to say, then, that the persistent problem for constitutional theory in the post-*Brown* era has been precisely the problem of "nonoriginalist" interpretation; it is the problem of explaining how a text can be "interpreted" once its meaning is not assumed to be equivalent to the meaning intended by its historical authors.

One response to this problem might be that a text can have meaning, and hence can be interpreted, without assuming or referring to *any* author. This response, however, is vulnerable to two powerful objections. First, the notion of authorless textual meaning ultimately rests on an untenable linguistic formalism; it assumes that a word—or, more accurately, a mark or a sound—can have a meaning even though no one uses it to convey that meaning. But it is hard to imagine how this could be so. What could it even mean to say that a mark or sound "just means" something?

To be sure, we often talk about the meaning of the text or the words without explicitly referring to any writer or speaker. But this is a sort of shorthand; we still make implicit reference to some author or speaker—if not to the actual speaker then to some other speaker, such as "the typical English speaker." Otherwise, such statements would be nonsensical: How could the marks W-A-T-E-R mean H_2O if no one had ever used the marks to communicate that meaning? One might think that the reference in such statements is to the audience; thus, to say that "*water* means the stuff that falls from the sky when it rains" would be to say that this is what most people understand or think of when they hear the word. Heidi Hurd notes that "the law commonly ignores what a speaker means and focuses, instead, on what that speaker's audience understands the speaker to mean."[34] As Hurd's statement reflects, however, an "audience understanding" account of meaning still necessarily refers to a presupposed speaker—at the very least something like "the typical English speaker." After all, why do most people think of the stuff of which rain is made when they hear the word *water* if it is not because they know that is what English speakers typically mean when they say "water"?

In this vein, even while denying that interpretation is bound to the meaning intended by a historical author or person, Ronald Dworkin acknowledges that interpretation necessarily makes reference to the presupposed intentions of *some* author or person: "For even if we reject the thesis that creative interpretation aims to discover some actual historical intention, the concept of intention nevertheless provides the *formal* structure for all interpretive claims. I mean that an interpretation is by nature the report of a purpose; it proposes a way of seeing what is interpreted . . . as if this were the product of a decision to pursue one set of themes or visions or purposes, one 'point,' rather than another. This structure is required of an interpretation even when . . . there is no historical author whose historical mind can be plumbed."[35]

Beyond assuming an implausible linguistic formalism, the notion of authorless textual meaning also generates a serious prudential objection. Suppose we could somehow explain how a text could have a meaning, and hence could be interpreted, without assuming or referring to any author. This explanation would merely revive the problem discussed above: even if it were *possible* to interpret a text without referring to any author, why would it be *sensible* to govern ourselves through such a procedure? As noted, the reason why governance through textual interpretation seems different and more defensible than governance through augury or astrology is precisely that texts are thought to be the expressions of mindful authors who have in some way considered and addressed the kind of problem or decision we are currently facing. If we could somehow explain how a text could mean something without presupposing or referring to the intentions of any author, then that distinction would disappear. Textual interpretation as a method of governance would then be on a par with augury or astrology.

It seems, then, that we face a dilemma. In the post-*Brown* era, we have chosen not to treat the meaning of the constitutional text as equivalent to the historical authors' meaning. But unless we link textual meaning to *some* authors' meaning, then making decisions by assigning meanings to texts seems impossible or, even if possible, no more rational or sensible than astrology. There may be an escape from this dilemma, however. We need, it seems, an author; and in constitutional law we cannot or will not simply accept the historical authors for this role. But if the author presupposed in textual interpretation is not the historical author who actually set pen to paper or fingers to keyboard, then why not invent an author? As Joseph Vining argues, if there is no actual author, the only alternative is to construct one. In this situation, "all the judge or lawyer can do is to construct, from the animating values alive in the air, a person to say what the statute says. . . . Even though that person may not exist."[36]

Resort to an artificial author may seem a dubious exercise in make-believe. But there is no reason to doubt that the intellectual operation called for is possible; indeed, it is quite familiar. We routinely suppose that we can talk cogently about what something would mean to fictitious characters: Sherlock Holmes would understand a message or clue in one way, whereas Watson would draw a different conclusion; Gandalf understands the writing on the door in a particular way, whereas Frodo does not understand it at all. In the same way, we might invent or construct an author for legal texts and then interpret the texts to mean what that artificial author intended them to mean.

The resort to a constructed author, though usually unacknowledged, is in fact common in constitutional interpretation. If a court's decision simply talks about what the text or the clause means, then unless the court is indulging in linguistic formalism, it is evidently making tacit reference to *some* author's intended meaning. But if that author is not the original framer or enactor of the text, then it seems that the tacit reference must be to an author constructed by the court.[37]

The role of the constructed author is perhaps most clearly recognized in the interpretive theory of Ronald Dworkin, who insists that legal interpretation "does not aim to recapture, even for present law, the ideals or practical purposes of the politicians who first created it."[38] As noted, however, he also maintains that any interpretation must be referred to an author and presented in the form of a reading of authorial intent. In short, Dworkin argues, first, that interpretation need not aim to discover the intent of any actual human author, but, second, that interpretation must be presented as an explication of the intent of an author. These two propositions make clear that the author whose meaning is discerned, or constructed, is an artificial figure. This conclusion is even more evident in Dworkin's insistence that all law, including statutes enacted and judicial decisions rendered by different bodies at different times over a period of decades or even centuries, should be understood, "so far as possible," as the work of a *single author*.[39] The dramatic departure from historical reality underscores the artificial or invented character of the author of legal texts in Dworkin's theory.

A Second Look: The Continuing Strangeness of Legal Interpretation

Earlier I suggested that a practice of interpretation makes sense only if it presupposes a mindful author who speaks through the text. The requirement that there be an author might conceivably be satisfied by the historical author of a legal text. In modern constitutional law, however, our interpretive practices appear to refer most commonly to a constructed author. This reference raises a fundamental question: Does the "constructed author" approach explain why our interpretive practices amount to a sensible or desirable way of directing our individual and collective affairs? Why, in other words, might we choose to be governed by decisions dictated by what our judges believe some imaginary author might mean by a set of legal texts?

At this point, the constructed author approach faces a dilemma that can be introduced in the form of another question: Is the constructed author a device that allows the interpreter—for example, the judge—to reach whatever decision she thinks best? Or does the constructed author constrain the interpreter, precluding her from reaching certain decisions even though she might prefer them? Either view underscores the strangeness and apparent irrationality of our practices.

Suppose, first, that the constructed author can be said to mean anything the interpreter wants the text to mean. If this is true, then constructed author interpretation is simply a way for the interpreter to decide a case as she thinks best and then present that decision as if it were derived from the interpretation of a text. And interpretation would be nothing more than a process, as Roscoe Pound caustically observed, by which the judge or scholar "puts a meaning into the text as a juggler puts coins . . . into a dummy's hair, to be pulled forth presently with an air of discovery."[40]

Such a process has little to recommend it as a method of making decisions; its apparent rationality is a sham. Imagine that you have a friend who tells you, "When I go to a restaurant, I don't just select something from the menu by whim, the way other people do. Instead, I use a more rational method. My method is this: Suppose there are 21 numbered items on the menu, and I prefer number 17. I don't just indulge my preference by ordering number 17. Instead, I take the square root of 100, multiply it by 6, subtract 11, divide by 7, subtract 6 again, add the number of the menu item I prefer, and subtract 1. Then I order the item corresponding to the result of this equation." This bizarre mathematical procedure seems manifestly senseless; it is simply an elaborate way of selecting the item that the diner preferred in the first place. What could be the point—unless it is deception (or self-deception)?

In the same way, if constructed author interpretation allows the interpreter to reach any decision he thinks best, interpretation becomes a misleading sham. Thus, Laurence Tribe and Michael Dorf argue that "the idea of an empty, or an infinitely malleable, Constitution" is "completely unsatisfactory." That is because the Constitution "would lose all legitimacy if it really were only a mirror for the readers' ideas and ideals."[41]

Conversely, the constructed author approach may *not* allow the interpreter to impose just any meaning on the text. Dworkin argues that his approach to interpretation does not allow the interpreter to reach any result at all: some results will be precluded even though the interpreter might regard them as the most just or desirable results.[42] Indeed, Dworkin concedes that if an interpreter can reach *any* result that his "convictions of justice" might recommend, then "he cannot claim in good faith to be interpreting" at all, and is instead "acting from bad faith or self-deception"[43]—which, it seems, is what some critics suspect Dworkin *is* doing.[44]

Unfortunately, this elaboration of the constructed author approach makes interpretation seem even less sensible than the version that would permit the interpreter to reach any conclusion he deemed best. If a particular decision seems most desirable or just, after all, then why should the decision maker be artificially precluded from reaching it? Why should the decision maker not be free to make his decision "the best it can be"?

To be sure, in many human situations and institutions, there are very good reasons for an individual to forgo making the decision that he might think best, and instead to defer to someone else's decision or interest. Someone else may have greater wisdom or expertise. Or a special need for unity or cooperation may require adherence to one person's decisions. In wartime, for example, a private should usually do not what he thinks best but what the general thinks best. In a democracy, officials may be obligated to make decisions that accord with the judgment or desires of the citizens or the people's elected representatives.

But to say that one may sometimes have good grounds to defer to the judgment of another real human being offers no reason at all to forgo the decision that one thinks best out of deference to some fictitious or constructed person or community. Thus, in Dworkin's theory, when a judge declines to reach the decision that he personally thinks is the most just, it is not because he thinks he should defer to the judgment of the actual legislators or the framers. On the contrary, as Dworkin makes clear, the purpose of interpretation is *not* to discover and then defer to the intentions of those officials.[45] Nor does the legal decision maker forgo his preferred result out of deference to the judgment of "the people": Dworkin's judge is plainly not in the business of simply implementing any conventional morality or political program.[46] Rather, the judge declines to make the decision he believes is best because he cannot plausibly attribute it to the fictitious "single author" of the whole body of law. The outcome that his convictions recommend is foreclosed not by the contrary judgments of real human beings, but by the will of a phantom.

This method of governing our collective lives is not obviously a sensible one. Indeed, it underscores the strangeness of our interpretive practices.[47] Perceiving this predicament, Joseph Vining wonders whether the lawyer "must be an illusionist, a magician, when he had thought he was entering the most rational of professions. . . . His position is worse than that of a courtier of the emperor who wore no clothes, passing a sock to him knowing all the while that there was no sock. At least there was an emperor."[48]

THE IMPULSE TO IDOLATRY

The preceding discussion began with a puzzle: How is it possible to explain our practice of allowing ourselves to be governed by meanings assigned to texts? Constitutional interpretation in particular, it seems, frequently treats the text as the expression of an imaginary, constructed author. This practice raises a basic question: Why is it sensible to treat as authoritative the will or expression of a fictitious lawmaker? The question raises what Joseph Vining calls "the issue of illusion and necessary self-delusion."[49] "Law," Vining observes, "must at least be aware of the possible value of illusion, the possible necessity of it."[50] Illusion might be necessary to save us from "liv[ing] without meaning and on the edge of despair"; a "public illusion" might be preferable to "madness." These reflections lead Vining to mention "the problem of idolatry."[51] The following discussion considers that problem.

The Demand for the Superlative

"There is in all men a demand for the superlative," Holmes wrote—adding, in Holmesian fashion, that this demand is so potent "that the poor devil who has no other way of reaching it attains it by getting drunk."[52] The almost universal character of the religious instinct provides powerful support for Holmes's view; in all times and cultures, it seems, most human beings have felt, at least on some occasions, the impulse to seek meaning, guidance, or help from some greater-than-human source. Mircea Eliade asserts that "nonreligious man *in the pure state* is a comparatively rare phenomenon, even in the most desacralized of modern societies. The majority of the 'irreligious' still behave religiously, even though they are not aware of the fact."[53]

This impulse to believe in a higher source can be understood in several ways. Three familiar kinds of explanations will be briefly noted here: the Freudian, the ethical, and the spiritual. Freud, in discussing the psychological origins of religious belief, stresses two factors: memories of the childhood experience of relating to a father, and "men's helplessness" and need for consolation in the face of nature, fate, and civilization.[54] These psychological conditions combine, he argues, to generate a belief in some entity possessing "superior wisdom" and "supreme goodness."[55] Religious beliefs, in Freud's view, are the product of "wish fulfillment"; they are "illusions, fulfilments of the oldest, strongest and most insistent wishes of mankind."[56] Thus, the Freudian explanation of the religious impulse to believe in a higher source associates that impulse with a prerational, immature psychological condition—one which, with the development of our rationality, we ought to outgrow.[57]

Contrary to Freud's position, an ethical explanation of the impulse to believe in a higher source may suggest that such belief is necessary in order to justify our ethical sense that there are "right" and "wrong" ways to live, and that moral judgments are not merely calculations of self-interest. In his now classic account of ethical philosophy, *After Virtue*, Alasdair MacIntyre argues that the "Enlightenment Project"—the "project of providing a rational vindication of morality" for a "world of secular rationality [in which] religion could no longer provide . . . [a] foundation for moral discourse and action"—has failed, and indeed was bound to fail.[58] MacIntyre's thesis provides a basis for the view that without a higher source, the distinction between "want" and "ought," or between what we would like to do and what we should do, is in danger of dissolution.

In an essay entitled "Unspeakable Ethics, Unnatural Law," Arthur Leff offers a provocative discussion of this problem. Leff asserts that "(a) all normative statements are evaluations of actions and other states of the world; (b) an evaluation entails an evaluator; and (c) in the presumed absence of God, the only available evaluators are people."[59] "A good state of the world," Leff insists, "must be good to *someone*. One cannot escape from the fact that a normative statement is an evaluation merely by dispensing with any mention of who is making it."[60] But if statements like "Charity is good" or "Cheating is bad" merely mean that these qualities are good or bad *to some human being*, then when people disagree on a moral question because different actions or characteristics benefit or disadvantage them differently, it becomes difficult or impossible to resolve the conflict—there is no other principle or higher source to appeal to. Much of Leff's essay addresses this problem and tries to show that there is no escape from it.

Beyond underscoring the problem of resolving moral conflicts among individuals or groups, Leff's argument makes the nature of moral statements problematic even for individuals themselves. What does it mean to say, for example, "Although I could cheat on my taxes and get away with it, it would be 'wrong' to do that"? The statement might mean that it is somehow not in my own long-term interest to cheat on my taxes, even if I can avoid detection. If so, however, the statement is not only dubious as a factual matter, it fails to capture the sense that moral statements are fundamentally different from statements of self-interest. Or perhaps the proposition means that although it is not in my own interest to pay taxes, it is better for the greater number of people, or for society as a whole, if I do so. But this rendering leaves a familiar and serious problem: Why should I sacrifice my own interest for that of society as a whole? Indeed, what does it even mean to say that I "should" sacrifice my interest for that of society? If this seemingly moral pronouncement is merely equivalent to a factual assertion that society will benefit from my sacrifice, then my response may be that I already knew that; but this factual assertion, although true, is not responsive to the important question: Why *should* I sacrifice my interest? The distinctively "moral" quality of the injunction to pay my taxes seems to have vanished.

The point can be put more generally: If there is no higher source of good or right, so that purely human goods are all we have, then the difference between moral decisions and calculations of individual or collective self-interest seems to disappear. And that conclusion creates severe difficulties in dealing both with the specific problem of egoism or selfishness and with the more general problem of explaining what it is that makes some kinds of discourse or counsel "moral" rather than merely "prudential."

Leff ends his reflections on a gloomy note:

All I can say is this: it looks as if we are all we have. Given what we know about ourselves and each other, this is an extraordinarily unappetizing prospect; looking around the world, it appears that if all men are brothers, the ruling model is Cain and Abel. Neither reason, nor love, nor even terror, seems to have worked to make us "good," and worse than that, there is no reason why anything should. Only if ethics were something unspeakable by us, could law be unnatural, and therefore unchallengeable. As things now stand, everything is up for grabs.

Nevertheless:

Napalming babies is bad.

Starving the poor is wicked.

Buying and selling each other is depraved.

Those who stood up to and died resisting Hitler, Stalin, Amin, and Pol Pot—and General Custer too—have earned salvation.

Those who acquiesced deserve to be damned.

There is in the world such a thing as evil.

[All together now:] Sez who?

God help us.[61]

This unhappy conclusion is a consequence of "the presumed absence of God." Leff stresses that "it is of the utmost importance to see why a God-grounded system has no analogues. Either God exists or He does not, but if he does not, nothing and no one else can take His place."[62] Thus, Leff's essay can be understood, as his final sentence may imply, as an oblique argument for the necessity of believing in a higher source if the status of our ethical beliefs is to be preserved.

The Freudian account of our need for a higher source suggests that the religious belief in such a source arises from nonrational psychological needs; the ethical account, by contrast, views such beliefs as rationally necessary in order to make sense of and uphold our pervasive beliefs about morality and the status of ethical judgment. A third, more "spiritual," account is openly religious, and for that reason controversial. For those who find this account credible, however, it explains the "demand for the superlative" in a way that subsumes the Freudian and ethical explanations. The spiritual account, which although familiar in Christian thought is not uniquely Christian,[63] maintains that the human soul is created by God, who is its true good. However, the soul has become estranged; its direct relationship with God has been severed. In this estranged situation, human beings experience spiritual yearnings to be reunited with God; no other, lesser goods can satisfy such yearnings.[64] In a chapter entitled "How God Alone Is Our True End," the Christian mystic Thomas à Kempis offers a characteristic expression of this view. The chapter describes the following counsel from Christ to the disciple: "My son, I must be your supreme and final End, if you desire true happiness. Fixed on Myself, your affection which too often is wrongly inclined to yourself and creatures, will be cleansed. For whenever you seek yourself, at once you become discouraged and desolate. Therefore, refer all things to Me, for it is I who have given all to you. Consider everything as springing from the supreme Good, since to Myself, as their Source, must all things return."[65]

The spiritual account of religious aspiration and belief can accept the Freudian explanation as a kind of half-truth. By this view, the psychological impulse to believe is real and significant. The recognition of this impulse, however, far from undermining religious belief or showing it to be irrational (as in Freud's account), in fact provides support for such belief; the impulse is evidence of our estranged state and of our inherent yearning to be reunited with God.[66] Similarly, the failure of secular ethics as described by MacIntyre, Leff, and others is, from the perspective of the spiritual account, fully to be expected. How could any theory of the good life hope to succeed when it takes no account of the highest human good or of the essential human need that other, lesser goods can never satisfy?[67]

The Freudian, ethical, and spiritual accounts all support, albeit in very different ways, Holmes's observation that humans feel a "demand for the superlative." The obvious ensuing question is how this demand is to be satisfied. One possibility, and seemingly the most satisfying one *if* it is available, is that the object of that demand is in fact attainable. Thus, a premise of much religious belief is that a higher source really exists and that human beings can receive help from, or achieve union with, that source.

Unfortunately, this answer to the demand for a higher source may be unavailable—either generally unavailable or unavailable in some circumstances. There may not be any higher source; or if there is, we may not have access to it (perhaps because of our own faithlessness). Hence, another possibility is that we should deal with the demand for the superlative by denying it—by frankly admitting that "we are all we have." This admission might be seen as a mark of maturity, as a liberating measure that will allow us to take control of our own destiny and take responsibility for our own conduct and future. Such a view is a prominent modern motif.[68]

There is, however, a third possibility. The "demand for the superlative," the impulse to find a higher source, may be more relentless than some modern thinkers have supposed. The failure of prophecies of imminent secularization in this country and the inability of Marxist regimes to suppress religion suggest that humans cannot so easily slough off their religious beliefs and yearnings.[69] Moreover, world history in this century, and indeed since the ideals of the Enlightenment became dominant in the eighteenth century, give reason to question the optimism exuded in humanist manifestos calling on us to take control of our destiny or to take responsibility for our future. These more sober reflections suggest a profound dilemma: We desperately need the help and guidance of a higher source, but that help is not available. In this situation, we might opt (as Freud suggests we *have* done) for the next best thing after an *actual* higher source—that is, the *illusion* of a higher source. More precisely, we might choose idolatry.

The Alternative of Idolatry

The term *idolatry* conjures up visions of primitive pagan rituals far distant from—and perhaps beyond the capacity of—our own culture. In its essence, however, idolatry is simply a practice in which humans take an object of human construction and, by an act of imagination, endow that object with superhuman wisdom, virtue, or power.[70] In this way the need for a higher source is satisfied—albeit by an object which, at least to one who looks at the practice from the outside, is merely a counterfeit.

The Old Testament narrative of the golden calf, perhaps the most famous account of idolatry, is helpful in identifying the basic features of idolatrous practice. In this biblical story, the community of Israel has been freed from slavery and led by Moses out of Egypt and into the inhospitable Sinai Desert. There is insufficient food and water in the desert, and the Israelites are forced to rely on God miraculously to provide these necessities. If this situation is an unhappy one, the alternatives are not necessarily preferable. In one direction lies Egypt, where the Israelites had been enslaved. In the other direction lies Canaan, the Israelites' intended destination. As they will soon learn, however, the Canaanites are reported to be fierce giants. In short, the Israelites depend entirely on divine aid both for their preservation and for their future prospects.[71]

As the story unfolds, the community of Israel receives divine aid through the help of God's prophet, Moses, who speaks with God face-to-face. Moses, however, has ascended Mount Sinai to meet with God and has been gone for some time. The Israelites now doubt that he will return. In this situation, the need to reestablish a connection with a greater-than-human source of help seems imperative. The Israelites approach Aaron, their leader in Moses's absence, with an urgent demand: "When the people saw that Moses delayed to come down from the mountain, the people gathered themselves together to Aaron, and said to him, 'Up, make us gods, who shall go before us; as for this Moses, the man who brought us up out of the land of Egypt, we do not know what has become of him.'"[72] Aaron responds by instructing them to bring him all their gold earrings. He then uses the gold to make a golden calf and presents it to them as an object of worship.

The biblical narrative describes both the merely human nature of the calf's construction and the imaginative act by which the Israelites endowed the idol with a supernatural quality. The description of the making of the idol indicates that there was nothing extraordinary about its construction: Aaron accepted their offering and *"fashioned it with a graving tool, and made a molten calf."*[73] However, when Aaron later relates the event from his own perspective, this mundane quality gives way to the miraculous: "And I said to them, 'Let any who have gold take it off'; so they gave it to me, and I threw it into the fire, and *there came out this calf."*[74] The biblical account also conveys the Israelites' sense of comfort, and indeed of jubilation, when they receive the golden calf. They accept the idol with feasting and rejoicing.[75] They dance, sing, and shout as they praise it.[76]

The story reflects the various aspects or stages of the practice of idolatry: the human need for superhuman help or guidance, the perceived lack of such help, the consequent fashioning of an object of worship by purely human means, the imaginative endowment of that object with superhuman qualities, and the sense of comfort or satisfaction received from accepting the idol. Once these characteristics are abstracted from the particular story, it becomes apparent that idolatry is a phenomenon not limited to the specific kinds of practices described in the Old Testament, or indeed to the worship of physical objects.

For example, in Plato's *Apology,* Socrates is described as giving what would appear to an outsider to be an idolatrous account of the poetry revered by the Greeks. Socrates describes his disappointment on questioning poets about their finest works and discovering that the poets could not explain the meaning of their own poems. "It is hardly an exaggeration to say that any of the bystanders could have explained those poems better than their actual authors."[77] Socrates concludes with an explanation possibly calculated more to appeal to the audience than to express his or Plato's actual belief: "I decided that it was not wisdom that enabled them to write their poetry, but a kind of instinct or inspiration, such as you find in seers and prophets who deliver all their sublime messages without knowing in the least what they mean."[78] This account would have the virtue of justifying the devotion that Socrates's contemporaries seem to have paid to the poems of Homer and others. Such respect would be warranted if the poems were not merely the work of talented but nonetheless mortal poets, but rather were in some sense divine.

Homer's is not the only literature to have been endowed with superhuman significance, and thus to have become an object of idolatry. For example, Hans-Wilhelm Kelling argues that the same thing has happened to the works of Goethe:

> Not only lay readers but also many specialists and scholars approach the renowned poet with unusual veneration and often regard him as an absolute authority on most matters of concern, particularly on questions of theology and religion. In Germany Goethe is revered as the perfect example of a Dichter, a creative artist who is much more than a skilled literary craftsman, laboring consciously and exerting rigorous effort to produce his art. The concept Dichter does not imply a hard working individual, but rather a unique being, quite unlike ordinary humans, who is endowed by a supernatural source with special insights, gifts, and intuitions enabling him to establish contact with transcendental spheres. The term denotes aspects of prophet, seer, revelator, leader of his people, one endowed with the gifts of God to an extraordinary extent, one set apart and participating in a divine spirit to whom the heavens are always open.[79]

In a related vein, numerous scholars have described the existence in this country of a "civil religion" in which the Constitution is revered as something approaching sacred scripture,[80] and not merely a political and legal document reflecting the deliberations and dealings of distinctly human delegates representing the interests of distinctly human citizens of a dozen states. Civil religion scholarship describes a phenomenon much like the idolatry that is the subject of this essay. Scholars seem to regard civil religion as an element of popular culture, however, and thus as something quite far removed from the more rational, self-aware deliberations of legal scholars.[81] The present essay suggests, on the contrary, that idolatry is a practice that permeates a good deal of recent constitutional theory and practice.

On the Uses of Idolatry

Biblical discussions of idolatry are never laudatory; perhaps no other inquiry is as fiercely condemned by Old Testament prophets. But the question whether idolatry is evil—like the question whether capitalism or democracy or the rule of law or the traditional family is evil—should imply another question: Compared with what? Biblical condemnations can be understood as asserting that, compared with the worship of the true God, idolatry is an unqualified evil. If one has the option of receiving help and guidance from a beneficent and all-powerful God, the alternative of seeking help from an impotent, man-made object has nothing to recommend it; from this perspective, idolatry is both impious and irrational. But if the alternative is to forgo worship altogether, the question becomes more difficult.

From the perspective of the political state, idolatry may be preferable to nonbelief. Rousseau made the essential argument: Because "no State has ever been established without having religion for its basis," the state should establish a civil religion, or a "purely civil profession of faith," in order to cultivate "sentiments of sociability without which it is impossible to be either a good citizen or a faithful subject."[82] This position need not be understood as tyrannical or self-serving on the part of those who control the state; indeed, the governors might promote idolatry solely in the interest of the governed. If the alternative to idolatry is the loss of community, or even civil chaos, then the interests of the citizens may require cultivation of an idolatrous civil religion.

It might seem that religious believers should reject this political rationale for idolatry, or at most tolerate it grudgingly as a necessary evil. But even from a religious perspective idolatry may be preferable to outright unbelief. The person who pays devotion to an idol is at least exercising his spiritual faculties; he is cultivating attitudes of reverence, humility, and faith. To be sure, from the religious perspective these faculties are misdirected—focused on an improper object. Still, the exertion of spiritual faculties, even though misdirected, may be a step toward a more pure or proper worship; when the true object of devotion is presented the idolater may be prepared to accept it.[83] In the unbeliever, in contrast, spiritual faculties might atrophy through lack of use, so that the unbeliever will be unable to accept a true object of worship when it is presented to him. (A counterargument might assert, of course, that by satisfying the individual's spiritual yearnings with a counterfeit object of worship, idolatry makes it less likely that the individual will seek or accept the true object of worship.)

In addition, religions often accept and even encourage the use of icons or images, physical objects or ceremonial displays that are not thought actually to possess divine qualities, but that symbolically represent spiritual realities or help to focus the believers' thoughts and feelings on those realities. Religious statues, paintings, music, architecture, and liturgies all attempt to serve this devotional purpose.[84] The use of images can lapse into idolatry if the believer slips from regarding the image as a mere symbol and begins to treat it as having divine qualities in itself.[85] Consequently, the use of images or icons has often generated controversy.[86] Beginning with Gregory the Great's defense of religious icons as the "books of the ignorant,"[87] Catholicism has historically been favorably disposed toward such practices. Conversely, Protestants have characteristically been suspicious and critical of them.[88]

The widespread acceptance of at least some religious images makes the condemnation of idolatry difficult. Ultimately it is only the deity and the religious believer herself who know whether she is treating a religious aid as idol or icon. Moreover, the slipperiness of the distinction suggests again the possibility that idolatry might be viewed as a step toward true worship. Just as the believer might slip from worship into idolatry, so too, in a contrary movement, the idolater might come to look beyond the idol, thereby elevating her devotion into true worship.

To be sure, the defense of idolatry can never be enthusiastic. To the rigorous believer, true worship will always be infinitely more rewarding than idolatry; to the devout rationalist, idolatry and the indulgence of illusion must always seem to be sinning against the cold truth. From any standpoint, therefore, idolatry falls far short of the ideal. But in a world that itself falls manifestly short of the ideal, idolatry might be, in some situations, the best available alternative.

IDOLATRY IN CONSTITUTIONAL PRACTICE AND SCHOLARSHIP

The preceding discussion suggests that the impulse to idolatry, far from being confined to primitive cultures, is better understood as a persistent feature of the human situation. If this is so, then even though law is not an inherently or necessarily idolatrous enterprise, it would be surprising if the impulse to idolatry did not manifest itself in this area. Law, particularly constitutional law, is a central locus both of coercive force and of symbolic meaning in our culture; and the desire to believe that law is in some way expressive of or responsive to a higher source of meaning would naturally be strong.

In this vein, Holmes argued that theories of natural law are an expression of the human demand for the superlative.[89] In at least some legal theories— Aquinas's classical natural law theory, for example—the link between a theory of law and a belief in a higher source is explicit and unapologetic.[90] In modern constitutional law, the connection is more veiled. I will argue, however, that the impulse to idolatry is discernible in modern constitutional interpretation.[91] In essence, much contemporary constitutional interpretation takes a human construction—the constitutional text—and endows it with superhuman qualities. The following discussion examines the familiar techniques by which this imaginative endowment occurs and suggests that an account of constitutional law as idolatry provides the most plausible explanation for much modern practice and theory.

A First Step in Idolatry: The Constructed Author

Insofar as interpretation attempts to discern the intention or understanding of actual human beings, there is nothing idolatrous about its practice. As noted, however, much constitutional interpretation appears to give authoritative status not to the understanding of historical, flesh-and-blood authors, but rather to the intentions of a constructed person or author. The practice of constructing an author does not by itself amount to idolatry; whether it deserves that label depends on the character and qualities ascribed to the constructed author. Thus, the constructed author might be almost human in her qualities. Much statutory construction arguably invokes a constructed author who is very much like actual human legislators except that she is more self-conscious and focused in her intentions and more meticulous in her expression and punctuation. For example, some canons of construction arguably contemplate this kind of more punctilious, barely better than human author.[92] Conversely, we might in theory suppose an incompetent or iniquitous author and, accordingly, adopt as a maxim of interpretation the idea that the most faithful construction—the construction that most likely captures this clumsy or demonic author's intent—is the one that makes the text "the worst it can be."[93]

If the technique of inventing an author is not equivalent to idolatry, however, it does facilitate the practice. So long as we are concerned with the intentions of actual human authors, idolatry is difficult. But if we can invent the author, then we gain the freedom to endow that author with qualities of our choosing—including, if we wish, superhuman qualities. Thus, the pervasive technique of the constructed author, although not idolatrous in itself, enhances the possibility of an idolatrous interpretive practice.

This possibility is heightened when an interpreter insists on seeing the Constitution, or law generally, as the work of a single author.[94] Such unitariness, of course, is not a necessary aspect of imagined authorship. Even if one concludes that the legal interpreter should look to an artificial author, the interpreter might nonetheless suppose that different statutes, judicial decisions, or constitutional provisions are the work of different artificial authors. In this view, if different legal texts appear to conflict, as they often do, then the interpreter's task would not be to construct an artificial unity, but rather simply to decide which of the conflicting provisions should prevail.

But multiple and perhaps clashing authors, although both possible and man-ifestly more consistent with the historical and political realities of lawmaking, make for a much messier realm of higher meaning. A collection of potentially disputatious authors would resemble the Greek pantheon of often warring deities. As Plato perceived, the spectacle of these divine disruptions is hardly one that inspires a healthy devotion.[95] A monoauthorial or monotheistic legal universe is more supportive of unqualified faith.

The Second Step: The Invocation of "Principle"

If law is to serve as a higher source, then it must be invested with greater-than-human wisdom or virtue. In modern constitutional theory and practice, the leading technique by which this endowment is achieved consists of the invoca-tion of "principle." Legal theorists of all stripes, from Herbert Wechsler and Alexander Bickel to Ronald Dworkin and Robert Bork, have insisted that the Constitution is in some sense a repository of principles.[96] Indeed, theorists often treat this Constitution-as-principles view as if it were axiomatic, as Michael Perry's statement reflects: "The fundamental reason any part of the Constitution . . . was ratified is that the ratifiers wanted to establish . . . a particular principle or principles: the principle(s) they understood the provi-sion to mean or to communicate either directly, by naming the principle, *or indirectly, by referring to it without naming it.*"[97]

Of course, not all of these theorists have understood principles in the same way. Typically, however, principles function to endow constitutional provisions with a wisdom that transcends that of either their flesh-and-blood authors or their mortal interpreters. *Brown v. Board of Education* provides a noteworthy example of this phenomenon. Legal scholars commonly acknowledge that the actual human framers and ratifiers of the Fourteenth Amendment did not believe that the amendment prohibited racially segregated schools.[98] Nonethe-less, these scholars have also argued that *Brown* was correctly decided because the Court properly applied the principle of the equal protection clause.[99] The conspicuous gap between the framers' conscious understanding and the princi-ple they adopted makes clear that the principle must have had moral content that exceeded the framers' own ethical or social vision.

Similarly, legal scholars do not accept the notion that *Brown* merely ex-pressed the political or moral judgment of nine men who happened to occupy the Supreme Court in 1954 and who therefore enjoyed the power to impose their political and moral views on the nation. Rather, scholars devote consid-erable effort to showing that *Brown* resulted from constitutional interpretation.[100] The *Brown* Court was applying "the law"—a law scholars conceive of as embodying a principle that evidently transcends the social vision or political judgment of both the citizens who wrote and ratified the legal text and the jurists who in 1954 were called on to interpret it. Tribe and Dorf explain: "It is not that the *meaning* of the Fourteenth Amendment had changed. . . . It took us longer than it should have to concede that segregating people in the public schools *amounted* to subjugating an entire race by force of law. But the basic principle remained constant."[101]

The reliance on principles that is so ubiquitous in constitutional interpretation today raises some troubling questions that are rarely addressed. One set of questions challenges the use of this technique in what purports to be a broadly originalist approach to interpretation. It is often argued that fidelity to original intent requires a court to implement the principle—or the concept or norm—adopted by the framers, rather than their more specific expectations or conceptions. In this way, a court can be said to have been faithful to original intent even when it reaches a specific result that the framers would not have approved.[102] But why should we suppose that the enactors of a legal text were adopting a principle, or a concept or norm, that was somehow implicit in but not expressed by the text? How did it come to be foreordained that constitutional provisions necessarily approve or embody a principle—even when they do so "indirectly, . . . without naming it"? If the enactors wanted to adopt a principle, why did they not do so explicitly instead of leaving the principle hidden in a text that says something else? Or, if the enactors *were* adopting a principle (and in some cases a legal text may be vague or general enough to make that supposition plausible),[103] how do we know that the current decision has selected the right principle? If the current decision deviates from the specific intentions or expectations of the enactors, is it not more plausible to conclude that the decision probably did *not* proceed from the same principle approved by the enactors?

It is sometimes said that the enactors might have been mistaken about the meaning or consequences of the principle they adopted.[104] If that is possible, other questions arise. Perhaps if the enactors had foreseen what were to them unwanted consequences, they would not have adopted the principle at all. So how much authority should a principle adopted by mistake carry for us? Is its force negated, or at least diluted, on a theory of legislative error?

These preliminary questions lead to a more fundamental, and ultimately ontological, question: What *is* a principle? Where, or in what form, can a principle be said to exist or to be real? It will be helpful here to consider three accounts of principle: the formalist, the conventionalist, and the realist.

The formalist account. This view explains what a legal principle is by its form. A principle is a general proposition that can be applied to the facts and can dictate outcomes in a range of cases, not merely in a single case. Herbert Wechsler's famous essay contains language suggesting some such conception. The target of Wechsler's criticism is the judicial decision based on "*ad hoc* evaluation"—or the decision maker who "simply lets his judgment turn on the immediate result"—and the remedy is to demand decisions that are "genuinely principled, resting with respect to every step that is involved in reaching judgment on analysis and reasons quite transcending the immediate result that is achieved."[105] Wechsler stressed that a principle is characterized by "neutrality and generality," so that it can be assessed by results it implies in a range of cases, not merely by the "instant application."[106]

The formalist account explains what a principle is; unfortunately, its conception renders the notion of "principle" largely useless for constitutional purposes. The problem is that it will *always* be possible purely as a formal matter to state a general proposition that dictates a particular result in a particular case and also supports satisfactory results in other cases. Consequently, a formalist requirement of principle provides no criterion for reaching one result over another, or for separating good decisions from bad ones.

Wechsler evidently supposed, for example, that a decision would be unprincipled if it were based merely on the fact that the claim was "put forward by a labor union or a taxpayer, a Negro or a segregationist, a corporation or a Communist."[107] But his supposition seems baseless. The proposition "Labor unions win" applies to a broad range of cases; it does not represent "*ad hoc* evaluation." Nothing stops that proposition from being, *in form,* a principle. Perhaps it is a bad principle, or one with no ground in the Constitution; but there is no remedy for that problem in the insistence that decisions be "genuinely principled."

Or perhaps Wechsler took it for granted that in fact no one would honestly favor the proposition "Labor unions win" in *every* case. But if that is so, then one need merely define the principle more carefully so that it covers only the cases in which one thinks labor unions should win. And if no conventional English terms seem ready at hand to describe the category of cases one wants covered, lawyers, of all people, could hardly object to the creation of a specialized vocabulary for the purpose. So the proposition might be something like "Labor unions win in cases of *perdorum*"—perdorum being a term of art coined to describe the category containing cases A, B, F, I, S, W, and X. From a purely *formal* perspective, this proposition's credentials as a principle are impeccable. It is, after all, a general proposition covering more than one case; and the person proposing this principle is presumably quite willing to endorse not only its "instant application" (to case F, say) but also its implications in the range of cases that it covers.

If we object to this sort of gerrymander, that is because we instinctively assume some kind of *substantive*, or content-oriented, constraint on what can count as a principle. Like Wechsler, in other words, we tacitly assume that in order to be a principle, a general proposition must somehow exist in something more than a merely formal sense. But in what deeper sense can a principle be thought to exist? The conventionalist and realist accounts address that question.

The conventionalist account. The conventionalist view holds that a principle is a general moral or political *belief* that is actually held by one or more human beings, and that principles therefore exist *in human minds* or in human culture. When we refer to the "principle of equality" or the "principle of humane punishment" or the "nonestablishment principle," we are not referring merely to the form of an idea; but neither are we describing an object that is in some sense "out there," and that thus enjoys some kind of extramental existence. Rather, we are referring to a general ethical belief held by some person or community.

The conventionalist account of what a principle is seems consistent with at least some of the uses to which the word is put. Unfortunately, a principle understood in this way still cannot do the work that much modern constitutional theory requires of it. If a principle existed in some objective sense independent of human beliefs *about* it, then it would be meaningful to say that someone accepts the principle but is mistaken or uninformed about the principle's content or consequences. That assertion would be analogous to saying that someone bought a car or a computer without understanding how the machine works or what it can do. But if a principle is nothing more than a kind of belief held by a person or group, the same assertion becomes problematic.

The "nonestablishment principle" adopted by the framers, for example, would by this account refer to certain beliefs held by the framers. To say that the framers misunderstood the meaning of that principle, therefore, could only mean that the framers were mistaken about what they themselves believed. They thought they believed something that they really didn't believe (or they really believed something they thought they didn't believe). It is not clear just how this enigmatic situation would arise, and it is in any event unclear how a contemporary court or scholar could ever be in a better position than the framers themselves to know what the framers "really" thought.

Similarly, if a principle has no objective status independent of human beliefs, then the explanation that a later decision implements the principle that the enactors adopted even though it deviates from their actual beliefs and conscious intentions borders on the nonsensical. If a principle is merely a belief existing in the mind of a person or persons, then if different groups hold different beliefs, those beliefs by definition do not constitute the same principle. Thus, if the specific beliefs that we associate with terms like *equality* or *religious freedom* are different from the specific beliefs that some earlier group associated with those terms, then by definition we are not talking about the same principles. By the conventionalist account, what we have in common with them is a term. If we pretend there is more than that or that "the basic principle [has] remained constant,"[108] we are simply equivocating; we are deluding ourselves with word games.

This point is typically deflected by the "level of abstraction" move, often using the familiar "concept/conception" distinction.[109] This move may be legitimate, but only if it assumes moral realism; hence, the move at least tacitly abandons a conventionalist account of principles in favor of the realist account (discussed below).

Suppose, for example, that convincing evidence shows the following: (1) in the eighteenth century, Americans generally believed that (a) "religious freedom," as they called it, was a fundamental right, and (b) prosecution for blasphemy was perfectly permissible; (2) in the late twentieth century, Americans generally believe that (a) "religious freedom," as we call it, is a fundamental right, and (b) blasphemy prosecutions are plainly *not* permissible. Legal scholars today, employing the level of abstraction move and the concept/conception distinction, might say that although our specific conclusions (or "conceptions") are in some sense directly contrary to those favored by our ancestors, at a more general level of abstraction we believe in the same principle (or concept)—that is, religious freedom.

What could this statement mean? One possibility is that the statement is simply asserting that we use the same words to refer to what are in fact quite different notions about the proper relations between government and religion. That assertion seems eminently plausible. But verbal similarity merely establishes verbal similarity—nothing more. It does not show that we and our ancestors share the same principle of religious freedom. The more accurate characterization would suggest that the same words are now used in different ways—that they are used, that is, to mean (at least partially) different things.

If talking about the "same principle" is to make sense—if it is to be more than a word game—then the "principle of religious freedom" needs to be something beyond both the words we use and the specific conceptions of religious freedom that we or our ancestors have held. If this principle is independent of both our words and our specific opinions about it, then it would be possible for our ancestors (or for us) to be wrong about the meaning or implications of the principle. It would also be conceivable that the same principle might dictate conclusion A (heresy prosecutions) in some circumstances but conclusion B (no heresy prosecutions) in very different circumstances. These possibilities depend, once again, on the principle having some reality or objective status beyond our opinions about it. If we make that assumption, however, we are no longer giving a purely conventionalist account of what a principle is.[110]

The realist account. The difficulties of a conventionalist account could be avoided by supposing that a principle enjoys some independent, perhaps Platonic, reality. We can, after all, hold conflicting opinions about the same moon or the same mountain, and we can sensibly say that we now know more about the moon or the mountain than our ancestors did. It makes sense to talk in this way because we suppose that the moon and the mountain exist independent of us and of our beliefs about them. If principles also enjoyed such an independent existence, the same possibilities should be available. Thus, a different, "moral realist" account of what a principle is might avoid some of the problems that attend the conventionalist account.

The moral realist account of principles would not answer all the questions raised by the invocation of principle. Thus, even if we assume that the framers approved a principle, and even if principles are in some sense independent of the framers' beliefs about them, it is still far from clear why contemporary decision makers should make a particular decision because an adopted principle supports or requires it, especially if that principle was adopted by mistake by framers who did not decide or intend to authorize this decision. It still might make more sense, or be more consistent with democratic assumptions, to implement the principle as the framers of the provision (mistakenly) understood it.

More fundamentally, few legal theorists or jurists today seem prepared to admit that principles enjoy any such extramental or Platonic reality. Confessing moral realists are relatively rare in the legal community.[111] In any event, it would not be enough merely to claim the label of "moral realist" and assert that "principles *are* 'real.'" That assertion by itself would still leave the ontological status of principles very unclear. *How,* or *in what sense,* are principles real? Medieval theology and philosophy might have been able to suggest answers to these questions—principles might have been said to be ideas in the mind of God,[112] for instance. It is debatable, however, whether modern secular thought possesses the metaphysical resources necessary to explain how principles could be said to exist independent of human beliefs.[113]

At present, therefore, two observations seem warranted regarding the pervasive invocation of principles in constitutional interpretation. First, principles are understood as operating to endow constitutional texts with meaning and wisdom beyond the finite capacities of their flesh-and-blood authors or readers. Second, this pervasive appeal to principles entails a suspension of disbelief and critical examination regarding fundamental difficulties that the invocation of principles would seem to generate. Together, these observations suggest that the practice of invoking and attaching considerable importance to principles is a modern instance of the imaginative act by which a merely human construction—in this case, positive constitutional law—is endowed with superhuman qualities.

An Example of Idolatry in Legal Theory: Dworkin's (Imaginary) Community of Principle

A yearning for community is conspicuous in much recent legal literature. At the same time, the purely human bonds that might make community possible seem increasingly tenuous. Alasdair MacIntyre argues that a genuine political community rests on "shared moral first principles" but that "our society as a whole has none." Consequently, our politics are not those of a genuine community; they are "civil war carried on by other means."[114] Under these circumstances, the desire to exalt the law, and thereby to transform it into a higher source, may take on a special urgency.

The need for community reflected in legal scholarship today can also be found in religious stories. Earlier I described the bleak situation of the biblical community of Israel after its release from Egypt. The community's dependence on providential assistance led to the idolatry narrated in the story of the golden calf. However, the earlier description neglected one essential aspect of Israel's dependence. The community depended on God's aid not merely for its physical survival but for its very character: Israel understood itself as having a special destiny or calling because of its special relationship to God. The Book of Exodus records God's proposition to Israel: "Therefore, if you will obey my voice and keep my covenant, you shall be my own possession among all peoples; for all the earth is mine, and you shall be to me a kingdom of priests and a holy nation."[115] The community enthusiastically accepted this proposition.[116] This calling gave Israel its special character as a people; without this sense of calling, the community would have been an aggregation of individuals with some common interests and, perhaps, a common geographical destination, but it would not have been a community in the full sense in which it understood itself. The community's knowledge that its identity and status were based on a relationship with God is an ongoing biblical theme: "Blessed is the nation whose God is the Lord, the people whom he has chosen as his heritage!"[117]

In legal scholarship, the law, endowed by principles with a transcendent wisdom, might create and guide a community in modern society, just as the biblical God created and guided the community of Israel. Robert Nagel argues that a religious yearning for community underlies the role that the Warren Court has played in modern constitutional thought. "The Warren Court is so enshrined because of a need for deeper roots in a political community," Nagel suggests. "Those who know the Court to be a wholly ordinary and unholy institution are demanding that it provide substitutes for political fellowship and religious conviction."[118]

But if we make the law serve a religious or providential function while at another level we know it to be a "wholly ordinary and unholy institution," then we make the law into an idol. This resort to idolatry as a ground for genuine community, and hence for the authority of law, is discernible in Ronald Dworkin's interpretive theory. In Dworkin's view, a theory of law must explain why the law "provides a justification for the use of collective power against individual citizens or groups."[119] Legal theory must deal, in other words, with "the puzzle of legitimacy"; it must account for the "moral authority of the law."[120] Dworkin criticizes and rejects conventional explanations of law's moral authority, such as the argument that citizens tacitly consent to be governed by law, arguing instead that law creates a kind of "associative obligation"—that is, an obligation that attaches by virtue of membership in a group or community.[121]

Not just any community will support this kind of associative obligation, however. Dworkin argues that only a "community of principle" generates such obligations and thus supports the authority of law. And in order to qualify as a community of principle, a group must meet stringent requirements. In particular, Dworkin argues that "people are members of a genuine political community only when they accept that their fates are linked in the following strong way: they accept that they are governed by common principles, not just by rules hammered out in political compromise."[122]

At this point in Dworkin's argument, the prospects for our own law and community look bleak. Our law lacks moral authority, we are told, unless it emanates from a rigorously defined community of principle. But our own political community, it would seem, falls woefully short of that standard. As a mundane empirical matter it is wholly implausible to suppose that we agree on and are governed by "a single, coherent set of principles."[123] To the contrary, it seems far more accurate to view a large part of our law, and even of our Constitution, as the result of "political compromise," or, in MacIntyre's gloomier assessment, "civil war carried on by other means." Does this lack of moral consensus mean that our law is condemned to illegitimacy?

Dworkin's response is, literally, an imaginative one; he constructs the necessary basis of legitimacy—the community of principle—through a series of imaginative acts. The first of these acts personifies the community. We must think "*as if* a political community were really some special kind of entity distinct from the actual people who are its citizens."[124] This "as if" community is defined by its adherence to a single coherent set of principles. And those principles are in turn understood as the principles that would guide or emanate from the constructed single author of the whole law—a being who, unlike any real human being, always acts and speaks in accordance with those principles. The community of principle is thus defined not by principle in the sense of conventional morality,[125] but ultimately by its allegiance to the ever consistent dictates of this higher (imaginary) author of the law.

In Dworkin's interpretive theory, the analogy to the biblical community is conspicuous even though not explicit. In each case, the community qualifies as a genuine community by virtue of its respect for a law that emanates from a single author who displays complete integrity and who stands above politics and conventional morality.[126] And just as the community of Israel communed with God through a prophet, Moses, so Dworkin's legal empire also has its "seers and prophets." The role of prophet does not belong to judges,[127] who for Dworkin are merely "princes"; rather, "it falls to philosophers, if they are willing."[128]

Although the parallels between the biblical prophetic community and Dworkin's community of principle are striking, there is an important difference. The biblical community consisted of real persons united by faith in what they believed to be a real God. Dworkin's community is, according to his own presentation, a personified abstraction defined by its allegiance to principles emanating from a concededly artificial author. Thus, Dworkin's theory is by its own terms a theology of legal idolatry. If it is also (as it may well be) the best and most elegant account of modern constitutional interpretation, then modern constitutional interpretation is likewise idolatry.

CONCLUSION

The religious concept of idolatry may provide a valuable insight into a good deal of modern constitutional interpretation as it is practiced by courts and justified by legal scholars. Interpretation begins with a human construction: the positive constitutional law. By an act of imagination, the interpreter then endows the constitutional text with qualities that transcend those of the mortal legislators, citizens, scholars, and judges who actually write, read, and vote for the text. The leading technique by which this imaginative act is achieved is the widely used device of the constructed author, given superhuman significance through the invocation of principle—a notion all the more useful because its ontological status is so mysterious. In this way, interpretation transforms constitutional law into an object that can satisfy the citizen's or scholar's "demand for the superlative." It also provides a way of constructing, imaginatively, the true community that many yearn for but that seems beyond our capacity to realize.

An account of law as idolatry illuminates central features of our interpretive practice and theory that are difficult to explain in more mundane rational terms, and thereby helps to explain the proliferation of theories of interpretation within law and constitutional scholarship.[129] The difficulty that generates such a proliferation of theorizing lies in the precarious status of idolatry in a world that aspires to secular rationality. Even in less secular periods, idolatry demands a kind of cognitive virtuosity. The idolater must endow a man-made object with superhuman powers and then forget or deny (even to himself) that he has done so. Once this cognitive feat is accomplished, however, the traditional idolater can enjoy a certain equanimity. Within *his* cognitive framework, what he is doing seems perfectly sensible: he is worshipping or seeking the help of an entity that, he succeeds in believing, is fully deserving of such attention.

In a culture that wants to regard itself as secular, in contrast, the maintenance of idolatry is a more arduous undertaking. The modern idolater still must do what idolaters have always had to do—endow a mundane object with supernatural attributes and then forget or deny the human source and the imaginary quality of those attributes. But the secular idolater must do more: he must deny not only the idol-making process but also its conclusion. In a legal world that aspires to be secular, no appeal to "transcendent authority" and no "Kierkegaardian leap of faith" are permissible.[130] Consequently, the legal idolater must at the same time tacitly affirm and explicitly deny (even to himself) the qualities that he imaginatively ascribes to law in order to make it worthy of being interpreted and obeyed.

The traditional idolater, in other words, must deny that he is an idolater—to concede that would be to spoil the illusion—but he can admit, and even proudly proclaim, that he is a worshipper. The modern legal idolater must deny even that. Legal idolatry thus depends on a kind of double denial, or persistent cognitive contradiction. This requirement imposes on the jurist or scholar a daunting—one might say "Herculean"—labor. In this situation, it is hardly surprising that legal scholars would be driven to develop a multitude of ever more sophisticated and abstruse theories of interpretation. Nor is it surprising that these theories sometimes seem to obfuscate more than they clarify. The practice of idolatry manifestly demands a certain amount of obfuscation— more so today than in openly devout times.

These difficulties might prompt one to repudiate the whole modern enterprise of constitutional theory and interpretation, much as early iconoclastic Protestants denounced prevailing practices of worship and sometimes physically smashed religious images and objects of veneration. Whether such an iconoclastic course is advisable would seem to depend, however, on the alternatives. For those who believe that a higher source is real and accessible, or, conversely, for those who think we can live with the knowledge that "we are all we have," idolatry in the law may be unnecessary and unseemly. But for a political community that needs to believe in something beyond itself but cannot acknowledge any actual higher source, the imaginative endowment of law with transcendent wisdom or moral meaning may be the only way to maintain an illusion too precious to be relinquished.

SECULAR FUNDAMENTALISM

Paul F. Campos

Government is a true religion. It has its dogmas, its mysteries, its priests. To submit it to the discussion of each individual is to destroy it. It is given life only by the reason of the nation, that is by a political faith, of which it is a symbol.—Joseph de Maistre[1]

NEAR THE BEGINNING of his influential book *After Virtue*, Alasdair MacIntyre notes that "the most striking feature of contemporary moral utterance is that so much of it is used to express disagreements; and the most striking feature of the debates in which these disagreements are expressed is their interminable character."[2] The interminable character of modern moral dispute is a product of the fact that "there seems to be no rational way of securing moral agreement in our culture." MacIntyre proceeds to give several examples of such disputes, one of which, concerning the legal and moral status of abortion, is particularly relevant to some of the claims put forth in John Rawls's *Political Liberalism*. MacIntyre asks us to consider the following "characteristic and well-known rival moral arguments":

(a) Everybody has certain rights over his or her own person, including his or her own body. It follows from the nature of these rights that at the stage when the embryo is essentially part of the mother's body, the mother has a right to make her own uncoerced decision on whether she will have an abortion or not. Therefore abortion is morally permissible and ought to be allowed by law.

(b) I cannot will that my mother should have had an abortion when she was pregnant with me, except perhaps if it had been certain that the embryo was dead or gravely damaged. But if I cannot will this in my own case, how can I consistently deny to others the right to life that I claim for myself? I would break the so-called Golden Rule unless I denied that a mother has a general right to an abortion. I am not of course thereby committed to the view that abortion ought to be legally prohibited.

(c) Murder is wrong. Murder is the taking of an innocent life. An embryo is an identifiable individual, differing from a newborn infant only in being at an earlier stage on the long road to adult capacities[;] and, if any life is innocent, that of an embryo is. If infanticide is murder, as it is, abortion is murder. So abortion is not only morally wrong, but ought to be legally prohibited.[3]

What characteristics do such arguments share that help make contemporary moral disputes in our culture so shrill and intractable? MacIntyre concentrates on two in particular. First, the arguments display what philosophers of science call "conceptual incommensurability." That is, although each argument is logically valid in that its conclusions do indeed flow from its premises, the rival premises themselves must at some point be taken as axiomatic. This would seem to make it impossible to measure the claims of each position against its rivals. In MacIntyre's hypothetical discourse, premises that invoke rights collide with premises that invoke moral universalizability; and, given the internal consistency of the arguments, there appear to be no objective criteria available for choosing between them.

MacIntyre's second point helps explain the significance of the first. These arguments all "purport to be *impersonal* rational arguments and as such are usually presented in a mode appropriate to that impersonality."[4] Statements of value claim to be about something other than the preferences of those who make them: such propositions depend on our assent to some moral imperative, the validity of which is supposedly independent of the beliefs of the person who happens to be making the argument. The interminable character of modern moral argument is thus a direct consequence of a kind of pragmatic contradiction. Moral claims at least appear to be in some fundamental sense subjective. One cannot, given the current epistemological obscurity of such claims, demonstrate that a woman's "right" to procreative autonomy is superior to an embryo's "right" not to be aborted; in the end, all such claims must have the flavor of arbitrary assertions. The advocate's belief in any particular moral position is therefore ultimately a matter of choosing to believe one claim rather than another. Yet the moral claims themselves continue to be made in language that appeals to objective standards of judgment. Hence, what might be explained away as a clash of antagonistic wills takes place in a vocabulary that not only demands rational assent, but does so precisely in those matters in which we cannot adduce any grounds for compelling such agreement.

After Virtue is perhaps the most celebrated of the recent attempts to grapple with what various modern thinkers have come to regard as the disastrous consequences of Enlightenment rationalism for all types of ethical discourse. Yet *Political Liberalism* does not merely ignore MacIntyre's work; it does not even acknowledge the existence of a counter-Enlightenment tradition in Western political thought. Indeed, if a reader's knowledge of moral and political philosophy were limited to Professor Rawls's four-hundred-page reply to the immense literature that has grown up around *A Theory of Justice*, that reader would conclude that the fundamental premises of liberal political theory were essentially incontestable. We should, I think, be taken aback when we discover that a book written by one of the preeminent philosophers in the English-speaking world—a book, moreover, that attempts to describe definitively the proper place for comprehensive moral theories in modern life—does not refer to the work of Marx, Nietzsche, Kierkegaard, or Heidegger, or indeed to any major European social philosopher who postdates Kant and Hegel. Even if such omissions can be credited to the institutional parochialism of Anglo-American moral philosophy, what are we to make of the book's failure to engage directly with the powerful criticisms of liberal ideology that have been made by MacIntyre, Michael Sandel, Charles Taylor and others, or to answer Robert Nozick's hyper liberal attack on the liberal welfare state?[5] Faced with such apparent complacency, certain critics have begun to ask a provocative question: What features of contemporary liberalism tend to make some of its academic champions so illiberal in their unwillingness to treat fundamental disagreement with their views seriously?[6]

In this essay, I argue that *Political Liberalism*'s central concept of "public reason" is empty, and that Rawls's analysis of political issues amounts to little more than the shamanistic incantation of the word *reasonable*. Specifically, as his discussion of abortion exemplifies, Rawls simply declares that some position is reasonable and then condemns opposing views for being not merely wrong, but contrary to the dictates of reason. The term *reasonable* thus serves the same performative function in Rawls's theory as that served by the term *God* in dogmatic religious argument. I then place Rawls's style of liberal belief into historical context and suggest that the success of this particular creed is best understood in essentially sociological terms.

II

Although it is, of course, extremely complex in its details, the central argument of *Political Liberalism* is fairly straightforward. According to Rawls, liberal theory faces a conundrum: "How is it possible that there may exist over time a stable and just society of free and equal citizens profoundly divided by reasonable religious, philosophical, and moral doctrines?"[7] The conundrum arises because Rawlsian liberalism posits that the supreme political value of social life is that people should have the freedom to make their own choices; however, those very choices will inevitably prove incompatible with the choices of other persons who do not share the same reasonable religious, philosophical, and moral doctrines. How is the state to decide which of the conflicting choices will be rewarded or prohibited without at the same time illegitimately interfering with the overriding moral imperative of allowing all persons to have "an equal right to the most extensive total system of equal basic liberties compatible with a similar system of liberty for all"? That is, how can a political regime give its citizens the freedom to make autonomous moral choices based on their own comprehensive belief systems? To resolve such conflicts, political liberalism needs some criterion of choice that is not itself the product of what Rawls characterizes as a reasonable comprehensive doctrine, for such a criterion would necessitate privileging one reasonable comprehensive doctrine over all the others.

Rawls's solution involves sharply distinguishing between the types of discourse which are appropriate to the public and nonpublic spheres in social life. When citizens decide really important questions—those involving "constitutional essentials"—they cannot invoke reasons drawn exclusively from their reasonable comprehensive doctrines, but only from what Rawls terms "public reason": "Our exercise of political power is fully proper only when it is exercised in accordance with a constitution the essentials of which all citizens as free and equal may reasonably be expected to endorse in the light of principles and ideals acceptable to their common human reason. This is the liberal principle of legitimacy."[8] This idea, as Rawls acknowledges, draws from the tradition in democratic theory that traces its roots to Rousseau's social contract, especially that thinker's concept of the "general will." For Rawls, a well-ordered society should never feature incorrigible political conflict between reasonable persons, at least as regards constitutional essentials, because all reasonable persons accept the requirements of public reason, and although "there are many nonpublic reasons [there is] but one public reason."[9] Therefore, the bewildering plurality of moral belief found in such a culture should in principle give rise to a satisfyingly monistic note of reasonable consensus on all truly fundamental political questions. The liberal conundrum dissolves when we understand that citizens may "by their vote properly exercise their coercive political power over one another" only to force all reasonable citizens to accept what their own reasonable comprehensive beliefs should have affirmed for them—that is, if they would but see what their own beliefs actually require them to affirm.[10] And if people insist on being unreasonable, then the neo-Rousseauist liberal can in good faith compel them to be otherwise.[11] Rawls goes on to say that "political liberalism also supposes that a reasonable comprehensive doctrine does not reject the essentials of a democratic regime. Of course, a society may also contain unreasonable and irrational, and even mad, comprehensive doctrines. In their case the problem is to contain them so that they do not undermine the unity and justice of society."[12] Obviously the crucial question then becomes, How do we determine the content of those essentials of a democratic regime that the idea of public reason requires all adherents of reasonable comprehensive doctrines to acknowledge? Here we can turn for guidance to Rawls's discussion of public reason and its application to one of the very few discussions of an actual political dispute found within the pages of *Political Liberalism*.

Rawls gives the following account of the requirements of public reason:

> It is only in this way [by accepting the dictates of public reason], and by accepting that politics in a democratic society can never be guided by what we see as the whole truth, that we can realize the ideal expressed by the principle of legitimacy: to live politically with others in the light of reasons all might reasonably be expected to endorse. What public reason asks is that citizens be able to explain their votes to one another in terms of a reasonable balance of public political values, it being understood by everyone that of course the plurality of reasonable comprehensive doctrines held by citizens is thought by them to provide further and often transcendent backing for those values. In each case, which doctrine is affirmed is a matter of conscience for the individual citizen. It is true that the balance of political values that a citizen holds must be reasonable, and one that can be seen to be reasonable by other citizens; but not all reasonable balances are the same. The only comprehensive doctrines that run afoul of public reason are those that cannot support a reasonable balance of political values. Yet given that the doctrines actually held support a reasonable balance, how could anyone complain? What would be the objection?[13]

This passage makes an extraordinary claim: those who hold comprehensive doctrines that cannot support a reasonable balance of political values on a particular issue have no grounds to complain when public reason rules against them, because, after all, other comprehensive doctrines do manage to support a reasonable balance of political values; and if a comprehensive doctrine is truly reasonable, it will recognize the need to give way in these circumstances. What is truly remarkable is the assumption that the answer to the question of whether or not a comprehensive doctrine supports a reasonable balance of political values on some particular question will itself be sufficiently transparent to provide a satisfactory answer to those whose comprehensive doctrines do not, in the interpreter's opinion, support such a reasonable balance.

The extraordinary nature of this assumption is magnified by Rawls's vague definition of reasonableness. Rawls defines the *reasonable* as "the willingness to propose and honor fair terms of cooperation" and the "willingness to recognize the burdens of judgment and to accept their consequences" for the use of public reason.[14] By "burdens of judgment" Rawls simply means that, given the epistemological problems inherent in moral and political reasoning, we must acknowledge the validity of the disagreements that can arise among reasonable persons.[15] "The willingness to propose and honor fair terms of cooperation" is more problematic. Whether it has any substance beyond signaling that the reasonable is not limited to rational choice means-ends analysis depends on how much content is given to the term *fair*. Yet even if *fair* is read as Rawls defines it within the context of justice as fairness in *A Theory of Justice*, this former definition is, as many critics have noted, so indeterminate that it gives the reader almost no guidance as to what, on any particular political question, a reasonable balance of political values might entail.[16] Just how remarkable Rawls's views are in regard to the interpretation and resolution of profound political disagreement in a pluralistic culture becomes clear when he elaborates with a rare concrete example:

> As an illustration, consider the troubled question of abortion. . . . Suppose . . . that we consider the question in terms of three important political values: the due respect for human life, the ordered reproduction of political society over time, including the family in some form, and finally the equality of women as equal citizens. (There are, of course, other important political values besides these.) *Now I believe any reasonable balance of these three values will give a woman a duly qualified right to decide whether or not to end her pregnancy during the first trimester. The reason for this is that at this early stage of pregnancy the political value of equality of women is overriding, and this right is required to give it substance and force.** Other political values, if tallied in, would not, I think, affect this conclusion. A reasonable balance may allow her such a right beyond this, at least in certain circumstances. However, I do not discuss the question in general here, as I simply want to illustrate the point in the text by saying that *any comprehensive doctrine that leads to a balance of political values excluding that duly qualified right in the first trimester is to that extent unreasonable.*[17]

---

*Readers sympathetic to abortion rights might want to consider the intellectual cogency of the following variation on Rawls's argument: The reason why abortion must be prohibited is that at every stage of the pregnancy the political value of the due respect for human life is overriding, and this prohibition is required to give that value substance and force.

It seems that, for Rawls, "reason" and "reasonable" fill the lexical space that in many other discourses would be filled by "God," or "the scriptures," or "moral insight." The concept of the reasonable becomes for Rawls what Kenneth Burke calls a "God term"; and the characteristics of this god remain, as perhaps befits its metaphysical status, somewhat mysterious.[18] That is, "reason" functions as the master concept that transcends the enumeration of particular reasons: *invoking* "reason" becomes equivalent to *giving* reasons. The obvious circularity of this argument illustrates how a discourse that presents itself as a model of rational explication is, rationally speaking, indistinguishable from the tauto-logical or emotive language games on which the coherence theorist and the moral intuitionist must more openly rely.

How, then, can we account for the startling disjunction between the apparent plasticity of Rawls's definitional structure and the certainty with which he states what public reason requires in the case of such a divisive issue as abortion? Moreover, what is the source of the author's surprising belief that his cryptic utterance as to what a reasonable balance of political values requires regarding this "troubled question" will be accepted by those whose comprehensive doc-trines would, in his view, support an "unreasonable" balance? The answer, I believe, can be found by historicizing the particular brand of political liberal-ism that has become the dominant ideology among much of the American intelligentsia.

III

Rawls notes in his introduction that political liberalism developed in reaction to the Reformation and its aftermath. After the savage religious wars of the sixteenth and seventeenth centuries, European civilization discovered "a new social possibility: the possibility of a reasonably harmonious and stable plural-ist society."[19] Before then, it seemed natural to believe that "social unity and concord require[d] agreement on a general and comprehensive religious, philosophical, or moral doctrine."[20] Rawls offers the plausible hypothesis that religious toleration developed because "it is difficult, if not impossible, to be-lieve in the damnation of those with whom we have, with trust and confidence, long and fruitfully cooperated in maintaining a just society."[21] This is an impor-tant point: if a culture truly believes that the roads to both heavenly salvation and eternal perdition are known and are accessible through acts of human will, then almost any measure to maintain individuals and nations on the path of deliverance will not seem merely justifiable, but will become a sacred duty. Liberalism, with its initial tolerance for many versions of truth, arises in part as a response to the decay of belief in a particular truth. It becomes, we might say, the faith of those who have lost their faith.[22]

Liberalism appeared in Europe as both a symptom and a cause of the collapse of various religious and sociopolitical orthodoxies. As liberalism gradually established itself as the legitimate ideology of the Enlightenment, various liberal theories adopted different justifications for rejecting the older sources of dogmatic authority. For instance, most versions of liberalism share some set of methodological assumptions about truth being best served through an exchange or clash of opinions. Yet beyond this common commitment to what might be termed tolerance as a methodological precondition, different types of modern liberalism rely on quite disparate justifications for allowing the propagation of what are believed to be false religious, philosophical, and political claims. At the risk of speaking too schematically, we can perhaps discern three general types of liberalism in postindustrial societies. (These, of course, overlap to produce many hybrids and variants.) *Political Liberalism* distinguishes itself from two of them and exemplifies the third.

One variety of liberalism finds its roots in a general skepticism about the entire concept of "truth" as applied to all types of value statements. Ontological skeptics doubt that statements of value are anything other than statements about subjective preferences. Epistemological skeptics, in contrast, believe that no way exists to determine adequately the objective status, if any, of such value claims. Both kinds of skeptics have good reasons—to the extent that this phrase means anything for a moral skeptic—for objecting to the social imposition of a particular "truth" on those who dissent from it. Given that moral skepticism is perhaps the most distinctive feature of modernity, it is only natural that it has come to be the basis for much of the support for liberalism in the modern world.

Political Liberalism refuses to rely on this justification, as indeed it must if it is to avoid imposing its own comprehensive doctrine on those whose comprehensive doctrines reject skepticism:

> Political liberalism does not question that many political and moral judgments of certain specified kinds are correct and it views many of them as reasonable. Nor does it question the possible truth of affirmations of faith. Above all, it does not argue that we should be hesitant and uncertain, much less skeptical, about our own beliefs. Rather, we are to recognize the practical impossibility of reaching reasonable and workable political agreement in judgment on the truth of comprehensive doctrines, especially an agreement that might serve the political purpose, say, of achieving

peace and concord in a society characterized by religious and philosophical differences.[23]

This statement might be understood to imply another reason for tolerating
what those who wield political power sincerely believe are deeply mistaken and
perhaps socially pernicious views on matters of fundamental importance. If the
nature of a pluralistic society makes reaching agreement on certain issues a
practical impossibility, then prudence might well dictate that we not even
attempt to create any sort of robust consensus on such questions. This brand of
prudential or pragmatic liberalism argues that, given the morally fragmented
quality of modern life, moral consensus on many questions could be achieved
only through coercive measures that would inflict severe damage on the basic
interests of the individuals and groups being coerced—a result that would be
bad in itself and would ultimately undermine the very consensus the measures
were designed to produce. On this view, liberalism operates as a kind of necessary modus vivendi within cultures that have lost the moral or religious coherence that would properly allow for the subordination of individual or group
interests to the demands of a single comprehensive political doctrine.

Despite what the passage quoted above might seem to suggest, Rawls does
not endorse this understanding of liberalism any more than he endorses a
conception of liberalism grounded in a morally skeptical view of the world. For
him, the overlapping consensus that enables a well-ordered society to answer
the most basic questions of political obligation through the use of public reason—rather than through recourse to any comprehensive doctrine—is not the
product of any mere prudential or pragmatic compromise. This overlapping
consensus is itself the social instantiation of liberalism as a kind of fundamental
moral view:

> A typical use of the phrase "modus vivendi" is to characterize a treaty
> between two states whose national aims and interests put them at odds. In
> negotiating a treaty each state would be wise and prudent to make sure
> that the agreement proposed represents an equilibrium point [between
> their respective interests]. . . . That an overlapping consensus is quite
> different from a modus vivendi is clear . . . [for] the object of the con-
> sensus, the political conception of justice, is itself a moral conception.
> And . . . it is affirmed on moral grounds, that is, it includes conceptions of
> society and of citizens as persons, as well as principles of justice, and an
> account of the political virtues through which those principles are embod-
> ied in human character and expressed in public life. An overlapping con-
> sensus, therefore, is not merely a consensus on accepting certain authori-

ties, or on complying with certain institutional arrangements, founded on a convergence of self or group interests. All those who affirm the political conception start from within their own comprehensive view and draw on the religious, philosophical, and moral grounds it provides. The fact that people affirm the same political conception on those grounds does not make their affirming it any less religious, philosophical, or moral, as the case may be, since the grounds sincerely held determine the nature of their affirmation.[24]

Rawls's vision of liberalism, then, is neither skeptical nor pragmatic; it is instead an example of what can be called "secular fundamentalism." The secular fundamentalist asserts that the supreme political value is to produce a political system that accepts liberal principles of political morality as embodiments of the supreme political value. The exclusion of reasonable comprehensive doctrines from the idea of public reason is then justified on the grounds that those reasonable comprehensive doctrines *are* reasonable only to the extent that they acknowledge that the role of a just political system is "to enable all members of society to make mutually acceptable to one another their shared institutions and basic arrangements, by citing what are publicly recognized as sufficient reasons."[25] This variety of liberalism is properly understood as fundamentalist in the sense that it denies the possible legitimacy of deep political conflict in what it considers a just social order. The overlapping consensus of reasonable comprehensive doctrines is held to produce the authoritative (and authoritarian) voice of a public reason that speaks ex cathedra, thereby eliminating the possibility of true conceptual incommensurability and its discursive offspring, interminable moral disagreement.

The irony, of course, is that in this triumphalist incarnation liberalism can begin to resemble the very dogmatic systems it once rebelled against.[26] Despite its highly abstract endorsement of moral and religious pluralism, *Political Liberalism* is ultimately a paean to a secular creed that has within it the potential to become every bit as monistic, compulsory, and intolerant of any significant deviation from the social verities as the traditional modes of belief it derided and displaced.

IV

In his *Philosophy of Right*, Hegel argues that "Plato's *Republic*, which is usually taken as the very model of an *empty ideal*, did nothing more than conceptualize the nature of Greek mores at the time."[27] Hegel's point is that Plato's utopian vision of the ideal political community was a product of the philosopher's struggle to come to terms with the actual conditions of the contemporary Greek state. The polis ruled by philosopher kings represents Plato's imaginative attempt to resolve what was perhaps the fundamental cultural crisis of fourth-century Hellenic society: the conflict between a longing for the traditional organic community of an idealized past, and what social conservatives such as Plato saw as the chaotic individualism and impiety of the Greek present.

Perhaps the most common criticism of Rawls's work has been that the stripped-down subjects of the original position are themselves "the very model of an empty ideal"—that such an asocial conception of persons as radically distinct from their ends is both metaphysically incoherent and sociologically absurd. These criticisms have much force. What they overlook is the extent to which the antiskeptical and nonpragmatic strains of liberal ideology actually *produce* the sorts of stripped-down subjects who find the remarkably impoverished vision of a pluralistic political community presented in *Political Liberalism* both plausible and attractive. What can one say to the modern liberal intellectual who writes that abortion cannot be prohibited in the first trimester because *any reasonable balance* of political values requires recognizing such a right, and then "explains" this conclusion by pointing out that "at this early stage of pregnancy the political value of the equality of women is overriding, and this right is required to give it substance and force"?[28] Such persons can no more be argued with than those who simply declare that a particular result is required because "God says so." At least the religious fundamentalist is alluding to a rich cultural and intellectual tradition that might give some warrant for believing that statements about rights and values have some kind of metaphysical significance. Liberal ideologues, who celebrate tolerance and pluralism while at the same time condemning any meaningful dissent from their own thin idea of the good as not merely wrong but contrary to the dictates of reason itself, cannot invoke even this meager excuse.

It involves a considerable oversimplification to say that the academic deployment of empty signifiers such as "the reasonable" in ways that gratify the moral prejudices of upper-class liberal intellectuals should be understood in sociological terms. Still, consider the following passage from the introduction to *Political Liberalism:* "I acknowledge a special debt . . . [t]o Ronald Dworkin and Thomas Nagel for many conversations while taking part in seminars at New York University during 1987–1991; and in connection with the idea of justice as fairness as a freestanding view, a rare illuminating midnight conversation in the deserted bar of the Santa Lucia Hotel in Napoli in June 1988."[29] No one with any interest in contemporary jurisprudence can have failed to notice how Ronald

Dworkin's work has both drawn on and influenced Rawls's writings. The similarities between *Law's Empire* and the essays collected in *Political Liberalism* are especially striking. Indeed, Dworkin's central claim that "law as integrity" consists of making the relevant materials congruent with the best public values is echoed by Rawls's beliefs that "in a constitutional regime with judicial review, public reason is the reason of its supreme court," and "the supreme court is the branch of government that serves as the exemplar of public reason."[30] Law as integrity parallels the idea of public reason legitimating the exercise of coercive state power "in accordance with a constitution the essentials of which all citizens may reasonably be expected to endorse in the light of principles and ideals acceptable to them as reasonable and rational."[31] As a formal matter, these concepts can accommodate any imaginable substantive outcome; in practice, both ideas are understood by their authors as requiring essentially the same narrow range of politically controversial results.

This convergence is not particularly shocking if we consider the social factors that in the end give content to such otherwise infinitely pliable concepts as "integrity," "reason," and "principle." The academic subjects who benefit from illuminating midnight conversations in the bars of fancy European hotels work at the same institutions, attend the same conferences, read the same newspapers, live in the same suburbs, and send their children to the same schools as their eminently reasonable interlocutors. Is it then so surprising that the servants of Law's Empire end up replicating the considered moral judgments handed down within the hermetic confines of Law's Reading Group?

LEVINSON. To switch questions fairly dramatically, the book, after the introduction, begins with Paul's catechism, which is couched as what I take to be a parody of the interrogation of Justice Ginsburg. And the question arises: Were you a senator charged to confirm a nominee—and on the judiciary committee with the power to interrogate a nominee—what sort of questions would you in fact ask, and what sorts of answers would be helpful to you in deciding whether somebody should be given a lifetime position on the Supreme—or, for that matter, any other—Court? Let me ask one other question linked to this. Is this something a law professor should even be asked? Is this a relevant kind of question? Should we have views on this sort of matter?

CAMPOS. I don't know that we should or not. I mean, I think it's perfectly legitimate to ask someone whether in fact he does have views on that question. I have to say that until two hours ago I had never considered that question. Following my own account of interpretation, I should now, as the author of that text, give a certain degree of contextualization which is not superficially available, and which might help situate it a bit more. The essay is a parody of the nomination process. It's also a parody of the Catholic catechism, and a kind of tribute to the "Ithaca" chapter of Joyce's *Ulysses,* which is also structured in that way. What questions would I ask if I were a senator asking a Supreme Court nominee? I think I would want to ask questions that would try to elicit from the nominee whether he or she had a dogmatic or zealous temperament, vis-à-vis law. I would prefer to have people on there who were less certain of themselves, knowing on some level that this desire is a little delusional because no doubt being in that job makes you more certain of yourself because you have to be in order to do the job, perhaps. But still, there is a distinction, ultimately, between the kind of dogmatism that somebody like Scalia or William Douglas manifests and the kind of temperament manifested by somebody like Robert Jackson, who seems quite willing to say, "I have considerable doubts as to whether I'm doing the right thing here. I'm in a position where I have to make certain decisions, but this isn't the pope speaking ex cathedra." I would try to see where on that spectrum of temperament this person falls. To reverse Potter Stewart's classic formulation, I know it when I don't see it, and what I don't want to see is this confident voice of the law in all of its grand, eloquent glory, claiming we are all obliged to follow it as a matter of basic political obligation or something.

SCHLAG. I'm puzzled by your question. You asked earlier whether it's an appropriate question to ask of a legal academic. To me, the question has a certain *fantastic* aspect. "What should a senator do in trying to question a nominee for the Supreme Court?" I am never going to be in that position. I probably will not talk to anyone who is in that position. If the question is asked of me, I now have to imagine myself a senator, which is an utterly fantastic picture, wildly indeterminate. So I get confused by the question. What is being asked here? There's a kind of radical acontextualism in asking that kind of question that renders it meaningless to me. How can it be meaningful to come up with a recipe of questions to be asked of a judicial nominee independent of who one is—a Republican, a Democrat, a senator with extremely liberal politics, a senator with extremely conservative politics? How can it be meaningful to come up with a recipe of questions independent of who the nominee is, and independent of national politics, and independent of one's status in the senate? I think that asking these kinds of radically acontextual questions is one of the problems with the normative fixation of the legal academy. Why is it sensible to demand of law professors and law students that they answer these questions when it's not clear, precisely, what is being asked or who it's being asked of?

SMITH. There are certainly a lot of constitutional law professors who have thought and written about the confirmation process and how it ought to work. Bob Nagel, I think, wrote an article in *New Republic* actually proposing some concrete recommendations as to how it ought to be conducted. So it seems to me that it's a perfectly permissible question to ask. On the other hand, with respect to that and a lot of similar kinds of questions, like "What do you think the law on this particular constitutional issue is, or should be?" I think you sometimes sense in our profession, particularly if you're in the area of constitutional law, that you have an obligation to be able to supply answers to questions like that. You're somehow remiss if you can't. I think that's wrong. The middle ground that I'm trying to strike here is that I think it is permissible to ask this question, but it should not be obligatory, in any sense, for people in this field to give answers. Many of us are probably better off not trying to engage with that kind of question.

LEVINSON. But this relates to something that I often suggest to my students—that the function of my course is to enable them to be a certain kind of dinner party guest. That is to say, I ask them to imagine being at a dinner party and somebody asks, "What do you think of that decision last week?" and one way of answering that question is to say, "Well, they decided X-Y-Z." And the person at the dinner party says, "I know that. I read the papers." And then next you say, "And the vote was five to four, and I think the next case that comes up, they're probably going to decide the same way"; and your companion's getting more and more irritated and says something to the effect of, "Look. You're a professional. I'm a layperson. I know what the Court said. I know what the vote was. I know what the probability is of their continuing to decide that way. What I want to know, is, was it a proper decision?"

SMITH. Just to see if I understand you, suppose you go ahead and say, "And I actually like that result." Your questioner will be dissatisfied with that, too, won't he? He'll say, "I'm not asking whether you like it or not, or whether as a legislator you'd vote for it."

LEVINSON. Right. You're an expert. Now, Pierre, I think, would say, "Whatever I'm an expert in, it's not in answering this sort of question, and it's simply an error to believe that I have anything useful to say about the provenance of this decision." Now, I think a lot of people would be surprised to be told at a dinner party that you literally had nothing to say about whether this was a sound decision or an unsound decision, correct or incorrect, or . . . But you're agreeing, as Pierre is agreeing, that . . .

SCHLAG. For the record, he's nodding yes.

LEVINSON. . . . . that you would leave your companion frustrated.

SCHLAG. Yes. I think it's because they have certain expectations of what it is a law professor does, and they have certain expectations of what the law is. I think among the lay public there is the supposition that there are correct answers in law and that we have a method for generating correct answers. This is a belief which is being sorely tested now. But it is still believed among the lay public. Now, I would remind, though, that the public has all sorts of beliefs about the law. During the Bork hearings, for instance, some poll showed that a large majority of the public believed that the Supreme Court justices ought to follow the framers' intent; a large majority also believed that the Constitution contains a right to privacy. So the fact that the public has certain expectations doesn't mean that they should or that they can necessarily be met. Now, I think that professors in the legal academy have pretty much the same expectations, too. In fact, just today I heard someone say about a case, "Do you think that case was correctly decided?" That is an unintelligible question to me. That is—since I don't think there is a method for deciding cases, at least none that is demonstrable—the whole question of whether a case was correctly decided is unintelligible, right? I think the supposition that one should be able to answer, as a law professor, the question of whether the court properly decided a case presumes objectivism—presumes an objectivist account of law—an account that is either radically underspecified or utterly implausible.

CAMPOS. I want to add something here which seems, perhaps, a bit confessional, but, listening to Pierre talk, I realize that the answer I gave to you about picking a Supreme Court justice is a really inauthentic answer—is an answer based on a sense of "I'm playing a particular social role, and I don't want to disappoint my questioner, and I also feel vaguely that I should have something to say about this, and that it would be really lame for me to say that I have nothing to say." But when I think about questions upon which I actually *do* have something to say, like "What does it mean to say that you're interpreting a text?" or "Was Mickey Mantle a better baseball player than Willie Mays?"—issues upon which I feel I have real knowledge that would allow me to say something useful and coherent, and I compare it to what I have to say about what kinds of questions I would ask a Supreme Court nominee, I realize I have *nothing* useful to say about what kind of questions I would ask a Supreme Court nominee, and for very much the reasons Pierre is talking about. Because I too, like him, really don't know at all what is meant by "Was that case correctly decided?" except on the very trivial level of "Do the results please me?"

LEVINSON. I'm assuming that your companion really believes that there are experts in the world about law. That's, after all, why people go to law school: to learn to be lawyers, to have informed opinions about the law. And if you teach law, then you really ought to . . .

SCHLAG. You ought to know something.

LEVINSON. . . . and most people at my dinner party, I think all of us agree, would be, at the very least, frustrated or surprised to receive these answers. I'm wondering, Steve, if you would also give the same sort of frustrating answer.

SMITH. Well, in fact, this isn't really such a hypothetical question. Here's just one example. As you probably know, in this state several years ago we passed an initiative known as Amendment 2, a sort of an anti–gay rights initiative, and there was a lot of discussion in the newspapers and elsewhere for a long time— still is, I suppose. It wasn't at all uncommon for people that I know outside the law school who knew that I was supposed to be a constitutional law professor to ask, "Well, what do you think? Is Amendment 2 really unconstitutional or not?" And my answer did tend to have to be, if they gave me a chance really to say what I thought, that not only did I not know the answer to the question, but I could not understand it. The question, I thought, was an unintelligible question. Now this does come as a real shock and surprise to people who say, "Well, I'm not even a lawyer, and it's a perfectly intelligible question to me. So how can it be that you're supposedly a constitutional law scholar and you can't even understand the question?"

Given enough time, one could explain, "Well, there are a number of things that you might mean by that question, and I could, perhaps, respond to some of them." But some of the responses would be the kind that you began by describing, Sandy, and then they would quickly say, "No, that's not what I mean." And as they got to what they meant, that's where the question would become most unintelligible. So this is an experience that isn't hypothetical. It happens a lot; it is a source of frustration to them, and it's a source of anxiety to me. A lot of your questions have been along the lines of "Isn't there something really subversive about the kind of analysis that's offered in these essays?" Maybe there is, and I think this is where you feel it the most. People could say, "Look. If this leads you to be incapacitated so that you could not even answer an ordinary question about something like this, isn't it likely that you're going to be infecting your students, over time, with the same kind of incapacity?" I don't have any quick answer to that.

SCHLAG. It's as if you were to ask people in religion departments, "Look. You're experts in religion. Now, I'd like to know: is there transmigration of souls or not?"—to which the answer might be, "Well, you know, in some religions they do believe in transmigration, in others they don't. Some people believe this, some people believe that."

LEVINSON. To play out the analogy, there's a difference between being a professor of theology and being a professor of religion. That is to say, state universities and most private universities don't have professors of theology. If I'm sitting next to a professor of theology, I will assume that person is in a denominational seminary and believes in the system, and so I might well ask— in fact, in an e-mail group I'm on I got into a vigorous discussion about whether Jews are damned in evangelical Christian thought, and some people were quite willing to say yes. Now, I can also imagine sitting next to a professor of religion in the secular department at a state university or private university, and I'd say, "Well, do souls migrate?" And the professor of religion says, "I don't have any view on that matter. I'm an atheist myself, but let me tell you the twelve different answers to this question." I can understand that. But if I said to a professor of theology, "Under Catholic theology, does the wine and the wafer turn into the blood and body of Jesus?" and the theologian says, "I have no view on that. I'm just a Catholic theologian," I would find that odd.

SMITH. Hold it. We might be able . . . any of us might be able to say, "Under

Holmesian jurisprudence, I would tell you that, in my opinion, Amendment 2 is unconstitutional."

LEVINSON. But any political scientist could do that. And I don't mean that sneeringly, but my colleagues in political science departments often know the way a number of jurisprudential systems work, and one of them would easily say, you know, "I don't believe in such things as correct or incorrect answers, but I can outline two possibilities." The part of the reality, maybe, of a law school is that it has a seminary aspect as well as the secular department of religion aspect, and it's in the seminary aspect that, I think, dinner party guests believe that you actually are willing to offer answers, even if you said, "Well, look. Don't confuse me with all Catholic theologians, my view is only my view. There are distinguished people on the other side. But, yeah, I really do believe that the wafer turns into the body," and so on and so forth, where one takes responsibility for stating an opinion; and all three of you seem very reluctant to do that.

SCHLAG. In law school, the seminarians pretend to be professors of religion. Now, if they were to remain seminarians and say, "We believe in law, but, you understand, it's just a matter of faith. It's basically legal dogmatics, but we believe," that would be fine. But they pretend to be professors of religion. So if we are going to have people in law school who are priests but who nonetheless claim to have the grounding of professors of religion, then it's perfectly fair game to point out: "No, this is just a faith that you have."

CAMPOS. I'd like to elaborate on that. Steve has a great metaphor for this situation. He talks of how law schools could be divided into departments of dogma and of rhetoric. Then people could ask, "Are you a dogmatist?" and people like ourselves could answer, "No, I'm on the rhetoric side."

LEVINSON. Let me try asking the question somewhat differently, then. At the dinner party your companion asks you, "Did you read the decisions in *X v. Y*?" And let's suppose that you did. And then he or she asks, "Well, which of the opinions did you find persuasive?" Can you answer that question? "Which as a law professor, as a professional, did you find persuasive?"

CAMPOS. Persuasive? I can't answer that question. I can say which I found more elegantly argued, which I found more attractive intellectually, which I found most boring, but most persuasive? Persuasive of what?

SMITH. And persuasive to whom?

LEVINSON. To you. I mean this as a straightforward question. I can ask you, "Are you phenomenologically persuaded by a legal opinion?" And if the answer is *no*, then, I think, we come back to a certain paradox as to what it is we're training our students to do, because one way of defining our role is as rhetoricians—to train them in the techniques of persuasive argument. But if then we

tell our students, "Look. I'm never persuaded by law talk. I can do these aesthetic analyses, or whatever, but I'm way too sophisticated, actually, to be
persuaded by any of this stuff," then I think students and others would find this
an odd thing for a law professor to say, and would wonder what's going on. Are
you training the students to persuade people less sophisticated than you are?
Are you saying, well, "You should be persuaded. You should learn that this is a
better argument than that, but, of course, I don't believe that," and so on and so
forth?

SMITH. In the abstract it's hard—for me, at least—to answer your initial
question yes or no. I think it might depend on the case. In other words, let's
suppose you could imagine a case of *X v. Y* . . .

LEVINSON. Have you read any constitutional law case decided the last term,
split opinion? The term limits case, the control of guns, high school campuses
case, or any of the racial districting cases, any cases that have been much in the
news with very sharply contending opinions? Go to the *Rosenberger* case. Five
to four on whether Virginia has a duty to finance an evangelical Christian
publication. Do you find yourself persuaded by one or another of the opinions?

SMITH. Well, as it happens, probably not, in a case like that. But I can
imagine I could say, "Well, some opinions are a little more persuasive," in
various terms. I mean, for example, if Justice Souter writes an opinion in which
he indicates that he's proceeding on original history assumptions, at least for
purposes of that case, and then makes an argument about original meaning
that I'm sure as a historical matter is not accurate, then I can say, "That's an
unpersuasive opinion." And conceivably, someone else, maybe Justice Thomas,
might write an opinion that I think is more accurate, and that's at least a
qualified persuasion. I realize there's a dispute about whether original meaning
should be determinative. But to the extent that that's one possibility, this opinion is more persuasive in terms of that assumption. That's one kind of judgment you can make, I think.

You can also make a judgment, I think, that one opinion is a more honest
and accurate treatment of the precedents that maybe the competing opinions
invoke, than another. And you can make a judgment, I think, about which is
more persuasive in terms of the future workability of a particular approach that
different opinions may advocate or criticize. One can be in doubt about a lot of
ultimate questions, to the point where, if someone—again, your dinner party
guest—just asks you in the abstract, "Is Amendment 2 unconstitutional?" you
have difficulty in answering or even understanding the question, because you
don't know what assumptions they might be making. But you might still be able
to make some judgment—maybe more lower-level judgments, but important

ones, perhaps—about given cases. I think this at least rescues you from the really pervasively skeptical position that you were describing a moment ago. I don't think the kind of critical perspective that some of our essays take necessarily leaves us in that position.

CAMPOS. I think I would agree with that. I think if you can narrow the question of what "persuasive" means to something along the lines of "Is this a persuasive argument about precedent?" or "Is this a persuasive argument about a historical question?" then you can make distinctions. But if you say, "Is this a persuasive argument as to whether this is correctly decided as a matter of law?" to me that question is, at this point, a deeply incoherent question, and then it's not persuasive on that level. But these narrower questions don't get to the issue of persuasiveness in the classical sense: Is this persuasive because it's law as opposed to not law?

SMITH. Or tells us what the Constitution really means on this question?

LEVINSON. But as I say, I'm assuming a series of questions like "Did you read the Supreme Court's opinions in X?" to which you answer, "Yes," and then you're asked, "Well, which opinion persuaded you most?" and at that point you would say, "Well, I can't answer that question."

SMITH. I thought I was suggesting that you might not be reduced to saying, "I just can't answer that question." You might be able to explain a lot of the more specific kinds of judgments I was talking about . . .

SCHLAG. I think there's a problem with the question, and I think it's probably what Steve has been talking about. I mean, one reads an opinion, and you ask, "Can you tell which of the opinions is more persuasive, persuasive to you?" Persuasive to you of what? That this is what the Constitution means? In that sense, I'm not really persuadable. I can give answers like, "Well, given the way the community of legal interpreters is constituted at present, this is likely to be much more persuasive to them than this other opinion." And so this is going to be a better argument, in my judgment, because right now within the community, the First Amendment is much more highly valued than the flag, for instance. And somebody turns around and says, "Yeah, but, I want to know: Was *Texas v. Johnson* correctly decided?" And they say, "I'm not talking about the community of legal interpreters, I'm talking about whether *you* think it was correctly decided." On that I really have nothing to say.

I can, of course, say that I like this opinion better than that one, but that will have to do with a lot of things that are contingent about me; about, for instance, my believing, for instance, that the First Amendment is much more important than the flag or vice versa. But it will have to do with contingent aspects of my beliefs, which aren't law. Is that intelligible?

LEVINSON. Sure. But at that point, it seems to me that the dinner party companion might be satisfied because you are saying, "On the one hand, here's my answer to your question. I found Justice X's opinion persuasive in a way that Justice Y's was not, but you ought to realize that this is in part because of who I am and certain general views and preferences that I have, but nonetheless I did find this a better example of the legal arts."

SCHLAG. But your dinner party companion is going to say, "No, no, no—you *still* don't get it. I'm not interested in *your* preferences as to which opinion you like better. I want to know which is the better opinion in terms of stating the law." So in terms of the answer that I have given, your dinner companion should still be frustrated.

LEVINSON. Then maybe at this point I flip over with you, because I would say, "Well I can't do anything more than tell you which opinion persuaded me and why I found it persuasive. But, look, there were four people on the other side. There is no reason to think they are blithering idiots or incompetent, and one's response to these questions will inevitably be a consequence of personal factors, political ideology, or whatever. And that is my view," and perhaps the companion would be frustrated. But this would be at least a different answer from saying, "Look, I just have nothing at all to tell you about which opinion persuades me because I don't recognize that as a coherent question."

CAMPOS. Well, I think this needs to be pushed on just a little bit more, because I think what Pierre would say is that he has certain political commitments, or moral beliefs, or whatever, which incline him to find certain legal conclusions more desirable than others. But I think he would see those—and tell me if I'm misstating your view here—but I think you would see those as being in some sense external to a question about law, per se. If the question is "Which opinion do you find persuasive?" in terms of which opinion comes closer to successfully determining the fact of the matter, when the fact of the matter is a fact of the matter about the identity and the content of law, then you have to say, "There isn't any fact of the matter."

SMITH. That question makes no sense.

LEVINSON. That there is no "fact of the matter" in that regard.

SMITH. That's right. I don't know if that's a gulf between us or not; because you might end up saying the same thing. Or you might have more worked-out notions than some of us do.

LEVINSON. I remain genuinely torn, because I have told my students that I want to enable them to be courteous dinner party guests, and I ask them when they read these opinions to be very self-conscious about what persuades them and why; that is to say, the course is not only teaching them the modalities of legal argument in a completely detached sense, but also is trying to engage them and force them to confront the question whether any of this stuff makes sense to them, or whether their response will be an entirely detached instrumental response, where you would tell your dinner party companion, "Look. This question really is nonsensical, but let me tell you, if you want to hire me to make arguments to a court in a way designed to persuade a judge, I'm very good at that." But that's a very different thing from telling you that I'm persuaded by any of this, because I'm much too sophisticated to find any of this stuff genuinely persuasive. And I do find that the dilemma of . . . the dilemma of teaching, because I really do try to figure out what it is that I'm doing and, as I said before, I can't find it plausible to tell students that I'm simply preparing them to be more effective advocates. But that could still be in this completely detached sense. They don't have to believe a word of it, but it's simply a set of rhetorical techniques that can pay them handsomely if they have certain skills in constructing well-formed sentences.

SMITH. This is an analogy, and I guess it's just another variation on your question about the "death of God," but suppose you're in a culture that has traditionally believed that it's very important to do the will of Zeus. There is some deity up there on Mount Olympus, Zeus, who somehow reveals his will in different ways, and it's very important to do his will. And there's a whole set of practices around discerning what his will is and doing it. But you're at a stage in this culture where, although the practice is still pervasive, it's hard to believe anymore—for you, at least, and for some people—that there is any deity up there on Mount Olympus called "Zeus." Nonetheless, you still may think these practices are serving valuable social functions, and you can speak this language, and you can even do it in at least a quasi-good-faith way, treating it as a sort of code for other kinds of things that you think are valuable and good. I think in some ways maybe that's the situation you, or we, are in. And I suppose there's no getting around the fact that there are certain bad-faith elements.

Maybe "bad faith" is too strong. But I think maybe in some situations we *are* in the position of having to say, "I'm too sophisticated to believe this in the same way these people are believing it." To some extent that should prompt us to feel the kind of angst that you were talking about earlier. I do think that's the kind of situation we're in. And we don't know how it's going to go in the future. We don't know whether these kinds of practices will continue in the same form. We probably can't control it, so for now we just live in the situation as well as we can, I think.

LEVINSON. Well, I'd like to perhaps conclude by returning to Paul, but I think it connects a number of these themes. A couple of times Paul has really pronounced himself, I think, an enemy of enthusiasm, of zealotry, of dogma-tism—has said that students really should not come out of his course confident that the law requires X or prohibits Y.

SMITH. And he said that with great passion and conviction.

LEVINSON. Right. But what I'm curious about is whether you want your students to have any views at all about what law requires, even if they're weak views. That is, even if they don't pound the table and say, "Well, the First Amendment means that you always have a right to say whatever you want: shouting 'fire!' in a crowded theater, calling for the assassination of the town mayor in front of the hall, whatever." But what if the students say, "I know these are really difficult issues—but I really do think, with all due modesty, that the best understanding of the First Amendment is that it protects this, under these circumstances"; or, "The best understanding of the Fourteenth Amendment is that it has this meaning." Can you make any sense of *that* enterprise—nice, modulated, full of recognition that other reasonable people can differ with you, but still willing to say, "The Fourteenth Amendment means this. The First Amendment means that"?

CAMPOS. Can I make any sense of it in the sense of—can I imagine that it would be socially desirable to have this practice?

LEVINSON. I suppose that's one way of reinterpreting the question, but it also has to do with your own relationship with the students who might believe, naively, that by the end of your course they should be able to articulate, with due modesty, what the Fourteenth Amendment, best understood—or, for that matter, if it's a statutory course, what the National Labor Relations Act, best understood—really means. Or if it's a common law course, what the best under-standing of some set of doctrines is. But nonetheless they say that they've got views, and you hear your students in a lunchtime conversation where your favorite student is arguing—but in a suitable, temperate way—with another student as to what the Fourteenth Amendment really means. And would you say, "Well, yes, I've done a good job of teaching that student," or would you say, "Well, as good as he or she is, there's just been this failure to realize that this form of conversation is bankrupt."

CAMPOS. I think it's necessary on some level to be a believer in law in order to do it at all. And this clearly ties in with the argument that we've been kicking around about what is the relationship between these kinds of views and teach-ing students.

LEVINSON. Teaching law students.

CAMPOS. Teaching law students. Because I have little doubt that if I were in the midst of a legal case—one in which I was representing someone or where I myself was being sued—I would, in fact, have strong views about the actual content of law under these circumstances. These views would be driven by certain emotional and psychological needs, but they would nevertheless be there, right? And it seems to me quite plausible that for students to actually be "good" lawyers, they must engage fully with the practice. Then, as they are engaging in that practice, they are committed to a certain metaphysic of the practice which, from an abstract and theoretical, outside, external view, I don't have. The analogy here would be: The basketball player is going up for the jump shot and the anthropologist of games suddenly runs out to the court and says, "While you're hanging up there, Mr. Basketball Player, you must realize this is really a kind of sublimated war game ritual." The player could properly object to this. He could say, "You know, when I'm shooting this shot I'm a basketball player. I'm also a lot of other things, and when I'm not being a basketball player, I have a different mindset and I can be somewhat abstracted from being a basketball player." That's part of the answer. The other part of the answer involves stepping back a little bit from the impression of total legal nihilism which I appear to be pressing here. I actually believe that there is content to law and that there are right answers to legal questions—it's just that they're not the kinds of questions that would ever be asked, certainly, in serious appellate court litigation. As long as law remains a set of background conditions, then there is sufficient commonality in the overall beliefs of the subjects who are subject to law about law's content. It's just that when you put social pressure on law to actually resolve legal disputes—once you get past the question you, Sandy, have addressed, of what is a frivolous legal claim, which, of course, is a very difficult question—then you are in this world of incoherence when you ask, "Is that correctly decided?" But if my dinner party guest says, "Look. What is the correct legal answer to the question 'Can a twenty-eight-year-old be elected president?'" I can, with confidence, reply that there is, in fact, a correct legal answer to that question. And not merely in the realist sense that you could predict that certain judges will act in a certain kind of way when presented with this case, but in the sense that there are certain entities out in the world—this is a little too objective of a metaphor—there are things out there that have content that provide an answer to that question, which is a correct answer. And the answer is just as real as the answer to the question "How many satellites does the earth have?" I think I'm completely with Pierre on the question of the live, legal dispute; but I might not be. I'm not sure about Pierre's views in this regard. I might not be with him on the view as to whether there's nothing there at all. I think there's stuff there, and that stuff really gives lots of good and perfectly adequate answers, they're just not adequate answers for the actual practice of law as that is usually understood. But I think the way the actual practice of law is usually understood is far too narrow an understanding of the social practice. The social practice, when it is invisible, when it is a background condition, works extremely well. It is only when we activate it in a conscious sort of way, when, we say, "Well, now we've really got this problem. We don't know what the answer to this question is about what the law requires right here. We just don't know. We're experts, we're lawyers, but we just don't know." Then the answer's just not going to be there. Then there's a kind of void. So, to put it in Derridean terms, law is a presence which becomes present precisely through its absence, and becomes absent when you try to bring it into presence, as it were.

SMITH. Tell me if this is right. I take your answer to be something like this. The ontological status of law lies in a certain set of social practices. Those practices often exhibit enough consensus and coherence that they are capable of answering certain kinds of legal questions that normally don't have to be asked. But if someone did ask, say, "Can a twenty-year-old be president?" they provide enough substance so that you can confidently answer that question.

CAMPOS. Right. Sure.

SMITH. It's just that these practices don't have the kind of substance and coherence that will allow us to answer lots of other questions, which are the kinds of questions we actually talk about most of the time. And then Sandy's dinner guest says, "Yeah, but what is the law on it?" That's where the question becomes unintelligible. Because it implies that you're talking about something beyond these social practices, and there *isn't* anything beyond those.

Maybe we're in this funny position of saying, "There is a reality to law; it consists in this social practice. But the odd thing about the social practice is that often, and maybe always, it depends upon a presupposition about a law that exists independent of the social practice. That law may *not* exist, and yet the belief in it is pervasive enough that a lot of times you can answer questions by reference to the social practice." But a lot of times you can't, and that's where the divergence may occur, because some people at that point will still think it's meaningful to say, "Yeah, but what is the law really?" Because they're enough immersed in the practice that they accept its presupposition. Others—I, and probably we—wouldn't accept that. And I think Pierre would go a little further in doubting the coherence of the social practice.

CAMPOS. But in a way the argument ends up being a bit at cross purposes. The dinner guest wants to know, for instance, about the rules of chess and says, "Now can the bishop move horizontally?" You say, "No, no, the bishop can't move horizontally." And he says, "Well, how do you know that?" And you say, "Well, because that's chess. Those are the rules of chess." "Well, how do you

know what the rules of chess are?" "Well, because there's an interpretive community—the people who play chess—and they have certain beliefs about the
rules of chess, and that's a belief that they hold about the rules of chess, and
therefore that constitutes the rules of chess." Now, wouldn't that be a satisfactory answer?

SCHLAG. But chess is not law. And the Levinson dinner party guest's interest
in what the rules of chess are is not the same thing as the dinner party guest's
interest in what the law is, even though in both cases we'll answer him by using
the term *rules.*

SMITH. Pierre's probably right, in part, on this. Where the difference appears, I think, is just in the situation where you say, "Okay, here's the question
that's been asked, and I can observe that there is no consensus within the
interpretive community. There are people advocating this and people advocating that." Or maybe, "The question hasn't really been considered before." And
then, as the dinner guest repeats the question, or presses it, the question really
does become nonsensical at that point. But the dinner guest doesn't think so.
Many people don't think so. He still thinks it's a meaningful question, and you
ought to be able to answer it. I think that does show some real differences in
assumptions between the dinner guest and you.

But for many questions, for a long way, although that difference is latent and
is potentially very important, you can avoid it. Finesse it. And you can give a
satisfactory answer in terms of your understanding of law having its reality in
this set of social practices.

But I think Pierre's right that there comes a point where these differences in
assumptions will manifest themselves. And someone might even go so far then
as to say, "That shows that you're not really answering the question even when
you pretend to be answering it in the easy cases," or "You're being a little
disingenuous, I think, in doing so, because you're not really answering the
question that the dinner guest is asking." That is a possible construction you
can put on that solution.

CAMPOS. But in terms of law, I think, sometimes, Pierre sounds a little bit
like a disappointed metaphysical realist, because he says, "Look. I want this
thing, I want it now, and I want it to be really solid. I want it to be like this table,
right? And then if it's not like that, which it really needs to be for a lot of
people . . ."

SCHLAG. No, it's not me. *They* want it to be solid!

CAMPOS. Well, okay . . .

SCHLAG. And you know, they don't want to call it law, if you introduce too
much of something that might be called "politics" or "the subject" or "person-

ality" or "conventions." You introduce stuff like that and . . . boom . . . it's not law anymore. . . . I resist the charge of being a disappointed metaphysical realist.

CAMPOS. Okay, well here's a metaphor, maybe this will catch something. There's a tightrope, and people walking on the tightrope, and they think there's a net under them. Now, as long as they believe there's a net under them, they will not test that net to see whether it will actually keep them from splattering—because if they believe that there's a net under them, there's no need for them to test it. Now, if what you mean by "Is there a net under them?" is "Do these people have the appropriate sets of beliefs that will keep them from splattering themselves?" the answer is "Yes!" Then, from what I realize is a kind of smarmy functional perspective, you can say, "For all practical purposes, there's a net under them," right? Now the problem is that when they start testing it, when they start jumping off, they start splattering. And then people like us start saying, "Hey, look. There goes another one. Boom-boom." I think that's what we're doing. I think we're pointing out that the people are splattering when they jump, and what's kind of funny is that after they splatter they keep claiming, "Oh, there really was a net there, it's just you're mistaking our situation. We may look rather bruised, but there really is a net and it caught us perfectly well."

SCHLAG. The net is binding. It constrains my fall.

CAMPOS. It constrains our fall. It's a disciplining net. It's going to keep us from hitting that concrete. And so, in a way, I'm trying to capture the sense that this thing works well precisely to the extent that you do not ask things of it. If you understand it as something that is in the background, it works really well in the way that the society wants and needs it to work, and then the argument about whether it's "really" there turns into this rather scholastic dispute about the ontological status of something that is working just as well whether it's really there or not. I think what we're all emphasizing is that when you start jumping, that net isn't nearly as much of a net as it's commonly imagined to be, and we disagree among the four of us as to precisely how much it's there or in what ways it's there, but we all agree that it's not there nearly as much as the traditional legal academic writers would say that it is.

SCHLAG. At this point, the text should read in block type, "Trust me, there's a net. Trust me, there's a net," over and over again.

LEVINSON. Well, thank you.

SCHLAG, CAMPOS, and SMITH. Thank you.

CLERKS IN THE MAZE

Pierre Schlag

IT MUST BE very difficult to be a judge—particularly an appellate judge. Not only must appellate judges reconcile often incommensurable visions of what law is, what it commands, or what it strives to achieve, but they must do this largely alone. What little help they have in terms of actual human contact, apart from their clerks, typically takes the form of two or more advocates whose entire raison d'être is to persuade, coax, and manipulate the judge into reaching a predetermined outcome—one which often instantiates or exemplifies only the most tenuous positive connection to the rhetoric of social purpose, legal doctrine, and moral value deployed by the advocates.

These are difficult—one might say unusual—working conditions. What makes them even more difficult is that, despite the origins of litigation in incommensurabilities, in contraries, and in contradictions, the judge must end on a note that is often monistic: judgment affirmed; judgment reversed. True, sometimes there is the possibility of deferral—as in, for instance, that last line of the opinion that reads "remanded." But even this is a qualified deferral—a time-bound deferral, a temporary reprieve from final judgment. The judge is thus a monistic figure, one who says what *the* law *is*. And this law is always announced in the singular: there is always, at the end, from the judge's perspective and the parties' perspective, just *one* law.[1] The mysteries of these metamorphoses, of these transformations, have something to do with violence.

The violence of judging. Not only do judges conclude their work on a note of violence—a death sentence, an incarceration, a compulsory wealth transfer—but, as Robert Cover observes, the entire ritualized process of argument over which judges preside is itself fraught with violence. Judges arrive at their decisions by killing off rival conceptions of law. As Cover puts it, "Confronting the luxuriant growth of a hundred legal traditions, they assert that *this one* is law and destroy or try to destroy all the rest."[2] Judges must destroy the worlds of meaning that others have constructed. Now, none of this, as Cover himself cautions, is a criticism of judges or judging.[3] Indeed, to criticize judging because it involves violence is to misunderstand or deny the character of judging; it is to criticize judging because it is not busy being something else—some other, more pacific activity. But even as it is inappropriate to criticize judges and judging for *this* implicit violence, and even if nothing can be done about *this* irreducible violence, this does not mean that we should overlook the law's violent character.

On the contrary, it is important to think about the violence implicit in judging because it greatly affects what judges construct as law. Indeed, once we recognize the violence implicit in the enterprise of judging, we are poised to understand that judges, far from having a neutral or a detached perspective on law, have instead a highly interested, partial perspective. Indeed, what judges take to be law is but a romanticized and inflated shadow image of all that law is and all that law does. Once we appreciate this point, we might even come to understand that the very elementary forms of the law of judges—the forms commonly known as "rules," "doctrines," "principles," and so on—are themselves already highly self-interested constructions.

The self-interested character of the law of judges may be seldom acknowledged in our public professional fora, but its existence is hardly surprising. On the contrary: it is obvious. Indeed, if, like a judge, one is continually engaged in destroying the worlds of meaning of others, if one is continually engaged in a practice fraught with violence, then one's needs for authorization and legitimation are likely to be intense. Judges quite understandably want their juridical identities, their roles, and their actions to be authorized. They want authorization in several senses. In one sense, judges want their own identities to be underwritten by a greater, grander power—a legitimating power like "The Text," "The Framers' Intent," "Justice," or, less grandly, "Doctrine." Not only do these "authoritative sources" help legitimate—a nonpejorative term here—the exercise of judicial power, they also help to diffuse and distribute judicial responsibility. It is in virtue of these authorities that the actions of the judge become the actions of the community. In a second and closely related sense, judges seek authorization in that they want a script to follow—a script that delineates as clearly as possible who they are and what they must do. Such scripts—and here we can think of the doctrinal script as an example—do not just guide and legitimate the actions of judges; they fashion the judge's very identity, perhaps even detailing his exact lines. The appeal of such a steady script in a rhetorical situation often fraught with uncertainty, unknowns, and violence is clear.

Now, again, and I want to insist on this point, there is no criticism of judges or judging here. But there is the beginning of a question as to whether judges are particularly well suited or well situated to think critically or deeply about law. Indeed, the judge's identity, role, and job tasks do not typically lead to asking questions in any intellectually sustained manner about the character of law—what it is, how it works, what it does, or how it should be. The only questions of this kind that can be asked from a judge's perspective must be formulated in such a way that the questions, the answering, and the answers do not threaten the validity or the value of the judge's own sources of authority. From the subject formation of the judge, the terminus of legal inquiry—whether concrete or theoretical—is always and already a foregone conclusion: there must be a noncontradictory answer, a satisfactory solution, which, however formulated, preserves and maintains the integrity of the authoritative sources and the authoritative methods. There is thus a very real sense in which the judge *wants not to see, wants not to understand, wants not to pursue certain lines of inquiry.* Indeed, the very construction of judges—that which enables them to be judges at all—will lead them in important senses not to see, not to understand, and not to pursue certain lines of inquiry.

All of this suggests that law, as constructed from the perspective of the judge, may well be a rather limited intellectual production—that is, one whose internal configurations and potential turn out to be intellectually rather limited. Now, what makes this law intellectually limited is not the abstract fact that there are certain things it does not want to see or understand or pursue. Indeed, all disciplines—even the most fertile—are constituted by a kind of formative forgetting. What is different about this law of judges is that the formative forgetting is given shape not by a desire to produce knowledge, insight, or understanding, but rather by that law's desire to hide from itself its own violent character.

The reason I mention all this is that it has been precisely the judge's perspective that has dominated and organized American academic legal thought for more than a century. Indeed, the persona of the judge has served as the single, unitary subject formation that enables the American legal academic representation of law. The prototypical legal academic has a strong identification with this judicial persona. For many legal academics this identification is cemented in the venerated and gateway tradition of the judicial clerkship. In this tradition, the young law graduate, soon to become an academic, is initiated into his first "real" law job by a judge who reveals to him what was withheld in law school: the "real" process of crafting a judicial opinion and a "real," even if exaggerated, experience of the power of the judge. For many legal academics, the clerkship is a defining moment—one from which they never recover. They become clerks for life.

Not surprisingly, the "law" of the academy bears the marks of the subject formation, the judge through which this law is metaphorically, allegorically,

and aesthetically constructed. This is true in an obvious, even if seldom acknowledged, sense: in the law school classroom, as in the casebook, as in the
prototypical law school exam, as in the prototypical scholarly work, all kinds
of law—statutory, administrative, customary, and institutional—are presented
and explored through the focused aesthetic and the specific problematics of the
judicial opinion.[4] The judicial opinion and the judicial persona provide the implicit framing and orientation for the presentation and elaboration of the law of
the academy. This point itself is rather obvious, but its implications are not. The
consequence of the legal academic's identification with the persona of the
judges has very serious implications for the construction of the law of the academy. As will be seen, the law of the academy is characterized by a profound
tendency to destroy cultural, intellectual, and thus legal, meaning. Moreover,
the law of the academy is constantly preoccupied with refashioning the rationalization of law's violence in such a way that reckoning with this violence is
continually deferred.

Indeed, the obvious dissonance between the law of the academy and the law
practiced by lawyers has nothing in particular to do with the embrace of
"theory" or the abandonment of "doctrine" in the academy. It has everything to
do with the fact that lawyers understand the violent, instrumental, and performative potentials of any given law while legal academics strive mightily—
whether they are doing "theory" or "doctrine"—to avoid such recognition. A
lawyer looks at doctrine and sees a tool, a vehicle, an opportunity, a threat, a
guarantee. A legal academic typically sees only a propositional statement.

The violence of the law of the academy is often not immediately visible. In part,
that is because the strategies that have been deployed to distance this violence
and to defer reckoning with this violence have already achieved success. Yet, for
those willing to notice, the violence implicit in the law of the academy is easily
retrieved—if only because it is inscribed everywhere.

Consider, for instance, the brilliant though destructive radical reductionism
of Christopher Langdell's famous preface to his first contracts casebook. In that
preface, Langdell reduces the law to a compendium of "certain principles or
doctrines."[5] Along the way, common law cases are reduced to mere vehicles for
studying the true essence of law, namely, "certain principles or doctrines." The
result of such formalist efforts is that the pluralism of common law narratives is
rudely reduced to certain "essential doctrines."[6]

The legal academy does, of course, recover somewhat from this foundational
destruction, and at various times recognizes law to be something more than
mere propositional statements; it is, for instance, a craft, a skill, a cognitive ca-

pacity, a social formation, an aesthetic, a politics, a social steering mechanism, and a dispute resolution process. But the recovery has been only partial. All these different perspectives on law, for all their potential richness, have nonetheless typically remained focused on rationalizing the Langdellian legal ontology of "certain principles or doctrines." The Langdellian destruction continues.

Indeed, this ongoing historical destruction of cognitive and interpretive possibility has become institutionalized in the law student's education. The first year of law school, as it is traditionally conceived, consists largely in imparting cognitive deficits to law students—an almost physiological incapacity to read "authoritative texts" in any but the highly delimited authoritative manner.[7] Karl Llewellyn, in 1930, described the first year in revealingly brutal terms. The physicality and violence of his nouns, verbs, and adjectives are almost palpable: "The first year . . . aims *to drill* into you the more essential techniques of *handling* cases. . . . The hardest job of the first year is to *lop off* your common-sense, *to knock* your ethics into *temporary anesthesia.* Your view of social policy, your sense of justice—*to knock these out* of you along with woozy thinking, along with ideas all fuzzed along their edges. You are to acquire ability to think precisely, to analyze coldly, to work within a *body of materials* that is given, to see, and see only, and *manipulate,* the machinery of the law."[8] It is no wonder that this sort of training produces the sense in many students that the Socratic method is "an assault."[9] As one former law student puts it, "The observation that students often respond physically and emotionally to questioning as though they were in the presence of a profound danger is simply *true.*"[10]

In jurisprudence, this violent and destructive tendency is often given expression and force in the famous distinction between the "internal perspective" and the "external perspective."[11] Here, the distinction is rendered by Ronald Dworkin:

> People who have law make and debate claims about what law permits or forbids. . . . This crucial argumentative aspect of legal practice can be studied *in two ways* or *from two points of view.* One is the *external* point of view of the sociologist or historian. . . . The other is the *internal* point of view of those who make the claims. . . .
>
> This book takes up the internal, participants' point of view; it tries to grasp the argumentative character of our legal practice by joining that practice and struggling with the issues of soundness and truth participants face. We will study formal legal argument *from the judge's viewpoint* . . . because judicial argument about claims of law is a useful paradigm for exploring *the central, propositional* aspect of legal practice.[12]

As Dworkin's telling and indeed representative statement reveals, the "internal perspective" is used to reduce law to the usual Langdellian object—forms, or what Dworkin calls "the *central, propositional* aspect of legal practice"—and to eliminate perspectives that might advance any troublesome learning not consonant with "the judge's viewpoint" or authority. Indeed, no sooner does Dworkin invoke the distinction than he immediately presses it into service to relegate history and sociology to the realm of the external, somewhere outside the realm of law.

This use of the internal-external perspective distinction is prototypical. Indeed, the distinction is typically used to patrol the borders of *Law's Empire.* It is used to rule out of bounds any perspective on law that is not consonant with what the judicial persona already takes to be law. In this uncritical deployment of the internal-external perspective distinction, the law is simply presumed to be separated from the rest of the world by a border that neatly divides the two into an inside and an outside. In this same move, the wielder of this distinction typically bestows on himself the authority to declare what belongs on the inside and what belongs on the outside. It is as if the legal academic could usefully pronounce on the value of an intellectual enterprise in the same way that a judge can rule from the bench on a motion to exclude evidence. Sometimes the internal-external perspective distinction is deployed in even cruder ways. Indeed, the destructive and violent effects of the academy's judge-centered vision are perhaps most easily seen in those academic writings that strive to rid the intellectual scene of certain inquiries or points of view by simply *declaring* them to be nihilistic.

While these kinds of brutal and blunt actions are one way the law of the academy exhibits its violent and profoundly anti-intellectual character, they are certainly not the only way. Much of the violence of the law of the academy is more subtle. Much of this violence involves the forced recasting of intellectual and cultural insights from other disciplines into *forms* and *uses* that accord with the aesthetics of the judge: the legal brief, the legal opinion, the thousand-footnote law review article. It is in this way that deconstruction is reduced to a legal reasoning technique. It is in this way that hermeneutics is crystallized into a method for advancing progressive legal thought. It is in this way that . . . is degraded into . . . Foreign disciplines and their insights do gain admittance to law, but only to the extent that they are recast to conform to the normative instrumental projects of the law of the academy. In general, foreign disciplines are to the law of the academy as expert testimony is to litigation: a largely instrumental display or simulation of intellectual authority and competence. This sort of normative instrumentalization of other intellectual traditions destroys the intellectual, perceptual, and aesthetic resources and capacities through which we (you and I) make sense of our world and our law. At the level of the individual, this normative instrumentalization destroys *cognitive capacity,* the ability to think in a wide variety of different interpretive, aesthetic, and cognitive frames. At the level of the social, this normative instrumentalization destroys *cultural and intellectual memory.* It puts cultural and intellectual resources beyond retrieval. It turns legal subjects into pawns. It makes the legal world flat—as if all truths worth knowing about law could be stated in the aesthetic, in the linguistic forms, in the normative persuasional grammar of the legal brief, the legal opinion, or the thousand-footnote law review article.[13]

I mention the violence at the heart of the law of the academy because it would seem to present significant difficulties for constituting or maintaining law as a vital intellectual discipline. With this sort of generic destructive orientation at the very heart of law, it is difficult to see how this discipline can achieve very much in the way of knowledge or insight. Its attitude toward the world and itself does not seem terribly open or curious or searching, or anything else that one might associate with a vital intellectual endeavor.

With so much violence at the heart of law, the discipline of law is, in some sense, constantly driven to try to escape from or deny its own violent ontology. Law is thus constantly in flight from itself—seeking to represent itself as some highly purified, chastened, idealized, or redemptive version of itself. This is why in the law of the academy we get so much *happy talk jurisprudence*—promises of law as a grand conversation, promises of law as subservient to progressive legal thought, promises of law as responsive to the imperatives of efficiency, promises of a law that is always already one way or another becoming the very best it can be. Of course, this desire for flight from the violent character of law is also why legal thinkers continually confuse and conflate *"really good"* legal thought with legal thought that makes them *feel really good.* Making the law feel really good—or, in more technical terms, "making the law the best it can be"—is not some mere side effect of legal academic enterprise: it *is* the legal academic enterprise. It is the perfected expression of a law that is in flight from its own violent ontology.

This same pattern is also enacted when we move from the normative celebrations of law to the normative criticisms of law. Indeed, the constitution of law as in flight from its own violent and destructive character helps explain why normative protests that law should be more self-conscious, more empathic, more moral, more sensitive to context, and so on always resonate with the academic audience and simultaneously always already miss their mark. These claims always resonate because law is always lacking in the humane qualities to which its academic custodians aspire. In this endlessly repeated observation, the academic custodians of the law could not be more right. But the claims also always already miss their mark because, as mere normative or epistemic criticisms, they leave the violent ontology of law completely untouched. Hence, whether cast as celebration or as criticism, the normative prescriptions of the law of the academy generally end up as part of the cheerful, happy, self-congratulatory celebration of a law whose violence and destructiveness thus become obscured.

All of this suggests great problems for the construction of law as a vital intellectual discipline. Indeed, if the generic generative gesture that gives rise to the law of the academy lies in transforming law into an idealized image of itself—whether as doctrine or theory or whatever—then we will have an academic discipline constituted as a continual attempt to escape from its own object.[14] Its very object of study will have been constituted as cheerful, idealized, purified simulation of the ostensible object of study. Hence, instead of studying law, legal academics will be studying doctrine, which, of course, they will call law. Instead of studying decision making, legal academics will be studying judicial opinions, which they will call . . . Instead of studying . . . (and so on). The critical ontological entities—rules, doctrines, principles, opinions, policies, and so forth—will have been from the very start treated as "real" law despite their obvious collective incompleteness and their radical individual underspecification. What regularity or groundedness these terms will offer over the course of centuries, decades, or the next fifteen minutes will depend on the legal academic's formative identification with the persona of the judge—a persona ineluctably given to acts of elaborate self-rationalization. Now, again, none of this is offered as a criticism of judges or judging. It does, however, make one wonder whether this is a sound constitutive matrix for the construction of a vital intellectual discipline.

This is hardly an auspicious beginning, but it does not get any better than this. On the contrary, the destructive tendencies of the law of the academy, together with its sustained drive to rationalize and legitimate what is already considered law, make it virtually impossible for the law of the academy to learn or produce anything new. Nor is this formative orientation likely to change easily. For one thing, the law of the academy cannot easily take cognizance of its own destructive and violent character because, like its organizing source-persona, the judge, it is constituted to deny this destruction and violence. Moreover, any chance encounters with intellectual or cultural insights that might enable the law of the academy to recognize its own violent character, and its tendencies to rationalization and legitimation, are immediately judged to be "external" to law or are otherwise slated for destruction.

The law of the academy—glittering with all sorts of normatively glowing representations of itself—is thus defensive and authoritarian. Indeed, what else could it be? Given the intellectually unstable character of the law of the academy as in flight from its own violent character, as in flight from its own object, all there is to protect this law from intellectual challenges is the disciplinary power of its constituting, organizing source-persona, the judge. Thus, when the law of the academy encounters new intellectual currents—everything from herme-neutics to poststructuralism to anthropology—the first contact tends to exhibit a sort of violent adjudicatory character. Typically there is no serious intellectual engagement. Instead, we usually get the academic equivalent of a ruling from the bench on whether the foreign insight or idea is or is not useful to law's empire. It does not augur well for an intellectual discipline if its constitutive disposition is basically to avoid learning anything new. This is not the sort of disposition that one would expect to produce a vital intellectual practice.

Now, if the law of the academy is prompted by a desire for flight from its own object, from its own violent character, and if its destructive and violent tenden-cies are manifested in an ongoing desire not to see, not to understand, and not to pursue certain lines of inquiry, then what have legal academics been doing all these years? This seems like a difficult question—until, of course, we realize that the answer has already been given. In their identification with the organizing source-persona of the judge, legal academics engage in the legitimation and rationalization of judicial opinions. In the first instance, it is the violence of judges and judging that they rationalize and legitimate. In the second instance, when these legitimations and rationalizations have taken hold and the violence of judges and judging have receded from view, legal academics simply rational-ize the rationalizations and legitimate the legitimations, and so on, reflexively. This practice is not as esoteric as it may first seem. On the contrary, it is downright commonplace. Consider, after all, that the prototypical doctrinal law review article is itself a legitimation of other legitimating artifacts—namely, judicial opinions. Consider also that the bulk of "law and . . ." work as well as most theory is itself often little more than a particularly abstract kind of mime-sis of the legitimating strategies of lower-order legitimating artifacts such as "doctrine" or "case law."

Nor is it the case that the legitimating strategies of the academy are par-ticularly illuminating—intellectually or otherwise. On the contrary, two rather simple legitimating strategies account for much of the law of the academy. The first legitimating strategy is *constrain and control*. For more than a century, legal thinkers have sought to fashion doctrine or other object forms of law that would not merely inform, but would constrain and control the actions of the judge. This legitimating strategy can be understood as a response to the implicit violence of judging. If the judge is not constrained and controlled, then the violence of judgment may well be wrought in illegitimate ways on nondeserving parties. The perennial focus of legal thinkers on constraint, restraint, binding doctrine, objectivity, and so on is an attempt to rationalize the violence of the law of judges by constraining it a priori to selected identifiable instances of legitimate use. Similarly, the fascination with observing procedural regularity, with the meticulous dissecting examination of what procedural regularity has produced, with gapless demonstrations of an unbroken chain between a decision and its origins in some canonical text or act or institution is also an attempt to secure, a priori, the rationality of the violence of judges and judging. This fascination with pedigree and provenance is inscribed everywhere—from sophisticated expression in the great works of the legal positivists, to the ordinary practice of stare decisis, to the internalized observance of exquisitely detailed, "authoritative" hierarchies in legal academic hiring, publication, and professional recognition. Not surprisingly, constrain and control produces a constricted form of thought. The attitude of this legal thinker is that of a sculptor working cautiously and carefully on the monument of law. He dare not have a creative idea, certainly not a big idea, lest it chip or crack the monument of law. The attitude is one of self-abnegation. Ironically, despite the constricted form of thought produced through constrain and control, there is one aspect in which it knows no limits, no restraint at all: it has an unbounded capacity to dissect and differentiate its own minute contributions to the edifice of law into even tinier analytical pieces.

The second strategy is *justify and redeem.* This strategy attempts to articulate the justifications or the redemptions that are to guide the development and deployment of law. Again, this strategy can be understood as a response to the implicit violence of judges and judging. If there are no justifications or redeeming virtues for law, then the violence of the judge may well remain unjustified. The perennial focus of legal thinkers on justification, on the offering of reasons, and on the formulation of normative prescriptions is an attempt to rationalize the violence of the law of judges by limiting its use to the achievement of good, widely shared ends. Similarly, the fascination with the question, "What should the law be?" and the fascination with the constant advocacy of goodness, rightness, and justice are also attempts to ensure that there is never a moment when the normative validity or the ethical identity of law might actually be in serious question. This fascination with moral totems is inscribed everywhere—from sophisticated expression in the philosophical theories of moralist thinkers like Ronald Dworkin, to the mundane practice of policy and principle justification in judicial opinions, to the idolatrous worship of sacred signifiers like "The Constitution," "Rights," "Progressive," or even "Transformative Action" among legal academics. It is inscribed in the very aesthetic structure of the usual law review narrative, which typically proceeds in a cheerful progression from inefficiency to efficiency, iniquity to goodness, oppression to liberation, or, to put it in generic terms, from insuperable illegitimacy to general moral wonderfulness. This moralizing tendency is inscribed as well in the political-intellectual syndicalism that organizes and regulates faction fights on faculties, hiring decisions, and the like. The justify and redeem strategy thus produces a conventionally politicized environment in which normativity is used to police or extinguish thought—all, of course, in the name of the very best values, the most worthy objectives. In the justify and redeem strategy, nothing can be said or thought about the law unless it demonstrably tends to advance conventionally sanctioned descriptions of the good, the just, the right, and so on. Not surprisingly, with the moral stakes so high, the legal thinker in the grips of this kind of legitimation strategy tends to worry a lot. For this legal thinker, the world and the law are things to wring one's hands over. In the justify and redeem strategy, the surface recognition of the potential of law for violence thus results in great angst-ridden displays of guilt and contrition, often compounded by grand demonstrations of profound and tragic moral concern, often accompanied by self-righteous and indignant outrage, which, ironically (though predictably enough), yield a kind of self-congratulatory feel-good jurisprudence. Like constrain and control, then, there is also one way in which justify and redeem knows no limits: it has an absolute and absolutely remarkable faith in the use and the usefulness of law and legal argument for the achievement of the good, the just, the right, and so on.

As legitimating strategies, constrain and control and justify and redeem have very appealing aspects. Hence, constrain and control can be seen as an entirely appropriate response to the potential of law for violence. The strategy recognizes that the law enforced by judges is not an appealing medium, that it is destructive, and that therefore it must be used sparingly, in the most limited and carefully monitored situations. Constrain and control thus finds its most perfected expression in standard conservative politics, which seek to minimize the use of law to regulate human affairs. If law is a destructive, undesirable, and painful mode of human association, then there is a certain amount of sense in trying to limit its use and its jurisdiction. How, then, does this legitimating strategy go wrong? It goes wrong in imagining that there is still some sector of life—some "private" sector—that remains relatively separate from, and impervious to, the mediating and regulative categories and grammar of the bureaucratic state. This is not our situation. Hence, the choice *is not*, as conservatives would want it, between use of law to regulate human affairs, on the one hand, and reliance on some idealized vision of private initiative untainted by legalism, on the other. And because, contrary to the political desires of conservatives, this *is not* the choice, constrain and control cannot effectuate a selection between a destructive legalism and something else. All it can do is effectuate a selection between one kind of destructive legalism and another.

Justify and redeem can also, at first, be seen as an appealing response to the problem of violence. Whereas constrain and control abandons the possibility of humanizing law and thus strives to restrict its use and jurisdiction, justify and redeem abandons the possibility of restricting law's use and jurisdiction and instead strives to humanize the law. If law has become America's civil religion, if it is all pervasive, if it has become a critical source of communal meaning and organization, then it might make some sense to strive to humanize this law. How, then, does this legitimating strategy go wrong? It goes wrong in imagining that by substituting the language of moral philosophy—of values talk—for the more technical language of doctrine and legal authority, the law might become more humane. Again, this is not our situation. Law, as it is practiced by lawyers, does not become more humane simply because its practitioners learn to use nicer, warmer signifiers (like "love" or "care"). Lawyers can be forced—a term deliberately used—to use nicer-warmer signifiers, but they will, of course, use these nicer-warmer, kinder-gentler signifiers in the same old coercive ways, to accomplish the same old performative tasks they were hired to do. The mistake here is roughly, but not exactly, the same as that of the constrain and control strategy. The constrain and control strategy imagines that there is some prelegal world of culture or self that is at once untainted and resistant to the bureaucratic state. The justify and redeem strategy imagines that there is a set of signifiers—signifiers usually associated with moral philosophy or value talk—that are not only impervious to, but that in fact will transcend the instrumentalist grammar of the bureaucratic state. This mistake is presently characteristic of the academic liberal-left. What the academic liberal-left does is treat its own favorite signifiers—like "politics" or "progressive legal change"—as somehow mysteriously exempt from social construction and still fully context transcendent after all these years.

Notice that both the constrain and control strategy and the justify and redeem strategy go wrong in much the same way. Both take their (intellectually antiquated) political desires as descriptive of their own situation. Neither is to be faulted for this. On the contrary: the institution of such deception, of such self-deception, is precisely what legitimating strategies are all about. Indeed, what else is to be expected from a legitimating strategy? The critical question is: How well are they doing it? The answer is: Not very well at all. Rather than experiencing either or both of these legitimating strategies as ethically generative or intellectually vital, our experience is altogether different.

Both legitimating strategies are, of course, quite constricting. Both are institutionalized forms of thought control. Not only do they limit what can be thought or asked about law, they organize and institute legal thought as a tedious repetition of—what else?—themselves. This is why, in the law of the academy, we seem always to be rediscovering the same old truths. This is why, in the law of the academy, if you have an idea, it is probably not law, and why, if you are "doing law," you probably have no ideas. This is why one often gets the feeling at legal conferences that virtually nothing is being said: Nothing *is* being said. Instead, legal thinkers are, for the most part, enacting the strategies of constrain and control and justify and redeem. They are sticking very close to the approved, cautious, incrementalist methods of constrain and control and very close to the conventionally sanctioned, normative narratives of justify and redeem. In the constrain and control strategy, legal thought is protected by elaborate burdens of proof, copious disclaimers, and very careful delimitations of the operative jurisdiction. In the justify and redeem strategy, legal thought is wrapped in an extensive padding of normatively wonderful signifiers and moral self-congratulation. Indeed, with all this institutional and rhetorical constriction and all this aura of destruction, the presentation of legal thought is framed very defensively. This is why legal thinkers are always taking "stances" and trying to "defend" their "positions." Indeed, with all this aura of destruction around, could one expect anything else?

Now, so far, I have described the world of academic law as (1) constituted by a desire for flight from its own violent character, (2) constructed so as to avoid learning anything new, and (3) given to rationalizing its own rationalizations. As a constitutive matrix for an intellectual discipline, this is, to say it again, not an auspicious start. But note that so far these three tendencies have been presented in a static frame. In order to understand our situation, it is necessary to present the matter dynamically. We need to consider what happens over time when both legal academics and judges are fashioned with these destructive, world-denying motivations and rationalizing tendencies and are then asked to train each other, to see and construct law in terms of the perspective of the other. Does law work itself pure?

This is not an idle inquiry. Consider that some of the very brightest people of each generation choose to work within the medium of the law of the academy. What happens when very intelligent people are asked to operate within this discursive world constructed as a flight from its own object, a discursive world given to elaborate, self-referential layers of self-legitimation and self-rationalization, a discursive world bent as far as possible on not learning anything new and reaffirming itself as the same? What happens when extremely intelligent people are asked to perform within this sort of discursive universe and are constructed through disciplinary power to observe this institutionalized and cognitively embedded etiquette? What do they do? What do they write? What is to be expected?

Fortunately, these questions are not hypothetical. We have more than a hundred years of answers to examine. Mostly what these extremely intelligent people do, it turns out, is construct extremely intricate and elaborate structures and then try to rationalize them. In short, they build mazes. Most of the time their schemes turn out to be something that might be called "doctrine"; sometimes they look more like what might be called "theory."[15] Either way, what we get is an extraordinarily variegated law—a law which is internally differentiated in multilayered, self-referential ways. We get a series of increasingly specific rationalizations linked to other rationalizations via an orderly system of rationalizations. Now, to the extent that one is operating within any of the currently available rationalization programs—efficiency analysis, ad hoc doctrinalism, ad hoc policy instrumentalism, ad hoc pragmatism, ad hoc whatever—the law of the academy makes a certain amount of sense. Indeed, it is extremely difficult to disprove the validity or value of any of these rationalization programs. Difficult because, at this late date, the hypertrophy of self-referential rationalization has obscured from view most of what might be called the referents. And since the logic of this self-referentiality consists mostly of self-congratulation, the rationalization programs are well defended. What is more, these programs are constructed in ways that authorize and legitimate the destruction of new nonconforming views and their relegation to the oblivion of the external perspective. How, then, could these rationalization programs possibly go wrong?

In some senses, it seems they cannot. These mazes built of massively overwrought doctrine, of sacred historical text fragments, of multilayered bureaucratic processes and sundry dominions of expertise, of massive economic or moral theoretical structures deployed to resolve picayune legal problems, are the mazes that legal academics run. While the mazes are all different, they are all aesthetically very much the same: they are constructed of repeated exercises of constrain and control and justify and redeem. What these mazes have going for them is that, over time, they produce certain cognitive and aesthetic deficits.

They produce subjects—legal subjects—who are so caught up in the rationalizations and the legitimations that they systematically conflate

the regulative ideal of thoughtful, searching,
and comprehensive judicial opinions
with
the regulatory bureaucratic noise of contemporary Supreme Court opinions;

the eternal form of law
with
the formative jurisprudential experience of their youth—(. . .);*

engaging in transformative or progressive political action
with
writing passionate law review articles in favor of transformative
or progressive political action.

Each of these conflations is in an important sense the *same* conflation, the *same*
confusion—a confusion that arises when the legal academic subject becomes so
immersed in and so suffused with the legitimations and rationalizations of the
law of the academy that he or she is no longer capable of distinguishing the referent from the simulation. In this discursive world, the *identity* and the *ontological* status of the main terms and the main grammar are at once almost
always beyond question, and yet almost always dramatically underspecified.[16]
As a partial preliminary list of such terms, consider the following:

The Law
The Rule of Law
Objective
Common Sense
Good Judgment
Transformative Action
Transformative Potential
Rights
The Constitution
The First Amendment
The Text
The Intent of . . .
Nihilism

*Pick one and insert as appropriate: (a) legal process, (b) formalism, (c) moralism, (d) taking over
the administration building, (e) (as yet unnamed).

Progressive Legal Change
Change
Contextual
Maximize
Deter
Cause

Now, among the appropriate legal academic audience, the invocation of these terms, in accordance with their usual accompanying grammar, will, with surprising frequency, *simply arrest thought on impact.* This dramatic arresting effect is part of the legitimation or delegitimation value of these terms. The terms are either so obviously true and good or so obviously false and wrong that their identity and ontological status are not and need not be questioned. Instead, whatever these terms may be missing in intellectual content—which, of course, is usually everything—is always already compensated through the legitimating or delegitimating projections of the appropriate legal academic audience.

The sort of desperate attempts that we see currently among leading legal academics to infuse vitality into these virtually empty signifiers—everything from "The Rule of Law" to "Progressive Legal Change" to "Politics"—is a testimony to their vacuity. The vacuity of these main terms should not surprise, for their accompanying grammar is generally vacuous as well. Indeed, consider that a great deal of the legal academic conversation can be understood as little more than an ongoing debate between generally conservative-right proponents of constrain and control and generally liberal-left proponents of justify and redeem. It has been, in short, a very long conversation carried on between two impossible visions, neither of which could possibly register in our present social circumstances—except, of course, as legitimations. Legitimations of what? Legitimations first and foremost of themselves. Legitimations secondarily of each other, for if one part of the opposition drops out, the other makes little sense: No Dworkin without a Bork. No Radin without an Epstein. No (. . .) without a (. . .), and so on. Third, what these legitimating strategies are legitimating is their own unconscious construction of an extraordinarily florid bureaucratic legalism that knows no limits in its internal differentiation or in its territorial acquisition of new subject matter to be submitted to the regimes of The Rule of Law, or Progressive Legal Change, or Politics, or whatever. In short, these legitimations are legitimations of the maze.

Is this surprising? Is it surprising that one day the grand legitimating strategies of law should appear vacuous? Is this surprising—given the constitutive desire of the law of the academy not to see, not to understand, not to pursue certain lines of inquiry? Is this surprising given the legal academy's sustained construction of mazes upon mazes of rationalizations of rationalizations? Is this surprising given the formative core of destructiveness and violence at the heart of the law of the academy? Is it surprising that the law of the academy should consume itself in this way—find itself one day in an extraordinarily extensive maze not knowing what to do or where to go and with only the most self-congratulatory versions of extradisciplinary knowledge available to help? Is this surprising?

No.

What might be, in one sense, surprising—though not according to this essay—is that the law of the academy, a law which has been bent on so much destructiveness and so much denial of its own destructive impulses, has been able to portray itself and its various mazes as somehow constructive. One can see how this claim is itself constructed if we look at the recent argument offered in Judge Harry Edwards's article "The Growing Disjunction between Legal Education and the Legal Profession."[17] Judge Edwards complains that various parties in the legal academy are contributing to the ethical corruption of young lawyers by supposedly abandoning doctrine in favor of theory. Now, this too might seem to be a surprising claim. Indeed, before the theorists or any of the younger intellectuals appeared on the legal scene, legal academics of Judge Edwards's generation and those before had been representing law as an idealized ordering of clean propositional statements, known as "certain doctrines and principles." They had developed an extremely intricate system of doctrines and cases and legal interpretation that successfully eclipsed the destructiveness and violence of law and judging. In order to maintain this intricate system of interconnected doctrines and rationalizations, they, of course, had to destroy the cognitive, aesthetic, and intellectual capacities of generations of students. They tried as much as possible to establish a system that would run by itself, a system that, through the legitimation strategies of constrain and control and justify and redeem, would severely limit the need for individual ethical judgment. They sought to transpose ethics from the realm of cognition and practice to what they saw as a more lasting and universal form—the form of rules, standards, and doctrines. They worked on projects like the Restatements and the ABA Code of Professional Responsibility. They sought to transform law and legal ethics into elaborate schedules of carefully drafted propositions. This they said was "constructive."

But now that they see what they have wrought, now that all their best intentions have turned into endless corridors of bureaucratic legalism riddled with instrumentalist opportunism, they blame their own jurisprudential failures on their offspring. This is sad.

These observations, of course, could easily be developed into a normative response to Judge Harry Edwards. In some sense, his inflammatory claims invite and merit such a response. But it is important to resist this sort of normative impulse. For one thing, it would just be another exercise in normative feel-good jurisprudence. For another, in its normative destructiveness it would simply be an expression of law's sameness. Besides, there is something more important to do here than simply return Judge Edwards's missiles back to sender. That something is to illustrate, one more time, a key argument of this essay: when an entire discipline like the law of the academy is constructed as a series of legitimations and rationalizations designed to avoid taking cognizance of its own violent and destructive character, when it is designed in such a way as to destroy indiscriminately new, nonconforming thought, it is easy for its practitioners to become ethically disoriented. One becomes ethically disoriented precisely because one has already lost the aesthetic and cognitive capacities to appreciate what is going on. One becomes ethically disoriented because one has become just another clerk lost in the maze.

I do not want to make a normative argument against the maze. I do not know about you, but in my experience, making normative arguments to social practices or to psychological formations to try to convince them to reform their own being is just not a terribly successful strategy. I have several views as to why this is. At least one of them is completely contrary to what is routinely taken for granted throughout virtually all contemporary American legal thought. This view—one that is described in this essay—is that *deficits in ontological condition will prompt epistemological and normative endeavors as compensation for those ontological deficits, and simultaneously render these normative and epistemological endeavors entirely ineffectual in correcting those ontological deficits.* Now, so long as this point is not understood, the normative and epistemological endeavors can keep going for a very long time—decades at least, possibly centuries. Of course, it is also true that if this point is not understood, those normative and epistemological endeavors will then seem, for inexplicable reasons, increasingly repetitive and increasingly boring.

This view is completely contrary to what virtually all contemporary American legal academics take for granted. If one takes seriously what they write and what they say, American legal academics seem to believe something like the opposite. It is not exactly the opposite, however, because it is not just a belief. Indeed, among American legal academics, the presupposition that normative or epistemological prescription is somehow competent to address and redress deficits in ontological condition is not merely a belief, nor even a sacred truth: it is a constitutive aspect of their very being as legal academics. Similarly, this constitutive aspect is critical to the construction of the legitimating strategies of American legal thought described above. In the context of this essay, it is easy to see why. If it were the case that normative and epistemological endeavors were not capable of transforming the ontology of law, then we, as legal academics, would be stuck with, and implicated in, what would then appear as the irreducible and unmediated violence of judges and judging. That, I take it, is something that American legal thinkers are constituted through and through to find absolutely intolerable, completely unacceptable. Hence, they believe that this violence can be transformed through constrain and control or justify and redeem into something else—something more palatable—like doctrine or normative theory or grand dialogue or neopragmatic sensitivity or (. . .). That, in short, is how legal thinkers get into and help propagate the maze.

Now, you can tell where this is going. I have been postponing the conclusion for some time now.

There is, of course, a way out. And it has been described throughout this essay. The difficulty with this way out, for most legal academics, is that it does not, indeed it cannot, reduce to a *prescription* or a *recommendation* or a *solution* or even a *criticism*. So, to the extent that one keeps looking for a prescription or a recommendation or a solution or a criticism, one will remain in the maze.[18]

But for those who find the way out, this is an extraordinarily exciting time in American legal thought. The social formations, the institutional norms, and the professional hierarchies that embody and enforce the orthodox jurisprudential strategies of constrain and control and justify and redeem seem to be losing some of their hold. Accordingly, for those who have the inclination and the capacity, the study of law provides extraordinary opportunities for intellectual creativity—opportunities that go way beyond the usual "law and . . ." strategies of reducing law to some foreign discipline or reducing some foreign discipline to the role of supporting cast for the reconstruction of the same old law. For those with the inclination and the capacity, there are a tremendous number of questions to answer—questions that, in virtue of the constrain and control and justify and redeem strategies, no one has yet *dared* to ask.

NOTES

INTRODUCTION

1 Pierre Schlag, "Normativity and the Politics of Form," this volume, at 98.
2 Citation omitted.
3 Paul Campos, "Against Constitutional Theory," this volume, at 139.
4 Steven D. Smith, "Idolatry in Constitutional Interpretation," this volume, at 189.
5 Pierre Schlag, "Values," 6 *Yale J.L. & Human.* 219 (1994).
6 *The Ages of American Law* (1974), 111.

NORMATIVITY AND THE POLITICS OF FORM

1 P. Bourdieu, *In Other Words* (1990), 178.
2 For a graphic demonstration, see C. M. Yablon, "Forms," 11 *Cardozo L. Rev.* 1348 (1990).
3 A. Sarat and W. L. F. Felstiner, "Lawyers and Legal Consciousness: Law Talk in the Divorce Lawyer's Office," 98 *Yale L.J.* 1663, 1685 (1989) (footnotes omitted).
4 See P. Schlag, " 'Le Hors de Texte, C'est Moi': The Politics of Form and the Domestication of Deconstruction," 11 *Cardozo L. Rev.* 1631 (1990); P. Schlag, "Normative and Nowhere to Go," 43 *Stan. L. Rev.* 167 (1990).
5 Notice that the generative metaphorical schema at work here is what Lakoff calls the "source-path-goal schema"; see G. Lakoff, *Women, Fire, and Dangerous Things: What Categories Reveal about the Mind* (1987), 275. The basic logic of this recursive schema is to go from a *source* to a *destination* on a *path*. As Lakoff puts it, "Purposes are understood in terms of destinations, and achieving a purpose is understood as passing along a path from a starting point to an endpoint" (ibid).

   Much of normative legal thought can be understood as structured by this source-path-goal schema. Teleological ethics are destination oriented, requiring the travelers on the journey to act in ways appropriate to achieve the destination. Deontological ethics, in contrast, are backward looking and source regarding, requiring the travelers to refer back to what has already transpired on the journey in order to decide what to do at each point.
6 See P. Schlag, "Cannibal Moves: The Metamorphoses of the Legal Distinction," 40 *Stan. L. Rev.* 929, 930 (1988).
7 For an argument that the "essential difficulties in social policy have more to do with *problem setting* than with problem solving," see D. Schön, "Generative Metaphor: A Perspective on Problem Setting in Social Policy," in *Metaphor and Thought,* ed. A. Ortony (1988), 254, 255.

8   For instance, the running feud between deontological and teleological ethics. For an early and sophisticated instantiation of this clash in the legal literature, see G. P. Fletcher, "Fairness and Utility in Tort Theory," 85 *Harv. L. Rev.* 537 (1972).

9   "Sedimentation" is a concept that arrives on the legal scene from Steven Winter, from Maurice Merleau-Ponty, from Husserl. See S. Winter, "Indeterminacy and Incommensurability in Constitutional Law," 78 *Calif. L. Rev.* 1441, 1487–88 (1990).

10 This is akin to what Bernstein calls "the Cartesian anxiety"; see R. Bernstein, *Beyond Objectivism and Relativism* (1985), 18. For expressions of this anxiety, see P. Carrington, "Of Law and the River," 34 *J. Legal Educ.* 222 (1984); O. Fiss, "Objectivity and Interpretation," 34 *Stan. L. Rev.* 739 (1982).

11 P. Schlag, "Normativity and the Politics of Form," 139 *U. Pa. L. Rev.* 801, 808–32 (1991).

12 See A. S. Brudner, "The Ideality of Difference: Toward Objectivity in Legal Interpretation," 11 *Cardozo L. Rev.* 1133, 1145 (1990): "Because it mistakes its own products for autonomous objects, ordinary [legal] consciousness remains an undeveloped interpretive process. . . . The task of understanding is to re-enact consciously the implicit creative activity of ordinary consciousness, interpreting the latter's objects as . . . realizations of a project." See also R. K. Sherwin, "Dialectics and Dominance: A Study of Rhetorical Fields in the Law of Confessions," 136 *U. Pa. L. Rev.* 729, 795 (1988); Winter, supra note 9.

13 It is, however, a very old business:

Plato's doctrine of "truth" is therefore not something of the past. It is historically "present" but not as a historically recollected "consequence" of a piece of didacticism, not even as revival, not even as imitation of antiquity, not even as mere preservation of the traditional. [Plato's doctrine of "truth"] is present as the slowly confirmed and still uncontested basic reality, a reality reigning through everything. . . . [M]an thinks in terms of the fact that the essence of truth is the correctness of the representing of all beings according to "ideas" and esteems everything real according to "values." *The decisive point is not which ideas and which values are set, but that the real is expounded according to "ideas" at all, that the "world" is weighed according to "values" at all.* (M. Heidegger, "Plato's Doctrine of Truth," in *Philosophy in the Twentieth Century*, ed. W. Barrett and H. Aiken (1962), 8:255, 269–70 (emphasis added).

14 We have been so accustomed to finding meaning *in* the text, *in* the restatement, *in* the doctrine, that, despite our most sophisticated theoretical attempts to avoid such naive objectifications, the object-form nonetheless continues to rule. Use of the preposition *in* often signals and effectuates an inside/outside distinction that serves to objectify the field. See, e.g., P. Schlag, "*Fish v. Zapp:* The Case of the Relatively Autonomous Self," 76 *Geo. L.J.* 37, 55–56 (1987). This inside/outside distinction, so common in law, effectuates what Lakoff and Johnson call the "container metaphor" effect. See G. Lakoff and M. Johnson, *Metaphors We Live By* (1980), 29–32; S. Winter, "*Bull Durham* and the Uses of Theory," 42 *Stan. L. Rev.* 639, 661–64 (1989).

15 "But there are several ways of being caught in this circle. They are all more or less naive, more or less empirical, more or less systematic, more or less close to the formulation—that is, to the formalization—of this circle" (J. Derrida, "Structure, Sign and Play," in *Writing and Difference* (1978), 278, 281 (referring to a "reasonably" similar circle).

16 A. E. Cook, "Beyond Critical Legal Studies: The Reconstructive Theology of Dr. Martin Luther King, Jr.," 103 *Harv. L. Rev.* 985, 1044 (1990) (emphasis added).

17 R. C. Post, "The Constitutional Concept of Public Discourse: Outrageous Opinion, Demo-

cratic Deliberation, and *Hustler Magazine v. Falwell*," 103 *Harv. L. Rev.* 603, 683 (1990) (emphasis added).

18 C. R. Sunstein, "Interpreting Statutes in the Regulatory State," 103 *Harv. L. Rev.* 405, 503–4 (1990) (emphasis added).

19 E. Chemerinsky, "Foreword: The Vanishing Constitution," 103 *Harv. L. Rev.* 43, 104 (1989) (emphasis added).

20 D. Laycock, "The Death of the Irreparable Injury Rule," 103 *Harv. L. Rev.* 687, 770 (1990) (emphasis added).

21 R. L. Hayman Jr., "Presumptions of Justice: Law, Politics, and the Mentally Retarded Parent," 103 *Harv. L. Rev.* 1201, 1268 (1990) (emphasis added).

22 J. B. Ames, "Purchase for Value without Notice," 1 *Harv. L. Rev.* 1, 16 (1887) (emphasis added).

23 F. J. Stimson, "Trusts," 1 *Harv. L. Rev.* 132, 143 (1887) (emphasis added).

24 L. M. Greeley, "What Is the Test of a Regulation of Foreign or Interstate Commerce?" 1 *Harv. L. Rev.* 159, 184 (1887) (emphasis added).

25 A. L. Lowell, "The Responsibilities of American Lawyers," 1 *Harv. L. Rev.* 232, 240 (1887) (emphasis added).

26 S. B. Clarke, "Criticisms upon Henry George, Reviewed from the Stand-Point of Justice," 1 *Harv. L. Rev.* 265, 293 (1887) (emphasis added).

27 W. H. Dunbar, "The Anarchists' Case before the Supreme Court of the United States," 1 *Harv. L. Rev.* 307, 323, 326 (1887) (emphasis added).

28 W. Williams, "A Creditor's Right to His Surety's Securities," 1 *Harv. L. Rev.* 326, 337 (1887) (emphasis added).

29 Schauer, "Constitutional Conventions" (Book Review), 87 *Mich. L. Rev.* 1407, 1409 (1989).

30 Rubin, "The Practice and Discourse of Legal Scholarship," 86 *Mich. L. Rev.* 1835, 1847–48 (1988) (footnote omitted).

31 Ibid. at 1853.

32 D. Kennedy, "A Rotation in Contemporary Legal Scholarship," in *Critical Legal Thought: An American-German Debate*, ed. C. Joerges and D. Trubek (1989), 353, 380.

33 P. Brest, "The Fundamental Rights Controversy: The Essential Contradictions of Normative Constitutional Scholarship," 90 *Yale L.J.* 1063, 1109 (1981).

34 The work of Steven Winter provides a general introduction to the metaphorical character of cognition, culture, and law that informs these observations. See Winter, supra note 14; S. Winter, "The Cognitive Dimension of the *Agon* between Legal Power and Narrative Meaning," 87 *Mich. L. Rev.* 2225 (1989); Winter, supra note 9; S. Winter, "The Metaphor of Standing and the Problem of Self-Governance," 40 *Stan. L. Rev.* 1371 (1988); S. Winter, "Transcendental Nonsense, Metaphoric Reasoning, and the Cognitive Stakes for Law," 137 *U. Pa. L. Rev.* 1105 (1989).

35 See Schlag, "Normative and Nowhere to Go," supra note 4, at 170–71.

36 One study found that "the number of citations [in Supreme Court opinions] to legal periodicals decreased from 963 in the 1971–73 period to 767 in the 1981–83 period. We find this decline substantial. . . . Our study suggests a decreasing judicial reliance on legal periodicals by the court that would seem to be the most receptive to the contributions of legal scholarship" (L. J. Sirico Jr. and J. B. Margulies, "The Citing of Law Reviews by the Supreme Court: An Empirical Study," 34 *UCLA L. Rev.* 131, 134–37 [1986] [footnote omitted]).

If anything, this decrease in the number of citations to law reviews probably understates their increasing irrelevance to judicial decision making. With the advent of increasingly bureaucratic modes of judicial decision making and the expanded role of law clerks, citation of law review articles becomes more and more a kind of window dressing and law review articles are less and less significant to the production of the actual decision. For discussion of the increased role of law clerks, see R. Posner, *The Federal Courts: Crisis and Reform* (1985), 102–19; E. N. Griswold, "Cutting the Cloak to Fit the Cloth: An Approach to Problems in the Federal Courts," 32 *Cath. U.L. Rev.* 787, 799 (1983); W. H. McCree, Jr. "Bureaucratic Justice: An Early Warning," 129 *U. Pa. L. Rev.* 777, 785–87 (1981); W. M. Richman and W. L. Reynolds, "Appellate Justice Bureaucracy and Scholarship," 21 *U. Mich. J.L. Ref.* 623, 626–28 (1988); J. Vining, "Justice, Bureaucracy, and Legal Method," 80 *Mich. L. Rev.* 248, 252 (1981).

37   See R. Dworkin, *Law's Empire* (1986).

38   Ibid. at 255.

39   See Schlag, "Le Hors de Texte," supra note 4, at 1660–64.

40   Though it is rarely self-evident when Dworkin means to advance his "concept" of adjudication as opposed to his "conception" of adjudication. See Dworkin, supra note 37, at 70–72.

41   Even CLS scholarship (in the early days of that movement) sought to arrange cases in the coherence of a stabilized pattern of "the fundamental contradiction." See J. M. Feinman, "Promissory Estoppel and Judicial Method," 97 *Harv. L. Rev.* 678 (1984) (arguing that theoretical and methodological developments exemplified in promissory estoppel cases represent failed attempts to overcome the fundamental contradiction of classical nineteenth-century legalism).

42   See R. Delgado, "Norms and Normal Science: Toward a Critique of Normativity in Legal Thought," 139 *U. Pa. L. Rev.* 933, 943–44 (1991) (describing the anxiety-reducing role of normative legal thought).

43   Here, I am referring to those surprising professions of faith that appear to be—even though perhaps they are not—inconsistent with the author's past professions of faith.

44   Consider the following passage: "So what is the value of another article on state action? First, I hope that change, at least in the long term, will occur if it is demonstrated emphatically and repeatedly that limiting the Constitution's protections to state action makes no sense. History shows that if doctrines and concepts are attacked long enough and hard enough they may begin to crumble" (E. Chemerinsky, "Rethinking State Action," 80 *Nw. U.L. Rev.* 503, 556 [1985]).

45   F. Michelman, "Law's Republic," 97 *Yale L.J.* 1493, 1513 (1988).

46   Ibid. at 1514.

47   See *The Republic of Plato,* trans. F. Cornford (1945), 106–7.

48   E. Warnke, "Rawls, Habermas, and Real Talk: A Reply to Walzer," 21 *Phil. F.* 197, 202 (1990) (emphasis added).

49   381 U.S. 479 (1965): "Would we allow the police to search sacred precincts of marital bedrooms . . . ?"

50   *L.A. Law,* NBC television broadcast, March 29, 1990.

51   Ibid.

52   This description resonates in autopoietic social theory: "Legal communications are the cognitive instruments by which the law as social discourse is able to see the world. Legal communications cannot reach out into the real outside world, neither into nature nor into society. They can only communicate about nature and society. Any metaphor about their

access to the real world is misplaced" (G. Teubner, "How the Law Thinks: Toward a Constructivist Epistemology of Law," 23 *Law & Soc'y Rev.* 727, 740 [1989]).

53   *L.A. Law,* supra note 50. This, of course, is preposterous, given that this case will be followed by an endless line of other cases—each also richly deserving of special treatment.

54   "The shadow law" is an expression taken from R. H. Mnookin and L. Kornhauser, "Bargaining in the Shadow of the Law: The Case of Divorce," 88 *Yale L.J.* 950 (1979).

     Of all criminal defendants convicted in the United States District Courts between 1986 and 1989, the percentage who pled guilty are as follows: 1989, 85.3 percent; 1988, 86.0 percent; 1987, 86.0 percent; 1986, 85.7 percent (from *Annual Reports of the Director of the Administrative Office of the United States Courts,* 1989, p. 279; 1988, p. 297; 1987, p. 120; 1987, p. 120, respectively).

55   The "favor bank" is a jurisprudential concept developed by Tom Wolfe. See T. Wolfe, *The Bonfire of the Vanities* (1987), 400–402.

56   *L.A. Law,* supra note 50.

57   Gillers notes: "I watched many hours of *L.A. Law.* The shows were uneven internally and from week to week. Some were heavy with adolescent humor and crude stereotypes. Others were admirable, occasionally masterful, in their depiction of legal and ethical issues. Lean and subtle, they could inspire class discussion" (S. Gillers, "Taking *L.A. Law* More Seriously," 98 *Yale L.J.* 1607, 1620 [1989]).

58   Sarat and Felstiner, supra note 3, at 1685.

59   A. Blumberg, "The Practice of Law as Confidence Game," 1 *Law & Soc'y Rev.* 15, 21 (1967); see also J. Carlin, *Lawyers on Their Own* (1962), 105–9 (discussing the mechanics of a small-scale, solo criminal practice).

60   Marbury v. Madison, 5 U.S. (1 Cranch) 137, 163 (1803).

61   A. Dershowitz, *Taking Liberties: A Decade of Hard Cases, Bad Laws, and Bum Raps* (1988), 2.

62   The discourse of lawyers is "a paradigmatic case of strategic, success-oriented communication" (M. Dan-Cohen, "Law, Community, and Communication," 1989 *Duke L.J.* 1654, 1668).

63   A. J. Moore, "Trial by Schema: Cognitive Filters in the Courtroom," 37 *UCLA L. Rev.* 273, 277 (1989).

64   J. Mitchell, "The Ethics of the Criminal Defense Attorney—New Answers to Old Questions," 32 *Stan. L. Rev.* 293, 299–300 (1980).

65   See Winter, "Cognitive Dimension," supra note 34, at 2272–74 (describing the ways the advocate's story line can persuade by tapping into an existing story line shared by his or her audience).

66   E. A. Dauer and A. A. Leff, "The Lawyer as Friend," 86 *Yale L.J.* 573, 581 (1977).

67   Dworkin, supra note 37, at 413.

68   O. Fiss, "The Law Regained," 74 *Cornell L. Rev.* 245, 249 (1989).

69   See R. Coombe, " 'Same as It Ever Was': Rethinking the Politics of Legal Interpretation," 34 *McGill L.J.* 601, 649 (1989).

70   Dworkin, supra note 37, at 405.

71   This point is suggested in R. Abel, "Why Does the ABA Promulgate Ethical Rules?" 59 *Tex. L. Rev.* 639, 667–68 (1981).

72   In the early days, Kennedy's articulation of the apologetic or legitimating character of academic legal thought was targeted at legal thought—in fact, at legal theory. See D. M. Kennedy, "Cost-Benefit Analysis of Entitlement Problems: A Critique," 33 *Stan. L. Rev.* 387, 387–89 (1981); Kennedy, "The Structure of Blackstone's Commentaries," 28 *Buffalo L. Rev.* 205, 209–11 (1979).

Quite possibly as the result of the typical identification that academics make between their legal thought and the law put out by courts, the legitimation thesis somehow became a claim about the function or role of law and the courts relative to the social order. But, of course, this slippage of the legitimation thesis from the academy to the courts, from theory to positive law, presented some serious conceptual problems (to say the least). It was no doubt prompted by the unconscious self-identification of legal thinkers with courts and judges, and by the presumption that they, like judges, are "doing law." They think that when they use the same three-letter word (*law*), it means the same thing in the academy as it does in the courts. This is wrong. It is a routine mistake.

73   On legitimation and apologetics, see Kennedy, "Cost-Benefit Analysis," supra note 72, at 444–45 (arguing that efficiency analysis is a kind of legitimation for the system of private law). For discussion of the less morally appealing roles of normative legal thought, see Delgado, supra note 42, at 947–55.

74   This is a slightly more gracious and slightly different way of saying what Stanley Fish has already said of Dworkin's theory: it's a nice piece of rhetorical work. As jurisprudence goes, it is in the genre of cheerleading. See S. Fish, *Doing What Comes Naturally: Change, Rhetoric, and the Practice of Theory in Literary and Legal Studies* (1989), 390–92; see also S. D. Smith, "Pursuit of Pragmatism," 100 *Yale L.J.* 409, 444–47 (1990) (suggesting that legal pragmatism is a kind of preaching, a kind of jurisprudence-as-exhortation).

75   See Dworkin, supra note 37, at 46–70. If one's basic motif for law is "courtesy," it's a pretty good (though not a sure) bet that the analysis is not going to take a searching self-critical turn.

76   L. Fuller, "The Forms and Limits of Adjudication," 92 *Harv. L. Rev.* 353, 360 (1979).

77   O. Fiss, "The Supreme Court, 1978 Term—Foreword: The Forms of Justice," 93 *Harv. L. Rev.* 1, 58 (1979).

78   See E. Weinrib, "Legal Formalism: On the Immanent Rationality of Law," 97 *Yale L.J.* 949, 982, 1003, 1012–13 (1988): "The forms of justice cannot be understood detached from the particularity of the external interactions that they govern and from the specific regimes of positive law that actualize them."

79   Several are noted in the following passage: "Convene a gaggle of lawyers and you will hear several varieties (and different intensities) of criticism of *L.A. Law*. The criticisms tend to focus on three aspects of the show: it makes lawyers' cases seem a good deal more significant than they are; it does not accurately recognize or describe the ethical issues lawyers face; it makes the work tasks of lawyers seem a great deal more exciting than they are" (Gillers, supra note 57, at 1607). What strikes me, however, is that the very same three criticisms apply obviously—and perhaps even more readily—to much of the normative legal thought that issues from the legal academy.

80   Some normative thinkers attempt to escape this problem by specifying that they are operating within the normative realm—hence, adopting normative conceptions of the person distinct "from an account of human nature given by natural science or social theory" (J. Rawls, "Justice as Fairness: Political Not Metaphysical," 14 *Phil. Pub. Aff.* 223, 232 n. 15 [1985]).

81   The point is made most globally by Alasdair MacIntyre, who demonstrates how the history of moral philosophy has evolved along tracks that have little relation to the aesthetics of our own social and psychological practices. See A. MacIntyre, *After Virtue* (1984).

82   How does normative legal thought imagine that it effectuates its recommendations and prescriptions? Its options are actually quite limited. The following list describes in increasing

order of sophistication the ways normative legal thought might without self-contradiction imagine that it produces its implications or effects:

1. Normative legal thought persuades judges to adopt the outcomes, principles, or values prescribed in the scholarship.

2. Normative legal thought provides rhetorical or stylistic comfort for judges who are already persuaded of the wisdom of the normative position but need something to cite as authority.

3. Because normative legal thought provides better, more compelling, more encompassing versions of the legal analyses that judges have already developed, it succeeds in extending the half-lives of judicial opinions and makes these opinions much more influential than they would otherwise be.

4. Normative legal thought influences courts by virtue of its political power.

5. Normative legal thought is influential, but only with very intellectual judges. Intellectual judges are a minority, but they are extremely influential among their peers.

6. Normative legal thought does not so much influence judges as it influences the moral-political belief systems of the community of eight thousand or so legal academics. The moral-political beliefs of this group are very important because they are teachers and their beliefs are transmitted to their students, who in turn act on these beliefs once they become lawyers.

These hypotheses share the presumption that normative legal thought is an authentic originary form of thought somehow distinct from the domains of power, psychology, and rhetoric. They share the presumption that the self-representation of normative legal thought is identical with normative legal thought itself. Ironically, this very (rationalist) way of thinking about normative legal thought is, as I will demonstrate later, itself a product of normative legal thought.

83 B. McDowell, "The Audiences for Legal Scholarship," 40 *J. Legal Educ.* 261, 273 (1990).

84 Certainly judges might have led them to believe so. Learned Hand said in 1925 that law teachers "will be recognized in another generation, anyway, as the only body which can be relied upon to state a doctrine, with a complete knowledge of its origin, its authority, and its meaning. We [the judges] shall in very shame, if we have sense enough, acknowledge that pre-eminence which your position and your opportunities secure" (D. B. Maggs, "Concerning the Extent to Which the Law Review Contributes to the Development of the Law," 3 *S. Calif. L. Rev.* 181, 187–88 [1930], quoting *Handbook of the Association of American Law Schools* [1925], 47).

85 What chance is there that judges are listening? Indeed, there is very little evidence to support the view that judges do in fact read or follow normative legal scholarship. Citation of scholarly articles in judicial opinions is probably the strongest piece of evidence that judges are reading them. But to conclude from the fact of such citations that judges are indeed persuaded by normative thought requires some significant leaps of faith. For one thing, it assumes that judges' understanding of the articles they cite has some strong correspondence to the understanding of the authors who actually write the articles. This correspondence is hardly self-evident; creative use of citations by judges is common. What's more, many noncreative citations of academic work are to marginal or obvious points that the academic author often considers peripheral to her enterprise. But even if these problems did not exist, it is still not clear that judges cite normative legal scholarship because they are persuaded.

It is at least equally plausible that judges (or clerks) deploy citations to legal scholarship in their opinions as a matter of style—in an effort to bolster already formed opinions. Indeed, in informal conversations with judges at both the federal and state level, judges have told me that this is often the case. If this is descriptive of the judicial practice of citing scholarly works, then normative legal scholarship might have marginal effectiveness. Thus, it might be the case that the existence of scholarly authority for a given normative position provides the intellectual comfort necessary for a court to adopt a given position or for a judge to write a dissent. See also supra note 82.

86   See Schlag, "Normative and Nowhere to Go," supra note 4, at 177.

87   On the boring, deadening quality of recent Supreme Court constitutional opinions, see R. Nagel, "The Formulaic Constitution," 84 *Mich. L. Rev.* 165, 177–82 (1985). On the boring, deadening quality of contemporary legal thought, see J. B. White, "Intellectual Integration," 82 *Nw. U.L. Rev.* 1, 5–6 (1987).

88   While I think that most students and law teachers would readily agree that the normative thought of legal academics does affect the normative orientation of students as well as other legal academics, this is not to claim that it has any effect on the normative character of their behavior. For instance, it is certainly conceivable that a thoroughgoing reading of Rawls could persuade some student or academic to drop her previous attachment to Nozick and embrace the difference principle. The student or academic might then say, perhaps even with great conviction, that she has become a Rawlsian. But apart from this new representation about her political beliefs, it is hardly self-evident that the behavior of the student or the academic will be affected in any other significant way. After all, the possibility of implementing the difference principle in legal practice, either explicitly or implicitly, is extremely remote. And this is my point exactly: most normative legal thought (and the vast majority of academic moral philosophy) is quite simply irrelevant to the kinds of concrete political and social choices confronting the academic, the law student, the lawyer, the judge, or the citizen. In our society, no one is authorized to operationalize most of what normative legal thought considers to be important. The issues are before neither the courts nor the legislatures, and they barely feature in our electoral campaigns and social life. Of course, the possibility that students and academics will become normatively sensitized as a result of exposure to this literature cannot be discounted, but the connection to any actual choice the student or the academic might make remains exceedingly remote.

89   Even when it is left-liberal, normative legal thought has a conservative effect. Normative legal thought recommends and proposes, and then attempts to make the recommendations and proposals seem appealing by taking the reader's presumed belief structures and showing how they logically entail the left-liberal solution or proposal. The left-liberal solutions or proposals typically drop off into the abyss because there is no social structure (i.e., no jobs) within the legal profession to put them into effect. And when the left-liberal recommendations drop off into the abyss, what remains is the performative reinforcement and reenactment of the reader's same old belief structures. Left-liberal normative legal thought is Sisyphean in character.

       These arguments are taken from or inspired by Duncan Kennedy's perceptive and insightful description of the politics of law school pedagogy and curriculum. See Kennedy, "The Political Significance of the Structure of the Law School Curriculum," 14 *Seton Hall L. Rev.* 1, 9–12 (1983).

90   See S. Winter, "Contingency and Community in Normative Practice," 139 *U. Pa. L. Rev.* 963 (1991).

91   When Michael Kuzak is telling the D.A. his provable facts about Stuart's drinking and arrest,

just what is the status of those statements? Is Michael saying: "You ought not go ahead with this case because, given these facts, the likelihood is that my client is not guilty and therefore should not be convicted"? Or is Michael instead saying: "Look, if you go ahead with your case, you are going to have to get around some fairly difficult obstacles that I have already put in your way—so you are going to be spending a lot of time trying to achieve something you probably won't get anyway"? See J. Austin, *How to Do Things with Words* (1975), 1–11.

92   Dworkin, supra note 37, at 413.

93   One striking example of this systemic discordance is the recent advocacy of civic republi-canism—a position that repeatedly bumps against the fact that there are no institutional mechanisms that could implement or otherwise host such a dialogic renaissance. For various formulations of this point, see R. Epstein, "Modern Republicanism—Or the Flight from Substance," 97 *Yale L.J.* 1633, 1637–38, 1640–41 (1988); H. J. Powell, "Reviving Republicanism," 97 *Yale L.J.* 1703, 1708 (1988).

94   See, generally, R. G. Lipsey and K. Lancaster, "The General Theory of Second Best," 24 *Rev. Econ. Stud.* 11 (1957).

95   This belief is already anticipated by the metaphoric expressions we use to describe linguistic acts—our language already leads us to describe linguistic acts as occurring within weightless, shapeless, unobstructed lines or "conduits" of communication. See M. Reddy, "The Conduit Metaphor—A Case of Frame Conflict in Our Language about Language," in *Metaphor and Thought,* ed. A. Ortony (1979), 284, 286–92.

96   True, the law may have to reckon with relativity—see F. Cohen, "Field Theory and Judicial Logic," 59 *Yale L.J.* 238, 270–72 (1950)—or even Heisenberg's uncertainty principle—see L. Tribe, "The Curvature of Constitutional Space: What Lawyers Can Learn from Modern Physics," 103 *Harv. L. Rev.* 1, 17–20 (1989). But normative legal thought apparently authorizes the legal thinker to think and write about both relativity and Heisenberg's uncertainty principle from the confident, secure framework of Euclidean geometry, within which the grounds of thought do not shift. The legal thinker remains in charge.

97   Richard Epstein, for instance, asserts that "it takes a theory to beat a theory" (Epstein, "Common Law, Labor Law, and Reality: A Rejoinder to Professors Getman and Kohler," 92 *Yale L.J.* 1435, 1435 [1983]).

98   R. West, "Progressive and Conservative Constitutionalism," 88 *Mich. L. Rev.* 641, 721 (1990).

99   Ibid. at 720.

100   This list was created with my friend and colleague David Eason and used in our seminar on power, ethics, and professionalism.

101   See, generally, MacIntyre, supra note 81.

102   Consider Michelman's discussion of what is required if we are to regard as possible "the historic American idea of constitutionalism":

> Given plurality, a political process can validate a societal norm as self-given law only if . . . there exists a set of prescriptive social and procedural conditions such that one's undergo-ing, under those conditions, such a dialogic modulation of one's understandings is not considered or experienced as coercive, or invasive, or otherwise a violation of one's iden-tity or freedom. . . . [This stipulation] contemplates, then, a self whose identity and freedom consist, in part, in its capacity for reflexively critical reconsideration of the ends and commitments that it already has and that make it who it is. Such a self necessarily obtains its self-critical resources from, and tests its current understandings against, under-standings from beyond its own pre-critical life and experience, which is to say commu-

nicatively, by reaching for the perspectives of other and different persons. (Michelman, supra note 45, at 1526–28; footnotes omitted)

I do not think that these conditions hold even among those individuals who have had the most privileged access to the cultural and intellectual resources to construct the kind of self described by Michelman. (Just consider the character of faculty meetings.)

103   D. Cornell, "From the Lighthouse: The Promise of Redemption and the Possibility of Legal Interpretation," 11 *Cardozo L. Rev.* 1687, 1689 (1990).

104   Precedents here include M. Ball, "The Play's the Thing: An Unscientific Reflection on Courts under the Rubric of Theater," 28 *Stan. L. Rev.* 81 (1975).

105   "Often what talkers undertake to do is not to provide information to a recipient but to present dramas to an audience" (E. Goffman, *Frame Analysis: An Essay on the Organization of Experience* [1983], 508).

106   See A. Gide, *The Counterfeiters* (1951); J. Fowles, *The French Lieutenant's Woman* (1969), 105–6. Yet, interestingly, Dworkin knows all about John Fowles. He says: "Intentionalists make the author's state of mind central to interpretation. But they misunderstand, so far as I can tell, certain complexities in that state of mind; in particular they fail to appreciate how intentions *for* a work and beliefs *about* it interact. I have in mind an experience familiar to anyone who creates anything, of suddenly seeing something 'in' it that he did not previously know was there. This is sometimes (though I think not very well) expressed in the author's cliché, that his characters seem to have minds of their own" (R. Dworkin, *A Matter of Principle* [1985], 155–56). Dworkin then cites the Fowles passage. But, of course, despite Dworkin's familiarity with this reflexive move, he seems to be quite incapable of critically examining the scene of his own writing, of his own productions.

107   See P. Schlag, "The Problem of the Subject," 69 *Tex. L. Rev.* 1627 (1991). There are, of course, counterexamples. See G. E. Frug, "Argument as Character," 40 *Stan. L. Rev.* 869, 921–27 (1988): "We come, then, to the question of the character of Argument as Character"; G. B. Wetlaufer, "Rhetoric and Its Denial in Legal Discourse," 76 *Va. L. Rev.* 1545, 1556 (1990): "In addition to the usual footnotes, the bottom of the page will also contain occasional 'rhetorical notes' in which I shall identify and sometimes reflect upon the rhetoric of the article that you are reading."

108   See, generally, R. Coase, "The Nature of the Firm," 4 *Economica* 386 (1937); R. Coase, "The Problem of Social Cost," 3 *J.L. & Econ.* 1 (1960).

109   See Coase, "Social Cost," supra note 108, at 18–19.

110   See G. Calabresi, *The Costs of Accidents: A Legal and Economic Analysis* (1970), 135; G. Calabresi and J. T. Hirschoff, "Toward a Test for Strict Liability in Torts," 81 *Yale L.J.* 1055, 1060 (1972).

111   Among law and economics thinkers, it is common to treat the market and its pricing system as an information dissemination device. See, e.g., S. Shavell, "Strict Liability versus Negligence," 9 *J. Legal Stud.* 1, 1–9, 22–25 (1980). For a general discussion of the informational character of pricing markets, see F. Hayek, "The Use of Knowledge in Society," 35 *Am. Econ. Rev.* 519 (1945).

112   Coase, by contrast, did attend to this problem. This is evident from his consideration of what he saw as the paradoxical tendency of academics to support a free market of ideas, but not a free market of goods: "What is the explanation for the paradox? . . . The market for ideas is the market in which the intellectual conducts his trade. The explanation of the paradox is self-interest and self-esteem. Self-esteem leads the intellectuals to magnify the importance of

their own market. That others should be regulated seems natural, particularly as many of the intellectuals see themselves as doing the regulating" (R. Coase, "The Economics of the First Amendment: The Market for Goods and the Market for Ideas," 64 *Am. Econ. Rev.* 384, 386 [1974]).

For another rare deployment of this kind of reflexive insight, see Epstein, supra note 93, at 1642 (stating that academics "applaud republicanism because it gives skilled academics a comparative advantage: this is the public choice explanation as to why intellectuals prefer politics to markets").

113   For the general argument tracing out this claim, see P. Schlag, "The Problem of Transaction Costs," 62 *S. Calif. L. Rev.* 1661 (1990).

114   W. James, "Pragmatism," in *Pragmatism and the Meaning of Truth* (1978), 104; see also Grey, "Holmes and Legal Pragmatism," 41 *Stan. L. Rev.* 787, 798 (1989); M. Minow and E. Spelman, "In Context," 63 *S. Calif. L. Rev.* 1597, 1599–1600 (1990).

115   The expression is borrowed from J. Derrida, "Freud and the Scene of Writing," in *Writing and Difference* (1978), 196.

116   For an early contribution linking the scene of writing to the character of its productions, see R. Delgado, "The Imperial Scholar: Reflections on a Review of Civil Rights Literature," 132 *U. Pa. L. Rev.* 561 (1984).

117   Minow and Spelman, supra note 114, at 1597.

118   See L. Ferry and A. Renault, *French Philosophy of the Sixties: An Essay on Antihumanism,* trans. M. Cattani (1990), 122–52.

119   J. Derrida, "Signature, Event, Context," in *Margins of Philosophy* (1982), 307, 329.

120   J. Balkin, "Deconstructive Practice and Legal Theory," 96 *Yale L.J.* 743, 786 (1987): "Deconstruction by its very nature is an analytic tool." See J. Balkin, "Tradition, Betrayal and the Politics of Deconstruction," 11 *Cardozo L. Rev.* 1613, 1629 (1990). I elaborate these points at greater length in Schlag, "Le Hors de Texte," supra note 4.

121   See Schlag, "Le Hors de Texte," supra note 4, at 1631–37.

122   See Schlag, "Le Hors de Texte," supra note 4.

123   See ibid.; Schlag, supra note 107.

124   The relatively autonomous self is a constructed self that concedes that it is socially and rhetorically constituted, yet maintains its own autonomy to decide just how autonomous it may or may not be. See Schlag, supra note 14, at 44.

125   Correspondingly, those persons most seriously committed to reason and to thinking are likely to be those most typically identified as irrational or nihilistic.

126   I illustrate the ways in which dualist representations of our thought are already very much pervaded by the decentering effects of pluralism in Schlag, supra note 6, at 962–63.

127   C. Fried, "The Lawyer as Friend: The Moral Foundations of the Lawyer-Client Relation," 85 *Yale L.J.* 1060, 1068–69 (1976).

128   See Schlag, supra note 107.

129   See P. Schlag, "Missing Pieces: A Cognitive Approach to Law," 67 *Tex. L. Rev.* 1195 (1989); Schlag, "Le Hors de Texte," supra note 4, at 1636.

130   See Schlag, "Missing Pieces," supra note 129, at 1204–5.

131   West, supra note 98, at 678 (emphasis added).

132   See ibid. at 678 n. 70 (citing M. Foucault, *Discipline and Punish: The Birth of the Prison* [1977]; M. Foucault, *The History of Sexuality* [1978]).

133   Ibid. at 678 (emphasis added).

134   And the intellectual source domain for this sort of conceptualization of political or social life is much less Foucault and much more some sort of power elite social theory. See, e.g., C. Mills, *The Power Elite* (1956), 3–4.

135   See supra notes 3–4 and accompanying text; see also M. Foucault, *Power/Knowledge* (1980), 112.

136   West, supra note 98, at 678 (emphasis added).

137   I understand that someone could ask, "Where do you stand to say all this?" and try to get me involved in some sort of performative contradiction (i.e., the ultimate in status degradation in the philosophy department of your choice). I have a few partial observations. The performative contradiction objection is currently taken in the legal academy to be a real killer move. But this move often imagines itself as resting on a secure foundation of knowledge, an a priori understanding of the form that intellectual activity should or must or does take. It also usually imagines (sometimes quite erroneously) that the truth games of the interlocutor (the questioner) and of the speaker (me) are the same—and that we stand relative to truth on the same epistemic footing or lack thereof. Elsewhere, I've suggested that these kinds of assumptions are products of a kind of disciplinary solipsism. See Schlag, "Normative and Nowhere to Go," supra note 4, at 181. I think the performative contradiction move is itself an exercise of power whose main effect is to police the bounds of intellectual inquiry in a way that reproduces the same old homeostatic matrices of rationalist thought. You'll notice that part of what I've done here is pull the reflexive move back on the hypothetical objection: "Where do you stand to ask where do I stand?" I don't want to dismiss the problem or the question of the performative contradiction. At the same time, I must admit that I am not nearly as troubled by it as I am apparently supposed to be.

When people say, "Well where can you go, what can you say if you are engaged in a performative contradiction?" I want to say, "Where don't you go, what don't you say if you are constantly avoiding performative contradictions?" If truth is understood, however tacitly, as representation, then performative contradiction is a problem. If truth, however, is a revealing, then the performative contradiction move loses a great deal of its bite.

138   West, supra note 98, at 678.

139   Schlag, supra note 107.

140   See, e.g., G. Binder, "On Critical Legal Studies as Guerilla Warfare," 76 *Geo. L.J.* 1, 1 (1987) (likening CLS legal thinkers with approval to guerrilla fighters).

141   See J. Rawls, *A Theory of Justice* (1971).

142   See "Symposium on the Public/Private Distinction," 130 *U. Pa. L. Rev.* 1289 (1982).

143   See M. Oakeshott, *Rationalism in Politics and Other Essays* (1962), 169.

144   See A. T. Kronman, "Precedent and Tradition," 99 *Yale L.J.* 1029, 1066 (1990).

145   See J. Baudrillard, *Simulations* (1983), i.

146   See J. Sartre, *Being and Nothingness* (1956), 573, 616–17, 625–26.

147   As Foucault observes: "What I am afraid of about humanism is that it presents a certain form of our ethics as a universal model for any kind of freedom. I think that there are more secrets, more possible freedoms, and more inventions in our future than we can imagine in humanism as it is dogmatically represented on every side of the political rainbow: the Left, the Center, the Right" (R. Martin, "Truth, Power, Self: An Interview with Michel Foucault" [Oct. 25, 1982], in *Technologies of the Self: A Seminar with Michel Foucault,* ed. L. Martin, H. Gutman, and P. Hutton [1988], 9, 15); see also Schlag, supra note 107.

148   See R. Delgado and J. Stefancic, "Why Do We Tell the Same Stories? Law Reform, Critical Librarianship, and the Triple Helix Dilemma," 42 *Stan. L. Rev.* 207, 208–9 (1989).

149   R. Barthes, *Mythologies* (1993), 150–51. Jamie Boyle provides a good example of this inoculation strategy in his description of H. L. A. Hart's attempt to protect legal thought from the
realist indeterminacy arguments. See Boyle, "The Politics of Reason: Critical Legal Theory
and Local Social Thought," 133 *U. Pa. L. Rev.* 685, 711 (1985).

150   Indeed, the main folk-intellectual inspiration informing CLS thought is the opposition of
structuralism and existentialist phenomenology. Jamie Boyle aptly describes how CLS attempts to pursue one of these lines of inquiry inevitably lead to consideration of the other.
See ibid. at 740–44; see also Schlag, supra note 107.

This is no accident: structuralism and existentialist phenomenology lead to each other
precisely because they are complementary parts of the same flawed subject-object map—that
which has channeled virtually all thinking in the American legal academy since its inception.
See Schlag, supra note 107. According to this view, CLS thought is the most advanced
expression of a flawed conception of subject-object relations. What Bourdieu says of Lévi-
Strauss seems easily applicable to orthodox CLS thought: "The main thing is that Lévi-
Strauss, who has always . . . been locked within the alternative of subjectivism and objectivism, cannot see the attempt to transcend this alternative as anything other than a regression
to subjectivism. He is, like so many other people, a prisoner of the alternative of individual
versus social phenomena, of freedom versus necessity, etc., and so he cannot see in the
attempts being made to break away from the structuralist 'paradigm' anything other than so
many returns to an individualist subjectivism and thus to a form of irrationalism" (P. Bourdieu, supra note 1, at 62).

151   H. L. A. Hart, *The Concept of Law* (1979), 86–88.

152   The "vacuum boundary" notion is developed in A. Katz, "Studies in Boundary Theory:
Three Essays in Adjudication and Politics," 28 *Buffalo L. Rev.* 383, 383–85 (1979).

153   Dworkin, supra note 37, at 12.

154   Ibid. at 12–13.

155   Ibid. at 13–14 (emphasis added).

156   With Dworkin situated in the very best place: the inside.

157   Dworkin, supra note 37, at 14.

158   As Steve Winter puts it: "Perhaps the single most identifying characteristic of the objectivist
model of rationality is the 'law of contradiction' that flows from the belief in essences. . . .
Thus, an object either has a property or it does not. Either a proposition or its negation must
be true" (Winter, supra note 14, at 652, 661).

159   Dworkin, supra note 37, at 14.

160   Dworkin recognizes that the legal actor will sometimes want to examine the historical record
to the extent that some historical fact may be germane to the litigation. See ibid.

161   Hart, supra note 151, at 86.

162   Ibid. at 88.

163   K. Greenawalt, "The Rule of Recognition and the Constitution," 85 *Mich. L. Rev.* 621, 663
(1987).

164   See ibid.

165   L. Friedman, "Law, Lawyers, and Popular Culture," 98 *Yale L.J.* 1579, 1581–82 (1989).

166   See "Clinical Legal Education: Reflections on the Past Fifteen Years and Aspirations for the
Future," 36 *Cath. U.L. Rev.* 337 (1987).

167   "Clinical courses originated on the fringe of the law school, not its core" (ibid. at 338; remarks
of Kandis Scott). (This is center/periphery imagery, not inside/outside, but close enough.)

"What was once the fringe, or, as one of the Presidents of the Association of American Law

Schools called it—'the side show'—now has become the main stream" (ibid. at 342; remarks of Dean Hill Rivkin).

"Life was very simple at that point. The big debate was between in-house or outhouse clinics" (ibid. at 347; remarks of Roger Wolf).

168   For elaboration on the structure of this self, see Schlag, "Le Hors de Texte," supra note 4, at 1667–73 (describing the relatively autonomous self).

169   Imagine, then, the confusion of the poor reader who has picked up this essay and engaged in precisely that practice.

170   It resonates, among other things, with Lakoff's source-path-goal schema; see G. Lakoff, supra note 5, at 275. As Steve Winter puts it: "We identify the subject matter of a lawsuit through the elements of the causal schema. The defendant's act is the *source*, the causal chain is the *path*, and the plaintiff's injury is the *goal*. The remedial *source-path-goal* metaphor is virtually a mirror image of the causal one: The individual's injury is the *source* of a process that has as its *goal* an order from the court redressing that injury; the *path* that connects them is the plaintiff's proof that the acts of the defendant caused the injury" (Winter, "Standing," supra note 34, at 1388; footnote omitted). For further discussion of the role of this schema in the context of our conceptualization of causes of action and adjudication generally, see ibid. at 1388–91, 1412, 1457, 1472–78, 1496.

171   Given that there is no case docketed and that the legal thinker is even further removed from the scene of action than the judge.

NONSENSE AND NATURAL LAW

This essay began as a comment on a talk by Roger Pilon presented at a conference titled "Natural Law and the Constitution," held November 1994 at the University of Southern California Law School.

1   "Anarchical Fallacies," in *Works*, ed. J. Bowring (1843), 2:501.

2   For a relevant, helpful discussion from a natural law perspective quite different from Pilon's, see Michael S. Moore, "Moral Reality Revisited," 90 *Mich. L. Rev.* 2424, 2469–91 (1992).

3   35 *Colum. L. Rev.* 809 (1935).

4   Karl N. Llewellyn, "A Realistic Jurisprudence—The Next Step," 30 *Colum. L. Rev.* 431, 449 (1930).

5   Ibid. at 443.

6   Francis Bacon, "The New Organon," in *The Complete Essays of Francis Bacon* (1963), 179, 202.

7   See A. J. Ayer, *Philosophy in the Twentieth Century* (1982), 114. Generally, see pp. 122–29.

8   See Hilary Putnam, *Reason, Truth and History* (1981), 105–6.

9   See *Charmides* (temperance), *Euthyphro* (piety), *Meno* (virtue), *Laches* (courage), *Lysis* (friendship), *Protagoras* (virtue), and *Republic*, bk. 1 (Justice). All citations to Plato's dialogues in this essay refer to the versions contained in *The Collected Dialogues of Plato*, ed. Edith Hamilton and Huntington Cairns (1961).

10   *Protagoras* 320d–328d.

11   See Gregory Vlastos, *Socrates: Ironist and Moral Philosopher* (1991), 57–58.

12   See, e.g., *Republic* 340d–341c (Thrasymachus suggests that Socrates is a "pettifogger" who uses "shyster's tricks").

13   See Terry Penner, "Socrates and the Early Dialogues," in *The Cambridge Companion to Plato*, ed. Richard Kraut (1992), 121, 126. See also *Theaetetus* 202b–d, 206c–207c. Although *The-*

aetetus is regarded as one of Plato's later works, it is like the earlier, more Socratic dialogues in its aporetic quality.

14   Penner, supra note 13, at 141, 168.

15   Ibid. at 168.

16   Compare T. H. Irwin, "Plato: The Intellectual Background," in *Cambridge Companion,* supra note 13, at 51, 69: "Socrates' efforts to define the virtues assume that objectively correct answers can be found, and that they must correspond to some objective realities independent of our beliefs and inquiries." For a similar statement from a later, non-Socratic dialogue, see *Laws* 627d: "The aim of our present inquiry into current language is to examine, not the propriety or impropriety of its phraseology, but the objective truth of falsehood of a theory of legislation."

17   Vlastos, supra note 11, at 58–60.

18   Compare *Republic* 498d (suggesting that conventional ethical and political discourse amounts to "the forced and artificial chiming of word and phrase").

19   *Gorgias* 489e.

20   Supra note 2.

21   Arthur O. Lovejoy, *The Great Chain of Being* (1936), 45–50.

22   Ibid. at 50–54.

23   Ibid. at 54–55.

24   Ibid. at 145–49.

25   Ibid. at 183.

26   Daniel J. Boorstin, *The Lost World of Thomas Jefferson* (1948; 1993), viii, 34–35. See also ibid. at 49: "The Jeffersonian was . . . impressed with the unique necessity of *every* animal and vegetable species to the large plan of nature. . . . He viewed himself as but a link, though the highest, in the great chain of beings, all the parts of which had been closely connected by the hand of the divine Maker."

27   Ibid. at 30. See also ibid. at 29: "In the familiar passage in the Declaration of Independence, the Being who endowed men with their unalienable rights is described as 'their Creator,' and throughout Jeffersonian thought recurs this vision of God as the Supreme Maker. . . . The Jeffersonian God was not the Omnipotent Sovereign of the Puritans nor the Omniscient Essence of the Transcendentalists, but was essentially Architect and Builder."

28   Henry F. May, *The Enlightenment in America* (1976), 295.

29   Boorstin, supra note 26, at 239: "The God invoked by the Jeffersonians was necessarily an intelligible being."

30   Ibid. at 3–11, 237. See also Richard K. Matthews, *The Radical Politics of Thomas Jefferson* (1984), 93–94: "Indeed, Jefferson perceives order, harmony, and purpose in the very nature of the universe. Beyond the teachings of an extraordinary man called Christ, Jefferson has no doubts concerning either the existence or the rational planning of a supreme creator."

31   For a similar argument by Plato, see *Phaedo* 97c–99d.

32   Boorstin, supra note 26, at 106.

33   Ibid. at 54.

34   See May, supra note 28, at 215:

> Despite their large range from [Samuel Stanhope] Smith and [John] Vaughn to Jefferson and [David] Rittenhouse, the active members of the [American] Philosophical Society shared a common view of nature and science. This scientific ideology reflected the common position of the Philadelphia elite of this period, balanced between the left of the

Moderate Enlightenment and the right of the Revolutionary Enlightenment. One and all, the liberal Christians and moderate deists who controlled the APS saw nature as designed by a wise creator for the use and edification of man. This view was more important to the deists, whose God depended solely on the evidence of nature, than it was to the liberal Christians, for whom nature merely corroborated revelation. As for the Bible, those more inclined to deism left it alone in their scientific utterances, while those more specifically Christian, from Rittenhouse to Samuel Smith, insisted that true science and Scripture could never be in disagreement.

35 Boorstin, supra note 26, at 30.

36 Ibid. at 31 (quoting Jefferson).

37 Thomas Jefferson, "Notes on Virginia," in *The Life and Selected Writings of Thomas Jefferson,* ed. Adrienne Koch and William Peden (1944), 187, 208.

38 Ibid. at 208–9: "To add to this, the traditionary testimony of the Indians, that this animal still exists in the northern and western parts of America, would be adding the light of a taper to that of the meridian sun."

39 Lovejoy, supra note 21, at 153–54, 242–43. Describing Spinoza's reasoning, Lovejoy explains: "We must, Spinoza says, conceive 'that God's omnipotence has been displayed from all eternity and will for all eternity remain in the same state of activity.' It would be an absurdity to imagine that at some former time he created a world different from that which he now creates; for this would imply that his intellect and will were then different from what they now are. . . . The existence of all possible beings at all times is therefore an implicate of the divine nature" (ibid. at 154; citation omitted).

40 Boorstin, supra note 26, at 155.

41 Ibid. at 140–41.

42 Ibid. at 171–72.

43 Ibid. at 190–91.

44 May, supra note 28, at 302.

45 Boorstin, supra note 26, at 196. See also ibid. at 194: "The word 'right' was always a signpost pointing back to the divine plan of the Creation."

46 Ibid. at 196.

47 James Boyd White, "Response to Roger Cramton's Article," 37 *J. Legal Educ.* 533, 533 (1987).

48 For a discussion of some of these complexities, see Steven D. Smith, "The Rise and Fall of Religious Freedom in Constitutional Discourse," 140 *U. Pa. L. Rev.* 149, 169–78 (1991).

49 Compare John Finnis, *Natural Law and Natural Rights* (1980), 205: "The modern vocabulary and grammar of rights is a many-faceted instrument for reporting and asserting the requirements of other implications of a relationship of justice *from the point of view of the person(s) who benefit(s) from* that relationship."

50 This example prompts the cogent rejoinder that in fact the First Amendment speaks of rights in the very way I am criticizing here—that is, as a conclusion. The amendment does not say, "Citizens have the right to freedom of speech," but rather, "Congress shall make no law . . . abridging the freedom of speech." I think this rejoinder is correct, and it tells us something significant about the Constitution: As designed, the Constitution did not primarily adopt a "rights" strategy but rather a jurisdictional, or "limited powers," strategy. Primary reliance on the rights strategy came earlier (in, e.g., the Declaration of Independence) and later (with, e.g., the "incorporation" of the Bill of Rights). For a relevant and helpful discussion, see Roger Pilon, "On the Folly and Illegitimacy of Industrial Policy," 5 *Stan. L. & Pol'y Rev.* 103,

108–11 (1993). See ibid. at 109: "Indeed, throughout the nineteenth century the debate was largely over powers—over whether Congress had a particular power—not over whether any rights might stand in the way of such powers, as in the modern debate (when there is a debate at all)." See also Roger Pilon, "Freedom, Responsibility, and the Constitution," 68 *Notre Dame L. Rev.* 507, 521–40 (1993).

51 Southern Pac. Co. v. Jensen, 244 U.S. 205, 222 (1917) (Holmes, J., dissenting).

52 John Austin, *The Province of Jurisprudence Determined and the Uses of the Study of Jurisprudence,* 4th ed. (1954), 134.

53 *Summa Theologica* I–II, Q. 90, Art. 4 (emphasis added), reprinted in *The Political Ideas of St. Thomas Aquinas,* ed. Dino Bigongiari (1953), 9.

54 Oliver Wendell Holmes, Jr., "The Path of the Law," 10 *Harv. L. Rev.* 457, 475 (1897): "The trouble with Austin was that he did not know enough English law." Regarding the sovereign lawgiver, see, e.g., Kawanakoa v. Polyblank, 205 U.S. 349, 353 (1907). "In societies like ours the command of the public force is intrusted to judges in certain cases, and the whole power of the state will be put forth, if necessary, to carry out their judgments and decrees" (Holmes, supra note 54, at 457).

55 See, generally, Lon L. Fuller, *The Morality of Law,* rev. ed. (1969).

56 Ibid. at 33–41.

57 Whether moral discourse itself becomes nonsensical outside a providential worldview is a question that need not be addressed here. For a well-known discussion within legal literature suggesting that moral discourse collapses without assumptions about God, see Arthur A. Leff, "Unspeakable Ethics, Unnatural Law," 1979 *Duke L.J.* 1229.

58 See, e.g., Pilon, "Industrial Policy," supra note 52, at 107: "The American vision . . . is guided by the idea that individuals have rights 'by nature.' . . . And that realm of moral rights is rooted in reason, not legislative will; the function of the legislature . . . is simply to recognize and declare the moral realm, not to create it."

59 Roger Pilon, "Individual Rights, Democracy, and Constitutional Order: On the Foundations of Legitimacy," 11 *Cato J.* 373, 381–82 (1992).

60 It is noteworthy that although rights and law exist in Locke's depiction of the state of nature, they are explained, as in the Jeffersonian worldview, by reference to God and the divine design: "The state of Nature has a law of Nature to govern it, which obliges everyone, and reason, which is that law, teaches all mankind who will but consult it, that being all equal and independent, no one ought to harm another in his life, health, liberty or possession; *for men being all the workmanship of one omnipotent and infinitely wise Maker; all the servants of one sovereign Master, sent into the world by His order and about His business; they are His property, whose workmanship they are made to last during His, not one another's pleasure*" (John Locke, "Second Treatise on Civil Government," para. 6, in *John Locke on Politics and Education,* Classics Club ed. (1947), sources 75, 78 (emphasis added).

61 The most extensive discussion in the sources I looked at is in Roger Pilon, "Ordering Rights Consistently: Or What We Do and Do Not Have Rights To," 13 *Ga. L. Rev.* 1171, 1176–82 (1979).

62 See Roger Pilon, "Moral and Legal Justification," 11 *Sw. U.L. Rev.* 1327, 1339–40 (1979) (emphasis added).

63 For a critical discussion of Kant's similar attempt to derive moral rules from formal rationality and the principle of self-contradiction, see Alasdair MacIntyre, *After Virtue,* 2d ed. (1984), 43–47.

AGAINST CONSTITUTIONAL THEORY

1   Jorge Luis Borges, "The Library of Babel," in *Labyrinths* (1964), 51, 57.

2   Jorge Luis Borges, "Pierre Menard, Author of the Quixote," in *Labyrinths,* supra note 1, at 36, 39.

3   Ibid. at 40.

4   Ibid. at 41.

5   Ibid. at 43.

6   Ibid. at 44.

7   The definition of *textual interpretation* put forward in this essay is essentially that advocated by Steven Knapp and Walter Benn Michaels in "Against Theory," 8 *Critical Inquiry* 723 (1982); see also S. Knapp and W. B. Michaels, "A Reply to Our Critics," 9 *Critical Inquiry* 790 (1983); S. Knapp and W. B. Michaels, "A Reply to Richard Rorty: What Is Pragmatism?" 11 *Critical Inquiry* 466 (1985); S. Knapp and W. B. Michaels, "Against Theory 2: Hermeneutics and Deconstruction," 14 *Critical Inquiry* 49 (1987). The first three essays are reprinted in *Against Theory: Literary Studies and the New Pragmatism,* ed. W. J. T. Mitchell (1985). Other relevant texts include Walter Benn Michaels, "Against Formalism: The Autonomous Text in Legal and Literary Interpretation," 1 *Poetics Today* 23 (1979); S. Knapp and W. B. Michaels, "Intention, Identity, and the Constitution: A Response to David Hoy," in *Legal Hermeneutics: History, Theory, and Practice,* ed. Gregory Leyh (1991); and S. Knapp, "Practice, Purpose, and Interpretive Controversy," in *Pragmatism in Law and Society,* ed. Michael Brint and William Weaver (1991).

8   This example is a variation on the "wave poem" illustration used by Knapp and Michaels in "Against Theory," supra note 7.

9   Michael Moore presents an elaborate defense of such an account of linguistic meaning in "A Natural Law Theory of Interpretation," 58 *S. Calif. L. Rev.* 277 (1985). Moore's account of linguistic meaning depends on the distinction, common in speech act theory, between the meaning of an utterance and the meaning of the sentence within which that utterance is encoded. He defines *sentence meaning* as "the meaning [a] type of utterance has, abstracted from any particular occasion of utterance." He asks us to imagine receiving a one-sentence anonymous letter "with no clue whatsoever about the motive, circumstances of transmission, or any other factor relevant to understanding the sentence *on the basis of its context of utterance*" (quoting Jerrold Katz, *Propositional Structure and Illocutionary Force* [1980] 14; emphasis added). The *sentence meaning* of the letter is defined as what we know about the letter's meaning "in such a contextless situation." The *utterance meaning* is the meaning that context *adds* to the sentence meaning. The problem with this account is that it assumes there can be such a thing as contextless meaning. Moore's own example decisively refutes this assumption. It involves an epistemological absurdity to assert that one could receive a one-sentence letter that contained no information "relevant to understanding the sentence on the basis of its context of utterance." For how would the recipient of this letter know (1) that it was a letter; (2) that it contained words, as opposed to marks that resembled words; and (3) that the words were those of a particular language—in sum, that these marks were an instance of an intention to undertake semantic communication—unless the reader brought a considerable number of assumptions about the context of utterance—about the author's intentions—to the act of reading? And all this information—in fact *all* the reader's conclusions about the text's meaning—depend on the assumptions he must necessarily make about "the

context of utterance." As Stanley Fish has demonstrated, the idea of a contextless sentence always involves a contradiction in terms; see Fish, *Is There a Text in This Class?* (1980), 269–92.

10 Henry Monaghan, "Our Perfect Constitution," 56 *N.Y.U. L. Rev.* 353, 375 (1981).

11 See Raoul Berger, *Government by Judiciary* (1977), 153–55; Michael Perry, "The Authority of Text, Tradition, and Reason: A Theory of Constitutional 'Interpretation,' " 58 *S. Calif. L. Rev.* 551 (1985); Mark Tushnet, *Red, White, and Blue: A Critical Analysis of Constitutional Law* (1988).

12 Borges, "Babel," supra note 1, at 53.

13 Ibid. at 55–56.

14 See Monaghan, "Our Perfect Constitution," supra note 10, at 374–77.

15 Ibid. at 383–84.

16 Ibid. at 376.

17 Ibid. at 382.

18 See Henry Monaghan, "Stare Decisis and Constitutional Adjudication," 88 *Colum. L. Rev.* 723, 767–72 (1988); Monaghan, "Our Perfect Constitution," supra note 10, at 382.

19 Michael Perry, "The Legitimacy of Particular Conceptions of Constitutional Interpretation," 77 *Va. L. Rev.* 669, 681 (1991).

20 Ibid. at 695–96.

21 Ibid. at 696.

22 Ibid. at 701.

23 Ibid.

24 Ibid. at 682. Compare Hemingway on the modern bullfight: "It is a decadent art in every way and like most decadent things it reaches its fullest flower at its rottenest point, which is the present" (Ernest Hemingway, *Death in the Afternoon* [1932], 68).

25 A moral realist such as Michael Moore would argue that the meaning of the statute had not changed. Moore would claim that the word *cruel* refers to certain practices that are objectively cruel, whether we believe them to be cruel or not. If capital punishment is "really" cruel, then my statute *always* banned capital punishment, whether I thought it did or not. By using the word *cruel*, I refer to *the actual meaning* of *cruelty*, not to my (possibly mistaken) conception of what is cruel. See, generally, Moore, supra note 9. Perry, on the other hand, seems to opt for the "deep conventionalism" advocated by Dworkin. According to this view, what gives the word *cruel* meaning is the *interpreter's best estimate* of what "it" means. Note how the ontological status of words becomes extremely fuzzy in the Dworkin/Perry world of concepts/conceptions and general/specific meanings. To a pragmatic conventionalist a word means what its author meant by it. To a realist, a word refers to some absolute reality of the signified, to what is "really" cruel. It is very unclear what, if anything, the words of an author (as opposed to the words of the author's reader) refer to in Perry's and Dworkin's accounts of linguistic meaning.

26 Perry, "Legitimacy," supra note 20, at 697.

27 Ibid. at 708.

28 Ibid. at 708–9.

29 Ibid. at 709.

30 To use Perry's own example: what kind of disfavored government conduct that disproportionately affects a discrete group could *not* be characterized as a product of "irrational prejudice"?

31   That is, if we consider the *text* of the Constitution to be the object of interpretation.

32   Ronald Dworkin, *Law's Empire* (1986), 348.

33   Ibid. at 348–49.

34   Ibid.

35   Ibid. at 350.

36   See Hans-Georg Gadamer, *Truth and Method,* ed. and trans. Garrett Barden and John Cumming (1975), 357.

37   Those limiting factors generate Dworkin's interpretive principle of "fit." See Dworkin, *Law's Empire,* supra note 32, at 230–32.

38   U.S. Constitution, amend. XIV, § 1.

39   See Berger, supra note 11, at 118–19.

40   See U.S. Constitution, amend. XIX.

41   See Bowers v. Hardwick, 478 U.S. 186, 195 (1986).

42   U.S. Constitution, amend. XIV, § 1.

43   See John Rawls, *A Theory of Justice* (1971), 511.

44   See Dworkin, *Law's Empire,* supra note 32, at 360–62.

45   See Ronald Dworkin, "Bork the Radical," *New York Review of Books,* Aug. 13, 1987, at 6.

46   Ibid. at 6–8.

47   Dworkin's theory requires a judge to employ the "best available political theory" in order to generate the necessary "interpretive fit." See Dworkin, *Law's Empire,* supra note 32, at 230, 350, 380.

48   See supra note 35 and accompanying text.

49   Borges, "Pierre Menard," supra note 2, at 43.

50   Ronald Dworkin, "My Reply to Stanley Fish (and Walter Benn Michaels): Please Don't Talk about Objectivity Any More," in *The Politics of Interpretation,* ed. W. J. T. Mitchell (1983), 310. Note that if reading *Hamlet*'s text "in a psychodynamic way" means "reading" it as if it contained a comment on Freud's particular understanding of what he called the Oedipal complex, then Dworkin is advocating reauthoring the text. If Dworkin means reading the text for clues about the author's own psychological state, then he is primarily interested not in the text's semantic meaning but rather in what indirect evidence the text's meaning provides about Shakespeare's personal psychology. A third possibility is that he means to say we can read *Hamlet* as containing insights about human psychology that were not yet captured in theoretical form. Although this last alternative is indeed a possible approach to authorial meaning, we should note that no analogous method appears to exist by which we could understand the equal protection clause "in a psychodynamic way," at least for the purposes of legal decision making.

51   See Dworkin, *Law's Empire,* supra note 32, at 358.

52   See, for example, Cass Sunstein's recent claims about statutory interpretation: "The words were enacted; the original understanding was not. . . . Words have passed through the constitutionally specified mechanisms for enactment of laws; intentions have not, and they are therefore not binding" (Cass Sunstein, *After the Rights Revolution* [1990], 129). For Sunstein, it is the *autonomous words themselves* that bind the legal decision maker.

53   After they initially offered their description of textual interpretation, Knapp and Michaels found themselves accused of, among other things, promoting "an ideology under which a privileged status quo would be secured against fundamental questioning," of creating a rhetorical effect that was "essentially nihilistic," and of clearing the way for "the long-established and well-heeled, native American, fly-by-the-seat-of-one's-pants, critical prag-

matists and know-nothings, who have been waiting in the wings ever since the late sixties for such boring annoyances as critical theory, feminism, affirmative action programs, and so forth to disappear" (see Knapp and Michaels, "A Reply to Our Critics," supra note 7, at 790, 799).

54 I use the term *meaning* here in the limited sense of "semantic meaning." In other words, the Grand Canyon is not a signifier.

55 See Dworkin, *Law's Empire,* supra note 32, at 154–60.

56 Several scholars have noted analogies between the rhetoric of constitutional interpretation and the exegesis of religious texts. See, generally, Robert Burt, "Constitutional Law and the Teaching of Parables," 93 *Yale L.J.* 455 (1983); Thomas Grey, "The Constitution as Scripture," 37 *Stan. L. Rev.* 1 (1985); Sanford Levinson, " 'The Constitution' in American Civil Religion," 1979 *Sup. Ct. Rev.* 123.

57 Any *human* text, that is. The Cabalists developed coherent procedures for dealing with Holy Scripture as an absolute (infinite, infallible, noncontingent) text. They reasoned that chance played no role whatsoever in the production of such a text: everything in it was meaningful, including the number of letters in each word and the letter each word begins with. "Let us suppose that Cervantes was the Holy Spirit (fortunately, he was not, and his work belongs to admirable human texts, imperfect but brilliant creations); then the fact that his book begins *En,* a monosyllabic word ending in *n,* and that it goes on to another, *un,* also ending in *n,* and then to *lugar* (place), a five-letter word, and then to *de la* (of the) would not have been accidental, because nothing can be accidental in an absolute text" (p. 68) (*Twenty-Four Conversations with Borges,* ed. Roberto Alifano [1984]). Compare Griswold v. Connecticut, 381 U.S. 479, 484 (1965): "Specific guarantees in the Bill of Rights have penumbras, formed by emanations from those guarantees."

58 Hans Walter Wolff, "The Hermeneutics of the Old Testament," in *Essays on Old Testament Hermeneutics,* ed. Claus Westermann (1979), 160.

59 John J. Davies, "Unity of the Bible," in *Hermeneutics, Inerrancy, and the Bible,* ed. Earl Radmacher and Robert Preus (1984), 640.

60 Edgar McKnight, *Post-Modern Use of the Bible* (1988), 102–4.

61 James Smart, *The Strange Silence of the Bible in the Church* (1970), 68–69.

62 Walter L. Bradley and Roger Olsen, "The Trustworthiness of Scripture in Areas Relating to Natural Science," in *Hermeneutics, Inerrancy, and the Bible,* supra note 59, at 283–84.

63 Henry Morris, "A Response to 'The Trustworthiness of Scripture in Areas Relating to Natural Science,' " in *Hermeneutics, Inerrancy, and the Bible,* supra note 59, at 335.

64 See Fernando Belo, *A Materialist Reading of the Gospel of Mark* (1981).

65 See Martin Buber, *Königtum Gottes,* 3d ed. (1956), 39.

66 See Virginia Mollenkott, *The Divine Feminine: The Biblical Image of God as Female* (1983).

67 See Phyliss Trible, *Texts of Terror* (1984).

68 See St. Thomas Aquinas, *Summa Theologica,* pt. 1, Q. 1, art. 10.

69 See Bernard Grebanier, *The Truth about Shylock* (1962).

70 See J. L. Cardozo, *The Contemporary Jew in the Elizabethan Drama* (1925).

71 See Frank Kermode, *Early Shakespeare* (1961), 224–25.

72 See Harold Goddard, *The Meaning of Shakespeare* (1960), 111.

73 See Marianne Novy, "Patriarchy and Play in *The Taming of the Shrew,*" in *William Shakespeare's The Taming of the Shrew,* ed. Harold Bloom (1988), 13.

74 See Coppella Kahn's essay in *William Shakespeare's The Taming of the Shrew,* supra note 73, at 41.

75 O. J. Campbell, "The Salvation of Lear," 15 *ELH* 107 (1948).

76 James Stampfer, "The Catharsis of *King Lear*," 13 *Shakespeare Surv.* 4 (1960).

77 Ibid. at 10.

78 A striking illustration of how sacred writings can work purely as cultural artifacts is provided by the Jews of Ethiopia. This religious community was until very recently cut off from the rest of the Jewish world. Nevertheless, they had the Torah (the most sacred book in Judaism) and they honored the Hebrew scriptures in their rituals. They were, however, unable to read a single word of the holy texts. See Claire Safran, *Secret Exodus* (1987), 25–28.

An even more germane example of a cultural artifact's ability to mimic a text is provided by the phenomenon of glossolalia, or speaking in tongues. Among certain charismatic Christian sects, God manifests Himself by infusing the soul of the believer with the ability to speak in unknown languages. The sacred words uttered under this inspiration are not recognizable as human speech; nevertheless, they can be "interpreted" by the religious community and transformed into meaningful evocations of belief. See, generally, *Speaking in Tongues: A Guide to Research on Glossolalia,* ed. Watson E. Mills (1986).

79 According to Freud, Shylock's character traits are best understood as "the first and most constant results of anal eroticism" (*The Complete Psychological Works of Sigmund Freud,* Standard Edition [1974], 9:171); see Samuel Taylor Coleridge, *Seven Lectures on Shakespeare and Milton* (1968); *Coleridge on Shakespeare: The Text of the Lectures of 1811–12,* ed. R. A. Foakes (1971); Samuel Johnson, *Johnson on Shakespeare,* ed. Bertrand H. Bronson (1986); Graham F. Parker, *Johnson's Shakespeare* (1989).

80 See Jacob Mann, *The Bible as Read and Preached in the Old Synagogue* (1996); Martin Luther, *A Commentary on St. Paul's Epistles to the Galatians,* trans. N. J. Westwood (1953); St. Thomas Aquinas, *On Law, Morality and Politics,* ed. R. J. Regun (1988).

81 See Gary Peller, "The Metaphysics of American Law," 73 *Calif. L. Rev.* 1151 (1985); Mark Tushnet, "A Note on the Revival of Textualism in Constitutional Theory," 58 *S. Calif. L. Rev.* 683–87 (1985); Andrzej Rapaczynski, "The Ninth Amendment and the Unwritten Constitution: The Problems of Constitutional Interpretation," 64 *Chi.-Kent L. Rev.* 177, 194–95 (1988).

82 Robert Cover, "Violence and the Word," 95 *Yale L.J.* 1601 (1986).

83 See St. Augustine, *On Christian Doctrine,* vol. 1, § 41: "But anyone who understands in the Scriptures something other than that intended by them is deceived, although they do not lie. However . . . if he is deceived in an interpretation which builds up charity, which is the end of the commandments, he is deceived in the same way as a man who leaves a road by mistake but passes through a field to the same place toward which the road itself leads."

84 George Orwell points out that these lines from Kipling were misattributed to Thackeray by John Middleton Murry in Murry's book *Adam and Eve.* Murry was (at that time) a Marxist who undoubtedly detested Kipling as the ultimate artistic symbol of British imperialism; he thus solved this particular interpretive conundrum with a neat bit of reauthoring. See George Orwell, *The Collected Essays, Journalism, and Letters of George Orwell,* ed. S. Orwell and I. Angus (1968), 193.

85 G. K. Chesterton, *G. F. Watts* (1904), 44.

IDOLATRY IN CONSTITUTIONAL INTERPRETATION

1 Notebooks for "A Raw Youth," ed. Edward Wasiolek, trans. Victor Terras (1969), 178–79; quoted in Ellis Sandoz, *Political Apocalypse: A Study of Dostoevsky's Grand Inquisitor* (1971), 177 n. 3.

2   "Twilight of the Idols," in *The Portable Nietzsche,* ed. and trans. Walter Kaufmann (1954), 463, 465.

3   Herbert Wechsler, "Toward Neutral Principles of Constitutional Law," 73 *Harv. L. Rev.* 1, 31–34 (1959).

4   Alexander M. Bickel, "The Original Understanding and the Segregation Decision," 69 *Harv. L. Rev.* 1 (1955).

5   See Bruce Ackerman, *We the People* (1991), 1:142–50; Robert H. Bork, *The Tempting of America* (1990), 74–84; Ronald Dworkin, *Law's Empire* (1986), 381–92; Laurence H. Tribe, *American Constitutional Law,* 2d ed. (1988), § 16-15, at 1475–78.

6   See, e.g., Thomas C. Grey, "The Constitution as Scripture," 37 *Stan. L. Rev.* 1, 1 (1984); Michael J. Perry, "The Authority of Text, Tradition, and Reason: A Theory of Constitutional 'Interpretation,' " 58 *S. Calif. L. Rev.* 551, 556 (1985) (advocating a "nonoriginalist conception of constitutional text and interpretation"); ibid. at 572 n. 68 (noting that his approach to constitutional adjudication could be interpretation because " 'interpretation' has no single, canonical meaning").

7   Sanford Levinson, *Constitutional Faith* (1988), 9–53; Grey, supra note 6, at 5–13.

8   Michael J. Perry, *The Constitution, the Courts, and Human Rights* (1982), 97–100; M. J. Perry, *Morality, Politics, and Law* (1988), 136–45.

9   Joseph Vining, *The Authoritative and the Authoritarian* (1986), 187–201.

10   Perry, *The Constitution,* supra note 8, at 97 (emphasis omitted). Perry's later work contains similar disclaimers: "I'm analogizing nonoriginalist constitutional interpretation to *the sort of interpretation of sacred texts that presupposes no more than that the texts are human artifacts and repositories of human wisdom*" (Perry, *Morality, Politics, and Law,* supra note 8, at 143); see also ibid. at 145: "If . . . the analogy between constitutional interpretation and the interpretation of sacred texts seems misleading, then ignore it. No argument in this chapter requires the analogy."

11   Vining, supra note 9, at 6, 64.

12   See ibid. at 160.

13   Joseph Vining, "Legal Affinities," 23 *Ga. L. Rev.* 1035, 1035–37 (1989).

14   Levinson, supra note 7, at 16 ("the metaphor of civil religion"); ibid. at 17 ("the analogy of the Constitution to a sacred text"); Grey, supra note 6, at 3 (Scripture is "an illuminating analogue to law"); ibid. at 17 ("analogy between Constitution and Scripture").

15   As Grey has explained, "We can learn practical lessons from both the similarities and the differences between scripture and constitution. Priests, prophets and believers are structurally parallel to but—given a secular conception of law and politics—importantly different from judges, politicians and citizens" (Thomas C. Grey, "The Uses of an Unwritten Constitution," 64 *Chi.-Kent L. Rev.* 211, 222 [1988]; see also Ackerman, supra note 5, at 159–60 (noting the "obvious analogy" between constitutional and scriptural interpretation but insisting that because ours is "a secular Republic" these disciplines are separated by a "hermeneutic wall").

16   Grey, supra note 6, at 20; see ibid. at 21–25 (concluding that this secular view is preferable to the alternatives). In a similar vein, after noting that "it seems worth asking whether the Constitution is indeed 'mysterious' in some genuine sense," Tribe and Dorf conclude that it is not. See Laurence H. Tribe and Michael C. Dorf, *On Reading the Constitution* (1991), 1. Indeed, one of their "main purposes . . . is to demystify the process of reading the Constitution" (ibid. at 4). They insist that the Constitution "is not mystical—and not even lost in the mists of the ideal" (ibid. at 18).

17   Vining, supra note 9, at 150.

18   Ibid. at 153.

19   The question is not ultimately whether we can explain our practice in terms of Martian criteria of rationality—criteria with which, I must confess, I am unfamiliar. Rather, the Martian visitor is simply a device for raising a question that we can, but typically do not, ask ourselves: Does our practice of legal interpretation "make sense," and if so, why? To be sure, the answer to that question, if there is one, will necessarily speak to values or criteria of rationality understandable by us.

20   Steven Knapp and Walter B. Michaels, "Against Theory," 8 *Critical Inquiry* 723, 724 (1982). For a more recent defense of their position with specific reference to constitutional interpretation, see Steven Knapp and Walter B. Michaels, "Intention, Identity, and the Constitution: A Response to David Hoy," in *Legal Hermeneutics: History, Theory, and Practice,* ed. Gregory Leyh (1992), 187.

21   Knapp and Michaels, "Against Theory," supra note 20, at 727–28 (describing an apparent Wordsworth poem hypothetically found on a beach).

22   Paul Campos, "Against Constitutional Theory," 4 *Yale J.L. & Human.* 279, 282–85 (1992).

23   Vining, supra note 9, at 14; see also ibid. at 158: "Running through legal discourse as a constant . . . is an insistence upon seeing, hearing, and feeling a person behind what is said."

24   Philip Soper, *A Theory of Law* (1984), 1, 7.

25   Henry David Thoreau, "On the Duty of Civil Disobedience," in *Legal and Political Obligation,* ed. R. George Wright (1992), 25, 26.

26   Vining, supra note 9, at 167–68.

27   Soper, supra note 24, at 80, 83–84.

28   See Brian Tierney, *Religion, Law, and the Growth of Constitutional Thought 1150–1650* (1982), 41 (noting "the universally held belief [in the Middle Ages] that all power came ultimately from God").

29   This description of statutory construction may, of course, be too complacent or naive. The task of discovering "legislative intent" presents familiar factual and conceptual difficulties. Criticizing various conceptions of legislative intent, Heidi Hurd argues that a legislature cannot be a "speaker"; her argument might be taken to suggest that it is futile to regard legislators as the natural authors of a statutory text that makes statutory interpretation a sensible activity (although this is not her point). See Heidi M. Hurd, "Sovereignty in Silence," 99 *Yale L.J.* 945, 968–76 (1990). Even if "legislative intent" can be adequately explained, moreover, common practices of statutory interpretation such as the use of "canons of construction" that arguably presume legislative omniscience (see Richard A. Posner, "Statutory Interpretation—in the Classroom and in the Courtroom," 50 *U. Chi. L. Rev.* 800, 811 [1983]), cast doubt on the proposition that courts are even trying to discover the actual intentions of human legislators. These doubts, however, do not undermine the present argument about *constitutional* interpretation. On the contrary, to the extent that the doubts are well founded, they suggest that the argument may be applicable to statutory construction as well.

30   Michael Klarman, "An Interpretive History of Modern Equal Protection," 90 *Mich. L. Rev.* 213, 253 (1991).

31   Ibid. at 253–54 (footnotes omitted).

32   Henry P. Monaghan, "Our Perfect Constitution," 56 *N.Y.U. L. Rev.* 353, 377–78 (1981).

33   Michael Perry adopts approximately this position, in which originalism and nonoriginalism collapse into each other. See Michael J. Perry, "The Legitimacy of Particular Conceptions of Constitutional Interpretation," 77 *Va. L. Rev.* 669, 710–19 (1991).

34   Hurd, supra note 29, at 976.

35   Dworkin, supra note 5, at 58–59; see also Hurd, supra note 29, at 993: "For Dworkin, interpretation must proceed with at least one eye to authorial intention."

36   Vining, supra note 9, at 123.

37   Sometimes, of course, a judicial opinion will explicitly refer to historical persons but attribute to them a meaning that they perhaps did not intend. Justice Brandeis's famous and eloquent concurring opinion in Whitney v. California, 274 U.S. 357, 372, 375 (1927) ("Those who won our independence believed . . ."), is an example of this technique. Once again, this technique can be viewed as a method of reading a text in accordance with the intention of an author constructed by the court.

38   Dworkin, supra note 5, at 227.

39   Ibid. at 225.

40   Roscoe Pound, "Spurious Interpretation," 7 Colum. L. Rev. 379, 382–83 (1907).

41   Tribe and Dorf, supra note 16, at 14.

42   Dworkin, supra note 5, at 255.

43   Ibid.

44   Tribe and Dorf, supra note 16, at 17: "The moment you adopt a perspective as open as Dworkin's, the line between what you think the Constitution says and what you wish it would say becomes so tenuous that it is extraordinarily difficult, try as you might, to maintain that line at all. How can one maintain the line—given the ambiguity of the Constitution's text, the plasticity of its terms, the indeterminacy of its history, and the possibility of making noises in the Constitution's language that sound like an argument for just about anything?" Some reviewers note that this criticism may in turn be deeply ironic, given its source. See, e.g., Frederick M. Gedicks, "Arrogance Cloaked as Neutrality," 65 St. John's L. Rev. 1235, 1236 (1991), reviewing Laurence H. Tribe and Michael C. Dorf, On Reading the Constitution (1991).

45   Dworkin, supra note 5, at 227.

46   Ibid. at 168.

47   Larry Alexander makes a related point:

Dworkin's theory was and remains quite bizarre. One can approach legal theory from a number of angles and ask, for example: what are the authoritative decisions that institutions have taken regarding what we ought to do? (the positivists' question); what should we predict officials will do in particular situations? (the legal realists' question); or, what ought judges or citizens to do in light of the authoritative decisions our institutions have taken? (the sophisticated natural lawyers' question). Dworkin's basic question is none of these. Rather, Dworkin asks: what are the most attractive political/moral principles that, if followed, can account for most of the coercive political decisions our society has taken? That is a very odd question, for unlike the other questions of legal theory, its relevance to any concern that anyone might have about "law" is quite opaque. Although Dworkin tries gamely in Law's Empire to make a case for his question's centrality, he never succeeds in dispelling the sense of the question's oddity.

(Larry Alexander, "Striking Back at the Empire: A Brief Survey of Problems in Dworkin's Theory of Law," 6 L. & Phil. 419, 419–20 [1987]).

I would put the point a little differently. I think Dworkin is asking a central and important question about the moral authority of law. He is asking a variant of what Alexander calls the sophisticated natural lawyer's question. What is curious is not the question but the answer. What would lead Dworkin, or anyone, to suppose that citizens who would question the moral authority of law in the first place would be satisfied by *imagining* that the law is the expression of a single author who always acts in conformity with a coherent set of principles, even though they know perfectly well that this is mere fantasy?

48   Vining, supra note 9, at 145.

49   Vining, supra note 13, at 1049.

50   Ibid.

51   Vining, supra note 9, at 200, 149, 198.

52   Oliver W. Holmes, "Natural Law," 32 *Harv. L. Rev.* 40, 40 (1918).

53   Mircea Eliade, *The Sacred and the Profane,* trans. Willard R. Trask (1957; 1959), 204. Although the disavowal of religious belief has probably become more common since the Enlightenment, Charles Taylor maintains that a complete lack of religious belief is still rare, and that "even unbelief is not all that it seems" (Charles Taylor, "Religion in a Free Society," in *Articles of Faith, Articles of Peace: The Religious Liberty Clauses and the American Public Philosophy,* ed. James D. Hunter and Os Guinness [1990], 93, 105). Taylor adds that

    faced with questions about death, about the ultimate meaning of life, about the deepest sources of moral goodness, many people who otherwise think of themselves as secular or agnostic turn to the religion from which they or their family emerged. Or groping for a language to mark or celebrate the crucial moments in life, such as birth, marriage, and death, they can only find it in the old faiths. For the hard-bitten atheists, these are lapses, regrettable moments of weakness, where the need for austere courage in the face of the dark and meaningless universe is forgotten. That is undoubtedly one way of reading these phenomena, but it is very far removed from the way the people concerned often understand them. (Ibid. at 106)

54   Sigmund Freud, *The Future of an Illusion,* trans. W. D. Robson-Scott (1949), 27–34.

55   Ibid. at 33.

56   Ibid. at 54, 52.

57   Ibid. at 85–87; see also ibid. at 92 (suggesting that "religion is comparable to a childhood neurosis" and that "mankind will overcome this neurotic phase").

58   Alasdair MacIntyre, *After Virtue,* 2d ed. (1984), 50; and ibid. at 36–78.

59   Arthur A. Leff, "Unspeakable Ethics, Unnatural Law," 1979 *Duke L.J.* 1229, 1233.

60   Ibid. at 1239.

61   Ibid. at 1249.

62   Ibid. at 1231.

63   The idea that the soul's true good lies in a reunion with God is not in itself distinctively Christian. A distinctive Christian element arises with the belief that Jesus is the redeemer who makes this reunion possible.

64   Augustine's ethics typify this view. Frederick Copleston explains Augustine's ethical position: "St. Augustine's ethic has this in common with what one might call the typical Greek ethic, that it is eudaemonistic in character, that it proposes an end for human conduct, namely happiness; but this happiness is to be found only in God. . . . [W]hen he said that happiness is to be found in the attainment and possession of the eternal and immutable Object, God, he was thinking, not of a purely philosophic and theoretic contemplation of God, but of a loving union with and possession of God" (Frederick Copleston, *A History of Philosophy* [1962], vol. 2, pt. 1, at 96–97).

65   Thomas à Kempis, *The Imitation of Christ,* trans. Leo Sherley-Price (1952), 104–5 (footnote omitted).

66   See, e.g., C. S. Lewis, "The Weight of Glory," in *The Weight of Glory and Other Addresses* (1949), 4–6.

67   See also Emil Brunner, *Christianity and Civilisation* (1948), 1:133: "The soul of man, created for God, can never be satisfied with finite things. That is why, cut off from God and lost in the world, it is insatiable and ever disappointed."

68   See, e.g., Freud, supra note 54, at 95: "From this bondage [of religion and illusion] I am, we are, free."

69   See, e.g., Andrew M. Greeley, *Religious Change in America* (1989), 11–12; Richard J. Neuhaus, Foreword to *Unsecular America*, ed. Richard J. Neuhaus (1986), vii.

70   An idol, it is important to note, need not be endowed with all the qualities ascribed to God in the Christian tradition, such as omnipotence, omniscience, and complete benevolence. Deities in some religious traditions have not enjoyed these qualities, as Greek mythology amply demonstrates.

71   A different, more spiritual dependence is discussed below.

72   Exodus 32:1 (Revised Standard).

73   Ibid. at 32:4 (emphasis added).

74   Ibid. at 32:24 (emphasis added).

75   Ibid. at 32:6.

76   Ibid. at 32:17–19.

77   Plato, *Socrates' Defense (Apology)*, 22b, trans. Hugh Tredennick, in *The Collected Dialogues of Plato*, ed. Edith Hamilton and Huntington Cairns (1961), 3, 8.

78   Ibid. at at 22c.

79   Hans-Wilhelm Kelling, *The Idolatry of Poetic Genius in German Goethe Criticism* (1970), 9. The concept of *Dichter* described by Kelling differs from that of inspiration described by Socrates; the *Dichter* apparently participates consciously in the transcendent revelation, whereas the poet or prophet described by Socrates is a mere conduit who has no idea what he is transmitting.

80   For discussions in legal literature of civil religion, see, e.g., Grey, supra note 6, at 21–25; Levinson, supra note 7; Sheldon H. Nahmod, "The Sacred Flag and the First Amendment," 66 *Ind. L.J.* 511, 535–41 (1991); and W. Tarver Rountree, Jr., "Constitutionalism as the American Religion: The Good Portion," 39 *Emory L.J.* 203 (1990).

81   Henry Monaghan notes that legal scholars who favor expansive, nonoriginalist interpretation "insist that they are aware of this history [of popular constitution worship], and that they neither worship the constitution nor view it as perfect" (Monaghan, supra note 32, at 357); see also supra notes 10–16 and accompanying text.

82   Jean Jacques Rousseau, *The Social Contract*, ed. and trans. Charles Frankel (1951), 119, 123–24. Compare Alexis de Tocqueville, *Democracy in America*, ed. J. P. Mayer, trans. George Lawrence (1969), 1:290: "What is most important for [society] is not that all citizens should profess the true religion but that they should profess religion."

83   In this way Erasmus, although stingingly critical of late medieval piety with its veneration of relics and images, nonetheless refused to endorse Protestant iconoclasm: "He argued that material objects of worship sometimes serve as 'signs and supports' of piety. They were necessary for those who were not ready to accept a more mature spiritual faith, for 'children in Christ.' His approval rested, he said, on the assumption that they are only steps that lead to a more appropriate means of salvation" (Carlos M. N. Eire, *War against the Idols: The Reformation of Worship from Erasmus to Calvin* [1986], 48).

84   See Adrian Fortescue, "Images," in *The Catholic Encyclopedia* (1910), 7:664. See ibid. at 671: "The sign in itself is nothing, but it shares the honour of its prototype. . . . [A]ll the outward marks of reverence, visibly directed towards the sign, turn in intention towards the real object of our reverence—the thing signified. The sign is only put up as a visible direction for our reverence, because the real thing is not physically present."

85   Protestants have typically regarded this sort of lapse as common and perhaps inevitable, whereas Catholics have taken a different view. Compare Paul Tillich, *A History of Christian Thought* (1968), 89: "The icons deserve veneration and not adoration. However, . . . in popular understanding veneration always develops into adoration," with Fortescue, supra note 84: "Nor is there any suspicion that the people, who were unconsciously evolving this ritual [of bowing to and kissing religious images], confused the image with its prototype. . . . [I]t is inconceivable that any one, except perhaps the most grossly stupid peasant, could have thought that an image could hear prayers, or do anything for us (at 668)."

86   For a discussion of the theological arguments about icons that divided Eastern and Western Christianity, see Jaroslav Pelikan, *The Christian Tradition: A History of the Development of Doctrine* (1974), 2:91–145.

87   See Eire, supra note 83, at 19.

88   Carlos Eire emphasizes that hostility to what they saw as idol worship was an essential part of the program of Protestant reformers such as Zwingli, Calvin, and Karlstaadt; Luther was more accommodating on this point. See, generally, Eire, supra note 83.

89   Holmes, supra note 52, at 40.

90   For a description of Aquinas's natural law jurisprudence, see Lloyd L. Weinreb, *Natural Law and Justice* (1987), 53–63.

91   Compare Campos, supra note 22, at 309 (suggesting that modern constitutional theory reflects "the human need for some semblance of communion with the divine").

92   But cf. Posner, supra note 29, at 811: "Most canons of statutory construction go wrong . . . because they impute omniscience to Congress."

93   Compare Pierre Schlag, "The Brilliant, the Curious, and the Wrong," 39 *Stan. L. Rev.* 917, 918 n. 2 (1987): "Dworkin insists that interpretation . . . 'seeks to make of the material being interpreted the best it can be.' My thought is that one can learn much from developing the least attractive interpretation" (citations omitted).

94   Dworkin, supra note 5, at 225; cf. Bruce Ackerman, "Constitutional Politics/Constitutional Law," 99 *Yale L.J.* 453, 459–60 (1989) (favoring "synthetic interpretation" that would treat the Constitution as a "principled doctrinal whole"). The power of this monistic approach is apparent in Suzanna Sherry's review of Ackerman's recent book. Although highly critical of most of Ackerman's analysis, Sherry finds Ackerman's discussion of "synthetic" interpretation to be the one appealing part of the book. See Suzanna Sherry, "The Ghost of Liberalism Past," 105 *Harv. L. Rev.* 918, 920–23 (1992), reviewing Bruce Ackerman, *We the People*, vol. 1 (1991). However, not all theorists favor this artificially unified approach to constitutional interpretation. See Tribe and Dorf, supra note 16, at 20–30 (criticizing "hyper-integration" in constitutional interpretation).

95   Plato, *Republic*, bk. 2, 378c–e, trans. Paul Shorey, in *The Collected Dialogues of Plato*, ed. Edith Hamilton and Huntington Cairns (1961), 575, 625.

96   See Alexander M. Bickel, *The Least Dangerous Branch* (1962), 23–28; Bork, supra note 5, at 143–60; Ronald Dworkin, *A Matter of Principle* (1985), 33–71; Wechsler, supra note 3; see also Ackerman, supra note 94, at 525 (the Constitution provides "a rich lode of principle").

97   Perry, supra note 33, at 690 (emphasis added).

98   See, e.g., Bork, supra note 5, at 75–76; Dworkin, supra note 5, at 360; Tribe and Dorf, supra note 16, at 12–13.

99   See, e.g., Bork, supra note 5, at 76; Dworkin, supra note 5, at 381–92; Tribe and Dorf, supra note 16, at 13.

100   See supra notes 3–5 and accompanying text.

101   Tribe and Dorf, supra note 16, at 13.

102   See, e.g., Ronald Dworkin, *Taking Rights Seriously* (1977), 135–37; Perry, supra note 33, at 695–98.

103   It may be, for instance, that principles are explicitly expressed in the Fourteenth Amendment. Compare Ackerman, supra note 94, at 522 (pointing out that the amendment's "first paragraph speaks the language of fundamental principle"). In contrast, if a principle of privacy is embodied in the First, Third, Fourth, or Fifth Amendment (see Griswold v. Connecticut, 381 U.S. 479, 484 [1965]), the principle seems at best implicit, not explicit.

104   E.g., Douglas Laycock, "Original Intent and the Constitution Today," in *The First Freedom: Religion and the Bill of Rights*, ed. James E. Wood, Jr. (1990), 87, 89: "The [constitutional] text states sweeping principles. . . . It is hardly surprising that the broad principles stated in the text turn out to have implications that the founders did not contemplate."

105   Wechsler, supra note 3, at 12, 15.

106   Ibid. at 15.

107   Ibid. at 12.

108   Tribe and Dorf, supra note 16, at 13.

109   See Dworkin, supra note 102, at 134–36.

110   To be sure, even if our conceptions diverge, there may still be a historical or genealogical connection between an idea that our ancestors denoted with the term *equality* or *religious freedom* and an altered or different idea that we denote with the same term. A historian might be able to show how our notions of religious freedom evolved—or, depending on one's point of view, degenerated—from notions held by our ancestors, perhaps by gradual or even imperceptible degrees. But it hardly follows that we are referring to the same idea or principle. I am descended from (and may have had the good fortune to inherit certain traits of) my grandfather, and I may even have been given his name. It does not follow that I *am* my grandfather, or that statements made about *him* are also about *me* (or vice versa).

111   Perhaps the leading proponent of moral realism in the legal academy today is Michael Moore. See, e.g., Michael S. Moore, "A Natural Law Theory of Interpretation," 58 *S. Calif. L. Rev.* 277, 376–81 (1985). Brian Bix points out that Moore's metaphysical realism runs contrary to "the way most of us currently think about language or the way most of us currently do (and teach) law" (Brian Bix, "Michael Moore's Realist Approach to Law," 140 *U. Pa. L. Rev.* 1293, 1330 [1992]). Similarly, Heidi Hurd defends moral realism (Hurd, supra note 29, at 1000–1006), but she acknowledges that this position is not dominant in the academy today. See ibid. at 1000: "Moral facts are right up there with Cartesian egos, moxibustion, and the Easter Bunny in the ranks of items . . . despised by most contemporary philosophers" (quoting William G. Lycan, "Moral Facts and Moral Knowledge," 24 *S.J. Phil.* 79, 79 [Supp., 1986]).

112   Despite significant differences in their epistemologies, both Augustine and Aquinas believed that universals rather than particulars are the immediate object of knowledge and that universals exist before and independent of individuals as ideas in the mind of God. See Steven Ozment, *The Age of Reform: 1250–1550,* (1980), 52–53.

113   For an interesting effort to defend moral reality, see Michael S. Moore, "Moral Reality Revisited," 90 *Mich. L. Rev.* 2424 (1992). My own doubt is whether Moore's account of moral reality in terms of "supervenience" is not nonsense in the same way that I have suggested modern natural rights talk is nonsense; see "Nonsense and Natural Law," in this volume.

114   MacIntyre, supra note 58, at 253.

115   Exodus 19:5–6 (Revised Standard).

116   Ibid. at 19:7–8.

117   Psalms 33:12 (Revised Standard).

118   Robert F. Nagel, "On Complaining about the Burger Court," 84 *Colum. L. Rev.* 2068, 2081 (1984), reviewing *The Burger Court,* ed. Vincent Blasi (1983).

119   Dworkin, supra note 5, at 109.

120   Ibid. at 190.

121   Ibid. at 192–93, 196.

122   Ibid. at 211.

123   Ibid. at 166.

124   Ibid. at 168 (emphasis added).

125   Ibid. at 168.

126   Compare ibid. at 400 (noting that, for the legal interpreter, "his god is the adjudicative principle of integrity"); ibid. at 183: "Integrity is our Neptune."

127   Compare Perry, *The Constitution,* supra note 8, at 98–99 (ascribing a "prophetic" function to noninterpretive judicial review).

128   Dworkin, supra note 5, at 407.

129   Of course, idolatry ultimately occurs within the hearts and minds of its practitioners. Hence, whether a particular devotee—or jurist, or legal theorist—is engaged in idolatry is not finally demonstrable through external evidence. It is always possible, for example, that even when a scholar's or jurist's language suggests idolatry, the language is calculated or deceptive. The apparent idolater might be a clear-eyed pragmatist who for what seem to him sufficient reasons will not admit to being merely a pragmatist. For an interpretation of Dworkin as a sophisticated, unconfessing pragmatist, see Steven D. Smith, "The Pursuit of Pragmatism," 100 *Yale L.J.* 409, 414–20 (1990).

Thomas Grey suggests a different escape from idolatry by resort to a "two-source" theory of constitutional law. For some constitutional decisions, Grey suggests, we should not pretend that the decisions are derived from the written Constitution; instead, these decisions come from some other source, such as tradition. See Grey, supra note 6. Significantly, jurists and scholars seem unable to reconcile themselves to this sort of account. Andrzej Rapaczynski observes that "judges sometimes admit that constitutional interpretation is sensitive to historical evolution and that history adds a 'gloss' on the text. But they never admit to deriving the authority for their decisions from outside the constitutional text.... Instead, any new result is unfailingly presented as a new and better *interpretation* of the text itself.... This behavior of judges is very significant because it expresses their belief that purely noninterpretive review would constitute an abuse of power and undermine the legitimacy of judicial review. In this belief, moreover, they are very likely to be right" (Andrzej Rapaczynski, "The Ninth Amendment and the Unwritten Constitution: The Problems of Constitutional Interpretation," 64 *Chi.-Kent L. Rev.* 177, 192 [1988]). Although he rejects Grey's two-source account and insists that constitutional adjudication must "interpret" the Constitution, Rapaczynski does not concede that such interpretation has a religious quality; on this point he agrees that "Grey is certainly right that judicial inquiry should be a secular enterprise" (ibid. at 203).

130   Grey, supra note 6, at 20.

SECULAR FUNDAMENTALISM

1   Joseph de Maistre, *Oeuvres Completes de J. de Maistre* (1884–87), 376; quoted in Isaiah Berlin, "Joseph de Maistre and the Origins of Fascism," in *The Crooked Timber of Humanity* (1990), 91, 125–26.

2   Alasdair MacIntyre, *After Virtue,* 2d ed. (1984), 6.

3   Ibid. at 6–7.

4   Ibid. at 8.

5   Ibid.; see also Alasdair MacIntyre, *Whose Justice? Which Rationality?* (1988); Michael J. Sandel, *Liberalism and the Limits of Justice* (1982); Charles Taylor, *Sources of the Self* (1989); and Robert Nozick, *Anarchy, State, and Utopia* (1974). Rawls does respond to one of Sandel's basic criticisms by emphasizing that the original position as set forth in *A Theory of Justice* is only a representational device and should not be understood to imply "a particular metaphysical conception of the person; for example, that the essential nature of persons is independent of and prior to their contingent attributes" (27). For Sandel's perspective on the evolution of Rawls's theory, see Sandel's review of *Political Liberalism,* 107 *Harv. L. Rev.* 1765 (1994).

6   See, for example, Peter Berkowitz's excellent review of Stephen Holmes's *The Anatomy of Antiliberalism:* "It is incumbent upon liberals and their friends to state that Holmes does liberalism no favors by flattering liberal vanities. Given the partiality and incompleteness of all things fashioned by human hands, it is doubtful that the principles of liberalism are secure when its champions are unable to discover anything of value about its weak points and unwise tendencies from [critics such as MacIntyre]" (Peter Berkowitz, "Liberal Zealotry," 103 *Yale L.J.* 1363, 1382 [1994]).

7   John Rawls, *Political Liberalism* (1993), xxv.

8   Ibid. at 214, 137.

9   Ibid. at 220.

10   Ibid. at 217.

11   Joseph de Maistre argues that "the inevitable consequence of faith in the principles of Rousseau is a situation in which the people is told by its masters 'You believe that you don't want this law, but we assure you that you do. If you dare reject it, we shall shoot you down in order to punish you for not wanting what you do want' and they then do so" (Berlin, "Origins of Fascism," supra note 1, at 150).

12   Rawls, supra note 7, at xvi.

13   Ibid. at 243.

14   Ibid. at 49.

15   Ibid. at 54–58.

16   See, e.g., Benjamin R. Barber, "Justifying Justice: Problems of Psychology, Measurement and Politics in Rawls," 69 *Am. Pol. Sci. Rev.* 663 (1975): "Rawls concedes that the precedence of liberty comes into play only after 'a certain level of wealth has been attained,' and that below this threshold, liberty may not only have to be weighted against but perhaps subordinated to other primary goods in whose absence freedom has no meaning. Depending on where the

threshold is established, even Marx might be comfortable with such a viewpoint!" (at 667 n. 9; citation omitted).

17   Rawls, supra note 7, at 243 n. 32 (emphasis added).

18   See Kenneth Burke, *Language as Symbolic Action* (1966), 46:

Many of [our] "observations" are but implications of the particular terminology in terms of which the observations are made. . . . Perhaps the simplest illustration of this point is to be got by contrasting secular and theological terminologies of motives. If you want to operate, like a theologian, with a terminology that includes "God" as its key term, the only sure way to do so is to put in the term, and that's that. The Bible solves the problem by putting "God" into the first sentence—and from this initial move, many implications "necessarily" follow. . . . I have called metaphysics "coy theology" because the metaphysician often introduces the term "God" not outright, as with the Bible, but by beginning with a term that *ambiguously* contains such implications.

19   Rawls, supra note 7, at xxv.

20   Ibid.

21   Ibid.

22   Isaiah Berlin describes the preliberal attitude toward dissent: "What Catholic in, let us say, the sixteenth century would say 'I abhor the heresies of the reformers, but I am deeply moved by the sincerity and integrity with which they hold and practice and sacrifice themselves for their abominable beliefs?' On the contrary, the deeper the sincerity of such heretics . . . the more dangerous they are, the more likely to lead souls to perdition, the more ruthlessly they should be eliminated, since heresy—false beliefs about the ends of men—is surely a poison more dangerous to the health of society than even hypocrisy or dissimulation, which at least do not openly attack the true doctrine. Only truth matters: to die in a false cause is wicked or pitiable" (Isaiah Berlin, "The Apotheosis of the Romantic Will," in *The Crooked Timber of Humanity,* supra note 1, at 207, 208).

23   Rawls, supra note 7, at 63.

24   Ibid. at 147–48.

25   John Rawls, "Kantian Constructivism in Moral Theory," 77 *J. Phil.* 515, 516 (1980). A significant ambiguity in Rawls's account concerns who should, as a practical matter, have the power to determine what counts as "running afoul of public reason," and what consequences, if any, should flow from such a determination. That is, if his prescriptions are merely precatory, we might want to ask what relevance they have to the political realities of "actually existing liberalism." On the other hand, if—as his comments on judicial review as an embodiment of public reason suggest—the account entails that some antidemocratic institutions have the ultimate power to determine what public reason in fact requires, then we have reason to worry that the author's supreme confidence concerning his ability to discern what he believes are the right answers to such questions will be replicated in the opinions of those appointed to safeguard the exercise of "public reason" (231–40).

26   If this resemblance seems implausible, consider how two other recent books by prominent liberal intellectuals have gone about addressing the abortion controversy. Like Rawls, Laurence Tribe and Ronald Dworkin emphasize the great and apparently intractable moral and political struggles that the Supreme Court's decisions in this area have occasioned. Yet all three writers reach the conclusion that a principled policy that adequately addresses the legitimate concerns of all parties is not merely available; in their view, such an ideal outcome is actually instantiated by the extant constitutional orthodoxy. See Ronald Dworkin, *Life's*

Dominion (1993), 168–72; and Laurence Tribe, *Abortion: The Clash of Absolutes* (1990), 204–8. The moral hubris of an established faith could hardly go further than this.

27   See Hegel's *Philosophy of Right*, trans. T. M. Knox (1952), 10.

28   Rawls, supra note 7, at 243 n. 32.

29   Ibid. at xxxi.

30   Ronald Dworkin, *Law's Empire* (1986), 225–27, 254–58; Rawls, supra note 7, at 231.

31   Rawls, supra note 7, at 137.

CLERKS IN THE MAZE

1   It may, of course, not be the same law that the parties or the judge read into the judicial opinion. But in each of their interested perspectives, they will each read one law.

2   Robert M. Cover, "The Supreme Court, 1982 Term—Foreword: *Nomos* and Narrative," 97 *Harv. L. Rev.* 4, 53 (1983).

3   Cover says that the balance of terror is pretty much the way he would want it. See Robert M. Cover, "Violence and the Word," 95 *Yale L.J.* 1601, 1608 (1986).

4   James B. White, *Heracles' Bow: Essays on the Rhetoric and Poetics of the Law* (1985), 108–12.

5   Christopher C. Langdell, *A Selection of Cases on the Law of Contracts* (1871), vi.

6   Ibid. at vii.

7   I make no claims here about whether this first-year violence is functional or not. Within a functionalist framework one could easily see the impartation of cognitive deficits as serving to create a class of professionals guaranteed to interpret any and all texts in the most highly delimited and stereotyped manner. People with such cognitive deficits could then be counted on to produce a relative stability or certainty in the fashioning and interpretation of legally significant acts.

8   Karl N. Llewellyn, *The Bramble Bush* (1930), 102 (emphasis added).

9   Duncan Kennedy, Note, "How the Law School Fails: A Polemic," *Yale Rev. L. & Soc. Action* (Spring 1970), at 71, 72–73.

10   Ibid. at 73 (footnote omitted).

11   H. L. A. Hart, for instance, found it useful to distinguish two points of view on legal rules: the external point of view, that of the "observer who does not himself accept" the legal rules; and the internal point of view, that of the "member of the group which accepts and uses them as guides to conduct" (H. L. A. Hart, *The Concept of Law* [1961], 86). Hart saw the external point of view as useful to predict the behavior of members of the group. What it cannot do, however, is reproduce "the way in which the rules function in the lives of certain members of the group" (ibid. at 88).

12   Ronald Dworkin, *Law's Empire* (1986), 13–14 (emphasis added).

13   This argument (with specific reference to deconstruction) is elaborated in Pierre Schlag, " 'Le Hors de Texte, C'est Moi': The Politics of Form and the Domestication of Deconstruction," 11 *Cardozo L. Rev.* 1631 (1990).

14   Indeed, much of academic law can be seen as successive attempts to enact and institutionalize precisely this escape. The "pure theory" decried by Judge Edwards can be seen, as he does, as one such attempted flight. See Harry T. Edwards, "The Growing Disjunction between Legal Education and the Legal Profession," 91 *Mich. L. Rev.* 34 (1992). But, of course, precisely the same claim can be made about what he calls "doctrine" or "legal process." Doctrine is simply

yesterday's successful theory. What it has going for it is that it has achieved success. What it has going against it is precisely the same thing.

15   To me it does not really matter much: the doctrine-theory distinction is vastly overstated. Much of what passes for theory in the academy is a kind of normative or normatively driven theory. It is, in short, a kind of metadoctrine, doctrine in waiting, a doctrine wannabe. It is a doctrine of the doctrine—which is, of course, entirely fitting given the age-old self-image of the legal academic as the judge of the judges. As for doctrine itself, its claims to be separate from theory are overstated as well. Doctrine is simply yesterday's theory successfully transubstantiated into an authoritative juridical artifact. Doctrine is simply the activity of theory reduced to artifactual status.

16   Could we be talking about God substitutes again? Sure. See Kenneth Burke, *A Grammar of Motives* (1945), 355: "For a God term designates the ultimate motivation, or substance, of a Constitutional frame." For my part, I call these little items "theoretical unmentionables." For a description of their structure and function, see Pierre Schlag, "Contradiction and Denial," 87 *Mich. L. Rev.* 1216, 1222–23 (1989), reviewing Mark Kelman, *A Guide to Critical Legal Studies* (1987).

17   Edwards, supra note 14.

18   Of course, from within the maze there are any number of very "moral" rationalizations available for remaining in the maze. But despite these rationalizations, remaining in the maze is far from ethically admirable. Consider that what the academic experiences as the dreariness of the thousand-footnote doctrinal or "interdisciplinary" law review article is echoed in the dreariness of contemporary Supreme Court opinions, which is echoed in the dreariness of the contemporary lawyer's bureaucratic practice, which is echoed in the dreariness of the bureaucratic mazes through which citizens must strive to push their lives. There is nothing ethically admirable about these massive self-referential corridors of rules, doctrines, or theories.

Why, then, do legal academics remain in the maze? Why do they extend it? Ironically, it is in part because they have an admirable disposition that leads them to want to help, to want to do something constructive. But, of course, *as an ethic,* this disposition is woefully incomplete. The thing to try to think about is help *whom*? Construct *what*?

Index

Paul F. Campos, Pierre Schlag, and Steven D. Smith are
Professors of Law at the University of Colorado, Boulder.

Library of Congress Cataloging-in-Publication Data
Campos, Paul F.
Against the law / by Paul F. Campos, Pierre Schlag, and
Steven D. Smith.
p.   cm.—(Constitutional conflicts)
Includes index.
ISBN 0-8223-1835-0 (cloth : alk. paper). —
ISBN 0-8223-1841-5 (pbk. : alk. paper)
1. Jurisprudence—United States.   2. Law—Study and
teaching—United States.   3. Law—United States—
Interpretation and construction.   I. Schlag, Pierre.   II. Smith,
Steven D. (Steven Douglas), 1952–   .   III. Title.   IV. Series.
KF380.C294   1996
349.73—dc20
[347.3]   96-22190 CIP